Praise for *Hamilt*

"*Hamiltonia* engages multiple learni
ing opportunity to flip traditional i
on real-world issues. Students develop a detailed understanding of the complexities of political decision making as they take the lead in designing their own state government and addressing pressing policy issues."

—David Redlawsk, University of Delaware

"In *Hamiltonia*, government is brought to life through creative and engaging simulations in which students craft a constitution, establish the powers of political institutions, and design policies. This book provides a comprehensive and practical approach for teaching state and local government and lessons that students will remember."

—Jennifer Clark, University of Houston

"Kaitlin Sidorsky and Kelly Smith breathe life into the concepts of state and local government by engaging students in the experiential process of building the fifty-first state of the United States from the ground up. *Hamiltonia: A State and Local Government Simulation* is a great addition to any state and local government course."

—Wendy Johnston, Adirondack Community College

"*Hamiltonia* allows students to learn state politics through a comprehensive simulation that provides an interesting and informative way to understand the importance of institutional structure, while capturing the complexities and variations of politics and policies throughout the fifty states. The text is a welcome addition to any state politics course."

—Jonathan Winburn, University of Mississippi

"What makes Sidorsky and Smith's comprehensive state and local politics textbook, *Hamiltonia*, truly exceptional is the comprehensive simulation that asks students to directly interact with important issues in state politics. Student interest, engagement, and learning is sure to increase with this remarkable new textbook."

—Shannon L. Jenkins, University of Massachusetts Dartmouth

"As student assessments become more complicated due to large language models (e.g., ChatGPT), simulation-based activities can be a great way to overcome these challenges. I highly recommend *Hamiltonia*, which gives a step-by-step guide on how to run a semester-length simulation of state governments that is thoughtful, well-designed, and just plain fun!"

—Eric Stokan, University of Maryland–Baltimore County

"State governments make many of the most important policies that affect students' day-to-day lives. But teaching state politics can be hard because students often enter the classroom with little understanding of state government. *Hamiltonia* to the rescue! This book blends a readable account of state politics with an innovative simulation that is sure to educate and entertain undergraduates."

—Michael Nelson, The Pennsylvania State University

"*Hamiltonia* provides an avenue for students to learn beyond lectures and fully engage with the intricacies of state governments. A resource such as this is greatly needed for state politics."

—Jordan Butcher, Arkansas State University

"*Hamiltonia* offers a unique combination of foundational knowledge regarding the politics of U.S. states, and an engaging simulation asking students to build the fictional fifty-first state of Hamiltonia. The perfect blend of content knowledge and simulation will significantly stimulate the engagement that instructors desire in the classroom."

—Paul Rutledge, University of West Georgia

Hamiltonia

A State and Local Government Simulation

Kaitlin N. Sidorsky
Ramapo College

Kelly B. Smith
Stetson University

ROWMAN & LITTLEFIELD
Lanham • Boulder • New York • London

Executive Acquisitions Editor: Michael Kerns
Associate Acquisitions Editor: Elizabeth Von Buhr
Sales and Marketing Inquiries: textbooks@rowman.com

Credits and acknowledgments for material borrowed from other sources, and reproduced with permission, appear on the appropriate pages within the text.

Published by Rowman & Littlefield
An imprint of The Rowman & Littlefield Publishing Group, Inc.
4501 Forbes Boulevard, Suite 200, Lanham, Maryland 20706
www.rowman.com

86-90 Paul Street, London EC2A 4NE

British Library Cataloguing in Publication Information Available

Library of Congress Cataloging-in-Publication Data
Names: Sidorsky, Kaitlin N., author. | Smith, Kelly B., author.
Title: Hamiltonia : a state and local government simulation / Kaitlin N. Sidorsky, Ramapo College, Kelly B. Smith, Stetson University.
Description: Lanham, Maryland : Rowman & Littlefield, [2024] | Includes bibliographical references and index.
Identifiers: LCCN 2024018702 (print) | LCCN 2024018703 (ebook) | ISBN 9781538192481 (cloth) | ISBN 9781538192498 (paperback) | ISBN 9781538192504 (epub)
Subjects: LCSH: Political science—Study and teaching—United States. | Simulation games in education—United States. | Women—Political activity—United States. | Local government—Study and teaching—United States. | State governments—Study and teaching—United States.
Classification: LCC JA86 .S53 2024 (print) | LCC JA86 (ebook) | DDC 320.80973—dc23/eng/20240710
LC record available at https://lccn.loc.gov/2024018702
LC ebook record available at https://lccn.loc.gov/2024018703

™ The paper used in this publication meets the minimum requirements of American National Standard for Information Sciences—Permanence of Paper for Printed Library Materials, ANSI/NISO Z39.48-1992.

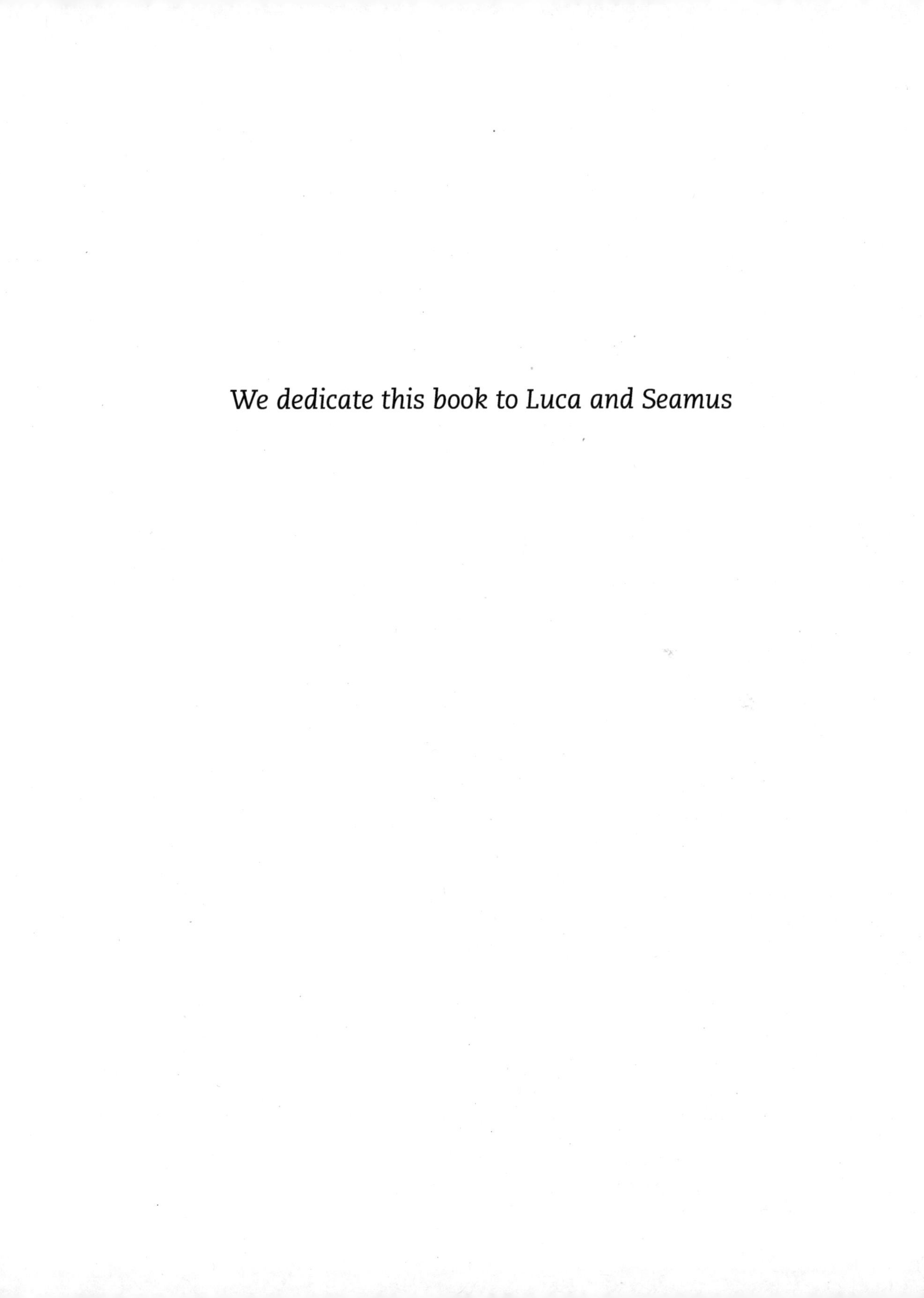

We dedicate this book to Luca and Seamus

Brief Contents

Contents

Tables and Figures

Tables

Figures

Preface

As professors of political science, we both noticed how much attention is afforded to national politics and government in the United States. Teaching our state and local government classes at our respective institutions has given us the opportunity to share with students the incredibly important role that these sub-national governments also play in the United States. From affecting licensing regulations for doctors, nurses, physical therapists, and hairdressers, to setting education standards and running Medicaid programs, state and local governments are integral to understanding U.S. politics and policy today.

We both also felt strongly about active learning strategies in the classroom as an important pedagogical method. But while we could easily find simulations on Congress, the Supreme Court, and local governments, we could not find any simulation on state-level government. There was no simulation that could do what we needed to do in our classes: teach students the differences in state and local institutions and cover various state and local public policies. So, in 2016 we created the fictional fifty-first state of America, Hamiltonia. This simulation is meant to teach students the differences in state and local institutional structures by debating and creating them and then actually living with these institutional structures by running for and working in the new government they created.

It has been a rewarding experience for us as we see students really debate why the Hamiltonia state legislature should be partisan or nonpartisan, or why the governor should or should not have a line-item veto power. We were able to have deep discussions with students about health care policy and their frustrations on why their class were not able to get a policy passed. We were also excited to see the strategy various students used as Speakers of the House, governors, and rank-and-file senate members as they bargained for policies they wanted to see enacted in Hamiltonia. Creating Hamiltonia has resulted in us learning as much as our students have, which is also why we decided to expand and publish *Hamiltonia* as a textbook for other instructors and students to benefit as we have.

We have included several features to help ensure that students get as much out of the book as possible:

- Each chapter starts with a list of **Learning Objectives** to guide students' reading and set their expectations for the material ahead.

- Chapter-opening **State Spotlights** follow because we want to drive home the real-world implications and catch students' attention with a story right from the beginning.
- After some introductory setting up of concepts, each chapter (starting with chapter 2) unfolds as instructions and guidance through the **Simulation** that is the core of this text.
- Callouts for **Action Items** are interspersed throughout the simulation section of each chapter, prompting students to make decisions about how they will structure the institutions, rules, and policies in their state.
- A **Key Terms** list at the end of each chapter helps students master the important language of politics.
- End of chapter **Assignments** provide instructors some helpful active learning exercises, either to extend the simulation game play or to provide tangential learning opportunities.

This book also includes online materials that can be utilized throughout the simulation including:

- Test banks for each chapter including multiple choice and short answer questions.
- PowerPoint lectures for each chapter to help guide students through the material.
- Worksheets for use during the simulation including forms to fill out for students running for elected office or seeking appointments in Hamiltonia. There is also a worksheet for each chapter with the action items for dissemination.
- A comprehensive instructor's manual that includes a sample syllabus, step-by-step instructions on how to run the simulation, and answers to common questions including class structure, adapting the simulation based on class size, and what to do when students are absent or the class is moved online.

Although our names are on the cover of this book, it was with the support of many people that we were able to get this book in your hands. We would like to thank our editor Michael Kerns and associate acquisitions editor Elizabeth Von Buhr at Rowman & Littlefield for their support of this textbook. Both Michael and Elizabeth were as excited and enthusiastic about Hamiltonia as we were; we cannot thank them enough for seeing our vision for this textbook and providing wonderful guidance as we started piecing it together.

We would also like to thank the reviewers of our textbook at various stages of this project, including Tiffany L. Bohm, Lake Michigan College; Mark D. Brewer, University of Maine; Jordan Butcher, Arkansas State University; Lisa Hager, South Dakota State University; Wendy L. Johnston, SUNY Adirondack; Jaclyn J. Kettler, Boise State University; Chad J. Kinsella, Ball State University; Malene A. Little, University of South Dakota; David Redlawsk, University of Delaware; Paul E. Rutledge, University of West Georgia; Kevin B. Smith, University of Nebraska–Lincoln; June Sager Speakman, Roger Williams University; Eric Stokan, University of Maryland Baltimore County; Matt Ulricksen, Community College of Rhode Island; Jonathan L. Wharton, Southern Connecticut State University; and others who wish to remain anonymous. The detail of their feedback was simply incredible. Their excitement for our textbook was also a great help to us when we felt overwhelmed by the scope of the project. We hope they see their contributions to this work throughout the textbook. We would also like to thank the students who tested out Hamiltonia throughout the years at Coastal Carolina University, Stetson University, and Ramapo College—their feedback was invaluable.

Kaitlin would like to thank her colleagues Michael Unger and Jeffrey Teigen as well as her Dean Susan Hangen who pushed her to think about turning Hamiltonia into a textbook during her job interview at Ramapo in fall 2023. She would also like to thank Wendy J. Schiller who as always is a wonderful mentor and friend. She thanks Ina Seethaler who provided thorough and helpful feedback on drafts of various chapters as well as for her support and friendship.

Kaitlin would also like to thank her family for their support for her professional goals. This textbook was written while she moved from North Carolina to New Jersey, started a new job, and lived through major home renovations. The work that went into this textbook does not exist without the encouragement and help of her sister Kimberly, sister-in-law Amanda, mother Cathy, and husband Ryan.

Kelly would like to thank her colleagues for their support and encouragement along the way. Thank you especially to Elizabeth Plantan for her feedback on chapters. Kelly thanks the Professional Development Committee at Stetson University and the provost for supporting this work through a faculty summer grant. She also thanks Elizabeth Buss for her helpful research assistance. She thanks both Susan L. Moffitt and Wendy J. Schiller for their mentorship during and after graduate school, and to her undergraduate mentors, Mark S. Hyde and William Hudson, for instilling a passion for state politics and public policy.

This book would not have been possible without the support and encouragement from Kelly's family and friends. She thanks her parents, Jeff and Maureen, and siblings for cheering her on in all her professional pursuits. She also thanks her close friends from Providence College who help her appreciate just how cool it is to have the opportunity to work on projects like this. Finally, she thanks her husband Kevin and son Seamus for being her biggest fans.

Democratic state Rep. Justin Jones of Nashville speaks prior to a vote on his expulsion from the legislature at the State Capitol Building on April 6, 2023, in Nashville, TN. He was expelled on a vote along party lines after he and two other Democratic reps led a protest at the Tennessee State Capitol building in the wake of a mass shooting where three students and three adults were killed on March 27 at the Covenant School in Nashville.

SOURCE: Seth Herald/Getty Images

Welcome to Hamiltonia!

1

Learning Objectives:

After reading this chapter students should be able to:

- Discuss the role of state governments in a federalist system.
- Explain the relationship between states.
- Describe the levels of racial, ethnic, and gender diversity among the states.
- Compare the new state of Hamiltonia to the other fifty states.
- Discuss the unique demographic characteristics, economics, and politics of Hamiltonia.

State Spotlight: Tennessee

Members of state legislatures in Tennessee and all around the country perform many important duties, from **oversight** of the executive branch to **constituent service**, to **sponsoring** and voting bills into law. Legislators also engage in advocacy and protest, sometimes right in the legislative chamber itself. This is exactly what happened following the March 27, 2023, mass shooting at The Covenant School in Nashville, Tennessee. The shooting resulted in the deaths of three children and three adults and left the Nashville community reeling from the senseless violence.

Following this shooting, Representatives Justin Jones, Justin Pearson, and Gloria Johnson broke **procedural rules** and protested on the lack of gun control on the floor of the Tennessee House of Representatives. Following this protest, the majority Republican House "employed a disciplinary tool little used since the 1800s to expel Pearson [and] Rep. Justin Jones, while sparing Rep. Gloria Johnson." The difference between the expelled members and Johnson? Race. Both Pearson and Jones are African American, and Johnson is white, a fact that was not lost on Johnson when asked why she was spared expulsion: "It might have to do with the color of our skin."[1]

When members of the Tennessee legislature are expelled, the choice for the replacements reverts to the local governing bodies in the district the members are from. On Monday, April 10, 2023, Jones was reinstated to his seat for House District 52 by the Nashville Metro Council and on Wednesday, April 12, 2023, the Shelby County Board of Commissioners reappointed Justin Pearson to his seat representing House District 86. Representatives Pearson and Jones's experiences is illustrative of the importance of state legislators and their role as representatives of their **constituents**, but also demonstrates the divisions present for people of color who serve their state governments.

The state of Tennessee is home to over seven million people. According to the U.S. census, 17 percent of the Tennessee population is African American, 6.1 percent identifies as Latino, and 73.1 percent identify as white. The Tennessee General Assembly, comprised of a Senate and House of Representatives, is 81.82 percent white, with 12 percent of the legislature identifying as African American and no legislators identifying as Latino. And despite 51 percent of the Tennessee population being women, there are only twenty women in the state legislature, amounting to only 15 percent of the legislative body. Are the lower levels of representation for marginalized groups in Tennessee part of the story of Representative's Jones and Pearson's expulsion?

There is only so much, however, stories and examples of government institutions can do to help students truly understand how state governments work and their impact on their citizens. This is why we have created *Hamiltonia: A State and Local Government Simulation*. Throughout the semester *you and your classmates* will be in the driver's seat of setting up the government of the fictional fifty-first state of the United States, Hamiltonia. The purpose of this simulation is to use the material you have learned in class about state government and apply it to a simulated case study. Throughout the course of this simulation your class will have to determine what the structure of the three branches of government will look like in Hamiltonia, and eventually move on to answer important and difficult public policy problems in the state. Each chapter of this textbook will provide the overview of the institution or public policy area you will be debating as well as structured questions for you and your classmates to address.

This chapter begins with a general overview of what state and local governments do and introduces you to what the state of Hamiltonia looks like as a starting point for the simulation. You will notice that there is a clear connection between the structure of the government you create and how that affects public policymaking in the second half of the simulation. The roles you create will be the roles you assume, so start thinking about what kind of "job" you want to assume in Hamiltonia and think about your political beliefs and what you stand for. There are only three ground rules for this simulation, although your instructor reserves the right to add to these rules as issues may arise. The ground rules are:

1. Students cannot violate the laws of the nation.
2. Students must remain within the bounds of realism.
3. Students must remain within one's role.[2]

Before jumping into the history and background on the state of Hamiltonia, let's discuss a little more about the importance of state and local government in our federal system.

The Importance of State and Local Governments

Americans are often captivated by national politics. From the fights on the U.S. Senate floor, to the hearings for Supreme Court nominees, to the biggest draw—presidential elections. And yet, despite Americans' fixation on federal-level politics, it is often the politics of state and local governments that most affects Americans' everyday lives. State governments are responsible for areas such as setting education standards, running elections, regulating professions such as barbers, massage therapists, and nurses, and maintaining roads, bridges, and tunnels. Many states collect taxes through income taxes or sales taxes, and they play an important role in applying for federal grants.

Local governments are often structured off a county system (except for Rhode Island and Connecticut due to their small sizes) and are considered creatures of state governments. Local governments also collect taxes and oversee services such as water, sewer, and sanitation, running schools, and **zoning laws**. Keep in mind that the relationships between the different levels of government are different. The federal government and state governments' relationship is one rooted in shared power called **federalism**. Look at Figure 1.1 for the difference in power dynamics between federal and state governments and state and local governments.

The arrows represent power, you will notice that power flows between the federal and state governments because they each have their own powers and they each share power. Think about the power of running elections. This is a power explicitly given to state governments in the Constitution. This is no different than the power of Congress to declare war—each level of government has its own list of powers. Most of state power is derived from the Tenth Amendment, which reads: "The powers not delegated to the United States by the Constitution, nor prohibited by it to the States, are reserved to the States respectively, or to the people." Running elections is one of the few powers explicitly given to state governments

Figure 1.1

Relationships between Federal, State, and Local Governments

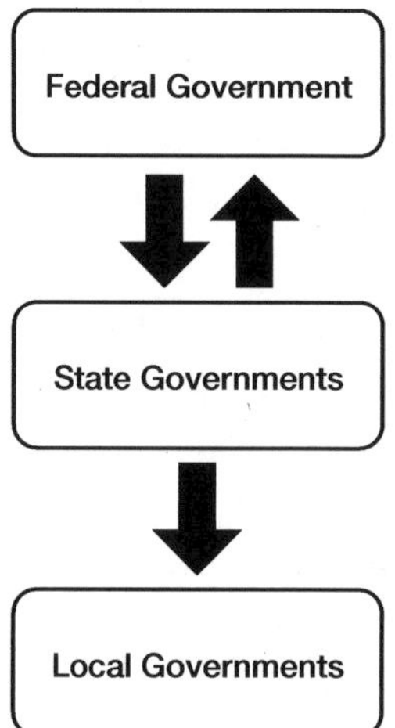

in the constitution, and it is known as the **Time, Place, and Manner Clause** (Article 1, Section 4). But there are also powers that both state governments and the federal government have, such as taxation. People pay state taxes and federal taxes; this kind of power is known as **concurrent powers**.

Now look at the relationship between state and local governments. Power is only flowing in one direction, from state governments to local governments. This is because the relationship between state and local governments is **unitary**—state governments allow local governments to use some of their power, but they can take it away or change it in whatever way they wish. Therefore, the power dynamics between local and state governments are very different than the power dynamics between state governments and the federal government.

There is one other power dynamic we want to discuss and that is the relationships that form between states. We want to highlight the relationships among states that border one another or may share major natural resources. Think about all the states that share access to the Mississippi River, one of the Great Lakes, or share a bridge that connects two states, such as the George Washington Bridge which connects New Jersey and New York. These states must work closely with one another to ensure access to these resources is equitable and that one state is not polluting or damaging the resource, impacting the citizens in other states.

The George Washington Bridge which connects the states of New York and New Jersey.

SOURCE: Getty

Let's look more closely at the relationship forged between New York and New Jersey. Over 100 years ago, in 1921, the U.S. Congress gave the states the authority to develop the Port Authority of New York and New Jersey. As an **interstate agency**, governors from both states each appoint six members to the board of commissioners, who are subject to state senate approval. According to the governing documents of the Port Authority, "commissioners serve as public officials without pay for overlapping six-year terms. The governors retain the right to veto the actions of the commissions from his or her own state."[3] The Port Authority oversees five major airports, four bridges, two tunnels, bus stations, the Path rail system, the Port of New York and New Jersey, as well as the World Trade Center. These kinds of relationships between states exist all over the country and are an important responsibility of state governments.

In addition to having relationships with each other, states can develop policies themselves and can be influenced by other states' policies. Supreme Court Justice Louis Brandeis famously wrote "It is one of the happy incidents of the federal system that a single courageous State may, if its citizens choose, serve as a laboratory."[4] Since then states have been studied as laboratories of democracy meaning that states can develop policy solutions that address their residents' needs and concerns. When states develop successful policy solutions, it is more likely that other states will adopt that policy.[5] This is called **policy diffusion** whereby policy innovations spread across governments. This means that policies developed at the state level, and not necessarily the federal level, can have widespread effects across the country. For example, at the federal level, marijuana use is illegal. However, in 1996 California legalized the medical use of marijuana. Since then, thirty-three states have followed California's lead and have legalized medical marijuana.[6] States have authority to create policy solutions to a variety of public problems in the United States. Sometimes these policy solutions can spread across state governments that has wide-reaching effects across the country.

Institutional Organization of State Governments

State governments are organized very similarly to the federal government. All state governments have three branches of government: the legislature (sometimes known as a general assembly), the executive branch headed by the governor, and the judiciary. It is the details associated with each branch that reveal differences between state governments and between state governments and the federal government. Take for example a comparison between the judicial branch of state governments and the federal judiciary. The federal judiciary has three levels: district courts, circuit courts of appeals, and the U.S. Supreme Court. Nine states, however, do not have three levels like the U.S. federal judiciary; they have no intermediate appeals court and simply have a trial court level and then a **court of last resort**, often called a state supreme court (New York calls their intermediate court the Supreme Court and their court of last resort the Court of Appeals). We will cover these differences throughout the simulation because you will have to decide what you want Hamiltonia's government to look like. Each decision you make not only affects other institutions in Hamiltonia's government but will also affect the scope of your powers once you assume a role in Hamiltonia's government in the second half of the simulation.

It is important throughout the simulation to keep in mind what each branch of government is responsible for, and how the institutional arrangements you create for Hamiltonia make fulfilling those responsibilities easier or harder. State legislatures are responsible for making the laws for the state as well as representing their constituents and keeping an eye on the executive branch of state government through oversight. The executive branch is responsible for implementing and enforcing the laws state legislatures enact. Governors, like presidents, can "check" the legislature through the power of the **veto**. Governor's also "check" the state judiciary in some states by appointing judges. Unlike the federal judiciary where the president has the power to appoint every judge on the federal bench (with the advice and consent of the U.S. Senate of course), not every state gives judicial appointment powers to governors. South Carolina, for example, gives judicial appointment power to the legislature. Finally, the state judiciary is responsible for interpreting and applying the law. This is an incredibly important role: most cases—both civil and criminal—in the United States will never be heard in the federal judiciary. This amounts to millions of cases making their way through state courts every year from the low stakes' cases in traffic courts to controversial cases surrounding the death penalty.

Because state government institutions are designed with a checks and balances system, sometimes these institutions can conflict within a state. In Florida, residents can vote on amendments to the state constitution. In 2018, residents did just that with 65 percent voting for Amendment 4.[7] Amendment 4 allows felons to have their voting rights restored "after they complete all terms of their sentence including parole or probation."[8] Controversy and conflict soon followed as to what "complete all terms of their sentence" meant. A few months later, a law was passed that required felons to complete all monetary portions of their sentences.[9] The governor and the legislature interpreted "all terms of their sentence" differently than the groups backing the amendment had. Governor DeSantis asked for an advisory opinion from the Florida Supreme Court. After hearing arguments, the court agreed with DeSantis' interpretation that "complete all terms of their sentence" included monetary terms of the sentence.[10]

Diversity among States

In each chapter we will delve into levels of diversity across the states. We want to begin the discussion of diversity by first acknowledging how different the populations of each state are in the United States, and how they face different challenges based upon location, geography, and culture. Figure 1.2 presents the racial and ethnic diversity of

Figure 1.2

Racial Diversity of American States, 2023

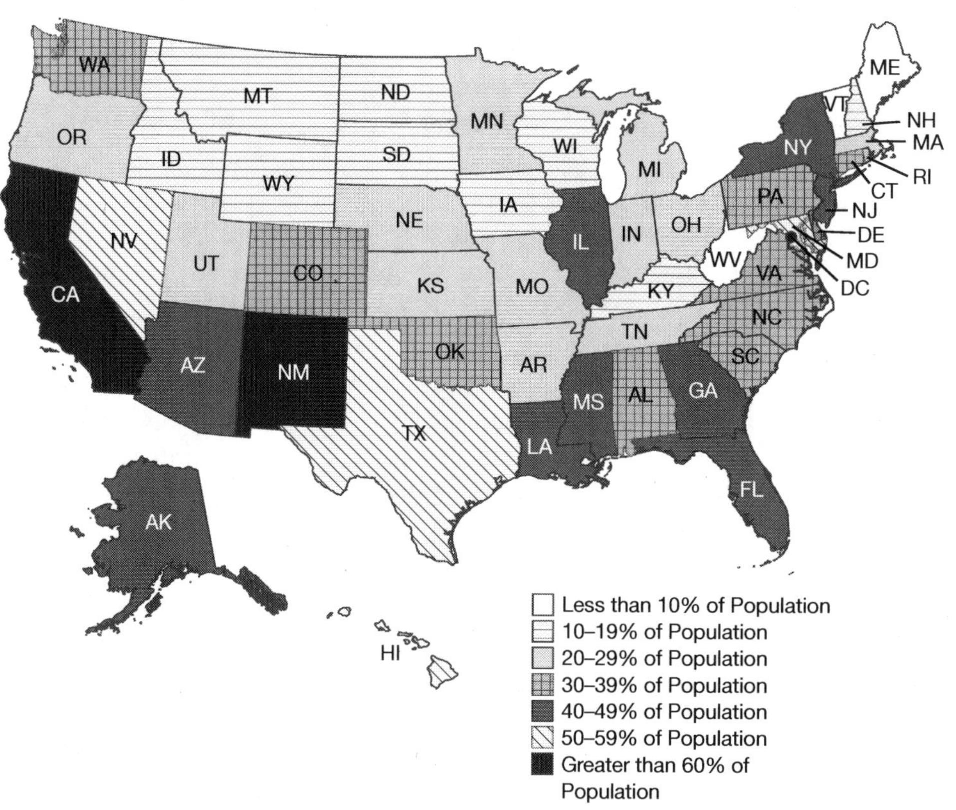

each state based upon data from the U.S. Census Bureau. States range widely in their racial and ethnic diversity, and this map does not even provide the number of different racial and ethnic groups nor their percentages of each state population. For example, the largest racial group in Hawaii is Asian while in New Mexico it is Hispanic.

We could also look at the states via different demographic variables, such as age. States with larger numbers of children versus people over the age of sixty-five face different public policy problems. Just over 21 percent of Florida's population is over the age of sixty-five, compared to Utah where only 11.7 percent of its population is over sixty-five. The cost, then, of providing Medicaid coverage between Florida and Utah is much different, and not only because Florida has a much larger population overall but also because a much larger proportion of their population will be relying on **Medicaid** which is partially funded by the state. On the opposite end of the spectrum, Utah has a higher percentage of people under eighteen: 28.4 percent compared to 19.7 percent in Florida. Here, education becomes a focus, because the states, through their local governments, are responsible for educating children through the twelfth grade.

So far, we have covered how differences in demographics of each state affect their governments. But we cannot forget there are also major geographic and climate differences among states. Think about hurricanes. States like Florida, Georgia, Louisiana, and South Carolina must not only create emergency response plans to address potential hurricanes that affect their citizens, but they also have to set aside money in their budgets each year to be able to help citizens and address damage. They also need to have strong lines of communication to federal agencies, such as the Federal Emergency Management Agency (FEMA), to call on them for assistance during and after natural disasters. States such as Oklahoma, Kansas, and Missouri, however, do not need to worry about hurricanes, but instead need to worry about tornadoes. Similarly, areas of Upstate New York, New Hampshire, and Vermont need to worry about blizzards.

A final area we want to mention is differences in state history and culture. Political scientist Daniel Elazar created a typology of state political cultures to help people understand the differences between states and how they feel about the role of government. Although his typology has been expanded over time, the original three political cultures he created, **moralistic**, **traditionalistic**, and **individualistic**, are helpful in understanding the underlying politics

Damage from Hurricane Katrina.
SOURCE: Getty

of each state. States in the South and Southwest typically identify as traditionalistic and often view government as purely maintaining the status quo. These states typically spend less money on government services and often are controlled by the Republican Party. On the other end of the spectrum are moralistic states often found along the West Coast and parts of the Midwest. These states see government as valuable and can be used to enact positive changes in society. Spending on government services is typically high in these states and public service and political involvement are valued. Finally, individualistic states are found in portions of the Northeast and the Midwest. Here, corruption is much more likely, and often accepted if it keeps government functioning. These states spend a moderate amount of money on government services, and the people often perceive the government as a service provider, instead of something to aspire to.

States differ from one another in a variety of ways. However, they also sometimes share similarities, particularly in the policy problems they seek to address. For example, all states play an active role in establishing and maintaining the public K–12 education system within their borders. Each of these states must establish a curriculum, keep track of student performance data, and more. Yes, these states may face different challenges in their education system due to geography, demographics, and other factors, but they do share a common authority to address policy problems. Sometimes these differences can cause states to take different approaches to solving policy problems.

Introducing Hamiltonia: The Fifty-First State of the United States

Now that you have been given an explanation of the role of state governments, their powers, organization, and differences, we can introduce our fifty-first fictional state, Hamiltonia. Hamiltonia is named after Founder and Framer Alexander Hamilton who was born on January 11, 1757, in Charlestown on the island of Saint Kitts and Nevis. As explained in numerous biographies as well as the very popular Broadway musical *Hamilton*, Alexander Hamilton made his way up the political ranks from relative obscurity to being one of the main authors of *The Federalist Papers* and serving as the Secretary of Treasury under the Washington Administration. Although Hamilton is often overshadowed by other Founders and Framers including George Washington, John Adams, James Madison, and Thomas Jefferson, the founders of the state of Hamiltonia felt it was time to give the recognition Hamilton deserved by naming the fifty-first state after him.

It is ironic that a state would be named after Hamilton, as he was known as a fierce proponent of federal power, while his political foe Thomas Jefferson was known to consistently fight for state's rights. Your class will ultimately decide just how powerful the state of Hamiltonia will be, as well as its political culture. Figure 1.3 provides a map of the state of Hamiltonia.

Hamiltonia is in the midwestern region of the United States. It is approximately 54,157 square miles: 230 miles (east–west) by 235 miles (north–south). Hamiltonia is landlocked with no major lakes but has two rivers that run through it—one in the western region of the state, the Elizabeth River, and a second in the central region of the state, called the Kings River. The state geography is relatively flat, with no mountain ranges. In terms of Hamiltonia's climate, it has an average temperature of 52 degrees Fahrenheit during the year, with the coldest month of January averaging a low of 17 degrees Fahrenheit and the hottest month of July averaging a high of 85 degrees. Hamiltonia receives an average snowfall of 28 inches, and an average rainfall of 37 inches over the course of the year.

Hamiltonia is a mid-size state with a population of 6,241,992 people. Its largest city is its capital, Charlestown, which has a population of 815,151 people. To put into perspective Hamiltonia's population size, Table 1.1 provides the 2023 census population estimates for the top ten states

Figure 1.3
Map of Hamiltonia

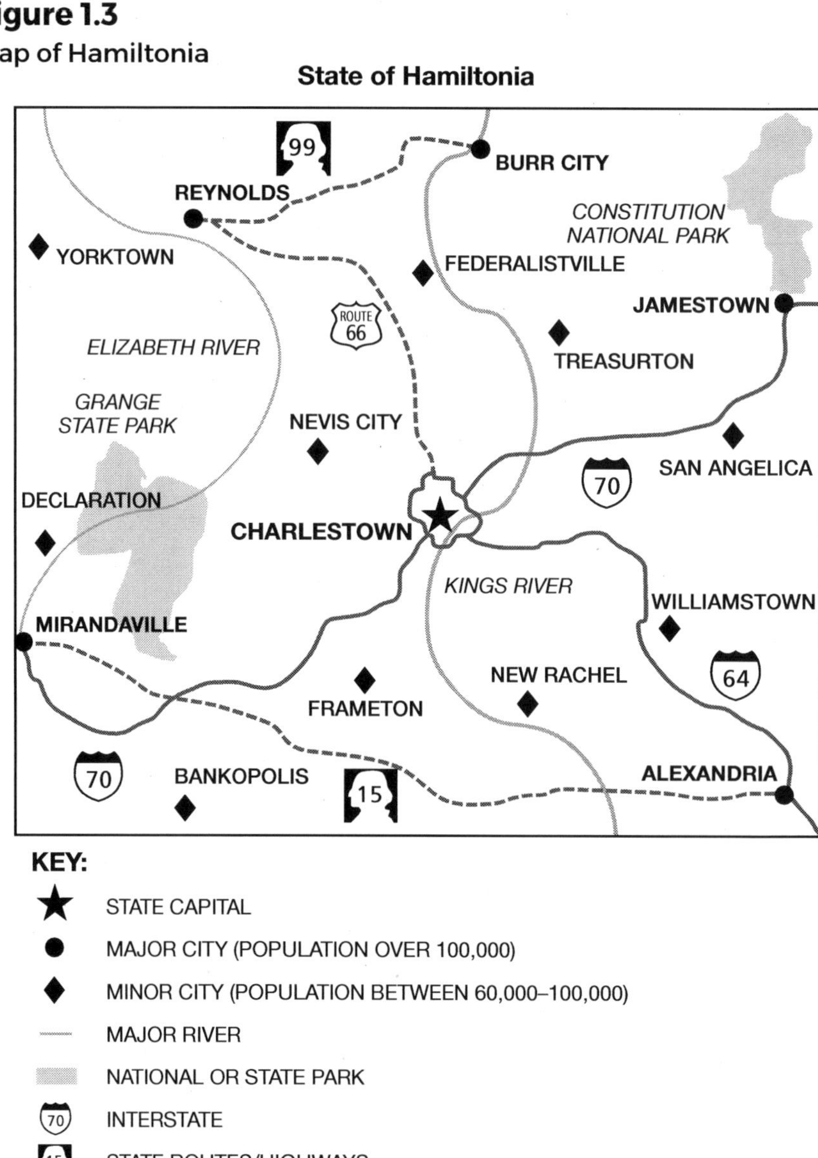

and cities in the United States. Hamiltonia would be the eighteenth-largest state in population and the city of Charlestown would be the seventeenth-largest city in the United States behind the cities of Charlotte and Indianapolis. There are four other major cities in Hamiltonia, each with a population over 100,000; they are: Burr City, Reynolds, Alexandria, and Mirandaville. Figure 1.4 includes the population sizes of each of

Table 1.1

Comparing Hamiltonia to Populations of Top 10 U.S. States and Cities

U.S. STATES BY POPULATION SIZE	U.S. CITIES BY POPULATION SIZE
1. California: 38,915,693	1. New York, NY: 7,888,121
2. Texas: 30,500,280	2. Los Angeles, CA: 3,769,485
3. Florida: 22,661,577	3. Chicago, IL: 2,608,425
4. New York: 19,496,810	4. Houston, TX: 2,264,876
5. Pennsylvania: 12,931,957	5. Phoenix, AZ: 1,651,344
6. Illinois: 12,477,595	6. Philadelphia, PA: 1,527,886
7. Ohio: 11,747,774	7. San Antonio, TX: 1,479,493
8. Georgia: 11,037,723	8. San Diego, CA: 1,374,076
9. North Carolina: 10,832,061	9. Dallas, TX: 1,259,404
10. Michigan: 10,030,722	10. Austin, TX: 966,292
18. Hamiltonia: 6,241,992	17. Charlestown, HA: 815,151

Figure 1.4

Population Sizes of Hamiltonia's Cities

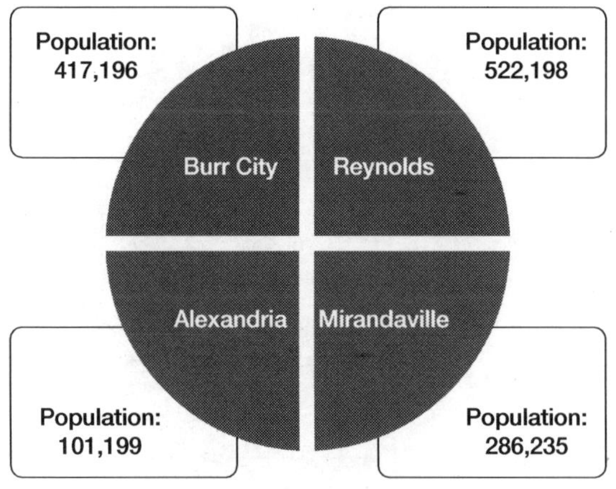

these cities. In addition to these five major cities there are ten other cities throughout Hamiltonia with populations between 60,000 and 100,000, and 900 towns and villages all with populations below 60,000. Hamiltonia is home to one national park, Constitution National Park, and seventy-five state parks. However, the largest and most well-known is Grange State Park.

Hamiltonia is also home to four military bases. There are two army bases and two air force bases. The first army base is outside of Yorktown in the northwestern part of the state. The second army base is just north of Bankopolis. The air force bases are both located on the eastern side of the state, with the first located between Alexandria and Williamstown and the second outside of San Angelica.

Figure 1.5 displays the racial and ethnic breakdown of Hamiltonia. About 33 percent of Hamiltonia identifies as non-white, with higher numbers of Latinos compared to African Americans throughout the state. About 50.5 percent of Hamiltonia's population is female. When it comes to the age of the people living in Hamiltonia, 6 percent are under five years old, 22 percent are under eighteen years old, and 17 percent are sixty-five years and over.

The final area of demographics we need to cover for Hamiltonia is economics. The median household income in Hamiltonia is $62,900, below the national average of $69,021. About 12.1 percent of people in Hamiltonia live in poverty (national average 11.6%) and the home

Figure 1.5

Racial and Ethnic Breakdown of Hamiltonia

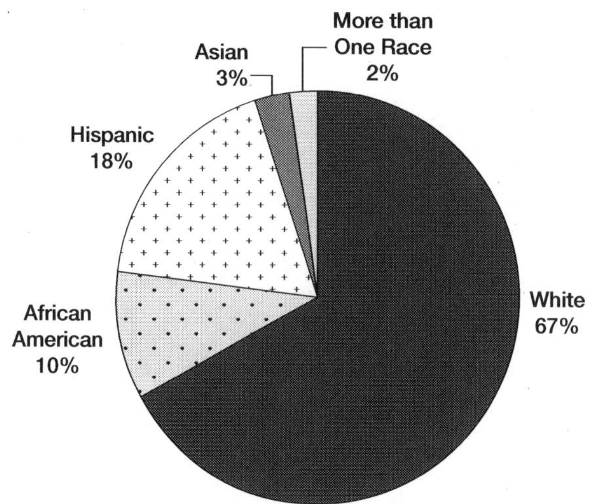

ownership rate is 66.4 percent. In terms of education, about 90 percent of citizens aged 25 and older have graduated high school, while 31 percent have a bachelor's degree or higher. Hamiltonia is home to 55 institutions of higher education, 15 of which are public four-year universities, 20 are public two-year universities, and 20 are private universities. The largest university is Hamiltonia State University (HSU) in the capital and annually enrolls about 17,500 students. The second-largest university is the University of Hamiltonia (UHA) located in Mirandaville with a student population of 15,250. These are both Division I universities and have a fierce rivalry.

Related to the economics of the state are the major industries in the state of Hamiltonia. Hamiltonia has a relatively diverse economy, with a slightly higher reliance on manufacturing than on other industries. While Hamiltonia has a relatively diverse manufacturing sector, two of the major areas in manufacturing are pharmaceuticals and electrical equipment including appliances. Figure 1.6 depicts Hamiltonia's gross state products by industry. Hamiltonia's gross national product (GDP) last year was $301.65 billion. The two major agricultural outputs are corn and soybeans.

Figure 1.6

Hamiltonia's Industries as Percentages of GDP

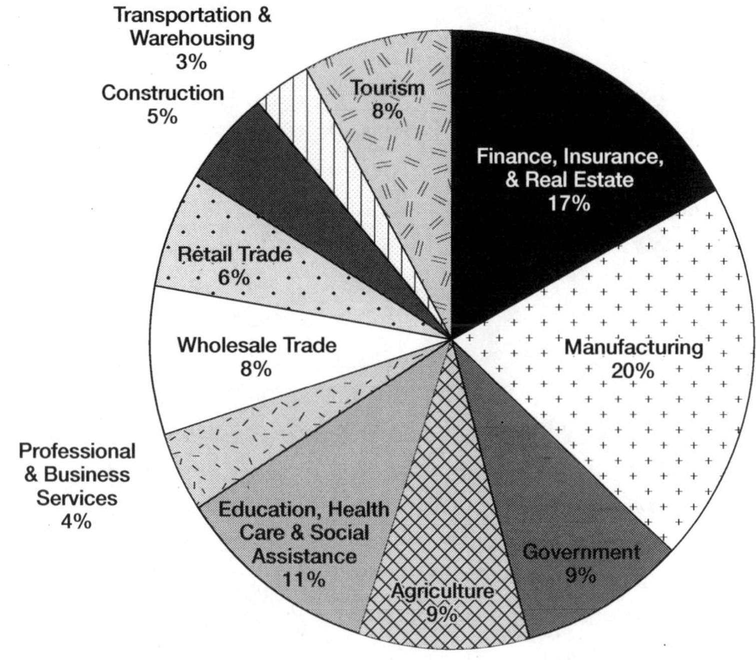

State governments also have policy authority in two major issue areas that affect residents: education and health. The constitution of Hamiltonia establishes a right to a public education. Hamiltonia contains 296 school districts serving 1.1 million K–12 students. Hamiltonia is in the middle of the pack in terms of student achievement. Hamiltonia is ranked nineteenth in the nation based on fourth grade reading scores and twenty-sixth based on fourth grade mathematics scores. Hamiltonia has a graduation rate of 85.96 percent and about 59 percent go on to a four-year college or university. Currently, residents have two major concerns about education in the state including access to and cost of early education and access to and cost of higher education.

In Hamiltonia, about 34 percent of four-year-old children attend preschool. A nine-month preschool program costs about $7,110 in Hamiltonia. Even for the families that can afford private preschool costs, spots are limited, and most childcare centers have waitlists. As mentioned above about 59 percent of Hamiltonia high school graduates go on to attend a four-year college or university. However, the cost of higher education can sometimes be prohibitive for students. The average cost of a public university is $10,000 for in-state residents and $19,000 for out-of-state residents, the average cost of a private university is $26,000, and the average cost of a community college is $5,500. Hamiltonia State Univerisity in the capitol costs $11,500 per year for in-state students and $27,800 for out-of-state students. With an economic shift away from manufacturing, Hamiltonia is focused on making sure it is preparing state residents for an economy of the future.

Health is also a major concern among Hamiltonians. In Hamiltonia, 10.2 percent of residents do not have health insurance, 52.2 percent have insurance through their employer, and 14.3 percent are on Medicaid (a state and federal program that provides insurance to low-income families). For those who do have health insurance, it has become expensive. The average yearly cost of health insurance for a Hamiltonia family is $7,643 and for an individual is $4,152. Hamiltonia is also facing several health problems including the opioid epidemic. In 2022, 2,263 Hamiltonians died from opioid overdoses including fentanyl. Yorktown and Frameton have been particularly hard hit by the opioid epidemic. Hamiltonia ranks twenty-seventh for teen suicide and has recently seen increases in teen depression and anxiety rates. About 9 percent of babies in Hamiltonia are born with low birth weight and 39.4 percent of residents are obese. The maternal mortality rate was 31.2 per 100,000 in 2022 and the Black maternal mortality rate was 68.9 per 100,000 live births. Overall, Hamiltonia ranks twenty-eighth in the nation for healthiest state.

Another area of importance to state governments is infrastructure. States are responsible for maintaining many kinds of infrastructure from roads to railways, airports, bridges, and drinking water. Every four years the American Society of Civil Engineers (ASCE) issues a national report card as well as a report card for each state across seventeen categories. In 2021 the United States was issued a grade of C– by the ASCE, which denotes that the "infrastructure in the system or network is in fair to good condition. It shows general signs of deterioration and requires attention. Some elements exhibit significant deficiencies in conditions and functionality, with increasing vulnerability to risk."[11] Nationally, the United States did not receive above a B in any category, with only two categories earning a B or B– (Ports and Rail), four categories earning a C+, C, or C– (Bridges, Drinking Water, Energy, and Solid Waste), and the remaining twelve categories earning a D+, D, or D– (Aviation, Dams, Hazardous Waste, Inland Waterways, Levees, Parks and Recreation, Roads, Schools, Storm Water, Transit, and Wastewater). Infrastructure has become such a problem that a typically polarized Congress was able to pass the Bipartisan Infrastructure deal in 2021 to address these issues.

A team of top civil engineers from Hamiltonia completed an independent review of the state's infrastructure across seven of the same categories reported by the ASCE. Below is the report card they issued:

1. *Aviation:* C+: According to the Bureau of Transportation Statistics there are 5,211 public airports throughout the United States. Hamiltonia is home to 215 of them, with nine being classified as major airports. Areas of deficiency include a below average percentage of airports meeting minimum runway length and width objectives, with some additional minor deficiencies in the pavement at the airport's runways and taxiways. Hamiltonia's airports report minimum delays.
2. *Bridges:* C+: In Hamiltonia 1,456 of the 14,953 bridges (10.27%) are structurally deficient. $57.90 million in bridge funds came from the Federal Highway Bridge Fund in the prior fiscal year. Approximately half of the bridges are owned by local governments, with the remaining bridges owned by the state of Hamiltonia.
3. *Energy:* C–: The overall health of Hamiltonia's energy generation and transmission system generally meets the state's current needs, but reliability and security concerns are posed by the state's dependence on coal and natural gas fueled generation.

Diversification of energy supply and investments in renewable energy and transmission system upgrades are needed to address these and other concerns such as fossil energy's contributions to global warming.

4. *Drinking Water: D+*: In the last fiscal year, Hamiltonia estimated that the drinking water systems needed an investment of $10 billion over the next twenty years to replace aging facilities and comply with safe drinking water regulations. Areas of investment include transmission and distribution, and treatment needs. There is a growing rate of water main breaks in the city of Charlestown: in the last year there were 1,756 main breaks in the capital with many others reported in the other major cities.
5. *Roads: C*: The last time the state of Hamiltonia passed a piece of transportation funding related legislation was in 2015. The funding generated by the bill allowed for 2,200 miles of the state's busiest highways to be smoother and safer, sped up fifty-five critical highway projects, and allowed $1.6 billion in new construction. The state has 131,978 public roads, 11,877 of which are major roads, and 10 percent of those are in poor condition. Hamiltonia costs motorists $1.6 billion a year from driving on roads in need of repair, which is $380 a year per motorist.
6. *Inland Waterways: C*: The state's two major navigable arteries, the Kings and Elizabeth Rivers and their tributaries, connect the state's eleven public river ports and over 100 private river terminals to river ports in fifteen states. Barge traffic is often delayed at Hamiltonia's docks due to abundant and unscheduled repairs, which can take months to completely resolve. Delays also occur due to low water, which results in light-loading barges and increased shipment costs. While delay times are generally low, they indicate an inability to effectively meet current demands. Budget cuts and depleted funds in the federal Inland Waterways Trust Fund threaten to set back Hamiltonia's water transportation infrastructure, including the new Federalist Lock, Hamiltonia's biggest water infrastructure project.
7. *School Facilities: C+*: There was a huge expansion in the 1950s where the number of schools in Hamiltonia more than doubled. These buildings are now sixty years old, and many need major repair or replacement. There is an estimated $4.6 billion in estimated school infrastructure funding needs.

8. *Rail: C–*: Hamiltonia has 2,900 miles of rail across the state. Many of these railways are for freight trains (2,515), with the remaining 385 miles dedicated to passenger rail. According to the American Society of Civil Engineers "passenger rail requires government investment and has been plagued by a lack of federal support, leading to a current state of good repair backlog at $45.2 billion."[12] Both passenger and freight rail safety need to improve in Hamiltonia and need to be expanded to better accommodate the state's needs.

The final area we need to discuss is public safety. Like all states, Hamiltonia is not without its public safety concerns. Public safety includes a wide-ranging array of crimes—from assault to theft to property damage. Table 1.2 contains the rankings of Hamiltonia on a series

Table 1.2
Public Safety Statistics in Hamiltonia

Public Safety (Overall Ranking)	20
Low Property Crime	15
Low Violent Crime	26
Corrections (Overall Ranking)	19
Low Incarceration Rate	10
Low Recidivism Rate	40
Sexual Violence in Prisons	15
Equality in Jailing	30
Gun Violence (Overall Ranking)	28
Firearm Deaths per 100,000 People	12.4 per 100,000
Total Firearm Deaths	775 (suicides: 436, homicides: 339)
Total Female Murders	35
Violent Crime Rate	339 per 100,000
Number of Mass Shootings Last 5 Years	3

of public safety measures in comparison to other states. Numbers closer to one mean the state is doing well on that measure (in other words they have a lower amount of that crime than other states). Numbers closer to fifty mean the state is doing poorly in comparison to that kind of crime as compared to other states.

The statistics on public safety are broken down into three major areas: overall public safety, which is comprised of property versus violent crime; corrections, which includes incarceration rates, recidivism, sexual violence in prisons and equality in jailing; and finally gun violence, which includes measures of firearm deaths, female murders to represent levels of domestic violence, and the number of mass shootings the state of Hamiltonia had in the past five years. In terms of overall public safety, Hamiltonia is in the top half of states, meaning they have lower crime levels. However, this is mainly driven by a lower level of property crime as compared to violent crime. In terms of incarceration, Hamiltonia has a lot of work to do on addressing recidivism, where they are ranked forty out of fifty states as well as equality in jailing. Hamiltonia also has an above average amount of gun violence, which is in part driven by suicides and female homicides, 50 percent of which are attributed to domestic violence.

There is one other area of public safety which includes the incidence of wildfires in the state. The National Interagency Fire Center reported 68,998 wildfires in 2022 which burned 7,577,183 acres. This was significantly higher than the number of wildfires in 2021. While western and southern states are particularly known for higher incidences of wildfires, they do occur in the midwestern states like Hamiltonia as well. Missouri had 136 forest fires in 2022 while Minnesota recorded 713 forest fires.[13] In 2022 Hamiltonia recorded 413 forest fires that resulted in 4,653 acres burned.

The Politics of Hamiltonia

Because Hamiltonia will be different based on each class that completes the simulation, we cannot say definitively the partisan composition of the state. However, there are some general patterns we can share regarding where registration is higher for certain political parties and which interest groups are most powerful in the state. Let's start with some of the patterns of political identification throughout the state. The cities of Reynolds, Burr City, Jamestown, Charlestown, Mirandaville, and Alexandria are known for their more liberal citizenry. This is particularly true for the capital of Charlestown and Reynolds. This follows patterns throughout the United States where urban areas typically have higher concentrations of members of the Democratic Party. The southern part of Hamiltonia between Mirandaville and Alexandria is where the majority of the agricultural industry resides and therefore is mainly rural farmland, this is where the Republican Party is the strongest, as well as on the eastern edge of the state between Jamestown and Alexandria. The western and northern regions of the state, outside of the cities, are full of small towns and villages with a relatively equal distribution of Republican and Democratic Party members.

When it comes to **interest groups** in Hamiltonia, there are quite a few that have influence in the halls of government. **Lobbyists**, who work to advance the needs of interest groups can be defined in different ways. The state of South Carolina, for example, defines a lobbyist as a "legislative agent ... who is employed, appointed, or retained, with or without compensation, by another person ... to influence in any manner the act or vote of any member of the General Assembly."[14] States regulate lobbyists to avoid improper relationships between organizations and people who work for the government. States typically require lobbyists to be registered with the Secretary of State's office, and many states require lobbyists or those who hire lobbyists to submit periodic disclosure reports "that identify how much money is spent on lobbying, what legislative issues are being lobbied, and for which officials' benefit the expenditures are made."[15] Table 1.3 compares the disclosure requirements of three states: Washington, West Virginia, and Maine.

The voice of farmers in the state is often heard through the Hamiltonia Farm Bureau Federation, part of the American Farm

Table 1.3
Lobbyist Reporting Disclosure Requirements

	WASHINGTON	WEST VIRGINIA	MAINE
Frequency	Monthly reports	3 times a year	Monthly reports while legislature is in session
Example Required Information	• Totals of all expenditures for lobbying activities • Listing of each contribution • Listing of each payment for an item over $50 to a state official	• Total amount of expenditures for lobbying • Subject matter of lobbying activities • List of public official or employee who received meals, beverages, living accommodations, travel, gifts, etc.	• Names of lobbyists for organization • Compensation for lobbying activities • Amount of indirect lobbying over $15,000 • List of legislative actions

Note: Information from the National Conference of State Legislatures (NCSL): https://www.ncsl.org/ethics/lobbyist-activity-report-requirements

Bureau Federation. There is also a chapter of the Sierra Club for the state of Hamiltonia. The Sierra Club's mission is to

> Explore, enjoy, and protect the wild places of the earth; practice and promote the responsible use of the earth's ecosystems and resources; Educate and enlist humanity to protect and restore the quality of the natural and human environment; Use all lawful means to carry out these objectives.[16]

Another interest group that has a strong presence in the state is the National Rifle Association (NRA). The NRA often ranks and grades both candidates and current office holders on issues surrounding the Second Amendment and gun control. Finally, keep in mind that major corporations such as Walmart and Amazon as well as educational institutions such as Hamiltonia State Univerisity and local governments act as interest groups as well. They will lobby their representatives as well as the governor and their cabinet to ensure laws are passed that benefit them, or in the case of educational institutions, they receive a certain amount of money from the state of Hamiltonia when the budget is created. Some of these groups have in-house lobbyists meaning that the lobbyists are employees of the company. Many others, however, use the largest lobbying firm in Hamiltonia called Burr and Associates. Burr and Associates represent many groups, causes, and companies in Hamiltonia.

Looking Forward

This chapter provided an overview of both the role of state governments in the American system as well as an introduction to the fifty-first state of Hamiltonia. In the next chapter we will be diving into the simulation, covering state constitutions and direct democracy.

Key Terms

oversight (2)
constituent service (2)
sponsoring (2)
procedural rules (2)
constituents (2)
zoning laws (4)
federalism (4)
Time, Place, and Manner Clause (5)
concurrent powers (5)
unitary (5)
interstate agency (6)
policy diffusion (6)
court of last resort (7)
veto (7)
Medicaid (9)
moralistic (9)
traditionalistic (9)
individualistic (9)
interest groups (21)
lobbyists (21)

Assignments to Learn More about State Governments

1. One area we did not cover was the state symbols associated with every state. This ranges from the official state flag to the state seal, to the official state bird, fish, flower, fruit, and beverage. In this table is a comparison of some of the state symbols of Montana versus Georgia.

SYMBOLS	MONTANA	GEORGIA
State Flag	Montana flag	Georgia flag
State Seal	Montana state seal	Georgia state seal
Nickname(s)	Big Sky Country; The Treasure State	Peach State, Empire State of the South
Motto	"Oro y Plata": Gold and Silver	"Wisdom, Justice & Moderation"
State Bird	Western Meadowlark	Brown Thrasher
State Flower	Bitterroot	Cherokee Rose
State Tree	Ponderosa Pine	Live Oak

IMAGE SOURCES: Getty

Hamiltonia needs these state symbols too. What should they be? Create the same state symbols for Hamiltonia as is provided for Montana and Georgia.

2. We provided the example of the New York and New Jersey Port Authority which helps to regulate and maintain the transportation-related relationship between the two states. Another example of an interstate agency is the Great Lakes Commission, which includes the states of Wisconsin, Ohio, Indiana, Illinois, Michigan, Minnesota, New York, and

Pennsylvania as well as the Canadian Provinces of Ontario and Québec. Research the Commission and explain both its history and the work it performs.

3. Throughout this simulation we will be looking into questions of representation in state government. What does good representation look like to you? How important do you think it is that Hamiltonia's government "looks" like its citizens in terms of race, ethnicity, gender identification, sexual orientation, and educational attainment?

Louisiana State Capitol, Baton Rouge, Louisiana

SOURCE: Getty

Creating a Constitution

Learning Objectives:

After reading this chapter students should be able to:

- Describe the purpose of a constitution for state governments.
- Explain what state constitutions typically contain.
- Compare the various ways state constitutions can be amended.
- Evaluate the utility of direct democracy at the state level.
- Decide whether Hamiltonia should have direct democracy mechanisms such as initiatives and referendums.

State Spotlight: Louisiana

Now that we have learned the background information necessary to start building a state government, you can officially start the Hamiltonia simulation! We begin the simulation where all state governments start: their state constitutions. Just like the U.S. Constitution sets up the roles and responsibilities of the three branches of government as well as the rules associated with amending the constitution, so too do state constitutions. What is fascinating about state constitutions is that unlike our federal constitution of which we have only had one, many states have had multiple constitutions throughout their history.

In fact, the state spotlight for this chapter is Louisiana which has had eleven different constitutions since it was admitted into the union in 1812. Georgia trails just behind Louisiana with a total of ten constitutions since 1777. Louisiana created a new constitution in 1845, 1852, 1861, 1864, 1868, 1879, 1898, 1912, 1921, and 1974. Why so many constitutions? In part it has to do with the Civil War. Four of the constitutions were created during the Civil War and Reconstruction, or just after. The 1862 constitution, for example, was created to show that Louisiana had seceded from the Union and recognized the Confederate States of America.[1] The 1864 constitution comes as the Union made inroads into Louisiana, so slavery became abolished in the parishes (what Louisiana calls counties) that were under Union control. Louisiana demonstrates the possibility of states reinventing their governments. On the other end of the spectrum, you have the Commonwealth of Massachusetts, which is the oldest constitution in the United States. That constitution was drafted in 1780 by none other than John Adams, and according to the Massachusetts government, "served as a model for the United States Constitution, which was written in 1787 and became effective in 1789."[2] Figure 2.1 describes how many states have adopted more than one constitution over their statehood.

State constitutions are like the federal constitution in that they lay out the institutions and the powers they retain. But they are also different from the federal constitution in that they are typically much longer (Alabama's constitution at a whopping 340,136 words compared to the 4,543 words in the U.S. Constitution[3]), contain specific public policies, and also outline the exact relationship between states and their local governments.[4] Unlike the federalist arrangement between the federal and state governments wherein power is shared, the relationship between states and their local governments is **unitary**, meaning all power originates from the state governments.

Figure 2.1
Number of State Constitutions

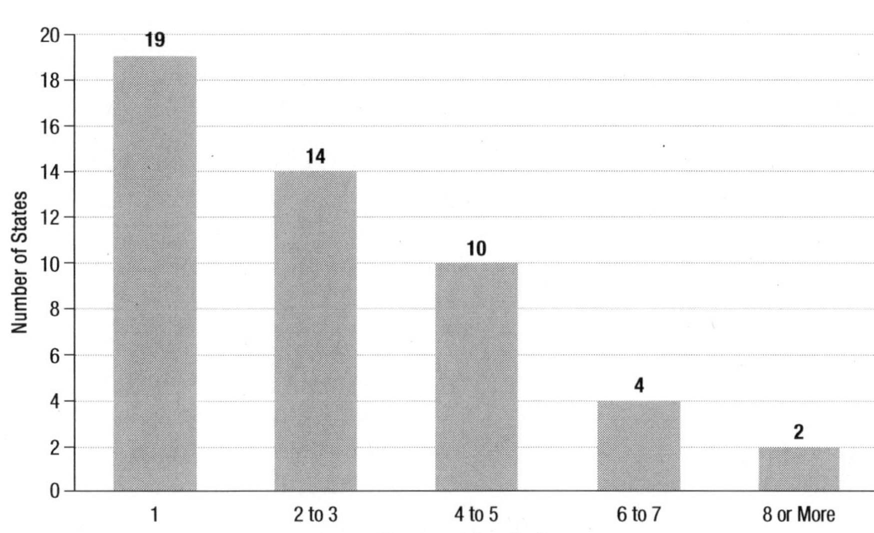

In this chapter we will be covering the key components contained within state constitutions as well as the myriad ways constitutions can be amended. We will also be guiding you through the decisions your class needs to make when it comes to Hamiltonia's constitution, including whether or not balanced budgets should be required in the constitution and whether you decide to adopt various direct democracy actions. Let's begin.

State Constitutions: What They Say and How They Say It

As we mentioned earlier, **state constitutions** lay out the institutions and policies associated with state governments. The first part of a constitution is the **preamble**, which sets out the broad political beliefs of the state. Here is the Commonwealth of Pennsylvania's preamble: "We, the people of the Commonwealth of Pennsylvania, grateful to Almighty God for the blessings of civil and religious liberty, and humbly invoking His guidance, do ordain and establish this Constitution."[5]

In comparison, South Dakota's preamble reads as follows:

> We, the people of South Dakota, grateful to Almighty God for our civil and religious liberties, in order to form a more perfect and independent government, establish justice, insure tranquility, provide for the

> common defense, promote the general welfare and preserve to ourselves and to our posterity the blessings of liberty, so ordain and establish this Constitution for the state of South Dakota.[6]

After the preamble, states differ on what they cover next in their constitutions. The U.S. Constitution sets out the three branches of government in Article I (Legislative Branch), Article II (Executive Branch), and Article III (Judicial Branch). Not all states do it this way. Some states, like Massachusetts, begin with a declaration of the rights of state residents, a bill of rights so to speak. In the First Part, Article I of their constitution, Massachusetts states that "all men are born free and equal, and have certain natural, essential, and unalienable rights; among which may be reckoned the right of enjoying and defending their lives and liberties."[7] Texas also begins their constitution with a Bill of Rights and protects the: Freedom and Sovereignty of the state, inherent political power, Republican form of government, equal rights, equality under the law, and religious tests among many other rights.[8]

Then there are sections of state constitutions dedicated to each branch of government. Oklahoma describes their legislative branch in Article 5 of their constitution, followed by the executive department in Article 6, and Judicial Department in Article 7. Figure 2.2 outlines the major sections of each of these articles. They set up how each institution is supposed to work, major positions, duties, and qualifications. Take a good look at what state constitutions say about their governmental institutions as you will be creating these same institutions as delegates of Hamiltonia's first constitutional convention.

You are probably wondering what else state constitutions cover if we already discussed the sections detailing the branches of government and a **bill of rights**. Remember from the beginning of this chapter we discussed how much longer state constitutions are. The reason for this is that many state constitutions outline public policy. For example, Article 6 of the Kansas Constitution concerns education. In this section of their state constitution Kansas says: "The legislature shall provide for intellectual, educational, vocational and scientific improvement by establishing and maintaining public schools, educational institutions and related activities which may be organized and changed in such manner as may be provided by law."[9]

The rest of this article outlines the creation a state board of education and state board of regents, a commissioner of education, and how education will be financed. States outline their responsibilities to a public education differently. These differences can have public policy consequences and determine how citizens can hold the

Figure 2.2

Articles 5, 6, and 7 of the Oklahoma Constitution

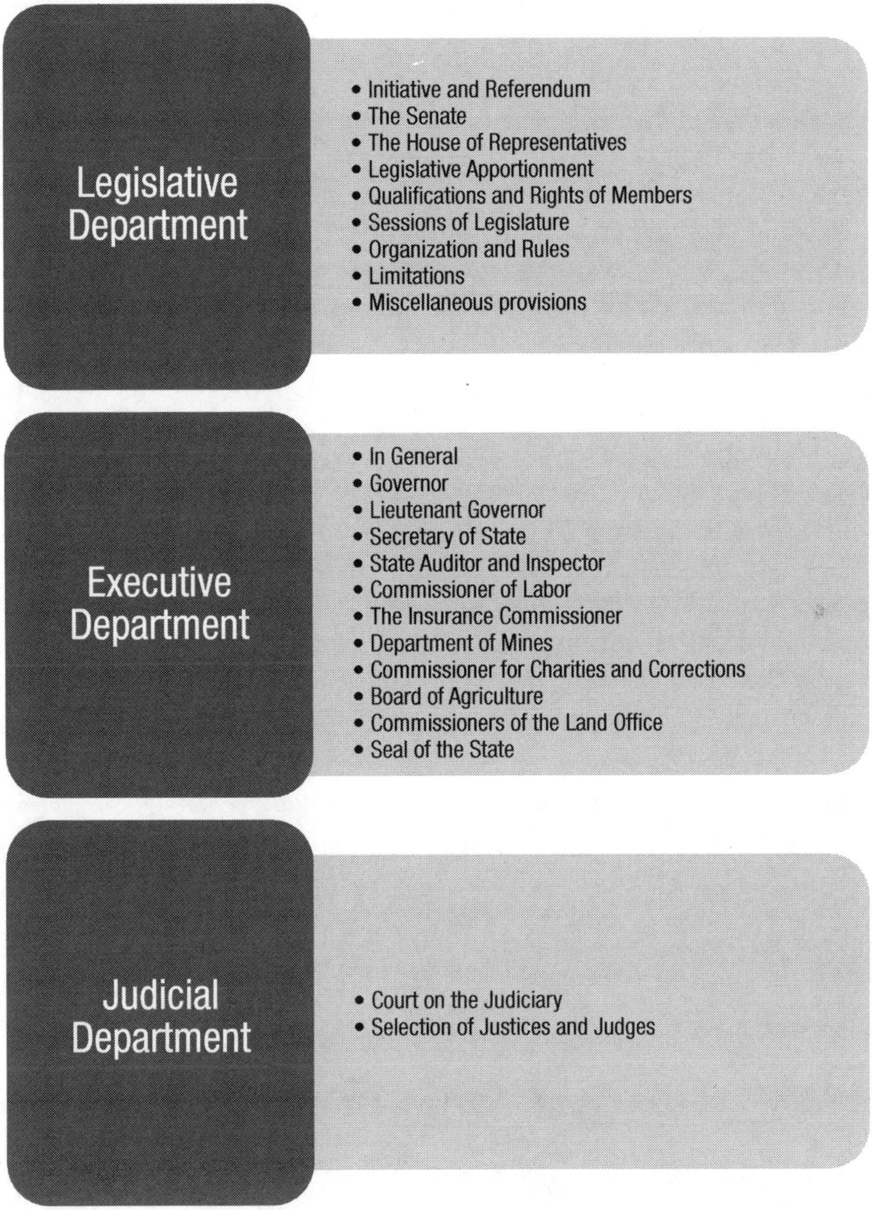

government responsible for providing this right. For example, the New Jersey Constitution states, "The Legislature shall provide for the maintenance and support of a thorough and efficient system of free public schools for the instruction of all the children in the State between the ages of five and eighteen years."[10] In the 1980s, the Education Law Center filed suit against the state, arguing that the way the New Jersey legislature was funding public schools was violating this clause in the state constitution because school funding was so unequal. This led to a series of court cases called the Abbott decisions that fundamentally changed education policy in the state and was instrumental in establishing a state pre-k program for children in some of New Jersey's school districts.[11] The New Jersey government was held accountable to the state constitution through these court cases.

Hawaii has a section of their constitution dedicated to public health and welfare. Article IX of the Hawaii state constitution states that the "state shall provide for the protection and promotion of public health," as well as "provide for the treatment and rehabilitation of handicapped persons."[12] There is also an interesting clause in Hawaii's state constitution regarding "Public Sightliness and Good Order," whereby "the State shall have the power to conserve and develop objects and places of historic or cultural interest and provide for public sightliness and physical good order."[13]

Finally, a substantial number of state constitutions also address local governments. As we will learn in chapter 3, the relationship between state and local governments is unitary, whereby local governments receive their power from their state government. Sections 156–168 of the Kentucky constitution concern municipalities. In these sections

Hawaii State Capitol, Honolulu, Hawaii.

SOURCE: Getty

of the constitution Kentucky describes how cities can be classified, the maximum tax rate for cities, counties, and taxing districts (cities with 15,000 people or more, no more than $1.50 for each $100, for example), and how members of local governments, such as mayors are to be selected. These sections in a sense authorize local governments to exist, and depending on the state, exactly how leaders of local governments are to be selected and what they can and cannot do.

Simulation

For the rest of the chapter, we will detail the various components of state constitutions and mechanisms of direct democracy. We begin with how states amend their constitutions.

Amending Constitutions

The first area you need to tackle as members of the first Hamiltonia Constitutional convention is how you will be able to change—or amend—it. Unlike the United States Constitution which has been amended only a handful of times (27, including the first 10 of the Bill of Rights), states vary drastically in the number of amendments they have associated with their state constitutions. From a low of thirteen amendments from Rhode Island's 1986 adopted constitution to a high of 977 from Alabama's 1901 adopted constitution, there is great variation in the total number of amendments adopted by states. Alabama's number of amendments is particularly interesting—and also another explanation for the state having such a lengthy constitution—in comparison to Massachusetts. Remember Massachusetts has the oldest state constitution with a ratification year of 1780. Over the course of their 243 years, they have only submitted 148 amendments to voters and adopted only 120.[14] Yes, you read that right—amendments have been submitted to the voters in the state of Massachusetts because in some states residents can vote directly on state constitutional amendments. We do not have this option at the federal level.

You may be wondering why states in comparison to the federal government have passed so many more amendments. One reason, again, is because state constitutions deal more with public policy, which are easier targets for amendments. A second reason is because many states have multiple ways a constitution can be amended. Let's first start off with how the United States Constitution is amended. The U.S. Constitution can be amended in one of two ways. Option one is an amendment that is proposed by two-thirds of both Houses of

Congress, which is the only way all twenty-seven amendments have been adopted. The second option is for a constitutional convention to be called by two-thirds of state legislatures.[15]

At the state level, the process looks very different. First, every state allows for amendments to be proposed by their legislatures, albeit with varying rules on the vote required for the proposal, whether consideration by two sessions is required, the threshold for **ratification**, and whether there is a limit on the number of amendments a legislature can submit in one election. Arizona, for example, requires a majority of legislators to review an amendment proposal, does not require consideration by two legislative sessions, requires a majority vote on the amendment, and does not limit the number of amendments to be submitted for each election. In comparison, Kentucky requires three-fifths of the legislature to review an amendment proposal, a majority vote on the amendment, and limits the number of amendments to be submitted for each election to four.

This is not the only way a constitution can be amended. Eighteen states allow for constitutional amendments via **initiative**. Initiatives are created and submitted by citizens, and in order to get on the ballot need a certain number of signatures which varies by state. Figure 2.3 provides examples from three states on their process for amendments via initiative. There is quite a bit of variation on the number of signatures required for the initiative to even make it onto the ballot, from 15 percent of the total votes cast for all candidates for governor in the last election in Arizona,

Figure 2.3

Constitutional Amendments by Initiative in Arizona, Illinois, and North Dakota

Arizona	Illinois	North Dakota
☐ 15% of total votes cast for all candidates for governor at last election.	☐ 8% of total votes cast for candidates for governor of last election.	☐ 4% of population of the state.
☐ Requires majority vote.	☐ Requires majority voting in election 3/5 voting on amendment.	☐ Requires majority vote.

to 4 percent of the population of North Dakota. To put that in perspective that is nearly 383,800 signatures in Arizona and 31,170 signatures in North Dakota.[16] There are also differences in what is needed for passage. Both Arizona and North Dakota require a majority vote, but Illinois requires majority voting in an election or three-fifths voting on the amendment. Furthermore, Illinois also limits what can be amended via initiative. The *Book of States* explains: "initiatives can only be used to amend substantive or procedural aspects of Article IV, the Legislature Article, and cannot be used to amend any other articles."[17] Figure 2.4 summarizes how many states have adopted this amendment mechanisms as well as the other mechanisms we are going to explain further.

Many states—44 to be exact—also allow amendments via **constitutional conventions.**[18] There are different variations of this process depending upon the state. Some states require that a ballot measure be issued after a certain number of years. New York asks their citizens every twenty years if they want to hold a convention. In 2017, 83 percent of voters said no to a convention.[19] The last time they held a convention was in 1967.[20] Other states allow for the legislature to call for a convention—sometimes with and sometimes without voter approval. Delaware allows amendments via

Figure 2.4

Constitutional Amendment Mechanisms

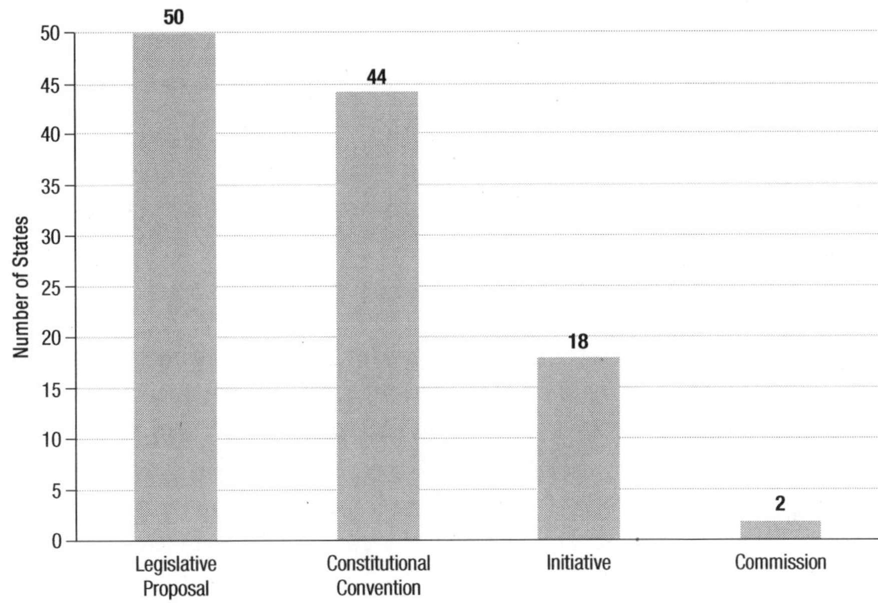

Data from *The Book Of States* (2021).

constitutional convention as long as two-thirds of both chambers of the legislature approve. However, Delaware is unique in that it is the only state that has a process whereby the General Assembly can amend the constitution without any vote held by the general public.[21]Another unique constitutional amendment procedure is Florida's. Florida has a Taxation and Budget Reform Commission that has the authority to propose amendments to the Florida Constitution. This group convenes once every 20 years. Florida also has a "Constitution Revision commission that convenes every 20 years since 1977."[22] Following in Florida's footsteps, New Mexico also has a commission that can create and propose constitutional amendments to the legislature.

This leads us to your first big decision as the delegation for Hamiltonia's first constitutional convention. Which mechanism or mechanisms will you adopt as a way for the constitution to be amended? Will you go the route Delaware has taken and allow amendments to be proposed and adopted all without popular consent? Maybe you like the idea of initiatives, which give the most amount of power to citizens of a state to change their constitution. Think carefully about who should be responsible for amending the constitution and the public's role in that process.

Action Item

2-1

How can the State Constitution be amended? Legislative proposals, ballot initiatives, conventions, or commissions?

Balanced Budgets and Tax and Expenditure Limits

An area unique to states is their adoption of balanced budget requirements as well as taxing limitations within their state constitutions. Let's start with **balanced budget requirements**. The Tax Policy Center, a joint organization formed by the Urban Institute and Brookings Institution, defines balance budget requirements (BBRs) as "constitutional or statutory rules that prohibit states from spending more than they collect in **revenue**."[23] The Tax Policy Center categorized BBRs in four ways: states that did not have a requirement at all, states with weak requirements, states with strong requirements, and states with statutory requirements. Here is how they describe their categories:

> A strong balanced budget requirement meets one or more of the following criteria: 1) requires the governor to sign a balanced budget; 2) prohibits the state from carrying over a deficit into the following year or biennium; or 3) requires the legislature to pass a balanced budget, accompanied by within-year fiscal controls or limits on supplemental appropriations.[24]

According to this definition, thirty-nine states have strong BBRs and nine states weak BBRs. North Dakota and Wyoming do not have any BBRs. Of the states that have strong BBRs, thirty-three of them have it in their constitution. If you are wondering why BBRs are so popular it is because they have been shown to effectively reduce spending, deficits, debt, and result in higher surpluses and faster spending adjustments during recessions.[25] However, the Tax Policy Center does note that sometimes states with strong BBRs may be under greater pressure during recessions because they have to either enact spending cuts to not go over budget or increase their revenues. This is the opposite of what should be done when a recession occurs. Figure 2.5 displays which states have strong versus weak BBRs based upon the Tax Policy Center's classification.

The second way states specifically restrict budgets is through **taxing and expenditure limitations**. These are exactly what they sound like: states limit the amount of money they can raise in taxes as well as how much of it they can spend. We again turn to the Tax Policy Center, which collected the number states that had these: 25 states limit spending, 21 limit revenue, and 13 limit both. For the states that

Figure 2.5

Strength of Balanced Budget Requirements across the United States

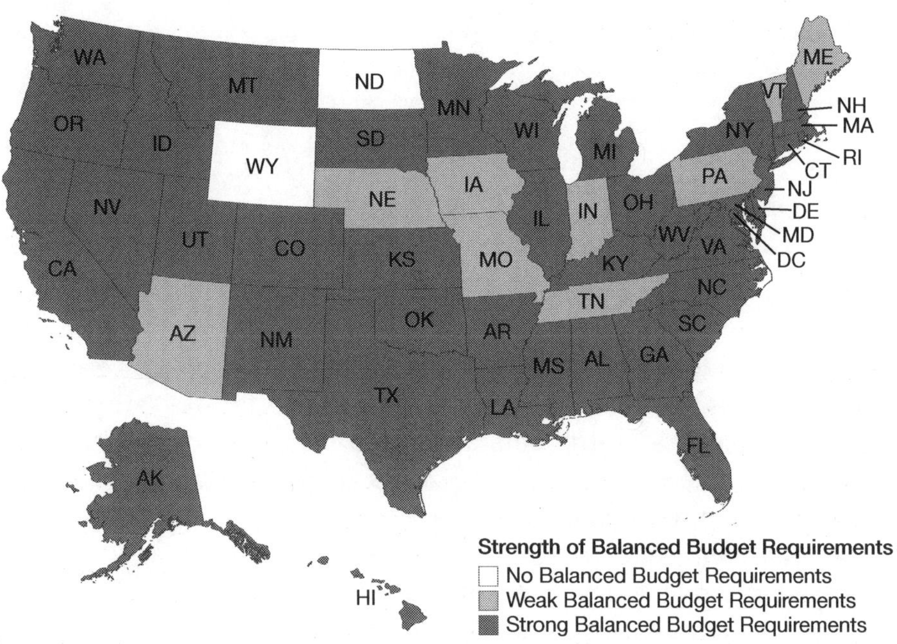

Based upon data from the Tax Policy Center.

limit revenue, most (19) require "a legislative supermajority to raise taxes."[26] States can either restrict their expenditures to a percentage of personal income or to a projected percentage of revenue. Furthermore, these taxing and expenditure limits can be placed within the state constitution, which is why we bring it up in this chapter.

You could even decide to be like Georgia, North Carolina, Texas, and Nevada and place a cap or ban on income taxes within the state constitution. This could be overridden by the legislature, but you would have to decide what the threshold is to override these laws. In the end, you may decide to keep balanced budgets and taxing and expenditure limits as a law that could be passed, instead of enshrined in the constitution. Keep in mind that makes them easier to change or get rid of entirely.

Action Item

2-2

Should there be a Balanced Budget requirement in the constitution?

Action Item

2-3

Should there be restrictions on raising taxes in the constitution? What should they be and how can they be changed?

Direct Democracy Mechanisms

Our next area to tackle is further ways that citizens of a state can be directly involved in legislation making and/or approval. Like the federal government, state governments are set up mainly to be **representative democracies**, whereby citizens elect representatives to create and pass legislation on their behalf. But unlike the federal government, some state governments allow citizens to be involved in this process in some way through initiatives or **referendums**, which are both forms of **direct democracy**.

Let's start with initiatives. We already know the first way initiatives can exist at the state level and that is through constitutional amendments. However, initiatives also exist in twenty-one states to change or pass new laws. There are two different ways initiatives can be presented: directly or indirectly. Let's start with **indirect initiatives** and use the example of Michigan. Michigan first adopted initiatives on statutes in 1908 and requires 8 percent of gubernatorial votes from the last election in order for the initiative to go to the legislature. If it meets that threshold, the legislature via a simple majority vote can approve the initiative as is, or they could propose a different initiative that is placed on the ballot at the same time to be voted on. Whichever they choose, they have to address the initiative within forty session days. If they do not, it goes on the ballot in the next general election. Nine states allow for indirect initiatives, with four states (Alaska, Michigan, Washington, and Wyoming) barring the governor from vetoing the initiative once approved by the legislature.[27]

Direct initiatives can be found in fourteen states (two states have both). In this process the legislature is not involved: sponsors of the initiative get the minimum number of signatures needed and then it goes on the ballot. Again, the required number of signatures varies from state to state. Arizona requires 10 percent of the votes cast for governor in the last general election while Arkansas requires 8 percent of votes cast for governor. Colorado bases their threshold of signatures on the percentage of votes cast for the secretary of state (5%), while Nebraska requires 7 percent of registered voters for a direct initiative to make it to the ballot. Requiring more signatures before an initiative can get on the ballot can make it more difficult for initiatives to get over that threshold.

Initiatives are not the only form of direct democracy present at the state level. The other kind of direct democracy measure are referendums. There are two ways we can think about referendums. The first is the most popular and is called a **veto referendum**. In a veto referendum the citizens have the opportunity to veto a law. Just like for the petitions for direct and indirect initiatives, each state has a minimum requirement of registered voters for the veto referendum to make it to the ballot. Twenty-three states have veto referendums, many of which can be found in the west. See Figure 2.6 for the map of states that have veto referendums. An interesting fact about veto referendums is that yes and no votes mean different things in different states. If you vote yes in a veto referendum in Alaska you are voting for the legislation to be repealed. If you are voting yes in a veto referendum in Missouri, you are voting for the legislation to be retained.[28] While we are not going to ask you to get this specific about whether you want a veto referendum, it is worth considering whether the process can be confusing to the average voter.

Figure 2.6
States with Veto Referendums

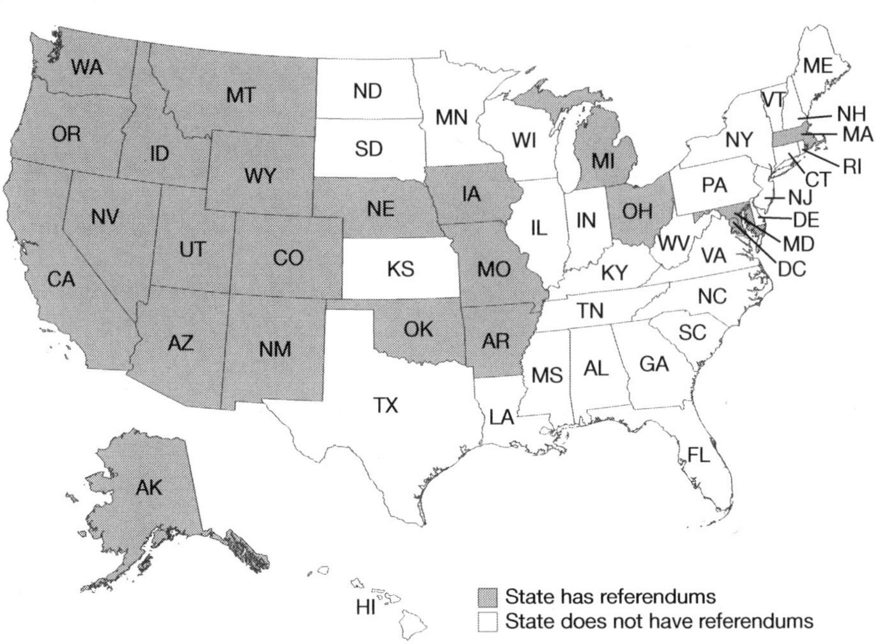

Referendums can also be used to approve laws. All but four of the states that have referendums (Arkansas, Idaho, Maine, and North Dakota) exclude specific subject manner from referendums. Massachusetts has a rather lengthy list of subjects that cannot be in referendums:

> Laws that relate to religion, religious practices or religious institutions; the appointment, qualification, tenure, removal, or compensation of judges; the powers, creation or abolition of courts; the operation of a particular town, city or other political division or to particular districts or localities of the commonwealth; or the appropriation of money for the current or ordinary expenses of the commonwealth or for any of its departments, boards, commissions, or institutions.[29]

Wyoming's list is much shorter: "laws related to dedications of revenue, appropriations, local or special legislation, or laws necessary for the immediate preservation of the public peace, health or safety."[30] Restricting the kinds of topics referendum can address places less power in the hands of the majority to shape laws in the state. You will need to decide whether or not you think Hamiltonia should adopt referendums and if you do, the process associated with getting one on the ballot. Remember, these direct democracy avenues are not available to us at the national level. Instead, states are an additional venue that state residents, including you, can have their voices heard.

Action Item

2-4

Should Hamiltonia allow direct democracy actions from citizens?

- Referendums
  - Will you limit it to veto referendums or allow for referendums for approval of legislation?
  - Will you limit the subject matter of referendums?
  - If you allow for referendums, what is the threshold that must be met for it to be on the ballot?
- Initiatives
  - Will you have direct initiatives?
  - Will you have indirect initiatives?
  - If you allow initiatives, what is the threshold that must be met for it to be on the ballot?
  - Will you allow initiatives passed by citizens to be overridden by the governor?

Larry Elder (Libertarian), a gubernatorial recall candidate for California against sitting governor Gavin Newsom (D) in 2021

SOURCE: Getty

Recalling Elected Officials

One final area of direct democracy is **recall elections**. Recall elections allow for voters to essentially fire their elected officials if they do not like how they are performing before the next election. A recent example of a recall election was for sitting Governor Gavin Newsom. Newsom was born and raised in California and has a long political resume including mayor of San Francisco (2004–2011) and lieutenant governor (2011–2019). He was elected governor of California in 2018, winning 61.9 percent of the vote against Republican John Cox.[31] There were multiple attempts to call a recall election against Newsom, with the one that was successful stating: "people in this state suffer the highest taxes in the nation, the highest homelessness rates, and the lowest quality of life as a result."[32]

In order for a governor to be sent for a recall election in California, there must be enough signatures to match "12% of the votes cast in the last gubernatorial election, with signatures from at least five separate counties equal to 1% of the votes cast in that county in the last gubernatorial election".[33] The petition can circulate for 160 days, and once the threshold has been met, a **simultaneous recall election** is held. This means that the sitting governor runs alongside challengers like Libertarian Larry Elder. Gavin Newsom won his recall election with the same exact amount he won by in 2018: 61.9 percent of voters did not want to recall him and elect someone else.[34]

According to the National Conference of State Legislatures (NCSL) the first ever recall election in the United States actually began in Los Angeles in 1903. Just five years later Michigan and Oregon would allow state officials to be recalled.[35] Figure 2.7 shows the four ways recall votes can be structured. The simultaneous recall election has two types: the first is when the election lists the governor and his or her challengers with the person winning the most votes becoming (or staying) governor. The second is what happened in California where voters are first asked if the governor should be recalled, and the second question asks who should replace the governor if a majority of voters want to replace the sitting governor.

In a separate **special election,** the process of recall and the potential election to replace them is separated. First the recall vote happens, then if a majority vote for recall, the governor leaves office and a special election is held to find a new governor. A **retention recall election** occurs similarly, except there is no election to select a new person to fill the governor's seat, but instead the next in the line of succession—the lieutenant governor—becomes governor for the remainder of the term.

Figure 2.7
Kinds of Recall Votes

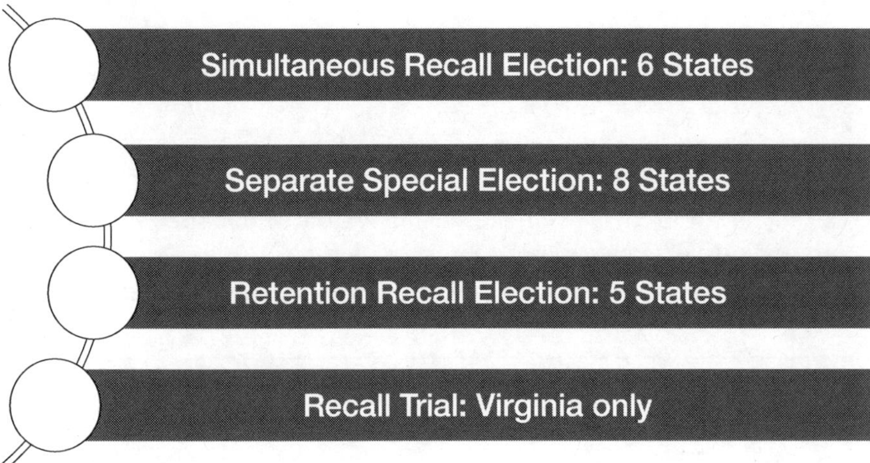

Finally, there is Virginia. Not only is Virginia unique in that the governor can only serve one four-year term, but it is also unique because it gets the courts directly involved in a recall. As Ballotpedia describes:

> The recall trial procedure ... involves the governor being tried before a circuit court. The governor has the right to request that the trial be heard before a jury, as well as to appeal the decision to the Supreme Court of Virginia. In the event that the court finds the complaints against the governor to be valid, the governor is removed from office and the constitutional successor takes place.[36]

There are two other aspects of recall elections we need to consider. The first is whether you want to specify the grounds for recall. Twelve states including Idaho and Michigan do not specify any grounds for recall. Minnesota specifies that there needs to be "serious malfeasance or nonfeasance during the term of office in the performance of the duties of the office or conviction during the term of office of a serious crime."[37] You will also need to decide the number of signatures required as well as the length of petition time. Alaska requires 25 percent of the votes cast in the last gubernatorial election with no time limit while Georgia limits the petition to ninety days and set the threshold to 15 percent of voters eligible to participate in the last gubernatorial election.[38] Recall elections are meant to allow state residents to hold elected officials accountable. As noted above, some states outline requirements such as serious malfeasance and others only require a certain number of signatures. Make sure you think about when and under what conditions the residents of Hamiltonia should be able to vote elected officials out of office *before* their term expires and how the threat of a recall may shape the behavior of elected officials.

Action Item

2-5

Will Hamiltonia allow for the recall of elected officials?

- If so, how will a recall be held: simultaneously, with a special election, retention election or trial?
- What is the required number of signatures and the length of time the petition can circulate?

Looking Forward

Congratulations! You have successfully started the Hamiltonia simulation by answering key questions of what you want in Hamiltonia's state constitution. You may have decided that direct democracy is important, and allowing citizens to make or vote on legislation will be a component of your state governmental institutions. Or maybe you decided to have only some or no direct democracy measures—you would not be the only state to do so. Whatever it is you choose, you are well on your way to creating a state government of your own. In the next chapter we will cover intergovernmental relations and how you want to create your local governments and the powers you will afford them.

Key Terms

unitary (26)
state constitutions (27)
preamble (27)
bill of rights (28)
ratification (32)
initiative (32)
constitutional convention (33)
balanced budget requirements (34)
revenue (34)
taxing and expenditure limitations (35)
representative democracies (36)
referendums (36)
direct democracy (36)
indirect initiatives (37)
recall elections (40)
simultaneous recall election (40)
special election (40)
retention recall election (40)

Assignments to Learn More about State Governments

1. The Preamble for the Constitution sets the tone of the document and generally outlines the fundamental beliefs of a state. South Carolina's Preamble, for example, says, "We, the people of the State of South Carolina, in Convention assembled, grateful to God for our liberties, do ordain and establish this Constitution for the preservation and perpetuation of the same." New Jersey's, however, says, "We, the people of the State of New Jersey, grateful to Almighty God for the civil and religious liberty which He hath so long permitted us to enjoy, and looking to Him for a blessing upon our endeavors to secure and transmit the same unimpaired to succeeding generations, do ordain and establish this Constitution." In no more than 100 words, write the preamble for the Hamiltonia Constitution.
2. In this chapter we reviewed the different kinds of direct democracy mechanisms states can adopt. The National Conference of State Legislatures (NCSL) contains the Statewide Ballot Measures Database which keeps track of all initiatives, legislative referendums, and popular referendums every year. Choose a state and compare two pieces of direct democracy from the last election. What was the referendum or initiative about? Was it successful?
3. There are different ways a state can amend their constitution. What way(s) does your state amend its constitution? When was the last time it was amended and what was changed?
4. One area of state constitutions we did not delve into too deeply were state bill of rights. What do you think states should protect in their bill of rights? Should they simply reiterate what is already in the federal bill of rights or protect something else? Why or why not? If you think the state should protect something else, what is it and why?

"Defund the Police" protests in Austin, Texas, on June 7, 2020.
SOURCE: AP

3 Local Governments and Intergovernmental Relations

Learning Objectives:

After reading this chapter students should be able to:

- Describe the power dynamics between state and local governments.
- Explain the responsibilities of local governments across the United States.
- Compare the different kinds of local governments.
- Understand why state governments limit local government powers on certain issues.

State Spotlight: Texas

We will discuss throughout this book how events that happen in one state can affect other states hundreds of miles away. This is exactly what happened with the murder of George Floyd in May 2020. George Floyd Jr. was arrested after being accused of using a counterfeit twenty-dollar bill. During his arrest he was held down via a knee to his neck and back, repeatedly telling officers he could not breathe. Eventually he died from the lack of oxygen, and video of his arrest and death spread far and wide and became the rallying cry for organizations fighting against police brutality as well as defund the police movements.[1]

Less than three months later and nearly 1,200 miles away in Austin, Texas, the **city council** reduced their police department budget by one-third. As the *Texas Tribune* explained:

> The Austin City Council unanimously voted to cut its police department budget by $150 million on Thursday, after officers and the city's top cop faced months of criticism over the killing of an unarmed Black and Hispanic man, the use of force against anti-police brutality protesters and the investigation of a demonstrator's fatal shooting by another citizen. Those criticisms coincided with protests across Texas and the country calling for reforms on police tactics and the "defunding" of law enforcement in favor of redistributing funds to social services and alternative public safety programs.[2]

The Black and Hispanic man the article refers to is Mike Ramos, who was killed in April 2020 by police. Ramos became a "rallying cry in Texas during the ongoing protests against police brutality and racial injustice following George Floyd's death in Minneapolis."[3]

In total the Austin City Council reduced the police department budget by $434 million which included eliminating three future cadet classes and the redistribution of victims' services and forensic sciences to other areas of government. While the reduction and redistribution of the police budget was supported by citizens of Austin, state government officials did not approve of the change in budget. Governor Greg Abbott said, "the council's actions represent the triumph of political agendas over public safety and vowed that the Texas Department of Public Safety will 'stand in the gap' to protect Austin until the state Legislature can take up the issue next session."[4]

And so, the legislature did. The legislature passed HB1900, which essentially fined local governments with residents of more than 250,000 that reduced their police department budgets.[5] The law—supported by Governor Abbott—went into effect on September 1, 2021, and resulted in the Austin City Council approving a new budget that would increase spending in the police department. Abbott argued that the Austin City Council became more focused on "political agendas than public safety."[6]

You may be wondering why the city of Austin was so quick to follow the new law, or why the state had the power to overrule a local decision. Unlike the federal system which says powers are shared between the federal government and state governments, the relationship between state and local governments is **unitary**. This means states hold all the power in their relationship with local governments and any powers that are given to local governments are done so at the discretion of their state government. This is why Austin, and other cities in Texas, can have their police department budgets dictated by the state government. Curious how this came to be? Let's go over the history briefly.

The Work of State and Local Governments

Local governments have a rich history in the United States, starting even before the American Revolution. Many towns in the Northeast were run by town or village councils that often made decisions that would affect residents' day-to-day lives. Why did the colonists adopt local government? The short answer is they came from a well-established system of local governments in Europe. What we often call counties in the United States, for example, is based on the shires of England, which are run by a sheriff.[7]

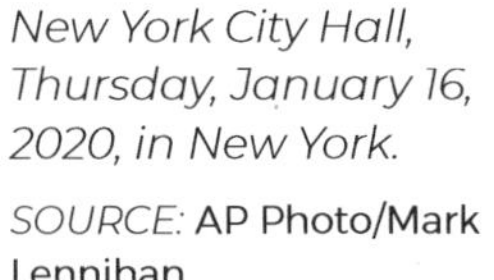

New York City Hall, Thursday, January 16, 2020, in New York.

SOURCE: AP Photo/Mark Lennihan

The history of local government in New York is illustrative of the evolution—and importance—of local governments in the United States. Although the Dutch set up a system of local government when they controlled New Netherland (aka New York between 1614 and 1664), the British quickly took over and adapted their local system. In 1665 a convention of delegates recognized seventeen towns and created the county of Yorkshire. The General Assembly of Freeholders in 1683 would further divide the colony into twelve counties which "became the basis of representation in the Colonial Assembly and also the unit of administration for the system of courts that was established at the same time."[8] Therefore it would be over a century prior to the adoption of the federal Constitution that local governments would become fully entrenched at the colonial, and then state level.

But what do local governments actually do? The answer is quite a lot. Again, we turn to New York which nicely explains the powers that are granted to local governments in their states.

> The granted powers include the power to: adopt ordinances, resolutions, rules and regulations; acquire real and personal property; acquire, establish and maintain recreational facilities; fix, levy and collect charges and fees; and in the case of a city, town or village, to adopt zoning regulations, and conduct comprehensive planning.

Need to get a permit to make renovations to your home? You'll need town approval for that. Interested in the ways schools set up their programming? Check out your local school district's school board meeting. Trying to understand why a Starbucks cannot be built in the middle of your residential community? You should review the zoning laws of your town or city. In short, local governments affect the amount of taxes we pay, how we educate our children, whether there are recreational facilities, and building codes and zoning laws. Because as great as a Starbucks sounds right next door, it really would not be advantageous to a residentially zoned neighborhood, both in terms of traffic and property values.

According to the U.S. Census Bureau there were 90,837 local governments across the United States as of 2022. Figure 3.1 summarizes the number of local governments per state. Notice that some small states—population-wise—have small numbers of local governments. Hawaii is ranked fortieth in terms of population and has the smallest number of local governments out of any state (21 to be exact). However, size does not always dictate the number of local governments. Kansas is ranked thirty-fifth in terms of population but has over 3,768 local governments. With 2,934,582 residents this totals to one local government for every 779 residents.

Figure 3.1
Number of Local Governments per State

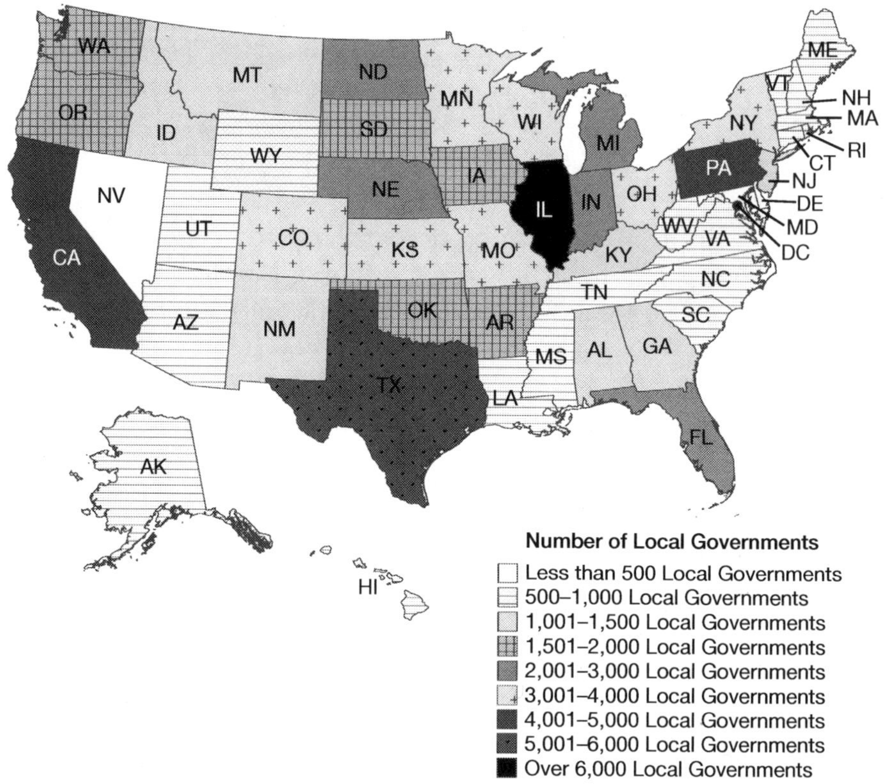

Data from the U.S. Census Bureau.

Simulation

We will now begin the simulation where we will discuss how state and local governments work together and the different forms of local government across the United States

The Relationship between State and Local Governments

There are two terms we have to go over in order to understand the relationship between state and local governments, and that is **home rule** and **Dillon's Rule**. Let's start with Dillon's Rule. Dillon's Rule is named after Iowa Supreme Court Justice John F. Dillon who, in *Clinton v. Cedar Rapids & M.R.R. Co.* (1868), outlined the power dynamic between state and local governments. In this case Dillon argued that while the U.S. Constitution provides for the existence of state government powers, it does not grant local governments powers. As Dillon stated, local governments are "the mere tenants at will of their legislature."[9] This reiterates that local governments do not have the same power vis-à-vis the state government as state governments have vis-à-vis the federal government.

On the other end of the spectrum is home rule. The Nebraska Legislature explains it as such:

> Home rule is granted by state constitutions or state statute and allocated some autonomy to a local government, if the local government accepts certain conditions. Home Rule implies that each level of government has a separate realm of authority. Therefore, state power should not infringe on the authority of local government in certain areas.[10]

Each state is different when it comes to home rule vs. Dillon's Rule. Let's use Nebraska as an example. Overall Nebraska is a Dillon Rule state whereby local governments have those powers only granted to them by the legislature. However, Article III, Section 18 of the Nebraska State Constitution prohibits the legislature from enacting certain local laws. Figure 3.2 lists examples of what laws they cannot pass. Furthermore, the cities of Lincoln and Omaha—the only two with a population over 100,000—are organized under a home rule charter, providing these cities with more control over their local decisions.[11]

Figure 3.2

Local Limitations of the Nebraska Legislature

Local Laws the Nebraska Legislature Is Not Able to Pass

- Granting divorces
- Locating or changing county seats
- Providing for the election of officers in townships
- Providing for the management of public schools
- The opening and conducting of any election, or designating the place for voting

The National Association of Counties (NACo) rates all the states from most restrictive (meaning strong Dillon's Rule) to Most Flexible (meaning strong home rule). They categorize seven states as being very restrictive (Wyoming, Nebraska, Texas, Vermont, West Virginia, Virginia, and Delaware) and nine states as being very flexible (Oregon, Kansas, Iowa, Indiana, Arkansas, Georgia, South Carolina, New York, and Hawaii).[12] Not a single one of the 254 counties in Texas has home rule, which is why it is considered a very restrictive state for local county powers. Compare this to New York, where all sixty-two counties have some form of home rule. As the NACo explains: "These broad home rule powers allow counties to regulate the quality of life and provide direct services for its residents. The provision of home rule powers to New York counties makes them full partners with the state in service provision."[13]

This discussion of home rule vs. Dillon's Rule leads us to our first big decision when it comes to state and local relations in Hamiltonia. You and your class will need to decide just how much power you want your local governments to have. Keep in mind, even in states with more home rule powers—like New York—the legislature still retains powers over many areas. For example, the home rule charter for Suffolk County, New York, still gives the state more power in the areas of "landfill closures, gifts or loans to private enterprise, sale of parkland, state-mandated moratoria and wetlands developments. The state mandates specific action in certain areas such as social services, elections and health."[14]

You therefore have a few decisions to make. First, will you have a more restrictive or flexible state–local relations in Hamiltonia? In short, will you lean more on Dillon's Rule or home rule? If you do decide to allow home rule, you need to outline the circumstances in which home rule is possible, and what exactly the power of home rule entails. Will home rule be limited to cities of a certain size—like in Nebraska—or will it be available to all counties regardless of size as it is in New York? Is there anything that you still want to limit explicitly in the home rule charter as New York does? Home rule does not mean that local governments are more powerful than their state governments. The **charters** simply lay out the powers the local government has as granted by the state government. Austin, which we referenced in the beginning of this chapter, is a home rule city, but it cannot violate state or federal law.[15] Once the state of Texas passed HB1900 penalizing cities for decreasing police budgets, the city had to fall in line.

Action Item

3-1

Will Hamiltonia lean more toward Home Rule or Dillon's Rule for relations with local governments?

- If you allow for Home Rule charters, are there any limits to which local governments can receive one (based on population, for example), or anything you feel should be specifically granted within the charters?

Now that we have a strong grasp on the power dynamics between state and local governments, we need to review the various kinds of local governments that can exist. We have mentioned thus far cities and counties but have not discussed towns/townships or special districts. We also need to discuss the variations in these kinds of local governments across states.

The Types of Local Governments

The U.S. Census Bureau breaks down local governments into five types: **county governments**, **municipal governments**, and **township governments** are considered general purpose governments. Special purpose governments include **special district governments** and **school districts**. We have already recounted the history of counties, which were formed after the shires of England. There are 3,031 county governments in the United States, but not every state has counties. Connecticut and Rhode Island do not have counties. Delaware and Hawaii only have three counties, while Texas has the highest number of counties at 254. Figure 3.3 summarizes how many states have a certain range of counties in the United States.

Action Item

3-2

Will Hamiltonia have county government?

- If yes, what will they be called, and how many will you have?
  - How will you set up county governments? Will you require that a county executive be elected or appointed or leave it up to each county?
  - Will you limit the minimum and maximum members of each county commission?
  - What will you call the people who are elected to the county commission?

Figure 3.3

Number of Counties across the United States

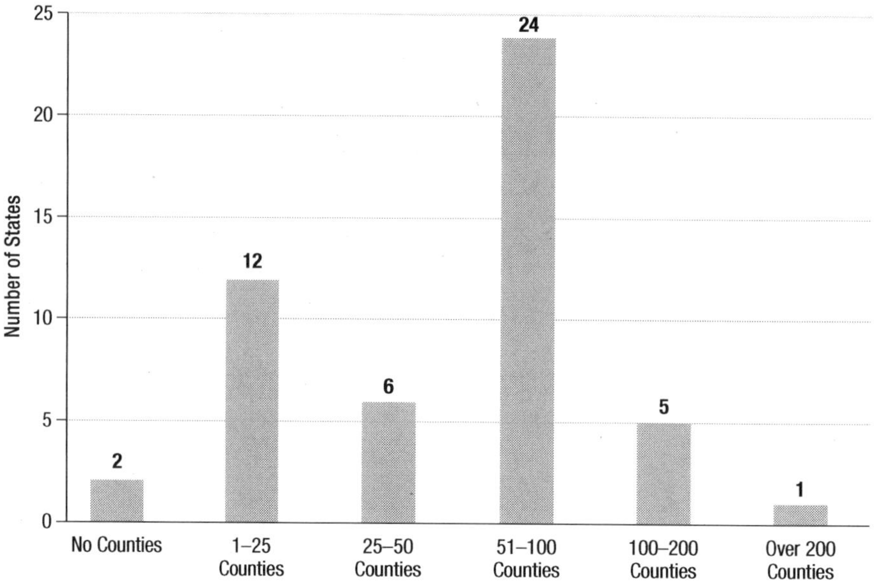

	No Counties	1–25 Counties	25–50 Counties	51–100 Counties	100–200 Counties	Over 200 Counties
Number of States	2	12	6	24	5	1

General-Purpose Governments

There is variation across states in how local governments run their county governments, specifically how they set up their county governments to function. The National Association of Counties (NACo) describes the structure of counties via two measures. First, whether the government form is traditional, mixed, or reformed (see Figure 3.4). Government form

> refers to the distribution of executive decision-making authority in a county. "Traditional" states mandate that counties exercise executive decision-making authority through a board of elected officials (commissioners, supervisors, etc.). "Reformed" states mandate that counties employ an elected or appointed county executive, manager or similar position to take on at least some of the county's executive decision-making authority. "Mixed" states have some "traditional" counties and some "reformed" counties.[16]

The second dimension NACo uses to describe the structure of counties is who has executive decision-making authority. At the state level, the governor has executive decision-making authority. But at the county level it can be an executive such as a mayor, which is what the borough (aka counties in Alaska) of Fairbanks North Star has, or it can be a board, a board/administrator, or some mixture of both. When

Figure 3.4

Number of States with Different County Forms of Government

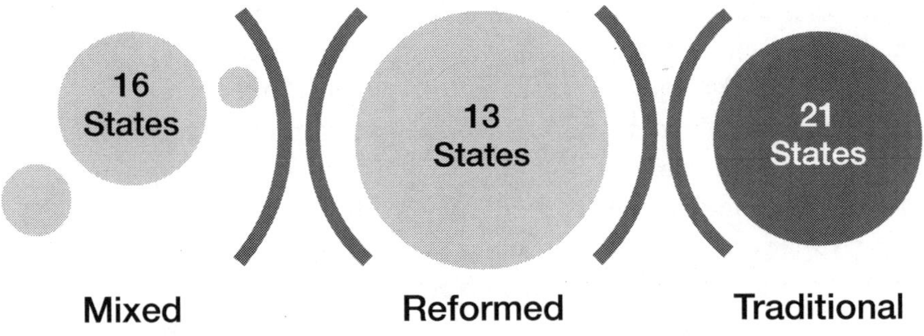

SOURCE: Data from the National Association of Counties (NACo).

it is a board (typically called a board of commissioners) then there is no separate "executive" authority, and the executive and legislative responsibilities are carried out by the board. When there is an administrator or some other form of executive authority than the executive responsibilities are split from the legislative functions of the board—although again, how much executive authority is given depends on each county, hence why NACo designates there can be a mix of both boards and administrators with executive authority.

There are also different rules governing whether the county executive is elected or appointed. In Alabama the executive can be elected or appointed depending on the county. In Arizona the county executive cannot be elected and must be appointed. And of course, to make things more interesting—and confusing—each state's counties have different names for their county board members and different minimum and maximum board sizes. County board members of Colorado are all called commissioners, but in Hawaii they are called councilmembers, in Iowa they are supervisors, and in Vermont assistant judges. Typically, the minimum board size is set to three members (unless you are Georgia which sets it to one or Wisconsin at zero), and the maximum varies greatly from no limit in North Carolina to fifty-one in New York.[17]

Let's pause for a moment to recap what we just covered about one kind of local government—counties. First, it is possible to decide that a state should not have counties at all, like Rhode Island or Connecticut, but this is unique to their smaller geographic size. Second, the structure of county government is different across the states. A state could decide to require that all executive officers—whatever they may be called—of county governments be appointed, or they may require they all be elected or some mixture of both. If they are appointed it is often the county elected board that appoints the executive. Or there may be no executives at all, and all executive and legislative authority resides with an elected board. Finally, a state may dictate the size of these elected bodies.

If you have not noticed, local government is complicated. So far we have covered the details about county government. Next, we must cover the other two general purpose governments: municipal and township. Municipalities include towns and cities. Townships are smaller units of local government subordinate to county governments whose functions vary widely from state to state. Figure 3.5 shows the number of municipalities across states as compiled by the U.S. Census Bureau. Figure 3.6 shows which states do and do not have townships, also retrieved from the U.S. Census.[18] Overall there are 19,491 municipal and 16,214 township governments across the United States.

Figure 3.5
Number of Municipalities across States

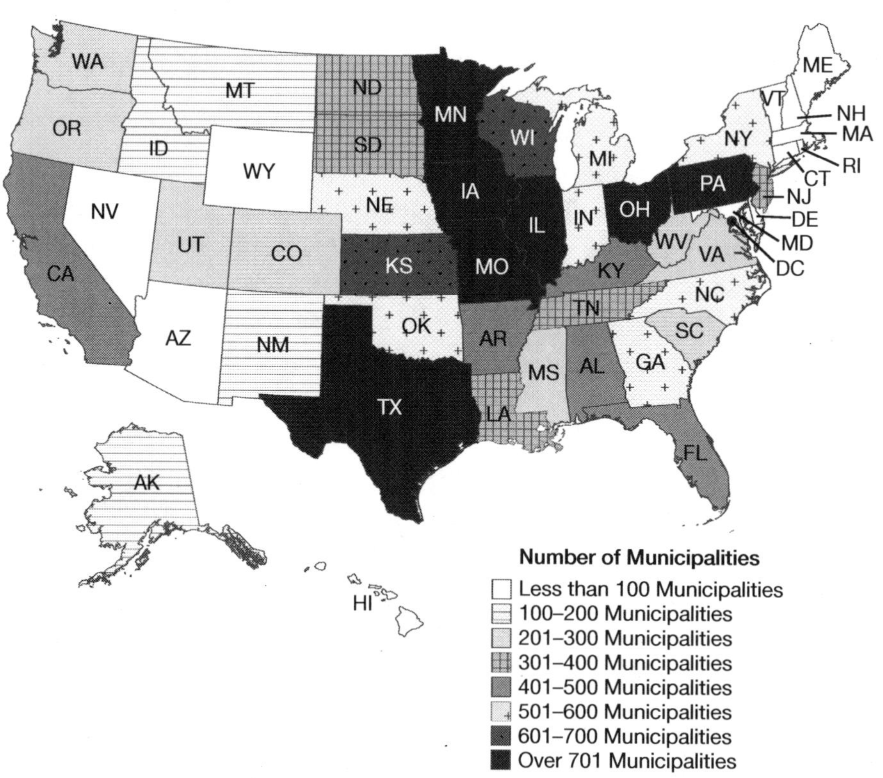

SOURCE: Data from the U.S. Census Bureau.

Figure 3.6

Presence of Townships across the United States

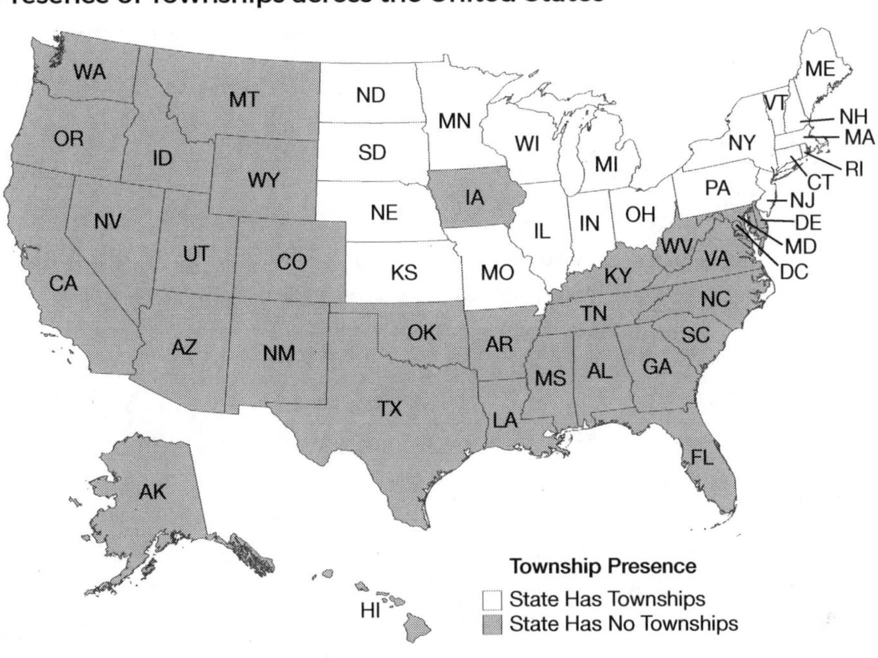

SOURCE: Data from the U.S. Census Bureau.

Wondering what cities and towns may do? In many places across the United States cities and towns, although particularly **cities**, offer a wide range of social services, and like counties, can have their own charters with the state. And like county governments cities have their own forms of government. The three kinds of city governments are: **mayor–council systems**, **council–manager systems**, and **commission systems**. Let's go over the differences in these kinds of systems to better understand how city governments work.

The **mayor** is the chief executive of a town or a city. Citizens vote for the mayor, but they also vote for a city council, which is the legislative branch of a city. However, mayors can be strong, or they can be weak. In a strong mayor–council system the mayor can veto actions of the city council as well as appoint individuals to leadership positions in city government. The mayor of New York was considered one of the most powerful mayors in the world in a 2013 BBC article about the position. The mayor of New York can "hir[e] and fir[e] the people heading the city's key agencies like police and schools, while also setting the budget. 'The California governor doesn't even have that power. And the mayor controls the education of one million children.'"[19]

But not all mayors are created equal. If there are strong mayor systems, then there are also weak mayor systems. In this system voters elect a mayor and city council members, but the mayor presides over city council meetings, does not oversee city departments, and does not have veto power. But remember, there may not even be a mayor at all. In a council–manager system there may be a weak mayor, or there is no mayor at all, and the voters elect a city council, and the council then hires a city executive. The city of Dallas, for example, has a weak mayor who presides over the city council meetings, but in terms of power, it is the hired city manager that runs the day-to-day operations of the city government. Figure 3.7 shows the organizational chart of Dallas' government. Notice the mayor is not in charge of the city departments—the city manager is.

The final kind of city government is the commission system. This form of government is not as popular anymore, because of issues with functionality. Commissioners are elected individually to head specific departments, but then come together to run the city. There can be a mayor in this system, but they are weak with no independent executive authority. Because commissioners run individual departments, it becomes difficult to see the needs of other departments outside their purview, hence why they are not as popular in city governments anymore.

In this section we have covered the different kinds of general-purpose governments: counties, municipalities, and townships. As you learned in chapter 1, Hamiltonia has five major cities (Charlestown, Burr City, Reynolds, Alexandria, and Mirandaville). Additionally, there are ten other smaller cities with populations between 60,000 and 100,000 and 900 towns and villages with populations below 60,000. How would you set up the city government of Charlestown versus a smaller city such as Federalistville? Would you adopt a commission system, council-manager system, or maybe-council system? What kind of powers would your mayor have—if you decided to have one, of course? Each of the decisions you make about the structure of your city governments will affect how they function and whether they flourish.

Figure 3.7

Dallas, Texas, Organizational Chart

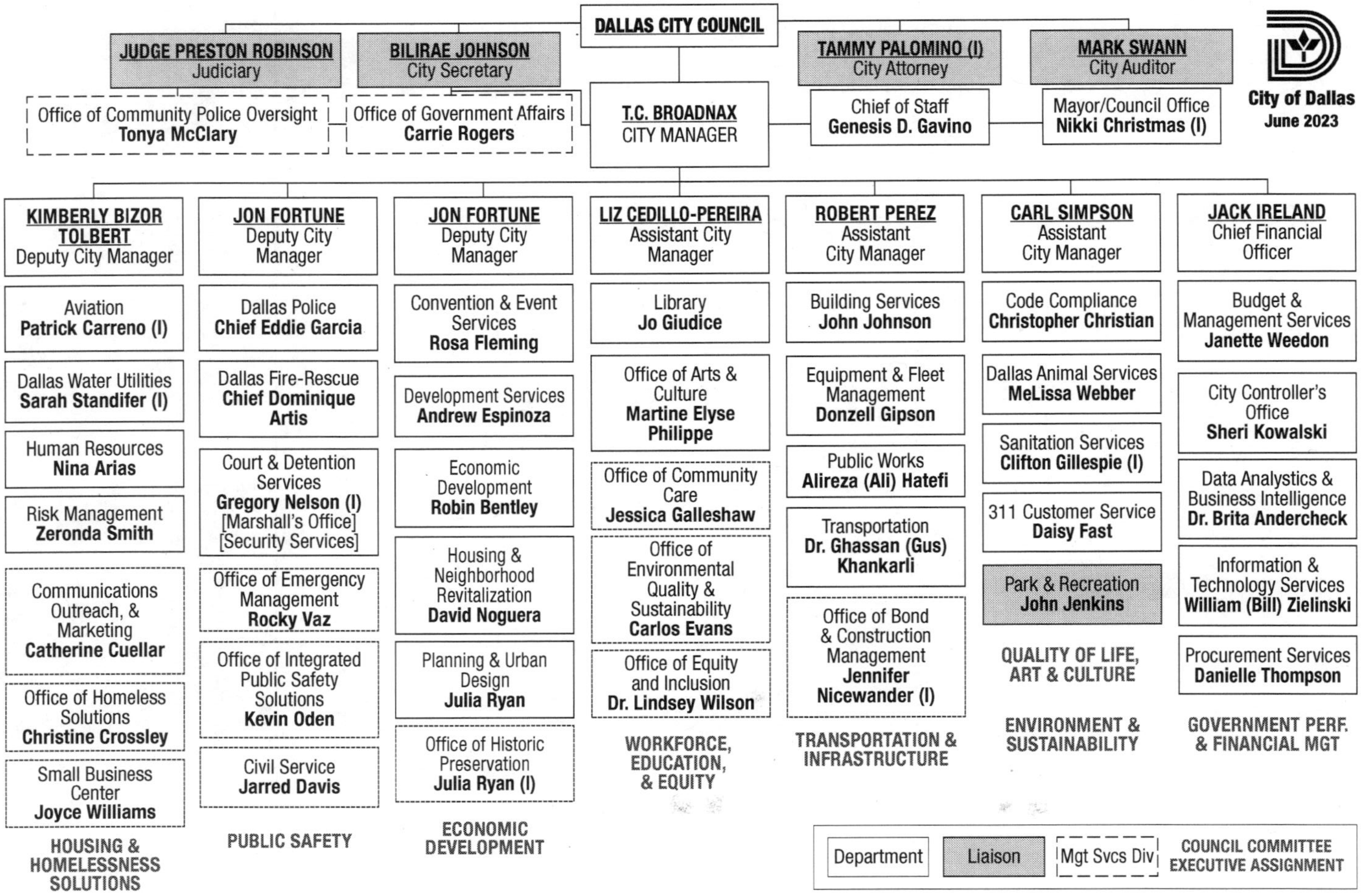

SOURCE: https://dallascityhall.com/government/citymanager/Pages/City-Manager.aspx chrome-extension://efaidnbmnnnibpcajpcglclefindmkaj/https://dallascityhall.com/government/citymanager/Documents/Org-Chart.pdf

Action Item

3-3

Consider the Capitol of Charlestown and the smaller city of Federalistville in Hamiltonia. Choose two different kinds of city governments for these cities and decide the following:

- Will these cities have mayors? If so, how powerful will they be?
- Will you go with a mayor–council, council–manager, or commission system for your cities?
- Will the mayors and/or council members have term limits, and if so what would they be?

Special-Purpose Governments

Special-purpose governments are divided into two types: special district governments and school districts. Special districts focus on one specific area of government, such as water districts. The Port Authority of New York and New Jersey that we discussed in chapter 1 is also a special district. Across the United States there are 39,552 special districts, with Illinois having over three thousand and Alaska and Hawaii having seventeen each. Figure 3.8 provides examples of special districts that can be found across the United States.

The other type of special district are school districts. School districts are locally based institutions that hire staff to run the schools and report to school boards who may be elected or appointed. The school boards set policy and the budget for the school district. The U.S. Census reports 12,546 school districts across the United States. Texas has the most at 1,070, closely followed by California which has 1,006. The census classifies Alaska, Hawaii, Maryland, and North Carolina as

Figure 3.8

Examples of Special Districts

Figure 3.9
Number of School Districts per State

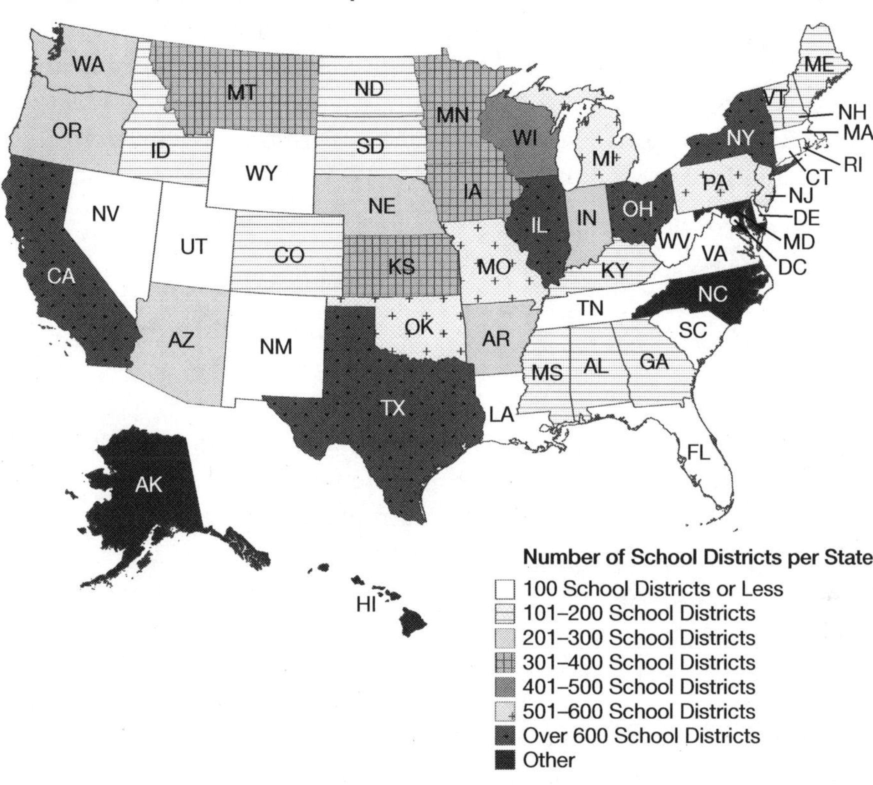

SOURCE: Data from the U.S. Census Bureau.

not having Independent School District Governments. This is because in North Carolina and Maryland, the counties run their schools and in Alaska and Hawaii their state governments mainly run their schools. Figure 3.9 displays the number of school districts each state has. As you will notice there is quite a bit of variation from state to state.

Action Item

3-4

What kind of special districts will Hamiltonia have?

Looking Forward

Learning about local government is incredibly important but can also be overwhelming. As we learned in this chapter, local governments are diverse as well as prolific. Unfortunately, not enough research is often directed at local governments because they are all so unique, making it difficult to generalize findings. Yet we know local governments have a direct impact on state residents, and as creatures of the state should not be ignored when creating a state government. In the policy chapters, beginning with chapter 9, "Fiscal Policy," we will devote a section to local government policy and ask you to think about how each of the policy areas will function locally in Hamiltonia. For now, we will move on to creating our first branch of government: Hamiltonia's State Legislature.

Key Terms

city council (45)
unitary (46)
home rule (48)
Dillon's Rule (48)
charters (50)
county government (51)
municipal government (51)
township governments (51)
special district governments (51)
school districts (51)
cities (55)
mayor–council systems (55)
council–manager systems (55)
commission systems (55)
mayor (55)

Assignments to Learn More about Local Government

1. Look up the town or city where your college or university is located. What kind of local government structure do they have? Is there a mayor? Are they strong or weak? Who is in charge of executive responsibilities of your local government?
2. How many local governments does your state have? Does your state have county government and if so is your state more or less flexible when it comes to local power vis-à-vis the state? What counties, if any, have Home Rule charters?
3. Look up two different special purpose governments in your state. What are they in charge of and how are they structured?
4. Look up the current mayor of New York. What kind of professional experience does the mayor have that prepared him to be the mayor? What are some of the major decisions that the mayor has made thus far in his tenure? How would you assess the mayor's job performance so far?

Illinois state legislators debate the state budget during session in the Illinois State Capitol in Springfield, Illinois, in May 2014.

SOURCE: AP Photo/Seth Perlman

Constructing a Legislature

Learning Objectives:

After reading this chapter students should be able to:

- Explain the historical background of state legislatures.
- Describe the levels of racial, ethnic, and gender diversity in legislatures across the United States.
- Compare the different kinds of legislative professionalism.
- Identify the steps of the legislative process.
- Discuss the varying eligibility requirements for state legislators.
- Create the Hamiltonia State Legislature.

Illinois' former Speaker of the House Michael Madigan speaks during a committee hearing Thursday, February 25, 2021, in Chicago

SOURCE: Ashlee Rezin Garcia/Chicago Sun-Times via AP

State Spotlight: Illinois

The Illinois state legislature is composed of a 118-member House of Representatives and a fifty-nine-member State Senate. Representatives convene in the state capital of Springfield every year to write legislation, vote on bills, and oversee the vast Illinois bureaucratic system. Just like the U.S. House of Representatives has a **Speaker of the House**, so too does the Illinois House of Representatives, except the Illinois Speaker of the House is unique because it has the longest serving Speaker of the House in state legislative history. Michael Madigan entered the Illinois House of Representatives in January of 1971 and served as the majority leader from 1977 to 1981 until the Democratic Party lost control of the chamber and he became minority leader from 1981–1983. After 1983 Madigan served as Speaker of the House for twelve years from 1983–1995 and then again from 1997–2021, totaling thirty-six years of service as the leader of a state legislative body.[1]

In 2017 the Illinois Policy Institute wrote an article about Madigan, noting the moment he surpassed the former record holder, Solomon Blatt, former Speaker of the House of the South Carolina House of Representatives.[2] Speakers of the House are generally powerful individuals within their House of Representatives, controlling who serves on **committees** as well as what legislation makes it to the floor for debate and votes. But the Illinois Speaker of the House is particularly powerful, with Illinois Policy noting several areas where the Illinois Speaker of the House was much more powerful than their counterparts in other states. The four powers that make the Illinois Speaker of the House powerful are: their ability to "dole out committee chair positions and the stipends that come with them, [controlling] who votes in committee, [controlling] what bills make it to a vote, and allowing the Speaker to be the only one to know when a bill will be called for a vote."[3]

While these rules may seem inconsequential to the outside observer, they give the Illinois Speaker immense power to influence the legislation that is passed in their chamber. The longer a member of the legislature serves, like Madigan, the more they understand these rules and how best to wield them to expand their power. This does not mean that legislative leaders are all powerful, because as we will learn later in this simulation, the business of lawmaking is difficult. It also does not mean that legislative leaders are always ethical. Madigan's term as Speaker of the House ended abruptly as he faced racketeering charges. Who knows how much longer Madigan may have served if he avoided such scandal.

You may become a member of the Hamiltonia legislature, or you may have to work closely with members of the legislature as a member of the governor's cabinet or as the governor herself! The next section provides a brief history of state legislatures in the United States to deliver a better explanation for why state legislatures have evolved to what they are today.

Overview of State Legislatures

State legislatures have a robust history in the United States as they are one of the first ways that colonists organized themselves. Some assemblies developed out of royal charters and allowed colonists an institutionalized way to try to govern themselves.[4] Essentially, state legislatures have long been a fundamental part of state governance.

In the United States, every state has a state legislature. Forty-nine states have two houses including a lower house (typically called the House) and an upper house (typically called the Senate). This amounts to having over 7,300 state legislators across the country! State legislators are making important policy decisions each year that affect your life. For example, state legislatures can determine whether and when you must register to vote prior to an election, whether you qualify for **Medicaid** and what kinds of benefits you receive, and whether and when you can access an abortion. The way that legislatures are designed and operate can affect how you are represented and what kinds of policies you experience.

State legislators are responsible for representing state residents. Over time, state legislatures have provided more equitable representation. As people began to move to cities, state legislatures overrepresented rural communities in their states and underrepresented urban communities. For example, in 1960, the state of Tennessee had not redrawn its legislative **districts** since 1901. Because urban communities had grown in population during this time, Tennessee legislators had vastly different numbers of **constituents**. This enhanced the voice of rural residents in the state legislature compared to the voice of urban residents. In a series of cases, the Supreme Court ruled that state legislators had to represent roughly equal numbers of constituents.[5] Since the 1960s, state legislative districts have been redrawn to better reflect the demographic changes of the state so that legislators *within* each state have the same number of constituents.

Even though representation has become more equitable within states over time, there is still a lot of variation across states in terms of how many constituents each legislator represents. For example, members of the Florida House of Representatives represent about 179,000 constituents, and New Hampshire legislators represent about three thousand constituents. This is determined by both the size of the state and the size of the legislature. Legislators in more populous states will represent more individuals than legislators in less populous states. This can be mediated, to some degree, by the size of the legislature. States with more legislative districts, and therefore more legislative seats, may be able to represent fewer constituents per district (depending on the population of the state).

Although legislatures are different sizes, in every state the lower body always has more legislators than the upper body, just like in the U.S. Congress. Additionally, no state legislature is larger than the U.S. Congress. New Hampshire has the largest House with 400 members but only 24 state senators. Texas has 150 house members and 31 senate members. While Texas has a much smaller house than New Hampshire, it is also a more populated state. These differences in size can also affect the functioning of the legislature itself. Larger state legislatures may need to concentrate more power in leadership positions to be effective, whereas smaller legislatures may grant individual legislators more power.

Diversity in the Legislature

States vary in their **descriptive representation** of their constituents as well. Descriptive representation is how well a representative body—like a legislature—reflects the demographics of a population, such as their race, ethnicity, sex, and age. Studying representation in the state legislature raises questions about the specific people who ultimately wind up holding state legislative office. State legislative seats are typically held by white, cisgender, heterosexual men. Let's take a look at the data on the number of women serving in the state legislature. The Center for American Women and Politics (CAWP) has tracked women's representation across multiple elected offices in the United States for many years. According to their database, 594 women serve in State Senates out of a total 1,972 seats while 1,820 women serve in State Houses out of 5,411 seats. This amounts to an average of 32.7 percent of state legislative seats being held by women. The vast majority of these female state legislators are affiliated with the Democratic Party (1,583 compared to 805). However, the average does not really show the range of women's representation in state legislatures as of 2023. A deeper dive into women's representation shows that only two states have reached **parity**—60.3 percent of legislators in Nevada are women and 50 percent of legislators in Colorado are women. However, seven states report fewer than 20 percent of their legislators are women: West Virginia (11.9%), Mississippi (14.4%), Tennessee (14.4%), South Carolina (14.7%), Alabama (17.1%), Louisiana (19.4%), and Oklahoma (19.5%).[6]

The National Council of State Legislatures (NCSL) provides data on the numbers of people serving in state legislatures by race and ethnicity. Approximately 66 percent of state legislators identify as white. After that 10.55 percent identify as Black, 6.24 percent identify as Hispanic, 4.16 percent identify as Asian, with the remaining legislators identifying as Indian, Native American, multi-racial, or have a race or ethnicity which is not identified.[7] Like gender, the racial demographics of state legislators vary a lot by state. For example, 26 percent of Californian state legislators identify as Hispanic, however less than 1 percent identify as Hispanic in Arkansas. In fact, less than 50 percent of California's state legislators identify as white compared to over 88 percent of Arkansas's legislators. See Figure 4.1 for a comparison between the gender and racial/ethnic breakdown of state legislators across the United States.

Figure 4.1

Gender, Racial, and Ethnic Breakdown of State Legislatures

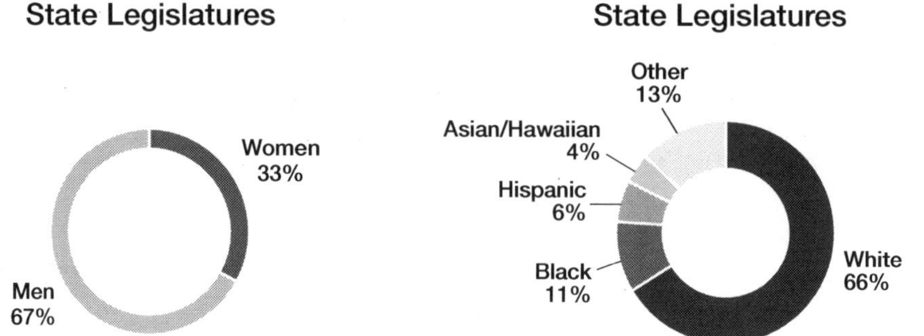

SOURCE: Data from the Center for the American Women and Politics (CAWP) and The National Council of State Legislatures (NCSL)

Finally, we should also consider LGBTQ representation across state legislatures. According to a February 2022 Gallup survey, just over 7 percent of Americans identify as LGBTQ.[8] As of 2021, 175 state legislators identify as LGBTQ, 168 of them identified with the Democratic Party and the vast majority identified as gay (78), lesbian (69), or bisexual/pansexual/queer (19). Only nine identified as transgender or gender non-conforming. Why does the demographic makeup of a state legislature matter? Research has shown considerable patterns of **party identification** and policy positions based upon one's demographics. For example, women legislators are much more likely to sponsor bills on issues such as welfare, education, and health care.[9] Similarly, African American women legislators have been known to focus more on domestic violence than other demographic groups in the state house.[10] Your class has its own demographic makeup—think about how the people in your class may determine the kinds of policies you debate and the laws your class ultimately adopts.

Legislative Professionalism

State legislatures have also professionalized over time. **Legislative professionalism** is a measure of state legislatures that consists of legislator salary, the number of staff, and the length of their legislative sessions.[11] States with high levels of legislative professionalism (i.e., they pay their legislators higher salaries, have more staff, and are in session longer) look and operate more like the U.S. Congress. Even though states have generally become more professionalized over time, legislative professionalism still varies across states. For example, more professionalized legislatures like in Massachusetts pay their state legislators $70,536 a year and meet from January to July or November depending on the year.[12] Other states like Arizona have a semi-professional legislature. They pay their legislators $24,000 a year and meet for 100 days out of the year.[13] See Figure 4.2 for a quick comparison of three states based on their level of professionalism.

State legislative professionalism has important implications for policymaking, representation, and more. Normatively, we desire that our elected legislators represent the people when making laws. States with more professionalized legislatures tend to have policies that are more congruent with the majority public opinion in the state.[14] More professionalized state legislatures are more likely to learn from successful policies in other states and adapt them for their circumstances at home.[15] Less professionalized legislatures, on the other hand, are also more likely to copy language from other states' bills.[16] This is especially true for divisive issues such as abortion and transgender rights laws where national funders are able to influence states' rights through national campaigns.

Legislative seats in more professionalized legislatures are typically seen as more prestigious. Therefore, it tends to be more difficult to get elected to a more professionalized legislature.[17] This can affect the background of our representatives. The most common occupation for state legislators is attorneys or business owners. However, this depends on the level of legislative professionalism. Legislators in states with less professionalized legislatures—because they meet

Figure 4.2

State Legislature Professionalism Snapshot

Professional: New York	• Meets year-round • Full time staff: 2,850 • Salary: $110,000
Semi-Professional: Arizona	• Meets January 9–April 22 • Full time staff: 621 • Salary: $24,000
Citizen: North Dakota	• Meets January 3–April 28 • Full time staff: 34 • Salary: $537 per month

less frequently and pay less in salary—may hold other jobs while also being a legislator. They are more likely to be in business or farming. Legislators in more professionalized legislatures are more likely to be from a political background or an attorney.[18] Incumbents in more professionalized legislatures are more likely to win reelection and weather external shocks in elections than incumbents in less professionalized legislatures.[19]

Legislative professionalism can also affect the power the legislature has vis-à-vis the executive branch. More professionalized legislatures may be more capable in engaging in oversight over state agencies.[20] If legislatures meet less often or have fewer resources, this can give the governor more power to pursue their policy initiatives.

Other Institutional Features

State legislatures vary in other institutional ways. State legislatures are different in the length of their terms, whether they have **term limits**, and the requirements to serve in office. Legislators in South Carolina's House of Representatives serve two-year terms and the legislators in South Carolina Senate serve four-year terms. This is the most typical arrangement across state legislatures with thirty-two states having two- and four-year terms for their lower and upper house, respectively.[21] Other states have legislators in both houses serve four-year terms or both houses serve two-year terms. In these states, the entire state legislature is going up for reelection at the same time.

States also differ in whether they have term limits and how restrictive those limits are. States began adopting term limits in the 1990s, and, currently, fifteen states have term limits. However, what those term limits are differs across states. Some states have lifetime limits meaning once a representative has served the maximum terms they may not return to the legislature. Other states have consecutive limits which allow the representative to return to the legislature after a specified period of time. Most states limit legislators to serving eight years in both houses, but some states like Louisiana and Nevada have twelve-year limits.[22] Term limits may have implications for who is in the state legislature and the power of the state legislature compared to the governor. Some studies have found that term limits may increase descriptive representation, but others have found no effect. However, term limits can affect legislator behavior and can weaken the legislature compared to the governor.[23] See Table 4.1 for a comparison between the states of California and Wyoming and their state legislative arrangements.

Table 4.1
Side-by-Side State Comparison

	CALIFORNIA	WYOMING
Size	120 total legislators	93 total legislators[1]
Professionalism	Professional Legislature	Citizen Legislature
Senate Qualifications	18 years old, citizen and state resident for 3 years, district resident for one year, and a qualified voter[2]	25 years, citizen of the US and Wyoming, and 1 year as a district resident[1]
Term Limits	12 consecutive terms in House and Senate	No Term Limits[3]
Term Length	Senate 4 years House 2 years[2]	Senate 4 years House 2 years[1]
House Committees	33 Standing Committees[4]	12 Standing Committees[5]
Leadership	*Senate:*[6] President of the Senate (Lt. Governor) President Pro Tempore Republican Leader Democratic Caucus Chair Republican Caucus Chair Secretary of the Senate *State Assembly:*[7] Speaker Speaker Pro Tempore Assistant Speaker Pro Tempore Majority Leader Assistant Majority Leader Majority Whip Assistant Majority Whip (2) Democratic Caucus Chair Republican Leader	*Senate:*[8] President Vice President Majority Floor Leader Minority Floor Leader Minority Whip Minority Caucus Chairman *House:* Speaker of the House Speaker Pro Tempore Majority Floor Leader Majority Whip Minority Floor Leader Minority Whip Minority Caucus Chairman
Districts	Single Member	Single Member

[1] *A Citizen Guide to The Wyoming Legislature*, Wyoming Legislative Service Office, https://wyoleg.gov/docs/CitizenGuidebook.pdf.

[2] *The Book of the States* (The Council of State Governments, 2021).

[3] "The Term-Limited States," National Conference of State Legislatures, April 19, 2021, https://www.ncsl.org/about-state-legislatures/the-term-limited-states.

[4] "Committees," California State Assembly, https://www.assembly.ca.gov/committees.

[5] "Joint and Standing Committees," State of Wyoming 67th Legislature, https://www.wyoleg.gov/Committees/List/2023/J.

[6] "Legislative Branch," California State Assembly, https://www.assembly.ca.gov/public-services/legislative-branch.

[7] "Officers of the California State Assembly," California State Assembly, https://www.assembly.ca.gov/assemblymembers/officers-california-state-assembly.

[8] "About the Legislature," State of Wyoming 67th Legislature, https://www.wyoleg.gov/Legislature/LegislatureAbout#:~:text=Leadership%20elected%20on%20the%20first,Pro%20Tem%20in%20the%20House.

States also differ in their requirements for office. Requirements can affect who is allowed to run for office and, therefore, who represents you. More restrictive requirements can make it more likely that people with certain characteristics are able to become legislators. South Carolina, for example, has an age requirement, a residency requirement, and a criminal background requirement. States typically vary on the age you can be when you run for office, the length of time you must live in your district or state, and whether you have to be a U.S. citizen. Just like at the federal level, the age limit is sometimes older for the upper house than the lower house. Some states, like Wisconsin, set their age limit at eighteen for both the House and Senate, and others are even older such as Mississippi where you must be twenty-one to qualify for a House seat and twenty-five to qualify for a Senate seat. The oldest limit is thirty in the senates of states such as New Hampshire and New Jersey.[24] Having to be older or be a resident for a longer period can prevent some individuals from running for office and, therefore, limit voters' choice.

The Legislative Process

The legislative process at the state level typically follows the same process as the federal level. Legislators are able to introduce bills. Typically, after the bill has been introduced and read it is referred to the appropriate committee. States vary on the number of committees they have and the topics they cover. For example, the California General Assembly has thirty-three **standing committees**. The committees range from Local Government, Military and Veteran Affairs, Transportation, Education, to Elections, and more. The standing committees typically have subcommittees that have a narrower legislative focus. Committees do a lot of legislative work in session. They actively discuss, research, and amend bills before sending it to the floor for a vote. Sometimes bills fail because they are never referred out of committee. See Figure 4.3 for the steps of the legislative process.

Figure 4.3

Steps of the Legislative Process

If a bill is referred out of committee, it typically has another reading and is voted on by the house where the legislation originated. If one of the legislative houses' votes "yea" on the bill, it must also be passed by the other body. Once the same bill has been approved by both chambers, it is sent to the governor's desk to be signed into law. State legislatures have the power to **override** the governor's veto, but the required votes needed to override are different across states. Some state legislatures can override a veto with a simple majority, others with three-fifths of the legislature, and the majority of state legislatures can override with a two-thirds majority.

Simulation

The remainder of the chapter will guide you through the various institutional decisions you will need to make for the Hamiltonia legislature. In the next section we begin with legislative partisanship and number of chambers.

Partisanship and Number of Chambers

This portion of the simulation begins with a discussion of the number of chambers the Hamiltonia legislature will have and whether they will be partisan or nonpartisan. Only one state out of fifty is nonpartisan and **unicameral** and that is Nebraska. Although it is rare for a state in America to have this institutional arrangement, it is possible. And just because legislators in Nebraska do not run under a political party does not mean they do not express their political ideologies through issue positions and endorsements from certain interest groups. You could also be unique and decide Hamiltonia should be **bicameral** and nonpartisan or partisan and unicameral. As you discuss and debate these institutional arrangements with your classmates, consider the impact a unicameral or bicameral and a partisan or nonpartisan legislature may have on the functioning of the Hamiltonia government. Do you favor having a nonpartisan legislature because it suggests a culture of unity over division? Or do you believe political parties play an important role in organizing people and making sense of public policy? Remember you will have to live with your choices in the simulation when you actually run Hamiltonia's government, so keep in mind how challenging it may be to be a legislator in the institution you create.

Size of the Legislature and Eligibility Requirements

Now that you have decided whether your legislature will have one or two chambers and be partisan or nonpartisan, you will turn to specifics regarding the number of people who can serve in the legislature, the length of their terms of office, whether they will have term limits, and the eligibility requirements to serve. Let's first consider the number of members in your legislature. As we discussed in the beginning of this chapter, there is quite a wide range of the size of legislative chambers across the United States. From the largest in New Hampshire with a total 424 legislators (24 in the Senate and 400 in House) to the smallest in Nebraska (unicameral—49) and Alaska (20 in the Senate and 40 in the House), states vary considerably in the size of their legislature.[25]

Why does the number of members matter? In part it affects how powerful each individual legislator is in the chamber. Being one of 400 legislators in New Hampshire means the chamber often relies on the parties to guide their votes and leaves little room for individual power, unless a legislator is in a leadership position. Being one of only twenty state senators in Alaska, however, means each senator retains a considerable amount of power and influence, as their vote is much more likely to be decisive in the chamber. While the size of the legislature for this simulation will depend on your class size, it is important to consider this question and its consequences for Hamiltonia even if you may not experience it in the legislature. Figure 4.4 displays the number of legislators in the House vs. Senate across state legislatures in the United States.

It is not just the size of the Hamiltonia legislature that you should consider, but the actual number and whether it is odd or even. An odd-numbered legislature, like the 163 members of the Missouri House, means no one has to break a tie vote. But in chambers that have even numbers, there need to be rules on how a tie vote is broken. In upper chambers—where even numbers are more common—the most common tiebreaker is the lieutenant governor, who is like the vice president of the U.S. Senate and can break a tie vote. There are several lower chambers, like the New Hampshire House mentioned above, that also have an even number of legislators. This affects everything from passing legislation to who becomes the leader in each chamber and therefore gets to decide who serves on which committee.

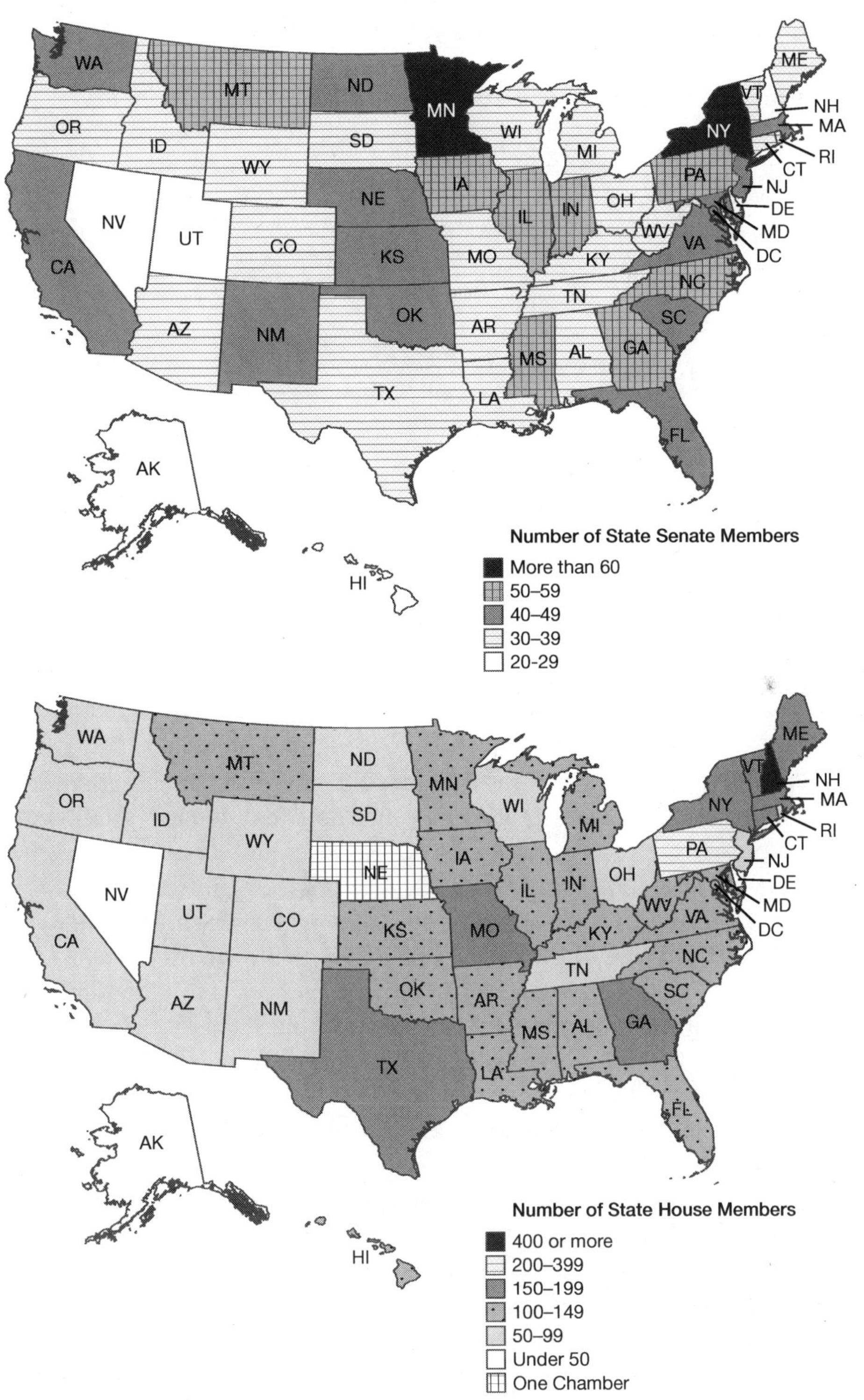

Figure 4.4

Number of Legislators in the House versus the Senate

What happens when there is a tie vote then? In the state of Montana an even split House of Representatives (50–50) means whichever party controls the governor's office gets to decide the leaders.[26]

Action Item

4-1

Should the Hamiltonia legislature be uni- or bicameral?

Action Item

4-2

Should the Hamiltonia legislature be partisan or nonpartisan?

Action Item

4-3

How many members will be in your legislature?

The next question your class will need to answer is the length of the terms of your legislators. If your class has decided the legislature to be unicameral, then you only need to decide the length of term for the one chamber. If, however, your class has decided that your chamber will be bicameral, then you will need to consider whether the length of terms should be the same or different between the two chambers. Legislative terms range from a low of two years to a high of four years, but this does not mean Hamiltonia couldn't have a term of six years, as the United States Senate has. Some states such as Alabama, Louisiana, and Maryland set both chambers' terms at four years, while states like Michigan, Minnesota, and Oklahoma set a four-year term for the upper chamber and a two-year term for the lower chamber. And yet still other states such as South Dakota, Vermont, and Maine set both chambers at two-year terms.

Conventional wisdom tells us that the longer a term the more time a legislator has to get legislation passed before going on the ballot again. Shorter terms may increase the pressure on state legislators to pass legislation as fast as they can so that they can claim credit for new laws and funding come election day. A longer term, however, may make legislators less responsive to the whims of their constituents, providing more of a buffer between when they vote on laws and when they seek reelection. In short, there are both good and bad consequences to deciding on term length. It is a good idea to consider the length of the legislators' term at the same time as you consider whether there will be term limits. About a third of the fifty states have implemented some form of term limits on their legislators. We discussed earlier in this chapter the different kinds of arrangements states have made for term limits, and you will need to decide how term limits will be implemented. Will it be a cap on the total number of years a legislator can serve regardless of the chamber? Or will the term limits be applied to each chamber separately? Keep in mind what you read earlier about what scholarship tells us about the consequences of term limits at the state level.

The final area of specifics on the legislators is what kinds of requirements you will place to serve in the legislature? The typical requirements are related to age, residency, and citizenship (see Figure 4.5). Will you require members of the Hamiltonia legislature to be a certain age before they can serve? Every state except for Vermont sets a minimum age to be qualified to run for their state legislature. The minimum age ranges from a low of eighteen to a high of thirty. How long do they need to be a resident of their district, or even the state, before they can be a legislator? Some states mandate being a state resident from anywhere from one (Colorado) to six (Kentucky) years. Do legislators need to be U.S. citizens? Most states require this in some way, but twelve do not require a person to be a U.S. citizen in order to run for their state legislature.

Action Item

4-4

How long will the terms of office be for your legislature? If you have two chambers will they be the same or different?

Action Item

4-5

Will the Hamiltonia legislature have term limits? If so, how will they be implemented?

Figure 4.5

State Legislature Comparison: Eligibility

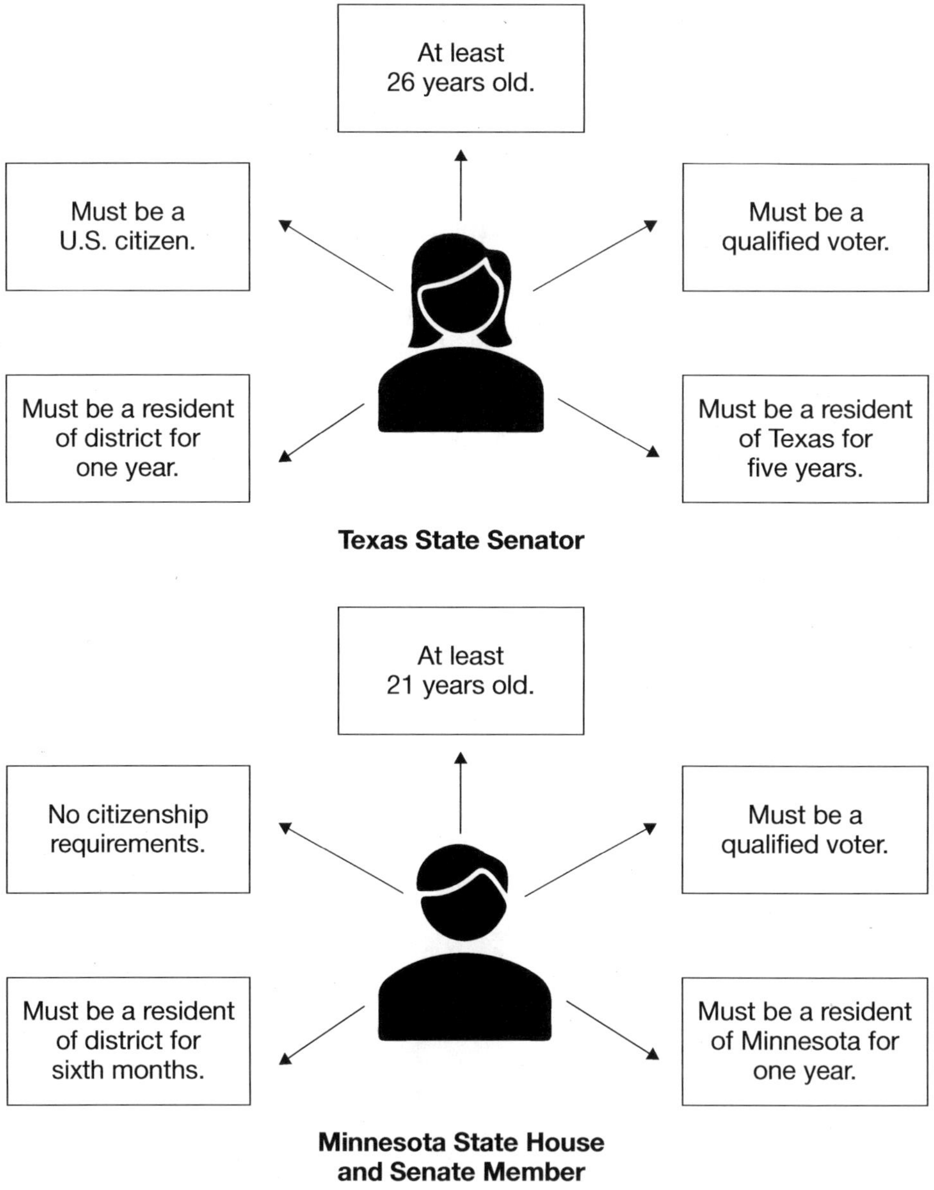

At least 26 years old.

Must be a U.S. citizen.

Must be a qualified voter.

Must be a resident of district for one year.

Must be a resident of Texas for five years.

Texas State Senator

At least 21 years old.

No citizenship requirements.

Must be a qualified voter.

Must be a resident of district for sixth months.

Must be a resident of Minnesota for one year.

Minnesota State House and Senate Member

Action Item

4-6

What are the eligibility requirements to serve in the Hamiltonia legislature? If you have two chambers, will the requirements be the same or different?

Legislative Professionalism

The introduction of this chapter provided an explanation of the components of legislative professionalism and the effects that has on state legislatures. Just like the other fifty states, you will need to decide whether your legislature is professional, hybrid, or a citizen legislature. You can discuss and debate this in two ways. First, you could have a broader discussion of the pros and cons of having a professional vs. hybrid vs. citizen legislature, then come to a consensus on which kind of legislature you want, and finally decide each individual component: length of legislative calendar, pay, and staff numbers that would typically fall within the kind of legislature you have chosen. Alternatively, you could debate each component separately and see what kind of legislature you create, whether that be professional, hybrid, or citizen.

Table 4.2 lists out each kind of legislature and where each of the fifty states falls. Most states are hybrid with the next most likely professionalism being citizen legislatures. However, even within each kind of legislature there is significant diversity. Consider the pay of legislators. Legislators in professional institutions should make a wage high enough so that they can live comfortably without having to have another job. But that wage depends also on the cost of living of the state. California legislators as of 2023 make $114,877 a year, yet legislators in Wisconsin, which also has a professional legislature, make a salary of $55,141 a year. Alabama legislators, who work in a hybrid legislature, make slightly less than Wisconsin legislators; legislative salary in Alabama is $51,734. On the other hand of the spectrum, we see a state like North Carolina, which has a hybrid legislature, paying their officials $13,951 a year, which is closer to citizen legislature states like Rhode Island ($16,636) and South Dakota ($12,851). Put simply, in an area such as salary, there is a bit of flexibility within each of the categories keeping in mind the size of the state and how expensive it is to live there.

Table 4.2
State Legislative Professionalism (Legislative Salaries)

PROFESSIONAL	SEMI-PROFESSIONAL	CITIZEN
Alaska ($50,400)	Alabama ($53,956)	Idaho ($18,875)
California ($119,702)	Arizona ($24,000)	Kansas ($88.66/session day)
Hawaii ($62,604)	Arkansas ($44,357)	Maine ($15,417 first regular session; $10,999 second regular session)
Illinois ($70,645)	Colorado ($40,242)	Mississippi ($23,500)
Massachusetts ($70,537)	Connecticut ($28,000)	Montana ($100.46/legislative day)
Michigan ($71,685)	Delaware ($48,237)	New Hampshire ($100)
New York ($110,000)	Florida ($29,697)	New Mexico ($0)
Ohio ($68,674)	Georgia ($17,341)	North Dakota ($518/month)
Pennsylvania ($95,432)	Indiana ($28,791)	Rhode Island ($16,835)
Wisconsin ($55,141)	Iowa ($25,000) Kentucky (188.22/calendar day) Louisiana ($16,800) Maryland ($50,33) Minnesota ($46,500) Missouri ($36,813) Nebraska ($12,000) Nevada ($164.69/calendar day up to 60 days) New Jersey ($49,000) North Carolina ($13,951) Oklahoma ($47,500) Oregon ($33,852) South Carolina ($10,400) Tennessee ($24,316) Texas ($7,200) Virginia ($18,000 senators/$17,640 delegates) Washington ($57,876)	South Dakota ($13,957) Utah ($285/legislative day) Vermont ($742.92/week during session) West Virginia ($20,000) Wyoming ($150/day)

Note: Legislative Salaries from the National Conference of State Legislatures: https://www.ncsl.org/about-state-legislatures/2022-legislator-compensation

The length of legislative calendars is a bit more rigid when it comes to the kinds of legislatures. Professional legislatures meet year-round or close to year-round, which helps to justify both their pay as well as their staff. There is a bit more flexibility in the differences in session length between hybrid and citizen legislatures. Florida, a semi-professional legislature, meets for 60 calendar days each year while Maryland, also with a semi-professional legislature, meets for 90 calendar days. The citizen legislature of New Hampshire meets for 45 legislative days while Wyoming meets for 40 legislative days in odd-numbered years and 20 legislative days in even-numbered years. The length of the session matters because the less days legislators have in session the less time they have to sponsor, debate, and vote on bills. This does not mean that citizen legislatures do not pass legislation, but because they are in session for such a short period of time—such as in Wyoming—the bills they have to debate, and pass are the ones that cannot be ignored—such as the budget. Add in the fact that many of the states that have such short legislative sessions also have no personal staff and limited committee staff, then this makes bill sponsorship very difficult beyond the most necessary bills to keep the government running. It is therefore not surprising that legislators in a state like New York which is professional and meets year-round sponsor many more bills than a state like Mississippi which only meets for 90 calendar days except in years after gubernatorial election when they meet for 125 calendar days.[27] Figure 4.6 shows the size of the staff in each state legislature.

Figure 4.6

Legislative Staff Size by State

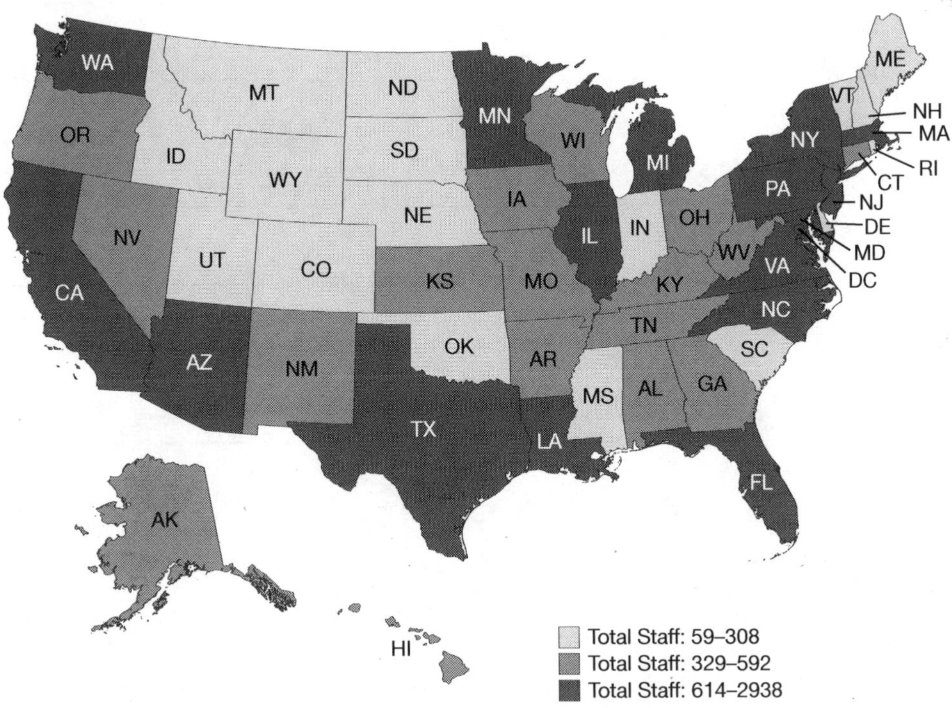

SOURCE: Data from the National Council of State Legislatures (NCSL)

If you are wondering what legislative staff does, it depends. If a legislator has staff dedicated solely to them, then their staff is used for constituent service, helping to research and write legislation, and organizing the legislator's day-to-day schedule including meetings and anything involving the press. New York State Assembly members maintain an office both in Albany and in their districts, therefore they need staff for both. In states where legislators don't have their own personal staff, then staff is shared, and typically can be found in legislative research offices and committees. These staff members help write and research legislation, but as they are shared among more than one legislator, this is somewhat limited.

Action Item

4-7

What is the salary you will pay Hamiltonia's legislators?

Action Item

4-8

What is the length of the legislative calendar?

Action Item

4-9

Will legislators have personal staff, and if so, how many?

Action Item

4-10

Based upon your class's answers to the previous questions, is your legislature citizen, semi-professional, or professional?

Legislative Powers: Overriding the Governor's Veto and Oversight

Different legislative chambers have more or less power vis-à-vis other government institutions. One power that legislatures may have over the governor is the power to override a veto. After the same bill has been passed by both chambers of the legislature, the bill is sent to the governor's office to be signed into law. Governors, however, can decide whether to sign the bill into law or to veto the bill. When a bill is vetoed, the legislature may respond by overriding the veto. This means that the bill can become law even without the governor's signature. In some legislatures, the requirement to override a veto is more or less cumbersome. For example, in Wisconsin the legislature can override a veto with two-thirds majority vote.[28] In Tennessee, however, the legislature can override a veto with a majority vote.[29] See Figure 4.7 on the breakdown of states and how they override gubernatorial vetoes.

The second major power of state legislatures is oversight over the other branches of government—particularly the executive branch. Remember, the state legislature enacts laws, but the executive branch implements them—the more vague a law, the more leeway **bureaucrats** have to affect the intent of the law. State legislatures want to ensure that the laws they pass are not only being implemented, but also that they are being implemented in the spirit with which the legislature intended. In addition to this, legislatures also want to ensure that money they **appropriate** to departments and agencies is being spent efficiently and effectively.

One way state legislatures oversee the executive branch is through the creation of **Administrative Rules Review Committees**. This is a committee within the legislature that checks the rules that state departments and agencies pass to ensure they are in line with the intent of the legislation. California, Colorado, Maine, as well as thirteen other states do not give the legislature the power to review proposed agency rules. The remaining states then provide varying levels of legislative oversight on proposed agency rules: thirteen states only allow for an advisory role. Of those thirteen, eleven require gubernatorial approval (Idaho and Kansas do not), while the remaining twenty-one states give the committees full

Figure 4.7

How State Legislatures Override a Gubernatorial Veto

The number of states that requires a majority of the legislature to override a governor's veto.

7

The number of states that requires three-fifths of the legislature to override a governor's veto.

37

The number of states that requires two-thirds of the legislature to override a governor's veto.

authority to reject proposed rules without any further approval from the full legislative body. Fourteen states (Louisiana and Massachusetts, for example) require gubernatorial approval under this arrangement while seven do not (Alabama, Connecticut, Iowa, Illinois, Michigan, Nevada, and Vermont).[30]

For the state of Hamiltonia you will need to decide how a legislature overrides a gubernatorial veto, as well as how powerful the legislature's oversight powers will be.

Action Item

4-11

What is required to override a gubernatorial veto?

Action Item

4-12

Will the Hamiltonia State Legislature have an Administrative Rules Review Committee? If so, will the committee be able to reject proposed agency rules under its own authority or will it require approval of the full legislature and/or the governor?

Legislative Leadership

Legislative leadership helps to run and organize state legislatures. Duties of legislative leaders typically comprise assigning legislators to committees including chair positions, presiding over daily session, and scheduling legislation including assigning it to specific committees. In the lower chamber of all forty-nine lower houses (remember Nebraska is unicameral) the head of the chamber is the Speaker of the House. For the upper chamber, typically known as the senate, there is more variation in leadership. The state of Alabama, Georgia, Mississippi, South Carolina, Texas, and West Virginia vest leadership of the upper chamber in the **lieutenant governor**. The lieutenant governor of Texas is unusually powerful and is able to appoint senators to committees and decide who becomes committee chair, and also decides which bills are considered, and the timing of when they will be considered.[31]

Other states call their upper chamber leader a president (such as Alaska, Minnesota, and Ohio), while still others call their leader a president pro tempore (Arkansas, North Carolina, and Vermont). New York calls the leader of their state senate a president or **majority leader**.[32] For the state of Hamiltonia, you will need to decide which leaders you want for your chamber(s) and which powers you will give them.

Action Item

4-13

Who will be the legislative leaders of your lower chamber if you decide Hamiltonia has one?

Action Item

4-14

What powers do your legislative leaders have?

Action Item

4-15

Who will be the legislative leaders of your upper chamber?

Action Item

4-16

What powers do your upper chamber legislative leaders have?

Action Item

4-17

Will Hamiltonia have single or multimember districts? If you have multimember districts, will voters be required to use all of their votes, or can they decide not to use all of them?

Legislative Districts

The final decision you have to make regarding Hamiltonia's legislature is how many elected officials will be assigned per district. The majority of states have single-member districts (SMD) where one legislator represents one geographical area. States with **multimember districts** allow constituents to vote for multiple legislators to represent them. Take for example the New Jersey State House. Voters receive a specific number of votes as there are open seats and can split up their votes for multiple candidates, give all of their votes to one candidate, or decide not to use all of their votes.[33] The state of Vermont is similar, except voters must use all of their votes.

You must decide whether you will have single or multimember districts and, if you decide on multimember districts whether you will set it up like Vermont or New Jersey in terms of vote usage. Research has shown that multimember districts promote more diversity of candidates. **Single-member districts** may have fewer diverse candidates but have a much stronger connection for voters because they have one representative, as opposed to multiple.[34]

Looking Forward

Nice work! You have fully formed a state legislature for the state of Hamiltonia. Whether you have one chamber, or two, are partisan or nonpartisan, or have single- or multimember districts, you have now decided the institutional arrangement of the Hamiltonia State Legislature. The way state legislatures are organized and the powers that they hold affects the ways in which the legislative and executive branches interact. Typically, as the legislature is more professionalized and has more power, the governor's power may be diminished. Likewise, as legislatures are less professionalized and are more limited in power, the governor's power grows. The way that you organize Hamiltonia's legislature has consequences for how powerful the governor can be. In the next chapter, you will be designing the executive branch for the state of Hamiltonia. It may be helpful to keep in mind how powerful the legislature is in Hamiltonia and whether you want the legislature or the governor to have more power.

Key Terms

Speaker of the House (62)
committees (62)
Medicaid (63)
districts (64)
constituents (64)
descriptive representation (65)
parity (65)
party identification (66)
legislative professionalism (66)
term limits (68)
standing committees (70)
override (71)
unicameral (71)
bicameral (71)
bureaucrats (81)
appropriate (81)
Administrative Rules Review Committees (81)
lieutenant governor (82)
majority leader (83)
multimember districts (84)
single-member districts (84)

Assignments to Learn More about State Legislatures

1. Write a newspaper op-ed for the *Hamiltonia Herald* on one of the institutional arrangements you believe the state of Hamiltonia should adopt.
   a. Try to keep your op-ed less than a thousand words: the shorter an op-ed is the more likely readers will read the entire article.
   b. Make sure you stay on topic and keep your argument as concise as possible. You have limited space, so try not to take on too much.
   c. For more guidance on writing an op-ed see:
      i. David Jarmul's "How to Write an Op-Ed Article": https://www.umass.edu/pep/sites/default/files/how_to_write_an_oped-duke_2.pdf
      ii. Harvard Kennedy School of Government's "How to Write an Op-Ed or Column":
      https://projects.iq.harvard.edu/files/hks-communications-program/files/new_seglin_how_to_write_an_oped_1_25_17_7.pdf

2. Choose two legislative districts and compare and contrast which issues may be particularly important to those constituents.
    a. Located in the instructor manual of this book is a description of each legislative district in the state of Hamiltonia. Choose two and look carefully at the demographic and economic makeup of each district.
    b. What issues do you think will matter most to the constituents of these districts? Why?
3. Choose a member of the state legislature from the state where you go to college and write a short biography noting the following:
    a. What their educational and professional background is,
    b. How long they have served,
    c. If they are subject to term limits,
    d. The committees/leadership positions they hold,
    e. The two most recent bills they have sponsored,
    f. An assessment of how well you think the legislator substantively and descriptively represents their district.

Alaska's Governor Mansion in Juneau, AK, since 1912.

SOURCE: Wikicommons

Generating the Governor's Office

Learning Objectives:

After reading this chapter students should be able to:

- Explain the formal powers of governors.
- Compare the different kinds of powers different states have.
- Discuss the historical background of the governor.
- Describe the levels of racial, ethnic, and gender diversity in the governor's office.
- Explain the varying qualifications for governors to serve.
- Create a state level governor's office.

State Spotlight: Alaska

What makes a governor powerful? Is it the powers they are given in their state constitutions? Or is it the amount they won their elections by? Maybe it is in part personality and ability to speak directly to the people? Is it how large the governor's mansion is? In many ways it is all of these things and more—except the size of the mansion. Let's take a look at a governor with a moderate level of **institutional powers** (also known as powers from their state constitution): Alaska. A governor's institutional powers range widely from state to state. There are five main categories that gubernatorial powers are typically measured: budget-making power, **veto** powers, appointment powers, how long they can hold office, and the number of separately elected executive-branch officials. Let's investigate each of these briefly for the Alaska governor and we will explain them further later in the chapter.

The governor of Alaska in 2024 was Mike Dunleavy (R). Governor Dunleavy spent a lot of his professional life as an educator. He was not only a teacher, but also a principal and a superintendent. He first ventured into politics by serving on a **school board**—a common entrance point into political life. After that he was an Alaska state senator from 2012–2018.[1] While in the state senate he chaired the education committee and served on the finance and transportation committees as well as others.[2] Although he was not born in Alaska, he has lived there for forty years.[3]

In Alaska only the governor and **lieutenant governor** are independently elected—meaning that they are elected in a statewide race. This means the governor does not have to compete with the constituencies of other executive branch officials because they were never elected. While the Alaska governor is limited to two four-year terms, this is still a longer tenure than other governors whose terms may only be two years (like New Hampshire), or who can only serve one term (like Virginia). However, this pales in comparison to a state like New York, which does not limit the number of times a governor can be elected to the position.

Appointment powers are an area where Alaska's governor powers shine. Although the governor may need to work with the legislature or an agency head to make **appointments**, they are involved in choosing not only the heads of major departments, but also hundreds of appointees that serve in lower levels, including boards and commissions. The positions governors can appoint to and whether the appointment has to be approved by other government institutions varies by state.

In addition to these appointment powers, the Alaska governor also has full responsibility over their executive budget without the legislature being able to increase it. The only power that the Alaska governor falls short on is the veto power, which is not to be taken lightly. In Alaska the governor only has veto power on **appropriations**, albeit with the high bar of two-thirds of legislators needed to **override**. Compare this to Alabama's governor, who has **line-item veto** power on appropriation amounts and language, but only a majority of elected legislators can override their veto. Keep in mind that a line-item veto is unique: it allows governors to block only parts of passed appropriations bills from becoming law. Appropriations bills tell state agencies—from boards and commissions all the way up to whole departments—how to spend their money.

Alaska Governor Mike Dunleavy (R) also has what we call **informal powers**. These are powers that give the governor political capital but are not necessarily outlined in the state constitution. Informal powers include components such as the amount the governor won his election by or what his approval rating is within the state. When the governor comes into office with a big electoral win and has strong approval ratings, he has more political capital to accomplish his goals. Dunleavy won the election in 2022 with over 50 percent of the vote with four opponents.[4] He is also the first Alaskan governor in about twenty-five years to win back-to-back terms.[5] But Governor Dunleavy only has about a 53 percent approval rating which may hamper his policy initiatives.[6] Informal powers of a governor are different across executive branches and can even change during a governor's tenure.

A great example of the changing nature of governors' powers is the COVID-19 pandemic. Governors ended up taking center stage in responding to the epidemic, helping to make decisions on not only where funding could be used but also becoming the central voices on mask mandates. While the federal government could mandate mask wearing on airplanes or trains—which are regulated by the federal department of transportation—they could not mandate that people wear masks in non-federally regulated areas or buildings. This meant governors stepped up to outline the conditions—if any—of mask mandates. Governors like Gavin Newsom of California instituted mask mandates early (June 2020) and kept them for a long time (March 2022). Governors like Ron DeSantis of Florida never issued a mask mandate, and in fact issued fines and penalties for local governments, including schools, from issuing mask mandates themselves.[7] This is just one example of how governor's powers can change in the blink of an eye.

In this chapter we will be discussing the role of the governor in the United States, and what the governor of Hamiltonia's powers will look like. Keep in mind how you created your legislature. If your legislature is citizen, the governor, who works year-round, may be more powerful in comparison. If you decide your legislature is professional and meets throughout the year, you may want to consider what powers you can give the Hamiltonia governor to balance out the power dynamic. In the end state governments, like the federal government, are set up to be a system of separation of powers with checks and balances. You will decide exactly what that will look like in terms of the governor's office in this chapter of the simulation.

Overview of Governors

Like state legislatures, governors have a history that predates the U.S. Constitution. Each of the thirteen colonies had a governor who was appointed by the king of England. As Batinski explains,

> The king appointed the governor. The governor remained in office at the king's pleasure. And governors appointed in England came to America with instructions to support the Church of England as the established church. They were expected to promote English economic interests even when they collided with the colony's welfare.[8]

Therefore, a key difference, historically between legislatures and governors is that many legislators were elected by the colonists prior to the American Revolution, while governors were the tools of a king living thousands of miles away. Colonial governors could convene legislatures, dissolve them, or veto any bills they passed in addition to numerous appointment powers.[9] These powers were eroded by colonial governments as they marched toward the American Revolution, and many governorships were significantly weakened following independence.

After the Revolution, governors become such a central figure in state government that the infamous *Federalist Paper* #69, written by Alexander Hamilton, consistently compares the new office of the president to governors of various states, attempting to ease the newly independent colonists' fears that the president is more powerful than the king of England or the governor of New York.[10] The governor's office is also often seen as a stepping stone to the presidency—seventeen out of the forty-five presidents that have served were governors of their states including Thomas Jefferson (Virginia), William McKinley (Ohio), Theodore and Franklin Roosevelt (New York), Ronald Reagan (California), Bill Clinton (Arkansas), and George W. Bush (Texas).[11] Like presidents, governors are the executive authority of their states, and as we briefly discussed in the beginning of this chapter, have a considerable toolbox to shape the policy landscape of their states not only during their terms, but also for years after their term ends.

Diversity in the Governor's Office

Unfortunately, like many political offices throughout the United States, governors have lacked diversity for much of their history. We are going to look at three different areas of diversity: gender, race, and sexual orientation. Starting with gender, the first woman to serve as governor was Nellie Tayloe Ross of Wyoming in 1925. Ross won a special election following the death of her husband—Governor William B. Ross. In fact, this was the only way the first women could serve as governors—they finished out the terms of their deceased or ineligible-to-run husbands. This happened to Miriam Ferguson (Texas, 1925 and 1933) and Lurleen Wallace (Alabama, 1967). It would take an additional fifty years for the first woman to be elected on her own; that honor goes to Ella T. Grasso of Connecticut in 1975.[12]

Figure 5.1 displays the party breakdown of the women who have served as governor in the United States. You will notice that there is a considerably higher percentage of women who have served as Democrats as opposed to Republicans. This pattern holds true for current governors as well—as of summer 2024, 12 women serve as governors with eight serving as Democrats and four serving as Republicans. Perhaps most interesting when it comes to gender and the governorship is the fact that 18 states

Figure 5.1

Women Governors by Party over Time

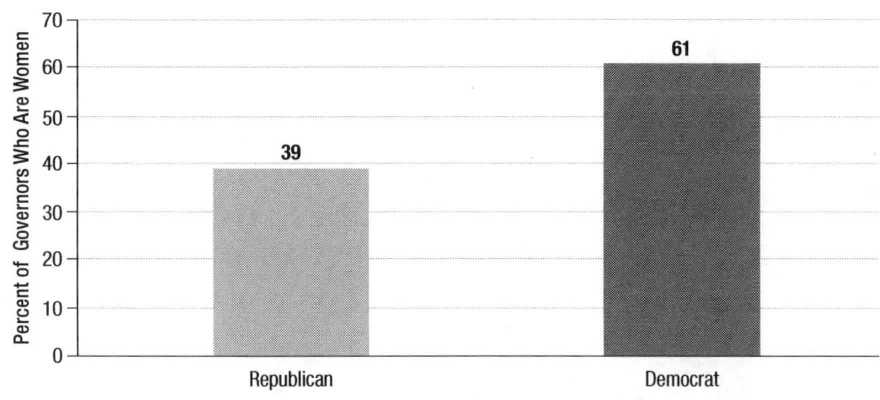

SOURCE: Data from the Center for the American Women and Politics (CAWP)

have still never elected a woman as governor, including more Democratic states such as California and Illinois. Overall, 49 women have served as governor in 32 states since the founding of the nation.[13]

Racial and ethnic diversity of governors is even lower than gender diversity. In 2023 only four governors identified as non-white: Michelle Lujan Grisham (D-NM, Hispanic), Kevin Stitt (R-OK, Native American), Chris Sununu (R-NH, Hispanic), and Wes Moore (D-MD, African American). Figure 5.2 displays the numbers of African American, Hispanic, Asian, and Native American governors that have served throughout American history. This includes governors who were never elected but may have been appointed to the office or assumed the office following a governor's death or **impeachment**. When you compare these numbers to the hundreds of governors who have served their states, the number of non-white governors is incredibly small.

The final area we want to cover when it comes to gubernatorial diversity is sexual orientation. The first openly gay governor was Jim McGreevey (D) of New Jersey, who revealed his sexual orientation in a speech regarding his resignation as governor after he faced sexual harassment accusations from the former Homeland Security advisor whom he had been engaging in an extramarital affair with. Jared Polis of Colorado was the first openly gay governor elected in 2018. Kate

Figure 5.2

Number of Non-White/Non-Hispanic Governors throughout American History

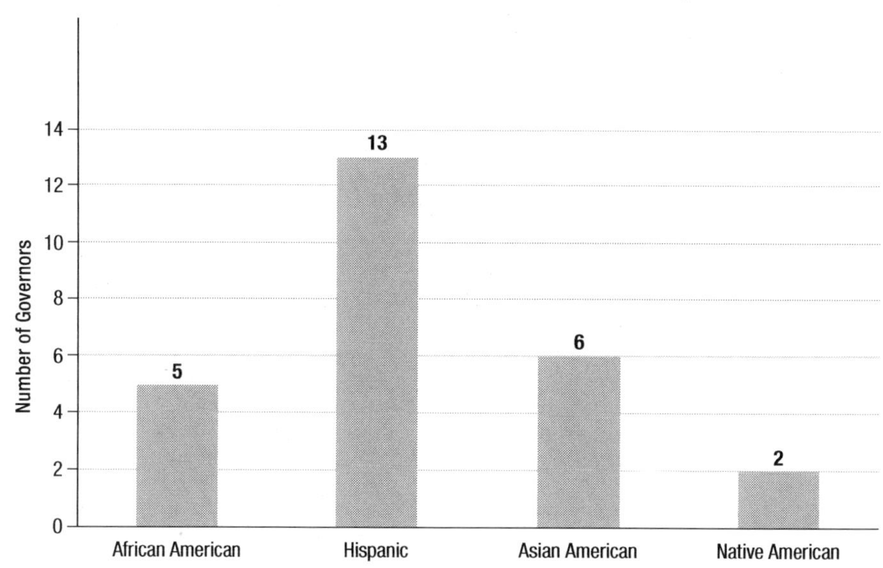

Brown was the first openly bisexual person to serve as governor after the previous governor resigned in 2015. She was elected in 2016. Finally, Maura Healey was the first openly lesbian governor elected for the state of Massachusetts in 2022. Thus far no transgender governor has been elected to serve as governor of a state. There are, however, eight openly transgender legislators serving throughout the United States.[14] Since the state legislature is a common pipeline to the governor's office, we may see more diversity in governor's offices soon.

Simulation

We will now cover the details of governor's powers and offices across the United States. By the end of this chapter, you will have created the office of the Hamiltonia governor.

The Details of the Governor's Office

We previewed gubernatorial powers in the beginning of this chapter. Now we will further explain each institutional power to keep in mind as you create the office of the Hamiltonia governor. Let's start out with the eligibility requirements your class may want to implement. Like the state legislature, there are three main eligibility requirements states set for their governors: age, residency, and citizenship. Only two states have no age requirement: Massachusetts and Kansas. Most states set the age at 30, with others setting it at 25 or 18. Oklahoma has the oldest age requirement, which is set at 31.

The other area of eligibility requirements are state citizenship, U.S. citizenship, and state residency. Some states do not have any state citizenship requirements, whereas others require state citizenship for as many as 7 years (we're looking at you, Alabama and Tennessee). In general, there is either no state citizenship requirements (24 states), state citizenship without specifying the number of years (12 states), at least 30 days (Rhode Island) or 6 months (Connecticut), or as many as 2 (4 states), 5 (6 states), or 7 years. All but four states (Kansas, Kentucky, Massachusetts, and Nevada) require U.S. citizenship, and many states require it for a significant number of years. Mississippi and New Jersey require 20 years of U.S. citizenship, while Georgia, Maine, and Missouri require 15 years of U.S. citizenship. Over half of the states require U.S. citizenship, but do not specify the number of years.

Finally, we get to state residency. Kansas and Tennessee are the only states that do not require residency requirements in their state to serve as governor. Connecticut, Massachusetts, Ohio, Washington, West Virginia,

Table 5.1
Comparison of Governor Qualifications

	KANSAS	ALABAMA
Minimum Age	No Minimum	30
State Citizenship	No Requirement	7 years
U.S. Citizenship	No Requirement	10 years
State Residency	No Requirement	7 years

SOURCE: The *Book of States*, 2021 Edition, Volume 53.

and Wisconsin require residency without a specified amount of time. The remaining states typically set residency requirements anywhere from 30 days (Rhode Island) to upward of 10 years (Missouri and Oklahoma). Take a look at Table 5.1 which compares the eligibility requirements of two states: one with low requirements and a second with high requirements.[15]

It is now your turn to decide the qualifications for the Hamiltonia governor. You should keep in mind the qualification requirements you set for the legislature. What made you set those requirements? Should the governor be different? Why? Many people will argue that with age comes more experience, while others do not want to limit a person from running for office because they may be young. On the other hand, people strongly believe that candidates should at least know the state they want to be governor for—that probably only happens if they are a state citizen or have lived in the state for a certain number of years. Alaska Governor Mike Dunleavy was not born in Alaska, for example, but moved there in his early twenties and didn't run for his first office until he was in his fifties. Keep in mind that no state requires that a governor have been born in the state, so you need to think about whether a person can effectively represent their state if you do not require citizenship or residency. However, it also may be unlikely that voters elect a person they do not know, or whom they know has not lived in the state for very long.

Action Item

5-1

What is the minimum age a person needs to be to be elected governor of Hamiltonia?

Action Item

5-2

Are there residency or citizenship requirements to be governor of Hamiltonia?

Term Lengths and Limits

Our next area to tackle is the length of the governor's term, whether or not the Hamiltonia's governor has **term limits**, and when you'd like gubernatorial elections held. Let's start with the length of the governor's term. Forty-eight states set the governor's term to four years; only New Hampshire and Vermont set the gubernatorial term to two years. At least for both states there are no term limits, despite having such a short term of office. Figure 5.3 compares the number of states that have each kind of term limit. You will notice that almost half of the states limit a governor to two consecutive terms, meaning that after they have served their second term they would not be eligible to serve for a third term right away. Thirteen states have no term limits, while Virginia stands out as the only state to limit the governor to one four-year term for life.

In terms of when gubernatorial elections are held, there is a bit more diversity. States like New Hampshire and Vermont who only give their governor two-year terms are always coinciding with midterm

Figure 5.3
Gubernatorial Term Limits

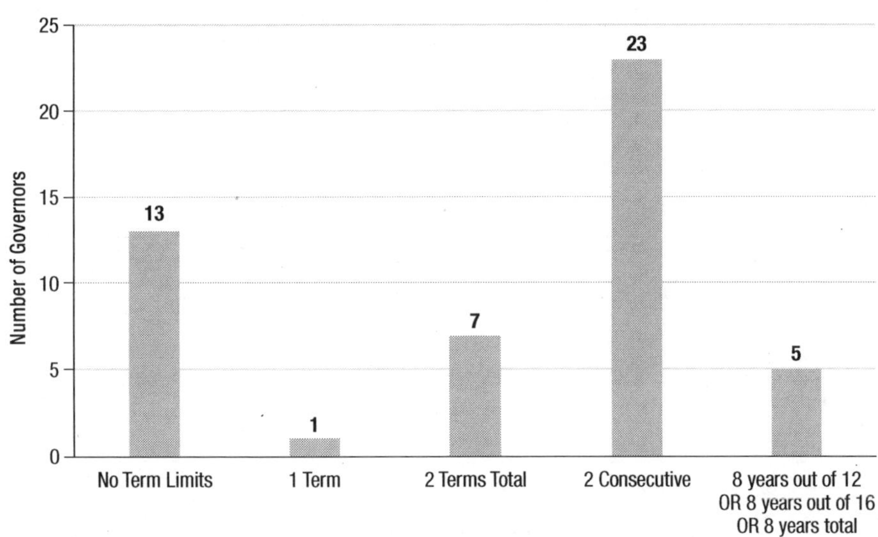

congressional elections and presidential elections. This also coincides with state legislative races as well. If you have designed your state legislature so that both houses have the same term length, it is possible that Hamiltonia could reelect its entire state legislature and the governor in the same election cycle. However, it is possible to hold elections in odd-numbered years, like Virginia, New Jersey, Kentucky, Mississippi, and Louisiana. Keep in mind that running elections is an important and expensive responsibility for state governments. Holding state elections at the same time as federal elections is much more cost effective. The downside is that state elections may be overshadowed by congressional and especially presidential elections. Holding elections on the odd-numbered year means voters can only focus on the state elections and their candidates. A downside to holding state elections on the odd numbered year, however, may be lower turnout—the highest turnout for any office in the United States is the presidency. Pairing gubernatorial elections with a presidential election (as nine states do) may result in higher turnout and therefore the opportunity for a newly elected governor to claim a mandate if they were to win by a substantial amount. It looks like most states—thirty-four—end up splitting the difference by setting elections for off-presidential years (2018, 2022, for example) to both save on the cost and also potentially garner higher turnout then if it was just a state-level election on its own.

This leads us to three more decisions you need to make for the Hamiltonian governor. Below you need to decide the length of the governor's term, whether there will be term limits, and when elections will be held. As we suggested above, keep in mind the decisions you made for your state legislative positions.

Action Item

5-3

What is the length of the governor's term?

Action Item

5-4

Will the governor be subject to term limits? If yes, what are they?

Action Item

5-5

When will gubernatorial elections be held? During presidential elections, midterm elections, or off-cycle elections?

Gubernatorial Line of Succession

Before we get into the details of gubernatorial powers, there is one other issue that you need to decide, and that is gubernatorial line of succession. In forty-five states the lieutenant governor would take over in the event that the governor was removed from office, resigned, or died. Arizona, Oregon, and Wyoming pass the torch to the secretary of state, while the Senate president takes over in Maine and New Hampshire.

This is important because you never know when the governor may have a catastrophic health event or be forced to resign from office. The importance of this question is relevant today. Governor Ralph Northam (D-VA) was under pressure to resign after racist pictures of him from medical school were revealed in 2019. During this time, if Northam had resigned the lieutenant governor would have succeeded him. There was only one problem—the lieutenant governor was under investigation after a sexual assault and rape allegation.[16] But the state of Virginia

Demonstrators hold signs and chant outside the Governor's Mansion at the Capitol in Richmond, VA, in February 2019. The demonstrators were calling for the resignation of Virginia Governor Ralph Northam after a 30-year-old photo of him in his medical school yearbook was distributed.

SOURCE: AP Photo/ Steve Helber

had thought this through. If the lieutenant governor was removed from office, the attorney general would take over the governorship. Yet again, Virginia was in trouble because the attorney general was also facing calls to resign after racist pictures of him were also revealed.[17] So what would happen if the governor and attorney general resigned, and the lieutenant governor was removed for misconduct? In Virginia, the Speaker of the House would be next to assume office. At this time, Virginia had a Republican Speaker of the House meaning that the party leadership of the state could potentially flip from a Democrat to a Republican governor. The Speaker of the House was Republican because the Republicans controlled the chamber with the slimmest of majorities—only one vote. The only reason the Republican Party controlled the chamber was because David Yancey's name was picked out of a cannister after a tie race for his district's seat.[18] Governor Northam stayed in office so the state of Virginia did not need to use the line of succession outlined in its constitution. However, this story illustrates the importance of states having a plan for who will take over the governor's office in the event of a resignation or death and the importance of a single vote in state legislative races. What will be the line of succession in Hamiltonia?

The line of succession is also important if a governor is impeached. Impeachment is the process whereby a public official may be removed from office. Impeachment for the president of the United States, for example, is decided by the House of Representatives and then a trial is held by the U.S. Senate where they decide whether or not to remove the president. The judge in charge of this trial is the chief justice of the United States Supreme Court. Like much of what you have already learned, states have different mechanisms for impeachment of their governors. Oregon is unique because it has "no provision for impeachment. Public officers may be tried for incompetence, corruption, malfeasance, or delinquency in office in same manner as criminal offenses."[19] The remaining forty-nine states all have provisions for impeachments.

When it comes to the process, forty-six states give impeachment power to their state house of representatives, while only three give that power to their senates (but remember one of those three is Nebraska which only has one chamber). If a governor is impeached, the trial is held by the Senate in forty-five states, by the House in one (Alaska), by the House and Senate in Oklahoma, by the State Supreme Court in Nebraska, or by a special commission of "seven eminent jurists to be elected by the Senate" in Missouri. There is even more diversity in the vote required for conviction: 13 states require a two-thirds vote by the present members, 29 states require simply two-thirds, and two states require two-thirds of majority members to convict. Iowa is the only state to require a majority of elected legislators to convict their governor during the impeachment process. While it is unlikely that an impeachment will come to pass during your simulation, this is an important process to decide for the future of Hamiltonia.

Action Item

5-6

Will there be a lieutenant governor of Hamiltonia? If you had decided in chapter 4 that a lieutenant governor was part of legislative leadership then this action item has already been decided.

Action Item

5-7

What is line of succession in the event that a governor dies, resigns, or is impeached from office?

Action Item

5-8

What is the process for impeachment of a sitting governor?

- Who holds the power of impeachment?
- Who conducts the impeachment trial?
- What is the vote required for conviction?

Gubernatorial Powers

Now we can cover the details associated with gubernatorial powers. Let's start with the governor's budget powers. Power over a state's budget is an important component of a governor's toolbox. Budgets determine what programs and initiatives get funded—the more influence a governor has over that process, the more they can make their vision for their state a reality. So, what exactly do gubernatorial powers over the budget look like? First, most governors have the power of estimating the next year's budget. Just over half the states give governors full responsibility over making the budget. In addition to this, thirty-four states give the governor line-item veto power over appropriation amounts and twenty-two states line-item veto power on appropriations language. See Table 5.2 for a breakdown of the number of states with line-item veto powers.

Table 5.2
Line-Item Veto Powers

LINE-ITEM VETO ON APPROPRIATION AMOUNTS	LINE-ITEM VETO ON APPROPRIATION LANGUAGE	NO LINE-ITEM VETO POWER
34	22	6

Note: The states with no line-item veto power are Indiana, Nevada, New Hampshire, North Carolina, Rhode Island, and Vermont. Source: *The Book of States*.

Let's pause for a minute to illustrate the power of the line-item veto. Line-term vetoes allow governors the option of rejecting portions of bills instead of whole bills. The president of the United States, for example, can only veto whole bills—even if there is only one small part of a bill they dislike. Governors get a lot more leeway with bills when they can use their line-item veto powers on final budget amounts (say they want to increase or decrease the budget by $500 million) or on the language of budget bills themselves, thereby changing exactly where the money goes and what it is used for.

Governors can get incredibly creative with their line-item veto powers. Governors in Wisconsin used to be able to strike individual letters in words to create new words (until 1990 when it was voted away by the public) and until 2008 were able to combine "parts of two or more sentences to create a new sentence." The first kind of veto was dubbed the "Vanna White" veto and the second was called the "Frankenstein veto."[20] However, this didn't stop Governor Tony Evers—a former teacher and state superintendent—from getting creative in his line-item veto in 2023 when he changed the wording of "for the limit for the 2023–2024 school year and the 2024–25 school year, add $325 to the result under par" by removing the hyphen and removing twenty so that the new bill read that education funding would increase until 2425.[21] As the *New York Times* explained: "because Mr. Evers's veto eliminated only entire words and digits, without combining two or more sentences to create a new sentence, it appeared to be legal." Therefore, being specific on the limits of the line-item veto, if you decide to give such a power to the governor of Hamiltonia, is something you should keep in mind.

The other side of gubernatorial vetoing powers is the legislative override. In the previous chapter you decided what would be required to override a gubernatorial veto, so keep this in mind as you decide below how extensive you would allow your governor's veto powers to be.

Action Item

5-9

Will the governor have full responsibility for the budget or share responsibility with the legislature?

Action Item

5-10

Will the governor have line-item veto power? If yes:

- Will the line-item veto power be on all bills or appropriations only?
- Are there specific limitations you want to apply to the veto?

Executive Orders

The next set of powers we need to cover are **executive orders**. Executive orders carry the force of law, and depending on how extensive they are, give the governor considerable powers over the executive branch. One area of a governor's executive order powers is her ability to reorganize the executive branch or create new agencies. Having such a power means the governor gets to have a lot of input on what a new agency's mission is, who leads it, and potentially its budget—and therefore the impact it may have on the state's government. Similar to this power is a governor's ability through executive order to create committees or commissions. There are thousands of state boards and commissions across the nation with varying responsibilities from licensing specific fields such as nursing to monitoring historic trails and buildings across the state. This is important because dedicating an agency or a committee to a specific issue or policy problem dedicates state resources and attention to that issue.

Let's look at the state of Vermont. Vermont is unique in that it is only one of two states to limit the years of a governor's term to two years. Vermont's governor is also relatively powerful in terms of executive orders: they have all the executive order powers except for emergencies beyond civil defense disasters, public emergencies, and energy emergencies, and cannot pass an executive order on state personnel administration. The governor is allowed to create advisory committees, such as the Governor's Emergency Preparedness Advisory Council that was created via Governor Philip B. Scott's executive order in 2019.

The "Council shall be to assess the State's overall homeland security and emergency preparedness programs, policies, and communications and provide for coordinated input by stakeholders in the preparation, implementation, evaluation and revision of the current systems."[22]

Members of this council include designees of the Secretary of Civil and Military Affairs, the adjutant general, as well as many other individuals who are crucial to emergency responses at the state level.[23] Other common gubernatorial committees and councils include advisory committees on the drug epidemic, disabilities such as blindness, and councils on fitness. As we will see in chapter 14, Governor Kasich (R) of Ohio created an Opiate Action Team to coordinate the state's response to the opioid epidemic.

In addition to the reorganization and creation of new agencies and/or boards and commissions, almost all governors except the governor of Alaska and Wyoming can pass an executive order for civil defense and disasters and forty states allow their governor to pass an executive order responding to federal program requirements. If you have ever lived in a state that has received damage from a hurricane or tornado, for example, governors who are able to will issue an executive order to send resources, such as various state first responders to the area affected to help those in need. Governors who have the power to pass executive orders in response to federal program requirements, get to directly impact how federal funding may be used in their state. This is of course limited by any specific federal regulations on such funding. Figure 5.4 summarizes the number of states that grant their governors each kind of executive order.

The use of executive orders by governors is not without controversy. In 2020, during the COVID-19 pandemic, Governor Gretchen Whitmer of Michigan issued an executive order declaring a state of emergency.

Figure 5.4

Governors and Executive Orders

36	48	46	40
Allow governors to reorganize the executive branch and create new agencies.	Permit the governor to issue executive orders pertaining to civil defense disasters and emergencies.	Allow the governor to create advisory, coordinating, or investigating committees/ commissions.	Permit the governor to respond to federal program requirements.

Whitmer, a Democrat, became limited by an April 30 deadline for the order passed by the Republican-controlled legislature. Whitmer expanded her executive order despite the legislature's limitation, citing two state laws that she argued granted her the authority to extend her executive order on the state of emergency. Unfortunately for Whitmer, the state Supreme Court in a 4–3 opinion struck down her executive order extension because it was "in violation of the Constitution of our state because it purports to delegate to the executive branch the legislative powers of state government—including its plenary police powers—and to allow the exercise of such powers indefinitely."[24] Therefore it is probably best to be as explicit as possible when it comes to Hamiltonia's governors' executive order powers to avoid such conflict in the future.

You will need to decide how powerful you would like your governor to be regarding executive order powers. Alaska's governor is one of the weakest when it comes to executive order powers, they are only allowed to issue executive orders related to creating committees and commissions. In addition to such restrictions on their executive orders, Alaska's governor is also one of only twelve states that require legislative review of executive orders, further limiting their power. Decide how extensive you want Hamiltonia's governor's executive order powers to be, and whether their powers will be subject to legislative review.

Action Item

5-11

Does the governor have the power to do any of the following via executive order?

- Reorganize the executive branch and create new agencies
- Address issues regarding civil defense, disasters, and public emergencies
- Power to create advisory, coordinating, study, or investigative committees or commissions
- Power to issue a public health emergency response
- Respond to federal programs and requirements

Action Item

5-12

Are any of the governor's executive orders subject to legislative review?

Lieutenant Governor

Our final area to tackle is that of the lieutenant governor. We discussed the lieutenant governor briefly in chapter 4, where you may have already decided that the lieutenant governor will preside over the senate. If that action item has been addressed, you can move on to the remaining action items. Remember that a few states, with Texas being the main example, give the lieutenant governor the power to appoint legislators onto committees. Although rarely given, it can elevate the position of lieutenant governor sometimes higher than the governor. You will also need to decide if the lieutenant governor can break roll-call ties (as they do in 26 states). Remember the U.S. Senate is an even-numbered body that at times results in a 50–50 split on votes. The vice president is the individual who breaks the tie. If you have decided in the previous chapter that your Senate is also even bodied, you will need to decide whether the lieutenant governor will be the person who breaks the ties.

Finally, a unique power you can give your lieutenant governor is to be able to assign bills to committee. We again bring up the Texas lieutenant governor who has this power and is in part what makes that position so powerful. If this is a power you have already assigned to a majority leader in the previous chapter, then you do not need to address this action item.

Action Item

5-13

Will there be a lieutenant governor of Hamiltonia? If yes:

- Will the lieutenant governor run on the same ticket as the governor or independently?
- Will the lieutenant governor preside over the senate?
- Will the lieutenant governor have the power to appoint legislators onto committees?
- Will the lieutenant governor break roll-call ties?
- Will the lieutenant governor assign bills to committee?

Note: You will only answer Action Item 5-13 if you decided in Action Item 5-6 to have a lieutenant governor. Portions of Action Item 5-13 may have already been addressed in the prior chapter of the simulation. Refer to your state constitution to see if you have decided this item already.

Looking Forward

Congratulations! You have shaped the governor's office for the state of Hamiltonia. Your governor may only be able to serve one term, or they may have an unlimited number of terms; you may have created the lieutenant governor's office, or you may have decided not to have a lieutenant governor. Whatever you decided, you just created the office of the governor for the state of Hamiltonia. However, the governor is just the tip of the iceberg when it comes to state-level executive branches. Governors are the leaders of vast state bureaucracies. In the next chapter you will be designing the rest of the executive branch for the state of Hamiltonia. Keep in mind the powers you have given your legislature and your governor as you embark on the next stage of the simulation.

Key Terms

institutional powers (88)
veto (88)
appointments (88)
school board (88)
lieutenant governor (88)
appropriations (89)
override (89)
line-item veto (89)
informal powers (89)
term limits (95)
impeachment (92)
executive orders (101)

Assignments to Learn More about State Governments

1. Look up the governor from the state where you go to college and write a short biography noting the following:
    a. What their educational and professional background is,
    b. How long they have served,
    c. If they are subject to term limits,
    d. The powers they have,
    e. The two most recent executive orders they have signed,
    f. An assessment of how well you think the governor substantively and descriptively represents their state,

   g. And an assessment of their informal power—how much did they win the election by? What point are they in their term? What is their approval rating?

2. Becoming governor can come with a lot of perks. Some states have designated governor's mansions, others provide governor's cars, airplanes, and even helicopters. Use *The Book of States* to see how many states provide access to transportation, provide an official residence, and the number of staff allowed for in the governor's office. Then decide what kind of perks you want the Hamiltonia governor to have and why.

3. As noted above, a number of governors have become U.S. presidents. The governor's office is an important training ground for national office. However, the transition from the governor's office to a presidential run is not always smooth. Recently, in the state of Florida, the legislature changed state law to allow a sitting governor to run in a presidential primary while still acting as governor of the state. Previously, the governor of Florida had to resign before running for president. Look up the governor from the state you were raised in or the state you attend college and answer the following questions:
   a. How many governors from that state have run for president? Have any of them been successful?
   b. Do governors in the state have to resign from office before embarking on a presidential run?
   c. Do you think the governor of Hamiltonia should resign if she runs for president? Write a new state law detailing what happens if the sitting governor runs for president.

4. Imagine you are the chief policy advisor to the governor of your home state. Write a policy memo describing what you think are the biggest three issues facing the state and what policies the governor should promote to address those issues. Make sure to consider the institutional powers available to the governor that could help her realize those policy goals.

Georgia Secretary of State Brad Raffensperger testifies before Congress regarding the 2020 election results.
SOURCE: AP Photo/J. Scott Applewhite

Building the Bureaucracy

Learning Objectives:

After reading this chapter students should be able to:

- Describe the role of the bureaucracy in state governments.
- Compare the responsibilities of attorneys general, secretaries of state, and state treasurers across states.
- Explain the different levels of racial and gender diversity in the bureaucracy.
- Review the differing eligibility requirements for various bureaucratic leaders.
- Create new bureaucratic departments and positions for the state of Hamiltonia.
- Choose selection mechanisms for various bureaucratic positions in Hamiltonia.

State Spotlight: Georgia

If we were to ask you what the **secretary of state** does, you would probably answer they are the chief diplomatic officer of the United States. This would be true if we were talking about the *federal* secretary of state. But what about your *state-level* secretary of state? Not so sure? Secretaries of state play important administrative roles for state governments: they oversee licenses for businesses, archiving state records, publishing state laws, and perhaps most importantly act as the top election officials of their state. In fact, secretaries of state became famous like never before following the 2020 presidential election, when then-president Donald Trump specifically called out secretaries of state across the nation for inaccurately certifying the election results. One of these secretaries was Brad Raffensperger of Georgia who came under fire from President Trump as well as Georgia's U.S. Senators David Perdue and Kelly Loeffler (both of whom were trying to win their runoff elections) who claimed election fraud.

Neither the senators nor Trump could provide any support for their claims. Raffensberger responded publicly to the allegations, saying:

> Both Senators and I are all unhappy with the potential outcome for our President. But I am the duly elected Secretary of State. One of my duties involves helping to run elections for all Georgia voters. I have taken that oath, and I will execute that duty and follow Georgia law... As a Republican, I am concerned about Republicans keeping the U.S. Senate. I recommend that Senators Loeffler and Perdue start focusing on that.[1]

We tell this story to show how a bureaucratic official normally shrouded in obscurity plays an essential role in the political process that has important consequences for state and federal politics. All but three states (Alaska, Hawaii, and Utah) have a secretary of state.[2] States have a number of important bureaucratic positions including the attorneys general, the chief law enforcement officer, the **state treasurer**, and the heads of major departments. We also cannot forget the thousands of men and women who serve in the **civil service**, ensuring state governments run smoothly—there are over 65,000 state employees in Georgia alone![3] The secretary of state in Georgia serves four-year terms. Not just anyone can be elected, however. The secretary of state in Georgia must be at least twenty-five years old. They also have to have been a state resident for four years and a U.S. citizen for ten years.[4] They serve as the chief election officer for the state among other duties including filing certificates of nomination or election and publishing administrative rules and regulations.[5]

In this chapter we will provide an overview of the major bureaucratic positions within state government, and then hand the reins over to you as you decide what Hamiltonia's **bureaucracy** will look like.

The Big Three: Attorney General, Secretary of State, and State Treasurer

Just below the governor and lieutenant governor are the next three major executive branch leaders: the secretary of state, the **attorney general**, and the state treasurer. Remember five states do not have a lieutenant governor at all. We got a glimpse at the secretary of state in the beginning of this chapter, but let's look a little closer at this position. Secretaries of state can have quite a long list of responsibilities, and they vary considerably from state to state. But as the National Association of Secretaries of State (NASS) explains, secretaries of state "revolve around a basic commitment to quality public service and effective, efficient, government."[6] One name you may recognize who served as a colonial secretary of state (in this case province) was Samuel Adams, who served from 1776–1780. Secretaries of state, therefore, predate our federal government.

Attorneys general (AG) seemingly go back even further. The National Association of Attorneys General (NAAG) lists all former AGs by state and year. The first AG of the colony of Rhode Island, for example, was William Dyer from 1650–1651 and in Massachusetts the first AG was Paul Dudley from 1702–1718.[7] The NAAG describes attorneys general as the "chief legal officers of the states… the role of an attorney general is to serve as counselor to state government agencies and legislatures, and as a representative of the public interest."[8] Attorneys general have become even more powerful in the last few decades, with many of them running for, and winning the office of governor following their tenure as AG. Some famous former AGs include delegate at the Constitutional Convention Edmund Randolph (VA, 1776–1786), President Martin Van Buren (NY, 1815–1819), and Vice President Kamala Harris (CA, 2010–2017).

Finally, if attorneys general are the chief legal officer of a state, state treasurers are the CFOs, or chief financial officers. As the National Association of State Treasurers (NAST) explains: "While their specific roles and responsibilities may vary, all State Treasurers play a critical role in overseeing their state's assets, investments, and overall fiscal well-being."[9] This includes tracking pensions and investments of state funds, maintaining unclaimed property programs, and managing 529 plans which are a state supported college savings plans for parents.

Jake LaTurner, former State Treasurer of Kansas.

SOURCE: Jill Toyoshiba/ *The Kansas City Star*/ Tribune News Service via Getty Images

These three bureaucratic officials along with the governor and lieutenant governors are some of the most visible leaders of the state executive branch. They protect and promote their state's financial, legal, and political security. As important as these positions are, they are not the only leaders of the executive branch, there are also the commissioners or secretaries of all the other major departments of each state government such as a state's department of education or **department of health** and human services.

States organize their executive branch distinctively, assign responsibilities across departments differently, and even call the same departments by various names as well. They do have some commonalities. For example, all states have a department of education. However, they may call the leader of their education department or the department itself by a different name. For example, in Wisconsin they have the Department of Public Instruction which is headed by the state superintendent of public instruction. In Georgia, the department responsible for schools is the Georgia Department of Education which is headed by the state superintendent of schools. Even though states may use different names or organize departments differently most states have departments that are responsible for health and human services, families and children, education, the environment, and more.

Secretaries and Commissioners of Various Departments in State Government

We have provided you with four additional secretaries for your simulation that you may or may not use depending upon the size of your class. Let's start with the **education secretary**. Although not one of the big three, we want to emphasize the importance of the person who leads a state's education department. Education is an incredibly important issue area for state governments—they get to set education standards, teaching certifications, and create policies on anti-bullying campaigns as well as address higher education standards. Education is one of the single largest expenses a state has, and the state is usually involved in early education all the way through higher education. You will learn more about education policy in chapter 10. But for now, think about the kind of person you would want to see running Hamiltonia's education department and your vision for what the state should be doing for its students.

The **environmental secretary** will address laws and regulations affecting Hamiltonia's environment, including air, water, and land management. Let's look at two different environmental departments to see how they can vary. First up is New Jersey's Department of Environmental Protection (DEP). The head of the department is known as a commissioner, and he is appointed by the governor. Figure 6.1 compares the major offices

Figure 6.1

Divisions of the New Jersey and Missouri Environmental/Natural Resources Departments

New Jersey DEP	Missouri DNR
• Fish & Wildlife • Parks, Forests & Historic Sites • Air, Energy, and Materials Sustainability • Climate Resilience • Contaminated Site Remediation and Redevelopment • Water Resource Management • Watershed and Land Management	• Air • Waste & Recycling • Water • Land and Geology • Energy • State Parks

SOURCE: The information in this chart came from the New Jersey Department of Environmental Protection and Missouri Department of Natural Resources websites.

of New Jersey's DEP to Missouri's Department of Natural Resources. The head of Missouri's Department of Natural Resources is called a director, and they are appointed by the governor with the approval of the senate. Sometimes states have separate environment versus natural resources departments and sometimes they have one or the other. In New Jersey they have the DEP which contains an office for natural resources while in Missouri they only have a Department of Natural Resources. You will see that they cover the main areas of the environment, with varying ways of addressing the same issue areas.

The ways that states organize their executive departments have important implications for policymaking. Dedicating an entire department to one issue can ensure that state resources will be devoted to that issue. It indicates that the state is taking important action on the policy problem. Oftentimes, however, public problems can be multifaceted and require coordination and input from a variety of people and experts. Having multiple issues housed inside one department may lead to more coordination to solve public problems. When designing Hamiltonia's executive branch consider the issues that need their own department but also how these silos may affect cross-department coordination.

Next up are state departments of health. State departments of health oversee responding to public health issues, addressing developmental disabilities, running state Medicaid programs, keeping track of the spread of diseases including sexually transmitted diseases, and regulating the licensing of medical facilities and workers. They are also on the front lines of addressing substance abuse, as we will learn more about in chapter 14.

Finally, the law enforcement, or **public safety secretary** could be responsible for both law enforcement as well as corrections. Corrections involves properly running jails and prisons. Jails are where people go while waiting for trial or those who are sentenced to short-term sentences. Prisons are for longer, more serious sentencing for felonies. Each state has different numbers of jails and prisons. Hawaii, for example, has four jails and four prisons. Florida, which states it has the third largest state prison system in the United States, has 143 facilities statewide.[10] Sometimes states do split up their public safety and corrections departments, which is something you could choose to do for the state of Hamiltonia as well.

Public safety departments can also be responsible for emergency responses to terrorist attacks or natural disasters. The Nevada Department of Public Safety, for example, includes the Capitol Police,

Highway Patrol, Investigation, State Fire Marshal, and Cyber Defense Coordination, among other divisions.[11] We recommend researching a few more public safety departments as a class, to decide exactly what you want your Public Safety Department to be responsible for.

Diversity in the Bureaucracy

Thus far we have covered diversity in the legislature as well as the governor's office. But we would be remiss if we did not cover diversity in the bureaucracy. As always, we turn to the excellent resource, the Center for American Women and Politics (CAWP), which has kept track of the number of women serving in state elective executive positions since 1969. Much of our discussion will focus on the elected positions, because unfortunately, not as much consistent attention has been given to the numbers of women in appointed executive positions at the state level.[12] Figure 6.2 displays the percentage of women in state elected executive positions since CAWP started tracking it in 1969, through 2023. The good news is that the trend is positive, more women have served in these positions over time. However, look carefully at the x-axis—we are at a current high of 31 percent women—which means not even a third of these positions are held by women. There is also

Figure 6.2

Percentage of Women in Elected Executive State Positions

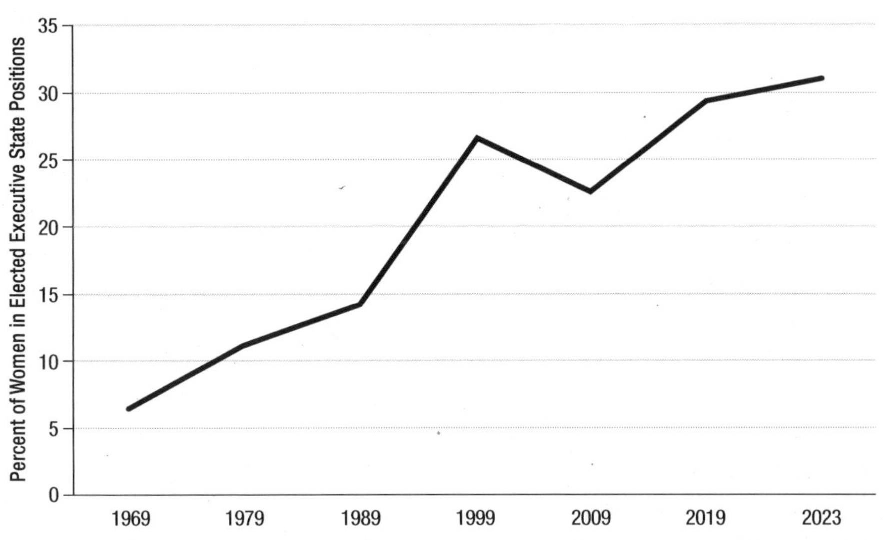

SOURCE: Data to generate this chart came from the Center for American Women and Politics (CAWP)

Attorney General Andrea Joy Campbell (right) speaks at joint committee of the legislature over wage theft bills held at the State House.

SOURCE: Staff Photo by Stuart Cahill/MediaNews Group/Boston Herald (Getty)

a slight partisan imbalance, as of 2023, 53 of the 96 elected executive positions held by women were Democrats (55%) versus the 41 that were held by Republicans (43%). Georgia has had three women serve as secretary of state—two Republicans and one Democrat.[13] It is important for women to serve in these critical state positions not only for representation purposes, but also because they may serve as a step to higher office such as lieutenant governor, governor, or even the presidency.

We also want to note the racial and ethnic diversity of the women in these positions. In 2023, twenty-three of the ninety-six women (24%) in these positions are women of color. There are four Asian Americans/Pacific Islanders: two are lieutenant governors—both Sylvia J. Luke of Hawaii and Aruna Miller of Maryland and two are state treasurers—Fiona Ma of California and Kimberly Yee of Arizona.[14] Additionally, there are ten African American women, eight Latinas, and one Native American woman in statewide elected executive office. According to the CAWP the positions with the highest numbers of women of color serving are lieutenant governor and secretary of state which have each seen eighteen women of color serving.[15] And we know from our state spotlight at the beginning of the chapter just how important state secretary of states are for state government!

Beyond gender, there are also prominent examples of people of color serving in state-wide elected executive offices. Vice President Kamala Harris, who identifies as both African American and Asian American, served as California's attorney general for ten years. There are currently seven African Americans serving as attorneys general in New York, Illinois, Nevada, Minnesota, Kentucky, Maryland, and Massachusetts. There are also three African Americans currently serving as secretaries of state in New Jersey, California, and Connecticut.

Simulation

For this part of the simulation, you will be building Hamiltonia's bureaucracy. We begin with the creation of new departments.

Bureaucratic Departments and Leadership

Just like we went over the details of the offices of governor and state legislator, we must also review the specifics associated with bureaucratic department positions. In this section we will detail how new departments are created, how their leaders are chosen, what these leaders do, and the term lengths and limits associated with these offices.

Creating New Departments

Hamiltonia already has education, environment, health, and public safety departments as part of the simulation. The first area we are going to tackle is whether you want or need to create new departments. If you are completing this simulation with a smaller-sized class, you can still create new departments, you will just be unlikely to appoint or elect students to these positions. Despite this limitation, it is still a good exercise to consider what departments you think are essential to running a state government. Table 6.1 lists out ten common state-level departments with the number of states that have them, to help guide you. Keep in mind that just because a state doesn't have a department for an issue area doesn't mean they do not address it. For example, Delaware does not have a commerce department, but the secretary of state oversees that issue area. Some states do not have a commerce department and instead have an economic development department, or vice versa. As we mentioned before, states organize their bureaucracy differently and call their executive departments different names but states all address—in one way or another—common issue areas.

These are just a small sample of the various departments you could create for Hamiltonia. For others, see *The Book of States*, or look at your state government's bureaucracy and see if there are any departments you would like to see in Hamiltonia as well. Remember you may want to consider what the most important public problems are in the state and create a department to cover that issue.

Table 6.1
Examples of Additional Bureaucratic Departments

DEPARTMENT	NUMBER OF STATES
Agriculture	50
Civil Rights	43
Commerce	40
Economic Development	39
Emergency Management	47
Labor	49
Mental Health and Developmental Disabilities	32
Social Services	32
Transportation	48
Welfare	36

Note: Data to generate this chart came from the 2021 *Book of States.*

Action Item

6-1

Are there any additional departments you want to create for Hamiltonia's government?

Selection Process of Bureaucratic Leaders

Now that you have decided what additional departments/positions you have chosen for Hamiltonia, it is now time to decide the selection process for these bureaucratic leaders. We briefly discussed the role of secretary of state in the beginning of this chapter, and while most states have this position, three do not. You must decide whether you want to have such a position in Hamiltonia, and if you choose not to, who will then oversee the secretary of state's typical responsibilities.

Action Item

6-2

Will Hamiltonia have a secretary of state? If so, are they elected or appointed?

If you have chosen to move forward with a secretary of state, you need to decide if they will be elected or appointed. If you choose **appointment**, then you must choose by whom. In fact, you have to make this same decision for the attorney general, state treasurer, and remaining executive branch leaders that we have provided to you and that you have created. Let's first compare the selection process of the big three across the fifty states. Figure 6.3 summarizes the selection methods of the secretary of state, attorney general, and state treasurer. You will see that most of the states elect these three positions, particularly the attorney general. However, there are several states for each position that have opted to appoint, instead of elect. Appointment can be different depending upon the state. For example, Texas is the only governor who has the power to appoint the secretary of state without any approval from the legislature. In Virginia, however, the governor has the power to appoint the secretary of state, but with approval from both legislative chambers.

Figure 6.3

Selection Methods of Secretary of State, Attorney General, and State Treasurer. (Not all states have each of these positions.)

Secretary of State	Attorney General	State Treasurer
• Elected by Public: 35	• Elected by Public: 43	• Elected by Public: 36
• Appointed: 9	• Appointed: 5	• Appointed: 8
• Elected by Legislature: 3	• Elected by Legislature: 1	• Elected by Legislature: 4
	• Elected by Court of Last Resort: 1	

SOURCE: Data to generate this chart came from the 2021 *Book of States*

In a few states, it is the legislature that has the power to elect the secretary of state, attorney general, and state treasurer. Maine is the only state that gives this power to the legislature for all three positions. We see more variation in appointment mechanisms for attorneys general and state treasurers. For example, in New Hampshire, the governor nominates the AG, but it must be confirmed by the Executive Council which is comprised of five members elected to represent their districts. We want to take a moment and point out that the Executive Council of New Hampshire is the only one of its kind in the nation. In fact, New Hampshire proudly promotes its unique form of government, by stating: "The New Hampshire Executive Council holds the distinction of being the first and the last of its kind in the nation. It is a vestige of the colonial era and a public reminder of the continuing indication of the basic distrust Granite State citizens have for dictatorial government."[16]

Why does the selection method matter? This may seem obvious, but whoever gets to choose the department head has more control over who serves in the position. Remember, these executive positions have a lot of power over how elections are run, what happens in public schools, and more. Whoever has the power to appoint an official can choose someone whose view of the policy problems and policy solutions match their own. Essentially, it gives them a bit more control over the policies the state will pursue. A governor may have to moderate her choice for an appointment if she needs to get the approval of the state senate. Likewise, if the legislature has the power to appoint, they can exert more control over the executive branch with their choice. Finally, if the people select the leader through election, the leader will be more beholden to the people rather than the governor or the legislature. You may want to consider these political dynamics when deciding the selection method for these positions.

Action Item

6-3

How will the attorney general be selected?

For state treasurer we want to note that two states do not have a state treasurer position. In Minnesota the responsibilities go to the Finance Department while in Texas it falls to the State Comptroller. In Georgia, it is the State Depository board that appoints the state treasurer. The Depository board is comprised of: "the governor, the insurance commission, the state accounting officer, the commissioner of banking and finance, and the commissioner of transportation."[17]

Action Item

6-4

How will the state treasurer be selected?

We have covered the selection process of the big three. But we also want to briefly cover the selection processes of three of the additional secretaries that we have created for Hamiltonia. We do this because there are many ways states select these executive positions. Table 6.2 provides the summary of the different kinds of selection mechanisms for these three positions. You will see the most common selection method typically involves the governor, usually with some kind of legislative approval. But there are also examples of other political bodies responsible for appointments, such as boards and commissions. This is particularly true for education secretaries (often referred to as state superintendents). State Boards of Education are typically involved in the process of choosing the leader of the state education department, although note that fourteen states do elect this position as well.

We also want to remind you of our discussion of gubernatorial power in chapter 5. Remember one aspect of a governor's powers is their appointment powers. The more appointments they have, the more influence they have over different aspects of the government they are leading, which means a higher likelihood of implementing their policy goals. It is no small power that the governor of Tennessee has the sole appointment power over the leaders of the education, environment, and health departments. This is in comparison to a state like Mississippi, that excludes the governor from selecting the head of the education and health departments, and instead gives that power to a board with senate approval. Therefore, you and your classmates should think carefully about how you want your executive leaders chosen and the influence you want the governor to have in that process.

We do not provide the selection mechanisms for the public safety/law enforcement secretary as there are quite a few ways state governments organize this area of the bureaucracy. California, for

Table 6.2
Selection Methods of Executive Branch Leaders

	EDUCATION	ENVIRONMENTAL	HEALTH
Board or Commission	19	4	2
Board/Governor	1	1	1
Elected	14	0	0
Governor	3	5	6
Governor with Legislative Approval*	11	27	29
Governor and Council or Departmental Board	0	1	1
Cabinet Secretary or Agency Head	0	7	1
Cabinet Secretary/Governor	0	2	4
Agency Head/Board	1	0	0
Agency Head/Governor and Council	0	0	1
Board/Senate	1	0	1
Civil Service	0	1	0
No specific Depart.	0	2	4

Note: Legislative approval could include approval from both houses, as Virginia requires for all three, approval from the appropriate legislative committee (Maine), either house (Connecticut), or the Senate, which is the most common approval (8 states for education, 23 states for environment, and 25 states for health). Data in table collected from the 2021 *Book of States*.

example, does not have a public safety department, but instead houses many of the common "public safety" duties with its Department of Justice (DOJ). Idaho and Illinois also do not have a public safety department and instead just have state police. Figure 6.4 provides a map of the ways states have organized this area of their bureaucracy. As delegates of Hamiltonia's constitutional convention, you should think about what you want your Law Enforcement/Public Safety Department to be called.

Action Item

6-5

What will be the selection process for the remaining leaders?

- Education secretary
- Environmental secretary
- Health secretary
- Law Enforcement/Public Safety
- Other secretaries you have created

Figure 6.4

Public Safety Departments by State

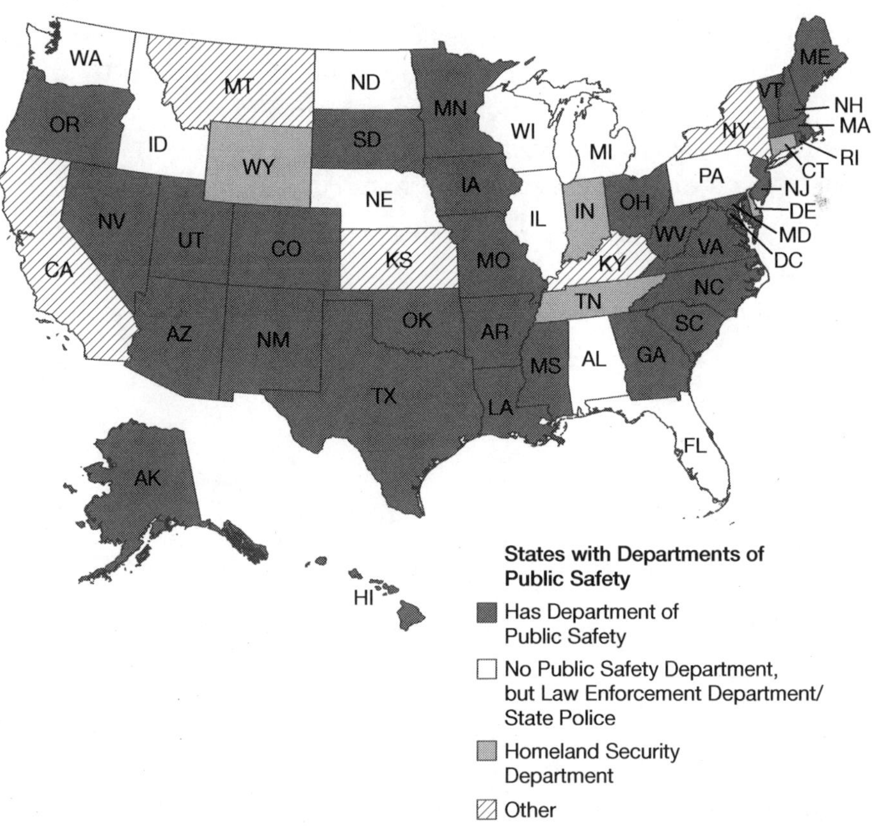

Qualifications for Bureaucratic Leaders

Now that you have chosen the myriad ways you could select your executive branch leaders, you will now need to determine their eligibility requirements. You should first refer to your state constitution and see the eligibility requirements for your governor as well as the line of succession. Why? Because it is likely the secretary of state, attorney general, and state treasurer may be part of it. You can set different eligibility requirements for the secretary of state, for example, than the governor. But if you do, then it means a secretary of state may be ineligible to take on the governor's position should the need arise. And states do this. Oregon is one of the three states where the secretary of state takes over if something happens to the governor. The age requirement to serve as governor is thirty. The age requirement to serve as secretary of state? Eighteen. Is it a likely scenario that the secretary of state is skipped over in the line of succession? Probably not. But in Oregon it is a possibility, which would mean the state treasurer (whose age requirement is thirty-one, by the way) would assume the office of the governor.

We have provided a series of figures that compare how many states set which age, citizenship, and residency requirements for secretary of state, attorney general, and state treasurer. If you look at Figure 6.5 first, you will see that state treasurers are most likely to have no age requirements, while attorneys general are more likely to have slightly higher age requirements of twenty-six and up.

Figure 6.5

Age Requirements for Secretary of State, Attorney General, and State Treasurer

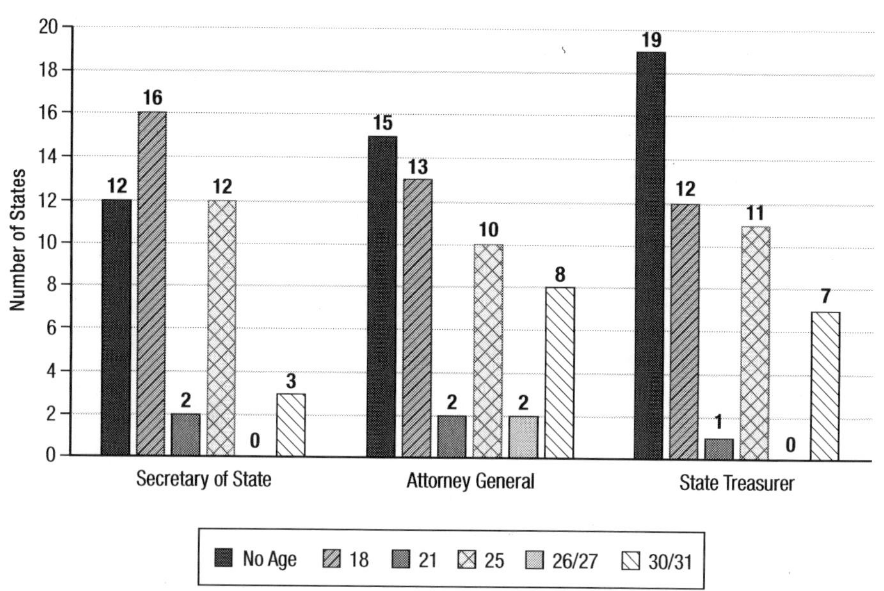

SOURCE: Chart created using data from the 2021 *Book of States*

Figures 6.6 and 6.7 show the citizenship vs. state residency requirements for each of these three positions. A similar number of states for each position set no citizenship or residency requirements to be eligible for office. Most states stipulate that a person has to be a citizen or state resident, but do not require it for any specified amount of time. About a third of states will set residency requirements of anywhere from one to five years, but very few are likely to set a time limit for citizenship on any of these positions.

You must also decide if there are any specific qualifications for the remaining leaders of the Hamiltonia executive branch. Many of these positions in state governments do not have minimum requirements. The Idaho Superintendent of Public Instruction, for example, is an elected position that does not have any age, citizenship, or residency requirements.[18] Georgia, however, requires the following of the state superintendent of schools: hold a four-year degree, no criminal convictions "involving moral turpitude," be at least twenty-five years old, a citizen for ten years, and a state resident for four years.[19] If you are setting any requirements for these positions, really think about why you are doing so. Hamiltonia does not want to exclude qualified individuals from being eligible from these positions, but there are good arguments

Figure 6.6
Citizenship Requirements for Secretary of State, Attorney General, and State Treasurer

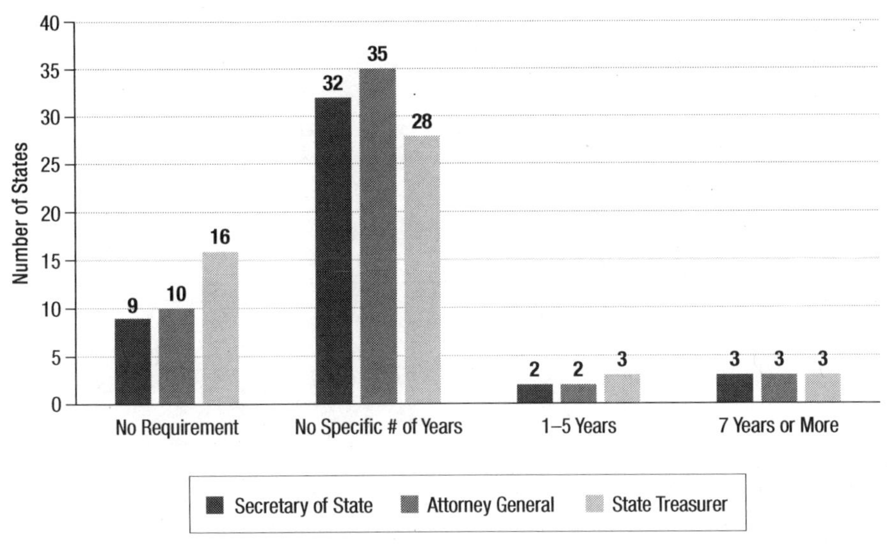

SOURCE: Chart created using data from the 2021 *Book of States*

Figure 6.7

State Residency Requirements for Secretary of State, Attorney General, and State Treasurer

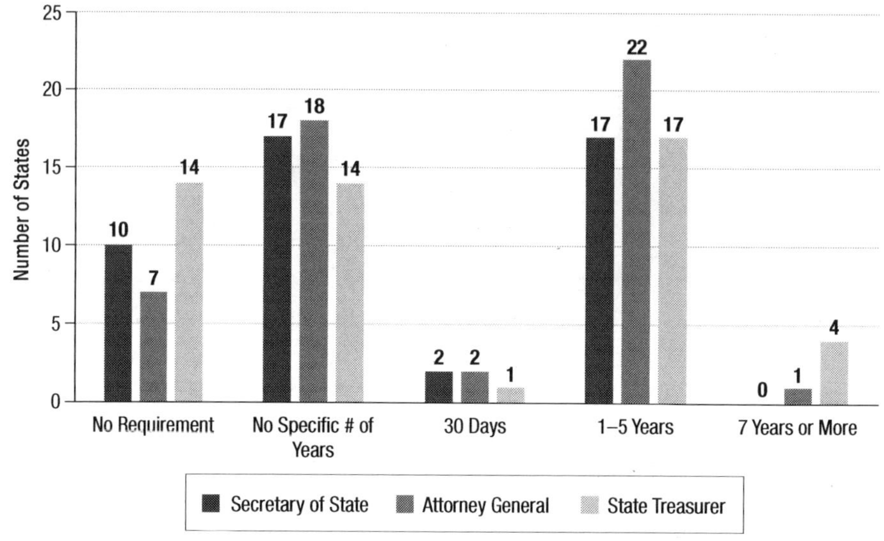

SOURCE: Chart created using data from the 2021 *Book of States*

to be made about why some people—state residents for example—may be better suited for a job versus those who do not hold the same qualifications.

Action Item

6-6

If you have a secretary of state, what are the eligibility requirements for that position?

Action Item

6-7

What are the eligibility requirements of the attorney general?

Action Item

6-8

What are the eligibility requirements of the state treasurer?

Action Item

6-9

What will be the eligibility requirements (if any) for the remaining leaders?

- Education secretary
- Environmental secretary
- Health secretary
- Law Enforcement/Public Safety
- Other secretaries you have created

Term Limits and Lengths

In the previous two chapters we have discussed the use of **term limits** for legislators and the governor. States are more apt to use term limits for the governor versus the legislature, but your class probably has an opinion on the utility of term limits at this point in the simulation. Some states do set term limits for their secretaries of state, attorneys general, and state treasurers. There are also term limits used at times for superintendents of education. Figure 6.8 displays the breakdown of term limits for secretaries of state. Most states do not set any restrictions on the number of terms. This is similar for attorneys general (34 states have no limits), treasurers (31 states have no limits), and state superintendents (45 states set no term limits).

Figure 6.8

Term Limits for Secretaries of State

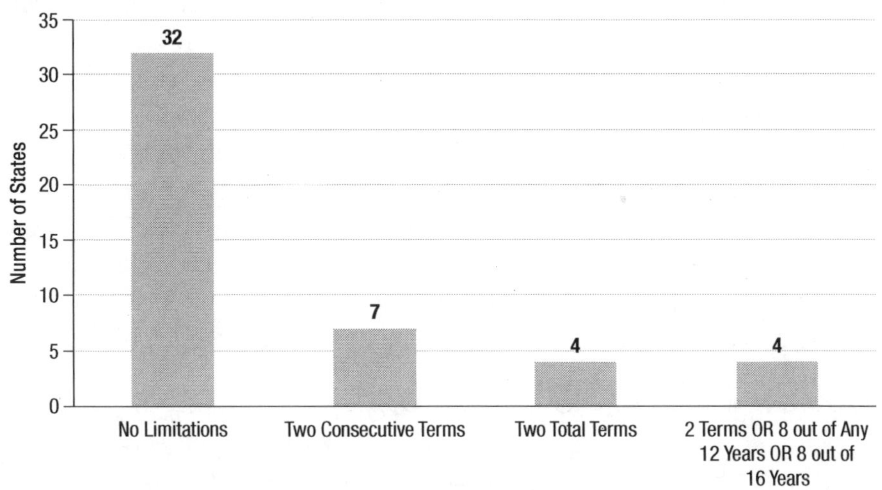

SOURCE: Chart created using data from the 2021 *Book of States*

There is even less variation on the length of the term of these executive officials. Remember only Vermont and New Hampshire had two-year terms for their governors. That was the only term length in the executive branch that New Hampshire shortened. All other executive branch officials in New Hampshire serve for four-year terms. Vermont kept their term lengths more consistent: the secretary of state, attorney general, and treasurer also have term lengths of two years.

Action Item

6-10

Will any of the executive branch leaders have term limits, and if so, what will they be?

Action Item

6-11

What will be the term lengths of your executive branch leaders?

Duties of Secretary of State, Attorney General, and State Treasurer

Up next we are getting into the nitty gritty of what the big three can do as part of their responsibilities as secretary of state, attorney general, or state treasurer. Each position has an incredibly long list of responsibilities, with of course variations from state to state. We have chosen the responsibilities that are most synonymous with these positions as well as those that are easiest to understand. We could have you decide, for example, whether the secretary of state should be in charge of filing candidates' expense papers (a responsibility of 22 secretaries of state), but think it is much more beneficial to really debate whether the secretary should be the chief election officer, or be able to register corporations, charitable organizations, or lobbyists.

We have followed *The Book of States* and their division of secretary of state responsibilities into the categories of elections, registration, custodial, publication, and legislative. While many of these duties may seem tedious, they are incredibly important for transparent government. The more transparent a government is, the easier it is to hold it accountable. We should not want a state government shrouded in mystery where it is hard to understand who is keeping track of lobbyists, and where administrative rules and regulations can be found.

One of the most important powers of secretaries of state is whether they are the chief election officers. As we learned in the beginning of this chapter, this is an essential responsibility, because in the end it is the secretary of state that would certify election results—confirming that free and

Figure 6.9
Number of States That Give Election Duties to Secretaries of State

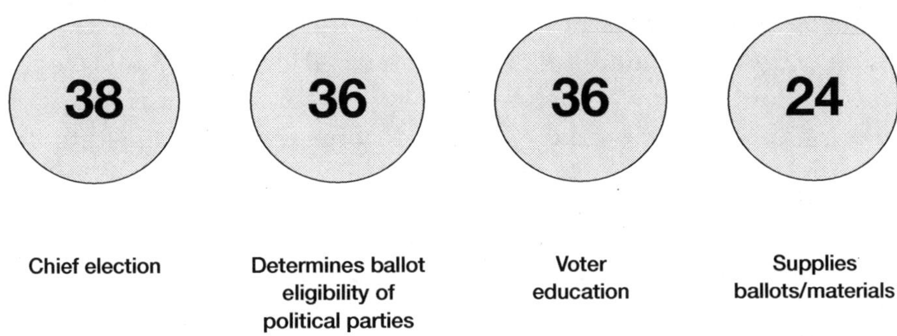

fair elections took place in their state. Figure 6.9 displays the number of states that give each of their secretaries of state the four election powers you may give. Remember that Alaska, Hawaii, and Utah do not have secretaries of state, so these numbers are out of forty-seven states.

Table 6.3 summarizes the number of states that give the secretaries the nine other duties that are associated with secretaries of state. We

Table 6.3
Secretaries of State and Their Duties

DUTY	NUMBER OF STATES
Register Corporations	42
Register Charitable Organizations	31
Archives State Records and Regulations	34
Files State Agency Rules and Regulations	34
Publishes Statutes	12
Publishes Administrative Rules and Regulations	27
Opens Legislative Sessions in Both Chambers	1
Retains Copies of Bills	38
Register Lobbyists	20

Note: Table generated using data from the 2021 *Book of States.*

counted a secretary as having one of these powers, even if they only partially had it. For example, the *Book of States* explains that the Indiana "Secretary of State's office receives and authenticates Bills and Enrolled Acts but does not keep or maintain them. Post-session legislative materials are maintained by the Indiana Public Records Commission."[20] Action Item 6-12 has you deciding exactly how many responsibilities you want your secretary of state for Hamiltonia to have.

Action Item

6-12

Will the secretary of state have any of the following duties?

- Elections:
  - Chief election officer,
  - Determines ballot eligibility of political parties,
  - Conducts voter education,
  - Supplies election ballots or materials to local officials.
- Registration:
  - Register corporations,
  - Register charitable organizations.
- Custodial:
  - Archives state records and regulations,
  - Files state agency rules and regulations.
- Publication:
  - Statutes,
  - Administrative rules and regulations.
- Legislative:
  - Opens legislative sessions,
  - Retains copies of bills,
  - Registers lobbyists.

Like the secretary of state, attorneys general have varying levels of responsibilities depending upon the state. We have broken down the attorney general's responsibilities into three major areas: local **prosecutions**, issuing **advisory opinions**, and **litigation**. Starting with local prosecutorial powers, attorneys general typically have the power to initiate local prosecutions, intervene in local prosecutions, assist in local prosecutions, or supersede local prosecutions. This power changes, depending upon

Figure 6.10

Attorney General Local Prosecution Powers

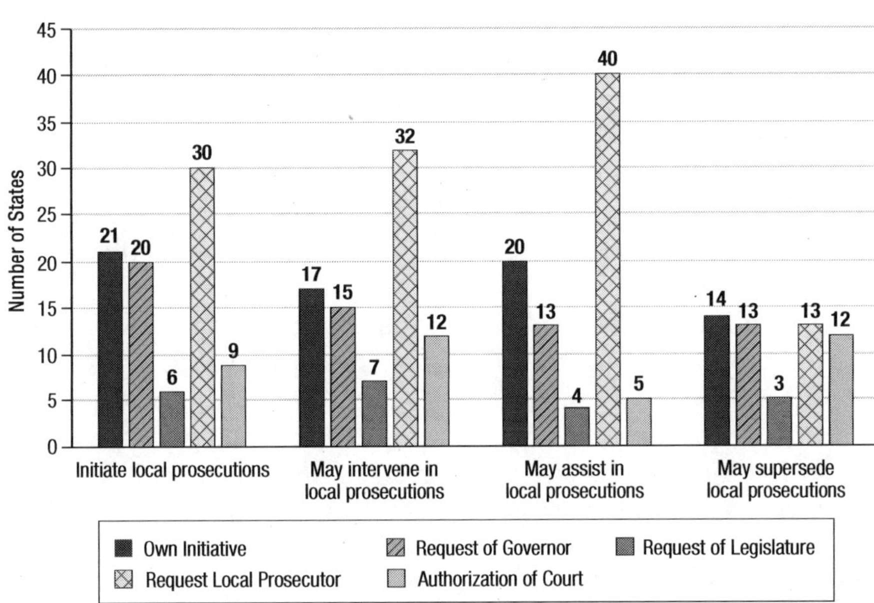

SOURCE: Chart created using data from the 2021 *Book of States*

whether the AG can do this on their own initiative or at the request of the governor, legislature, or local prosecutor. AGs who can do it on their own have more power, but as you can see this only happens in less than half of the circumstances of local prosecutorial powers. The most likely instance where an AG will become involved in local prosecutions is at the request of the local prosecutor. Figure 6.10 provides the breakdown of the number of states that allow the AG to have local prosecution powers and the circumstances under which they can execute them.

Another important area of responsibility for attorneys general is who they can issue advisory opinions to. The National Association of Attorneys General (NAAG) explains that issuing advisory or legal opinions is an important component of the AGs responsibilities. They explain:

> Because most public officials are not lawyers and it can be difficult to determine the meaning of a law without the application of legal training, attorney general offices provide legal opinions to their clients every day in a variety of ways. Formal written legal opinions of the attorney general answer questions of law from state agencies or officials about the agency's or official's legal duties. Commonly known as attorney general opinions, these opinions are prepared by and reviewed by attorneys in the office, including the attorney general, through an established process and have the authority of the office behind them.[21]

All AGs have the power to issue advisory opinions to state executive officials. Nevada, New Jersey, and Pennsylvania are the only states that do not allow their AG to issue an advisory opinion to legislators, although Connecticut restricts it to leadership (such as the Speaker of the House) and in South Carolina it has to be requested by the legislature. Seven states do not allow advisory opinions to go to local prosecutors and less than half allow their AGs to issue opinions on the constitutionality of bills or ordinances. And although there are many different ways AGs can be involved in litigation, we have asked you to consider two: whether the AG should be involved in **rulemaking** (36 states) and whether they review rules for legality 37 states).

Rulemaking is a core function of the bureaucracy. After a law is passed by the legislature and signed by the governor, the bureaucracy takes over to figure out how to implement it. Maybe the legislature updated licensing requirements for physicians, or home inspectors. The bureaucratic agency will need to create a rule that implements the bill, including allowing for a public comment period so that interested parties, such as the state medical association, can comment on the proposed rule. The agency will also conduct an impact analysis to explain how the new rule will affect citizens and the industries directly involved. Having AGs involved in the rulemaking process, or at least reviewing the rules for legality, means bureaucracies can try to avoid any questions of constitutionality of the rules they create. Is this a power you want the Hamiltonia AG to have?

Action Item

6-13

Will the attorney general have any of the following duties?

- Local prosecutions:
  - Can the AG initiate local prosecutions, intervene in local prosecutions, assist local prosecutor, or supersede local prosecutor on their own, at the request of the governor, at the request of the legislature, at the request of local prosecutor, or on authorization from the court?
- Issue advisory opinions:
  - To state executive officials, legislators, local prosecutors, or on the constitutionality of bills/ordinances.
- Litigation:
  - Is involved in rulemaking,
  - Reviews rules for legality.

Last, but not least, we need to cover the responsibilities of the state treasurer. We have narrowed the considerable amount of responsibilities of state treasurers to three that we want you to consider for Hamiltonia: investment of retirement funds, managing college savings programs, and managing unclaimed property. Let's start with the investment of retirement funds. Thousands of people across the United States are employees of state governments. This includes state police officers, college professors, and tax auditors among many other positions. All of these people set aside a certain amount of their salaries into a retirement system, typically a state pension system. According to the National Association of State Treasurers (NAST), treasurers were responsible for over $3.3 trillion in pensions and investments.

In addition to that large sum of money, state treasurers also manage **529 college savings plans**, which are "tax-advantaged savings plans designed to help families set aside funds for future education costs."[22] As of 2020 treasurers managed 14.83 million 529 accounts and invested $425 billion into the plans. You may be one of the many college students who have benefited from such a plan. Note that just over half the states give responsibility of 529 plans to their state treasurers.

Finally, thirty-five state treasurers are responsible for unclaimed property management. If you think this is a small amount think again. In 2019 alone, state treasurers returned $3.14 billion in unclaimed property to their owners. The North Carolina state treasurer is one of the treasurers who has the responsibility over unclaimed property. Unclaimed property can include outstanding checks, credit balances, and deposits among other items. The Unclaimed Property and Escheats Division within the state treasurer's department of North Carolina invests any unclaimed property "to maximize the greatest earnings for utilization by the North Carolina State Education Assistance Authority in order to provide grants and low interest loans to North Carolina students in state supported schools of higher education."[23] Figure 6.11 lists how many states give their state treasurer each of the

Action Item

6-14

Will the state treasurer have any of the following duties?

- Investment of retirement funds
- College savings
- Management of unclaimed property

Figure 6.11

Responsibilities of State Treasurers

Investment of Retirement Funds: 19 States

College Savings: 28 States

Unclaimed Property: 35 States

responsibilities we covered here. You and your classmates now need to decide whether you want Hamiltonia's state treasurer to have any of these responsibilities.

Formal Cabinet

As we near the end of creating Hamiltonia's bureaucracy, we need to decide whether all of these bureaucratic leaders you have created will be a part of the governor's formal cabinet. The cabinet can advise governors on policy decisions.[24] Only twenty-two states have a formal provision in their state constitution for a cabinet. Georgia, Mississippi, New Hampshire, Oregon, and Texas have no formal cabinet system at all. Nevada has a unique cabinet system which includes the governor and directors or leaders of Nevada's "top agencies, departments, institutions, and the National Guard."[25] So first, you need to decide whether there will be a formal cabinet. If you decide not to have a formal cabinet, then you have completed all of the agenda items for the bureaucracy section. If you do want Hamiltonia to have a formal cabinet, then next you must decide who will be the members, how frequently they will occur, and whether the meetings are open to the public. Figure 6.12 provides the common frequencies of cabinet meetings within states.

If you think it is common for these cabinet meetings to be public, think again. Only seven states (Alaska, Florida, Montana, North Dakota, Pennsylvania, Rhode Island, and South Carolina) have open cabinet meetings regularly. Illinois allows some cabinet meetings open to the public, but not all. Interestingly, the cabinets that do publicize their cabinet meetings either only meet at the governor's discretion (AK, PA, and RI) or monthly (MT, ND, and SC). Florida is the only state that meets one or two times per month and makes their meetings public. Public meetings may make the cabinet decision-making more transparent to state

Figure 6.12
Frequency of Cabinet Meetings

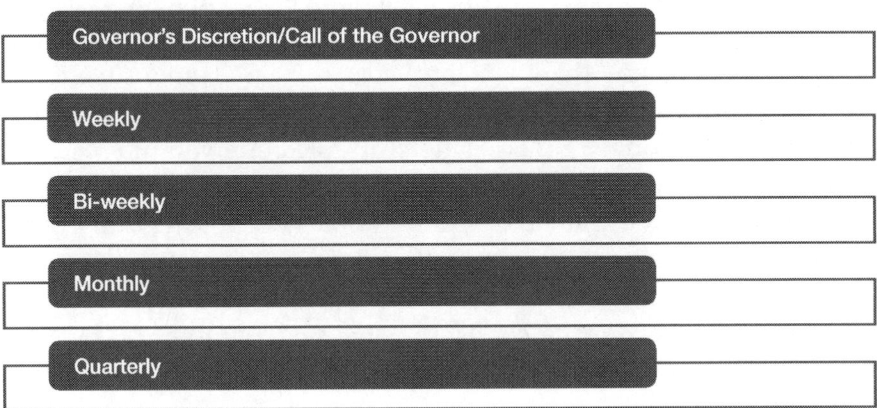

residents. However, if they are public, cabinet members may not advise the governor in a certain way. How do you think Hamiltonia should balance government transparency and open dialogue among cabinet members?

Action Item

6-15
Will there be a formal cabinet that the governor convenes?

Action Item

6-16
Who will be members of the cabinet?

Action Item

6-17
What is the frequency of cabinet meetings?

Action Item

6-18
Are cabinet meetings open to the public?

Looking Forward

Phew! That probably felt like a marathon of deciding exactly what you wanted Hamiltonia's executive branch to look like. While it was a lot of work, we hope it gives you an appreciation of just how extensive state bureaucracies are, and the important work they are responsible for. In just a few chapters you will be deciding whether you want to pursue one of these executive branch leadership roles. Are you interested in law? Maybe consider running for attorney general. Do you like to keep things organized and value transparency? Maybe consider seeking out the position of secretary of state—that is if you created it of course. Each of the executive branch roles you have created are important, and if you want to provide counsel to the next Hamiltonia governor, these are good positions to keep in mind as you move forward in the simulation.

Key Terms

secretary of state (108)
state treasurer (108)
civil service (108)
bureaucracy (109)
attorney general (109)
Department of Health (110)
education secretary (111)
environmental secretary (111)
public safety secretary (112)
appointment (117)
term limits (125)
prosecution (128)
advisory opinions (128)
litigation (128)
rulemaking (130)
529 college savings plan (131)

Assignments to Learn More about Bureaucracies

1. The big three of secretary of state, attorney general, and state treasurer play incredibly important roles in state governments around the country. In part due to time constraints, we were only able to cover a portion of each position's responsibilities. In Figure 6.13, we list additional responsibilities that you could have debated in the simulation. What do you think about them? Do you think the Hamiltonian leader for each specific position should have had one of these powers? Why or why not?

Figure 6.13

Additional Responsibilities of the Secretary of State, Attorney General, and State Treasurer

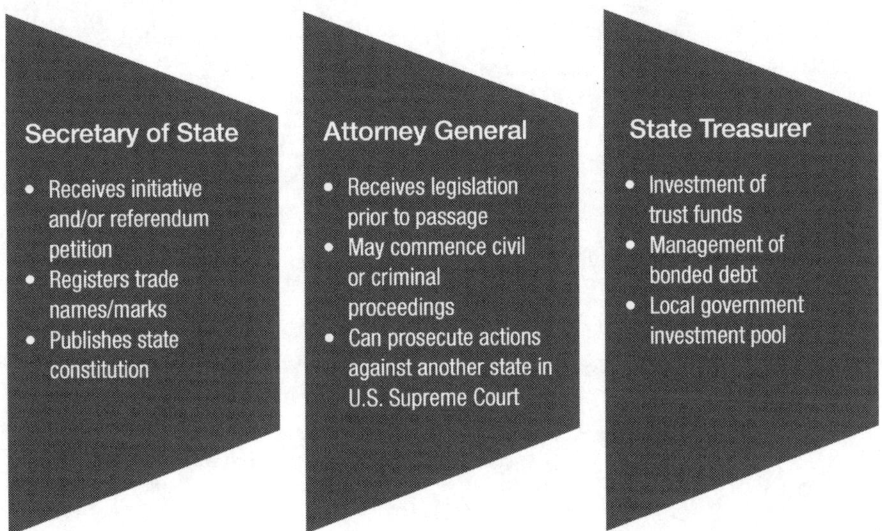

2. We reference *The Book of States* a lot throughout the simulation because it is an excellent resource for all things state government. One area we did not cover was annual salaries. Table 4.11 in *The Book of States* displays the salaries of all executive branch leaders. In the previous chapter we had you consider the governor's perks, although we did not have you consider her salary. Now we want you to think about all the executive branch leaders and how they are compensated. What should their salaries be? Should they be higher than the governor? Why? Based on the perks you awarded the governor, should that affect their salary? In Table 6.4, we provided three state examples of the salaries of the governor, lieutenant governor, secretary of state, attorney general, state treasurer, education, health, and environmental secretaries for reference.
3. There are two other major executive branch officials we did not discuss in this chapter: State auditors and comptrollers. Forty-four states have an auditor, and thirty-nine states have a comptroller. Research each of these positions. What are they responsible for in state government? Why do some states like Tennessee have a comptroller, but not a state auditor? Should Hamiltonia have either of these positions?

Table 6.4
Salaries of Executive Branch Officials 2021

OFFICIALS	COLORADO	MISSOURI	NORTH CAROLINA
Governor	$92,700	$133,821	$154,743
Lieutenant Governor	$164,009	$86,484	$136,699
Secretary of State	$93,360	$107,746	$136,699
Attorney General	$107,672	$116,437	$136,699
State Treasurer	$93,360	$107,746	$136,699
Education	$283,416	$225,831	$136,699
Environment	$106,596	$114,433	$144,048
Health	N/A	$147,223	$232,188

Note: Data collected from *The Book of States* (2021), Table 4.11.

4. Choose one of the big three executive positions in your state. Who currently resides in that office? How long have they been in office? What kind of work or positions have they done previously?
5. Choose three states and explore their state transparency websites. Does the state have a transparency website? Which agency is in charge of the website? What kind of information does it have and do the three transparency websites provide the same information? Think about which transparency website was easiest to use and which one you think makes it easiest for the public to hold the government accountable.

Anti-abortion demonstrators outside of the South Carolina State Supreme Court.

SOURCE: Photo by Sean Rayford/SOPA Images/LightRocket via Getty Images

Creating the Courts

Learning Objectives:

After reading this chapter students should be able to:

- Compare the different institutional arrangements between state courts.
- Explain the role of the judicial system at the state level.
- Describe the levels of state courts and their responsibilities.
- Create a state level judicial system.
- Discuss the effect diversity on the bench has on state level cases.
- Describe the different qualifications states set for judges.

State Spotlight: South Carolina

Thus far in the simulation you have decided whether Hamiltonia will have direct democracy through the adoption of referendums or initiatives, and you have created a legislature and an executive branch as well. But now it is time to create the last major institution of state governments, the judicial branch. Next to the bureaucracy, the judicial branch is probably the institution of government that citizens have the most contact with. Got a traffic ticket? You'll have to go to traffic court. Know someone getting divorced? They will have to go through the courts to be granted the divorce. Suing a company for breach of contract? You guessed it, you'll be going to the courts. Even if a citizen does not directly interact with the courts over the course of their lifetime, decisions by the courts can impact them directly. Let's take the recent example of abortion rights. The U.S. Supreme Court removed the right to abortion via the *Dobbs v. Jackson Women's Health* case in 2022. In the time since the case was decided, legislatures across the nation enacted restrictive abortion laws, whether that was restricting abortions before a certain time in a pregnancy (such as six weeks) to criminalizing abortion procedures for both medical staff and the patients who sought the procedure. State courts have played an important role in the constitutionality of these laws, as many people and organizations have sued these laws in court.

Let's look more deeply into the South Carolina judicial branch, which provides an excellent example of the role courts can play in protecting the rights of its citizens. The South Carolina State Supreme Court is unique in that it is only one of two **state courts of last resort** (the other being Virginia) that select their justices via legislative appointment.[1] There are five justices on the court, and they serve for ten-year terms. South Carolina is a predominately Republican state, with the 2023 legislature comprised of 30 Republicans in the Senate out of 46 seats (65%) and 88 Republicans out of 124 in the House of Representatives (71%).[2] It was therefore very surprising that such a conservative state had not passed stronger abortion laws following the fall of *Roe* in the summer of 2022. But it wasn't for lack of trying.

The legislature passed and Governor Henry McMaster—a Republican—signed a law that prevented abortions after a heartbeat was detected. Known as a "heartbeat bill," it essentially restricts abortions when fetal cardiac activity can be detected, which is typically after the sixth week of pregnancy. Like many of these laws, abortion activists sued the state, and it was appealed all the way to the South Carolina Supreme Court, which at the time was led by **Chief Justice** Kaye Hearn—the only female on the bench. In a 3–2 decision, Justice Hearn wrote in the majority opinion that the six-week abortion ban was unconstitutional because it violated the right to privacy found in the state constitution. Therefore, this case also exemplifies how we live under two constitutions—federal and state.

But in South Carolina, like in other states such as Massachusetts, there is a retirement age for justices, which is set at seventy-two. Chief Justice Hearn hit that mandatory retirement age shortly after the court struck down the abortion law. And because the legislature oversees selecting justices, they were able to choose her predecessor. Despite two women being nominated out of three nominations by the legislative commission, the General Assembly (a majority male body with less than 15% of the seats held by women) chose the male candidate Gary Hill to create the only all-male state Supreme Court.[3] And although it was not clear how Hill would decide an abortion case, many legislators felt he would side with the legislature on restricting abortion access, as Republican Representative Micah Caskey said: "There are certainly people who voted for Judge Hill on the basis of their understanding of where he would be on abortion."[4] In June 2023 the new all-male

Court of Appeals Chief Judge Kaye Hearn, foreground right, acknowledges the legislature in the House of Representatives after the General Assembly elected her as a state Supreme Court justice. Her daughter, Kathleen, stands by her side.

SOURCE: AP Photo/The State, Tim Dominick

Supreme Court heard essentially the same six-week abortion ban written in a new bill. In August they released their decision overturning the case and allowing the six-week abortion ban to stand.[5]

This story is illustrative of the important role of the state judicial system. It also demonstrates the importance of representation on judicial bodies—citizens should pause when they see a Supreme Court with not a single woman on the bench. This story also illustrates the positive and negative consequences of mandatory retirement ages: on the one hand it could result in more diversity on the bench, but it can also result in less diversity. In the next section we will further explain the role of state courts, their responsibilities, and institutional makeups. We will then move on to the simulation, where you will be able create Hamiltonia's judicial branch.

Overview of State Courts

State courts handle the majority of cases that make their way through the U.S. legal system. They handle everything from traffic violations to murder trials, and cases where there are disputes over constitutional rights. The courts of Hamiltonia will play an important role ensuring that the state constitution—which you are in the process of making—is protected in addition to supporting the rights of all citizens of Hamiltonia. Most states have three levels of courts—similar to the federal court system. These are typically a **general jurisdiction court**, an **appellate court**, and a state supreme court. We discuss each of these levels below.

The lowest level of courts are known as general jurisdiction and **limited jurisdiction** courts—or what we often refer to as **trial courts. Limited jurisdiction** courts only handle specific kinds of cases. Family courts, for example, only handle cases dealing with child custody and other areas related specifically to families. They are not going to be hearing traffic violations. General jurisdiction courts handle many kinds of cases. For example, they may handle cases including robbery, assault, and money laundering.

Let's go back to South Carolina to better help us understand how state courts can be set up. The general jurisdiction courts of South Carolina are known as Circuit Courts. In other states they may be known as District Courts (such as Texas), or Superior Courts (such as Vermont). The Circuit Court has "a civil court, the Court of Common Pleas, and a criminal court, the Court of General Sessions."[6] **Civil cases** involve things such as personal injury, property damage, divorce, and adoption. **Criminal cases** involve things such as assault, murder, or robbery. South Carolina also has four limited jurisdiction courts: family, magistrate, probate, and municipal. Figure 7.1 displays the South Carolina court system.

Wondering what some of these limited jurisdiction courts do? **Magistrate** courts are in many ways on the front lines of the judicial system. Magistrates are not judges but do have to pass a certification exam. As the South Carolina judicial branch explains:

> Magistrates generally have criminal trial jurisdiction over all offenses subject to the penalty of a fine, as set by statute, but generally, not exceeding $500.00 or imprisonment not exceeding 30 days, or both. In addition, they are responsible for setting bail, conducting preliminary hearings, and issuing arrest and search warrants. Magistrates have civil jurisdiction when the amount in controversy does not exceed $7,500.[7]

While magistrates are appointed for one-year terms in South Carolina, Probate Judges are popularly elected for four years, and they address areas such as the handling of minor's settlements, involuntary institutional commitment for the mentally ill, estates, and marriage licenses.[8] Finally, municipal courts are located within towns or counties and handle all offenses if they do not have large fines or long imprisonment.

Although the trial courts of the South Carolina judicial system are a bit complex, the next two levels are simple. Above the trial courts is the Court of Appeals. Like the Supreme Court, the nine justices of the Circuit Court of Appeals are elected by the General Assembly. These judges hear cases in panels of three judges, or as a whole court. And finally, above that, as we explained in the beginning of this chapter is the State Supreme Court of five justices elected by the General Assembly. The State Supreme Court hears appeals from the appellate courts, and they may have **original jurisdiction** (meaning the case would come to the Supreme Court first) in

Figure 7.1

South Carolina Trial Courts

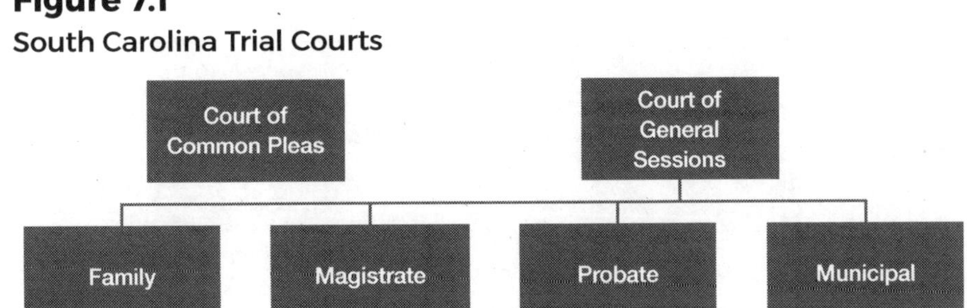

certain situations. In fact, the case above discussed in the state spotlight was filed with the South Carolina Supreme Court under original jurisdiction. Figure 7.2 displays the hierarchy of the South Carolina courts.

The interesting, albeit sometimes frustrating part about state courts is they are all very different. We just spent the last two pages explaining what the South Carolina courts look like, but other state courts look very different. Take Texas for example. They also have three levels of courts, but instead of having one state court of last resort, they have two. Texas has a Supreme Court, and they have a Court of Criminal Appeals. They also have different limited jurisdiction courts at the trial level: Constitutional County, Probate, County at Law, Justice of the Peace, and Municipal.

Perhaps no state court system is more unique—or complex—than New York. The first way New York is unique is that they do not call their court of last resort a Supreme Court, but a Court of Appeals (way to be confusing, New York!). They then have two appeals courts: the Appellate Divisions of Supreme Court and the Appellate Terms of Supreme Court. Finally, they have a complex network of trial courts. Three are general jurisdiction (Supreme, County, Claims), and seven are limited jurisdiction (Surrogates, Family, District, City, NYC Civil, NYC Criminal, and Town & Village Justice Court).[9] While we do not necessarily recommend creating such a complex network of courts for Hamiltonia, you can see it is not without precedence, as is the case with New York.

Figure 7.2
Levels of State Courts

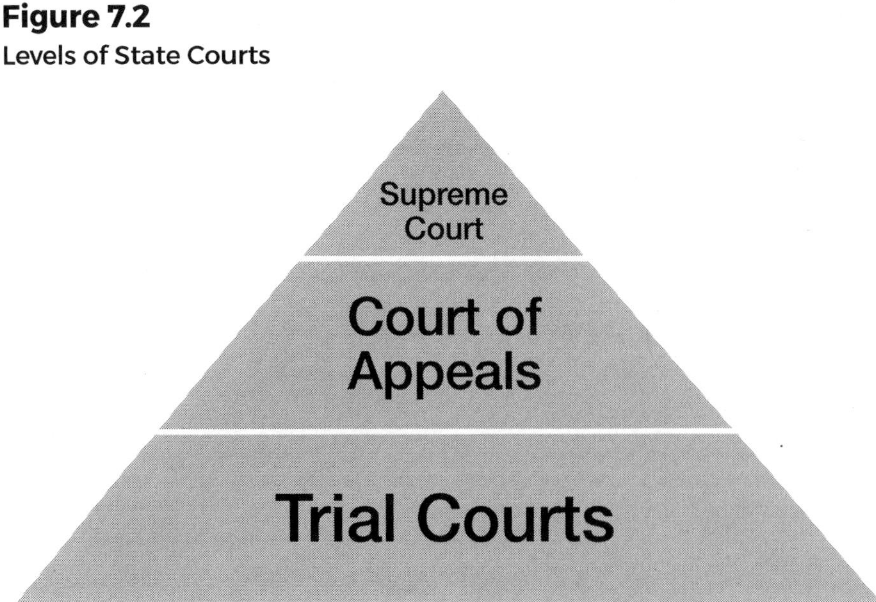

Diversity on the Bench

We started this chapter with a story of the South Carolina Supreme Court and how it went from a body of one female justice to an all-male body. Just as we have covered diversity in the legislative and executive branches across the United States, we must also discuss diversity on state benches. In 2022, the Brennan Center for Justice published a report on the gender, racial, and ethnic diversity of state supreme courts. Figure 7.3 shows that almost half of the state supreme courts have no people of color on the bench.

To think of this another way, the Brennan Center reports that "across all state high courts, just 18 percent of justices are Black, Latino, Asian American, Native American or multiracial. By contrast, people of color make up over 40 percent of the U.S. population."[10] When it comes to gender diversity, the numbers look a little better. Remember that the Brennan Center data is from 2022, before Chief Justice of South Carolina Kaye Hearn's retirement. Therefore, at that time there were no state high courts that did not have a woman serving. In 2022, 59 percent of state supreme court seats were held by women, with nine states only have one woman on the bench. Figure 7.4 displays the top five states with racial and gender diversity on their state courts of last result.[11] The nine states that are at 57 percent women are New York, Maryland, Ohio, Arkansas, Michigan, Minnesota, Nevada, California, and Oregon. Note that many of the same states pop up for gender and racial diversity.

Figure 7.3

Racial Diversity on State Supreme Courts

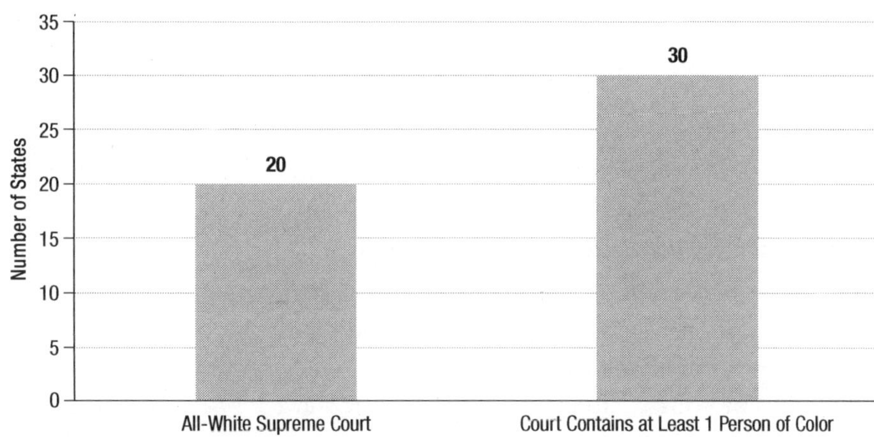

Figure 7.4

Diversity on State Supreme Courts

Note: Data from the Brennan Center for Justice

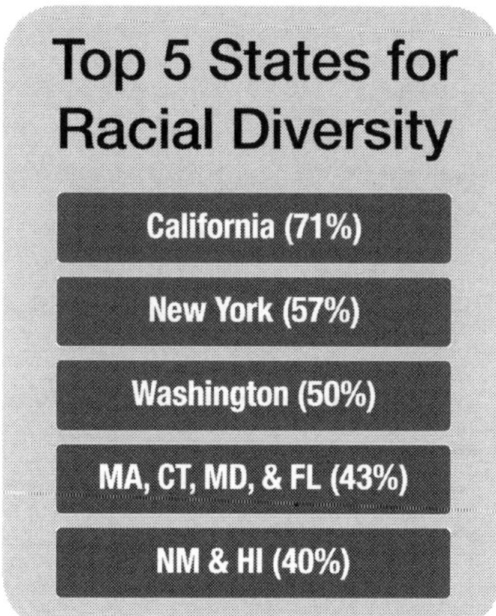

Unfortunately for our purposes, we cannot share much data on women in courts lower than state courts of last resort. Some scholars have studied the levels of women versus people of color in these positions, but have only focused on elected positions, or the research is more than a decade old and out of date.[12] In general it is still conventional wisdom that more men and white people serve as judges even in intermediate courts and trial courts across the United States.

Simulation

In this chapter we will be building the Hamiltonia judicial branch from the ground up. This will include deciding how judges are chosen as well as the requirements associated with serving as a judge. We begin this section with deciding the number of levels of state courts in Hamiltonia.

Levels of State Court Systems

We have now come to the point where we have some decisions to make when it comes to the Hamiltonia Judicial Branch. First, let's look at the number of levels we want for the judiciary. Nine states only have two levels of courts, meaning they do not have a state intermediary (or appellate) court. The states that do not have intermediary courts are Delaware, Maine, Montana, New Hampshire, Rhode Island, South Dakota, Vermont, West Virginia, and Wyoming. When a state does not have an intermediary court, then appeals would go directly to their court of last resort.

Why would states decide to have three levels of the judiciary instead of two? Nevada is a great example as to why. Nevada is the latest state to have created an intermediary court, the Court of Appeals via popular vote in 2014 on an amendment to the Nevada Constitution. As the Nevada courts explain:

> Before 2014, the Supreme Court heard all appeals, including everything from murder convictions to appeals of driver's license revocations. For decades, the Supreme Court struggled to keep up with its caseload. This was demonstrated by the number of pending cases before the court, which prevented speedy resolution of appeals. The idea for the Court of Appeals was born out of the concern that "justice delayed is justice denied." The truth of this old adage was painfully apparent when families had to wait for an appeal in a child custody case, or when decisions on proposed ballot initiatives were slowed by the backlog of cases. With the voter-approved Court of Appeals, parties waiting for their appeals to be heard now have their cases resolved more quickly... The Court of Appeals hears most matters that are not precedent-setting and take less time to prepare. This allows the Nevada Supreme Court to spend more time on the cases that merit published opinions and take more time to prepare.[13]

Therefore, as the Nevada courts explain, intermediary courts take some of the pressure off courts of last resort to hear appeals that really don't handle larger legal or constitutional questions. Now the Nevada Supreme Court has more time to rule on cases involving disputes among the branches of their state government, new laws that are unclear, and public policy more generally. What do you think you will decide when it comes to the levels of Hamiltonia's state courts?

Beyond deciding whether or not you want two or three levels in your judiciary, you also need to think about whether or not you want one or two courts of last resort and one or two intermediary courts (if you have chosen to create one of course). Oklahoma and Texas have two state courts of last resort, they are called the Supreme Court and Court of Criminal Appeals. Additionally, some states that do have intermediary courts have two: Alabama, Indiana, Tennessee, and Pennsylvania have two intermediary courts of appeal. In Alabama they break up their intermediary court into a court of civil appeals and criminal appeals, in Indiana they have the Court of Appeals and Tax Court, and in Pennsylvania they have the Superior Court and Commonwealth Court. You need to decide for Hamiltonia how many levels of courts, how many of each court you will have, as well as the names of these courts. The vast majority of states name their courts of last resort "supreme court" with the exception of New York and Maryland, who call theirs Court of Appeals, and West Virginia which somehow merged both names to be the Supreme Court of Appeals.

Included in your decision on the number of courts is specifically the number of general jurisdiction courts Hamiltonia will have. Alabama's general jurisdiction courts are called circuit courts and there are forty-one of them. California has fifty-eight general jurisdiction courts called superior courts, and they are set within each county. Sometimes states have more than one general jurisdiction court. Oregon has a general jurisdiction circuit court based upon districts and a tax court. Tennessee has four general jurisdiction courts: circuit, chancery (civil cases such as contract disputes), criminal, and probate.[14]

Action Item

7-1

Will there be two or three levels of courts in Hamiltonia?

Action Item

7-2

What will the names of these courts be?

Action Item

7-3

How many of each court will there be?

Judicial Selection Methods

Next up we must tackle judicial selection methods. There are five different ways that judges can be selected: legislative appointment, partisan elections, nonpartisan elections, merit, and gubernatorial appointment. Table 7.1 summarizes the number of states for each selection method for state courts of last resort and intermediary courts.

Let's take a moment to explain what each of these selection methods looks like. We have already covered the selection method of **legislative appointment** in the beginning of this chapter, because South Carolina is only one of two states that select judges this way. **Gubernatorial appointment** is similar: The New Jersey governor appoints judges to the state supreme court and intermediary court, while the Maine governor appoints judges to the Maine State Supreme Court—there is no intermediary court in Maine. In both states the nominees must be confirmed by the state senates. **Partisan elections** are no different than partisan elections for other positions throughout the United States. Candidates run affiliated with a political party, therefore as either Democrats or Republicans. In **nonpartisan elections** candidates do not run with any party affiliation, it is simply their name on the ballot.

Table 7.1
Judicial Selection Methods

JUDICIAL SELECTION METHOD	NUMBER OF STATES COURT OF LAST RESORT	NUMBER OF STATES INTERMEDIARY COURTS
Legislative Appointment	2	2
Gubernatorial Appointment	2	1
Partisan Elections	8	8
Nonpartisan Elections	15	12
Merit Plan	23	18

Note: Only 41 states have intermediary courts of appeal. North Dakota's Supreme Court appoints the intermediary court judges.

Finally, **merit plans** (sometimes called the Missouri plan) are the most popular judicial selection method at the state level. This is an interesting process because it typically starts with a nominating commission whose job it is to recruit and evaluate judges on—you guessed it—their merits. This could include their length of service, educational background, or where they have served (in terms of which courts). In merit systems judicial nominating commissions can be incredibly powerful governmental bodies. They are usually comprised of representatives from the governor's office, legislative leadership, and even the state bar association. Take the Connecticut Judicial Selection Commission, for example. There are twelve members of the commission: six are appointed by the governor and the remaining six are appointed by various leaders of the legislative branch such as the Speaker of the House and the minority leader of the Senate.[15] Conversely, the Kansas Supreme Court Nominating Commission has nine members, one lawyer and one nonlawyer from each of the four congressional districts. The "Nonlawyers are appointed by the governor. Lawyers are elected by other lawyers within their congressional districts. The chairperson is elected by lawyers statewide."[16]

The commissions narrow the applicant pool of judges down to a set number of names, typically three, that they send to the governor to choose to appoint. Therefore, even in merit selections the governor does have influence over the nominees through both having a nomination on the selection commissions and choosing the final nominee from a list that was provided to him. If you want to give the Hamiltonia governor more power, giving her more appointments on a judicial selection committee is one way to do so.

A final aspect of selection mechanisms that you must consider is the possibility of **retention elections**. Retention elections can be used in a couple of these judicial selection methods—usually partisan elections or merit plans—and mean the judge goes on the ballot with no opposition and must get a majority vote to stay on the bench. You may have faced this scenario as a voter yourself. If you live in a state with retention elections, you may have had a ballot that stated "Do you wish to retain Judge Smith" with the option of yes or no. New Mexico is one of the few states that require more than 50 percent of voters to approve them for retention election. The argument for retention elections is that they are a good popular check on the behavior of judges that had been selected prior. Most of these retention elections end favorably for the judge. An article covering retention elections in Arizona in 2022, for example, said that there had only been three judges who lost their retention elections in the almost fifty years since Arizona adopted retention elections. Interestingly the number would double after the 2022 election when three judges from Maricopa County were not reelected to their positions.[17] Therefore you need to decide whether Hamiltonia will have retention elections, and if so after how many years of their original appointment to the bench. This can be anywhere from one (Wyoming) to ten years (Pennsylvania) or more depending upon what you and your classmates decide. See Figure 7.5 for retention elections across the United States.

Figure 7.5

Judicial Retention Elections across the United States

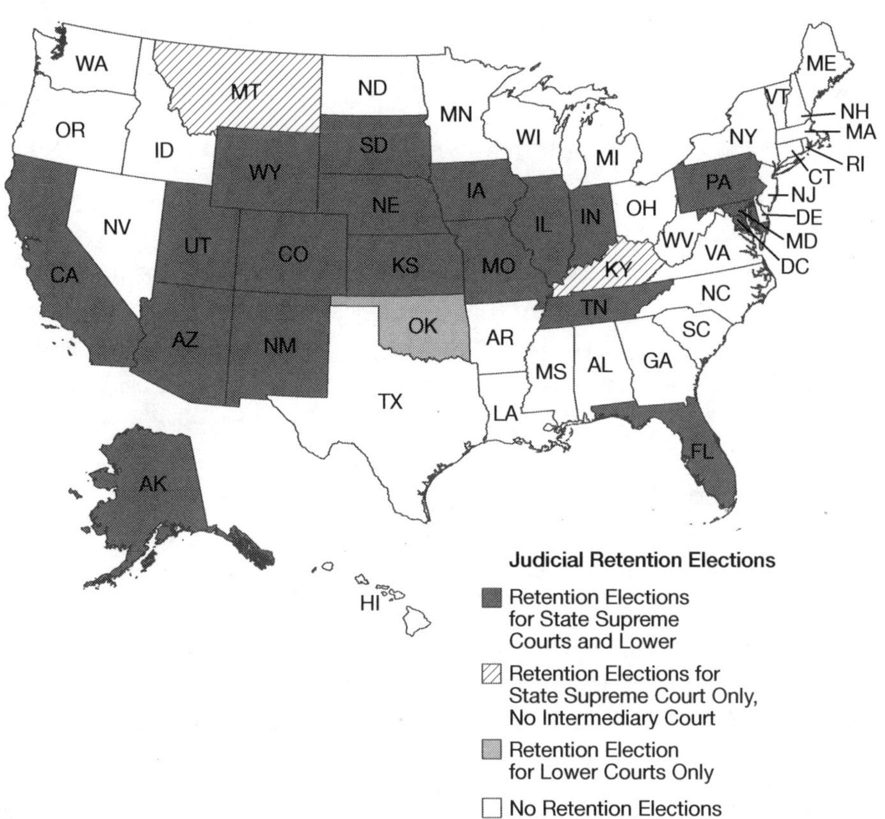

Action Item

7-4

How will judges for each level of Hamiltonia's courts be selected?

- Legislative appointment
  - Will there be retention elections? If so, after how many years?
- Partisan Election
  - When will the election be held? On or off cycle?
- Nonpartisan Election
  - When will the election be held? On or off cycle?
- Merit
  - If there is a judicial commission, who is on that commission?
  - Will there be retention elections? If so, after how many years?
- Gubernatorial appointment
  - Does the appointment need to be approved by the state senate?
- Will there be retention elections? If so, after how many years?

Judicial Qualifications

Now that we know *how* judges are selected for the Hamiltonia courts, we need to know *who* is eligible for these positions. There are three main areas for qualifications that are often set for state judges: residency, age, and whether they are a member of the state bar, a practicing attorney, a licensed attorney, or "learned in law." Let's start with state residency requirements for courts of last resort and appeals courts. Less than one-fifth (9 to be exact) of states set no residency requirement for these judges. Eighteen states require residency, but do not dictate a specific length of time. The remaining 33 states set residency requirements from as low as 28 days (Wisconsin) to as high as 9 years (Missouri). Most states also do not set any minimum age requirements—Rhode Island has a minimum age of 21, Nevada a minimum age of 25, and then an additional 15 states set the age at 30 or more.

The reason states may avoid using age qualifications is because many of them use some kind of legal credential requirement. Since most people are not graduating law school and passing the bar below twenty-five years of age, there is already a built-in age minimum through the credentials alone. Figure 7.6 displays the number of states that have each kind of legal credential. You will notice that

Figure 7.6

Qualification Requirements for Courts of Last Resort and Appellate Courts

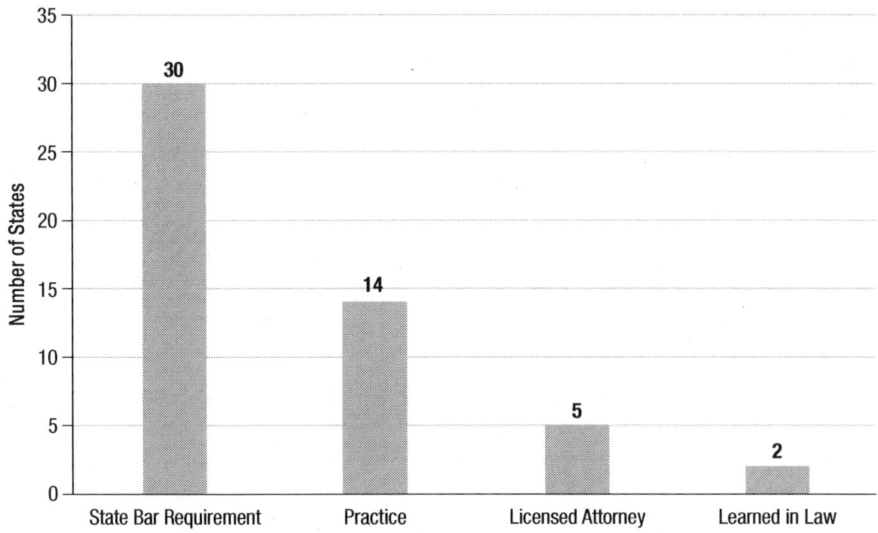

the total adds up to more than fifty because some states like Nevada require two credentials. In their case judges must have bar membership and be a practicing attorney for ten years. States set these credential requirements from anywhere from five years to up to ten years.

Qualifications look very similar for state trial courts. Eight states set no residency requirements while seventeen do not require residency for any length of time. Residency requirements on the upper end are lower for trial courts then higher-level courts: no state requires more than five years of residency to be eligible. The minimum age requirements are slightly more common for trial courts—twenty states require a minimum age of anywhere from eighteen to over thirty. Finally, states expand their legal credential qualifications for trial court judges—for higher courts Illinois requires judges to be licensed attorneys and Wyoming requires their judges to have nine years of practice. But their legal credential requirement for their trial court judges is to have a law degree.

Judges are the final public official that you will have to decide eligibility requirements for. At this point your class has decided who can serve in the legislature, who can be governor, and who is eligible to serve in numerous bureaucratic leader positions. Did you keep your eligibility requirements different for each branch? If you didn't, why were the minimum ages you set, for example, different for the legislative versus executive branches? Should judges be held to a different standard? Why or why not?

Action Item

7-5

Will there be residency requirements to serve as a judge? Is it different depending on the level of the court?

Action Item

7-6

Will there be a minimum age to serve as a judge? Is it different depending on the level of the court?

Action Item

7-7

Will there be legal credential requirements to serve as a judge? Is it different depending on the level of the court?

Judicial Tenure and Terms

So far you have decided the levels of Hamiltonia's courts, how judges are selected, and their qualifications to serve. But we have not specified term length for the judges, and something unique to state judicial branches, whether there should be a mandatory retirement age. Remember the federal judiciary appoints judges at all levels for life. That is not true for state courts of last resort. In fact, only one state—Rhode Island—appoints justices for life. Figure 7.7 displays the term length for State Supreme Court justices by state so that you can get an idea of how long they tend to be.

Term lengths for judges on intermediary courts is anywhere from one year (North Dakota) to up to seventy years of age (Massachusetts). Most states (19) set the term length to six years. General trial courts have terms starting at four years going all the way up to serving for life in Rhode Island (remember Rhode Island does not have an intermediary court). Half the states set the term length for trial courts to

Figure 7.7

Supreme Court Justice Term Length by State

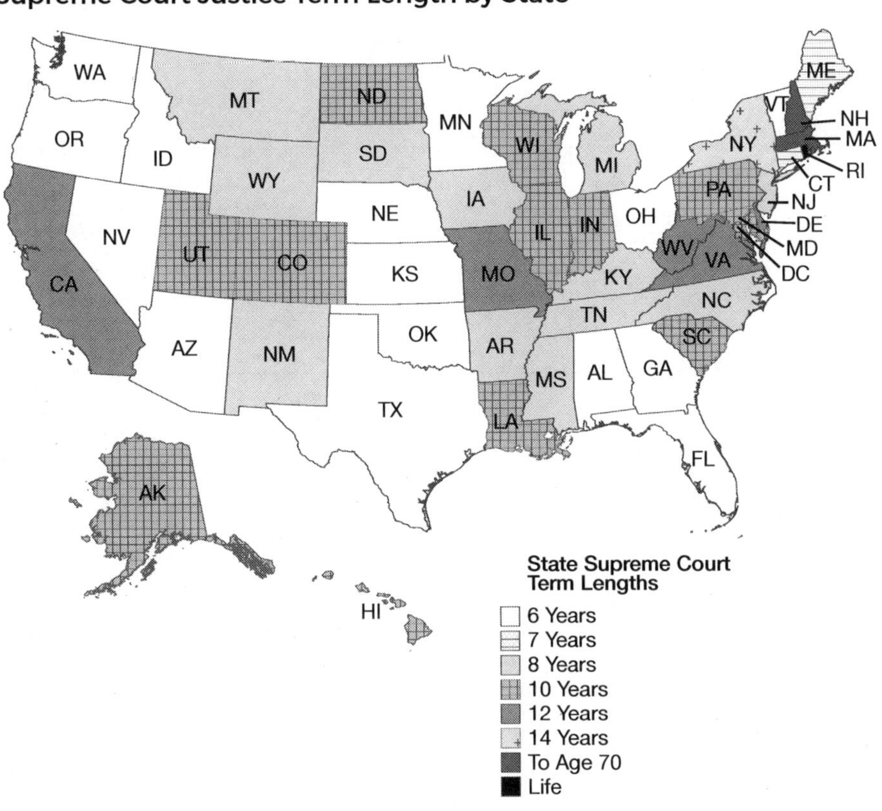

six years. While state judges do not have term limits like other public officials, some states have enacted mandatory retirement ages. Massachusetts, New Hampshire, New Jersey, and South Carolina set mandatory retirement for their justices (70 for MA, NH, and NH, 72 for SC). This does not exist in the other two branches of government; should it be a limitation for judges?

The question of term length should be taken into consideration with what you have previously decided about judicial selection method and whether you created retention elections. If you chose a merit plan for your judges, then you may want to consider terms that are shorter so that voters can approve the judges regularly in retention elections. However, if you are concerned about politics affecting judicial decision-making—which probably means you haven't chosen the election route at all—then you may want to consider longer terms so that judges can be insulated from voters and thus politics. If you are questioning the mental capacity of judges once they reach a certain age, then you should take mandatory retirement ages seriously, as this is one argument for why retirement ages should be applied to the judicial branch.

Action Item

7-8

How long is the term for the justices for each level of the judiciary?

Action Item

7-9

Will there be a mandatory retirement age for any level of the judiciary? If so, what will it be?

Chief Justice of State Courts of Last Resort

We cannot forget an important position on state courts of last resort—the chief justice. Chief justices play important administrative roles not only for their courts, but also the courts below them as well. For example, the Wisconsin Supreme Court chief justice takes part in long-range planning, creating new initiatives such as the Children's Court Improvement Program and improving relations with both the public and legislative and executive branches.[18] Most courts choose their own chief justice (22), with some chosen by partisan and nonpartisan elections, or gubernatorial appointment with confirmation from the legislature or judicial commission. Figure 7.8 also displays the term lengths for chief justices, which can be different than associate justices. How long will you set the chief justice's term and how do you think they should be chosen in Hamiltonia?

Action Item

7-10

What is the term length of the chief justice of the state court of last resort?

Figure 7.8
Term Length for Chief Justices

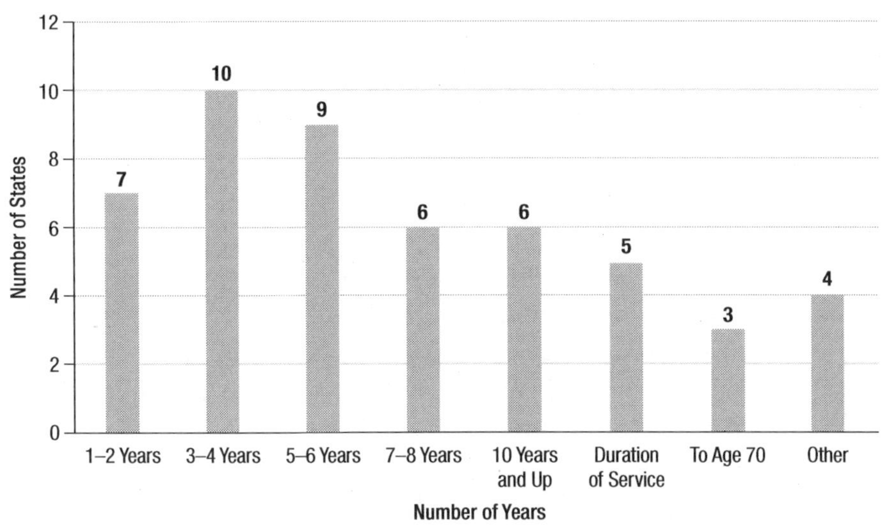

Action Item

7-11

How are chief justices of state courts of last resort chosen?

State Courts of Last Resort

Alabama Supreme Court Justices talk while awaiting the arrival of Gov. Kay Ivey to give her State of the State address, Tuesday, March 7, 2023, in Montgomery, AL

SOURCE: AP Photo/Julie Bennett

We have two more areas to discuss when it comes to state Supreme Courts. First is the number of justices you want to serve on the court. Remember that both Oklahoma and Texas have two state courts of last resort. Oklahoma's Supreme Court has 9 justices while its Court of Criminal Appeals has 5 justices. Both of Texas' courts of last resort have 6 members each. As Figure 7.9 shows, most state courts of last resort have 7 justices, followed by 17 having 5 justices. Only four states—Alabama, Georgia, Mississippi, and Washington—have 9 justices on their only state court of last resort. Depending upon your selection mechanism, a higher number of justices means potentially more appointment power for the legislature or governor (if you decided to go that route). It could also mean more opportunity for diversity in the court and more perspectives on each case. Remember South Carolina from the beginning of this chapter—they only have five members of their supreme court and removing the one woman from the bench and replacing her with a man resulted in an all-male court.

You will also want to think about how many justices need to agree to hear a case. For the United States Supreme Court there is the rule of four, which says that 4 out 9 justices need to agree to grant the writ of certiorari for the case to be heard before the court. Very few cases every year ever reach that threshold. Likewise, the vast majority of state level cases will never make it past the trial level. California has also set the number of justices who need to agree to hear a case at 4—but this bar is actually much higher than the U.S. Supreme Court because California's Supreme Court only has 7 justices.[19] Indiana's

Figure 7.9
Number of Justices on State Supreme Courts

Supreme Court, which only has 5 members, requires 3 out of the 5 justices to hear the case.[20] These are the final two decisions you have to make about Hamiltonia's Supreme Court; think carefully about how you want the court to look.

Action Item

7-12

How many justices will serve on the state court of last resort?

Action Item

7-13

How many justices are needed to agree to a case to be heard before the court?

State Trial Courts

You are the end of your decisions for Hamiltonia's judicial branch. We have one final area to discuss for Hamiltonia's court system—specifically the **trial court** level. We went over South Carolina's general versus limited jurisdiction courts, but as we have seen time and time again with state governments, each state has their own number and type of limited jurisdictions. Let's compare the four states located in Table 7.2 and their limited jurisdiction courts. Some states have limited jurisdiction courts tied to specific cities or towns, see Louisiana's City and Parish and mayor's courts. Others may have separate juvenile or family limited jurisdiction courts. Finally, there are some states that have more specialized limited jurisdiction courts such as Rhode Island

Table 7.2
State Limited Jurisdiction Courts

COLORADO	LOUISIANA	MICHIGAN	WEST VIRGINIA
County	Justice of the Peace	District	Magistrate
Municipal	Mayor's	Probate	Municipal
	City & Parish	Municipal	Family

which has Workers' Compensation and a Traffic Tribunal limited jurisdiction. You could also be on the other end of the spectrum and be like California which has no limited jurisdiction courts, although it is only one of a handful of states to set up their judiciary this way.

If you are wondering the reasoning for limited jurisdiction courts, it may help judges who are deciding these cases. Why? Well, if a judge is serving in a limited jurisdiction court, then they become experts in that area of the law. If they are serving in a general jurisdiction court, then they must be prepared to handle cases from civil disputes potentially all the way up to murder trials. This may also help the court system move more efficiently because the judges know the laws and procedures much better, and inherently some kinds of cases, such as small civil disputes, may move quickly as compared to the more in-depth criminal trials. What will you and your class decide when it comes to the limited jurisdiction courts Hamiltonia will have?

Action Item

7-14

What limited jurisdiction trial courts do you want Hamiltonia's judicial branch to have?

Looking Forward

It may have seemed like a long time ago, but just five chapters ago you started piecing together Hamiltonia's state constitution. We had you begin with creating the details of the constitution including amendment procedures, how taxes could be raised, and whether you would allow any direct democracy measures. We then moved onto the three branches of Hamiltonia government. You created the legislature with either one or two chambers, you crafted the terms of the legislators—deciding their term lengths and whether they had term limits. You then moved onto the governor's office, where you learned the powers of the governor, and decided on the strength of the governor in the Hamiltonian government. You shaped the executive branch the governor leads: you created departments, decided eligibility requirements, and selection methods. And finally, in this chapter, you created the courts, choosing the number of levels, justices, and selection methods of the judicial leaders of Hamiltonia.

In short, you and your classmates have created a state government from the ground up. This is no small feat, and hopefully an exercise that has helped you truly understand the different institutional arrangements of state governments, including their positive and negative attributes. But we are now at a turning point for the Hamiltonia simulation. We have spent the first half of this simulation *creating* the government, now it is time to *run* the government. In the next chapter you will be tasked with seeking out the offices you created during the Constitutional Convention. We hope that a few positions have caught your interest along the way, and you have started to think about what you may bring to the table for Hamiltonia government.

Once elections and appointments have been settled, you will be choosing the policy agenda for the remainder of the simulation. You will be deciding Hamiltonia's budget, and creating policy in the areas of education, criminal justice, environment, and health. As you address each of these areas as members of the Hamiltonia government we urge you to also think about the roads not taken. Would your debates on opioid addiction have been different if you had decided that the override for the governor's veto was a simple majority? Would you have set the budget differently if you had only created one legislative chamber—like Nebraska—instead of two? The Hamiltonia simulation provides you the unique opportunity to create a government and immediately see the consequences of your choices as you become the government. We look forward to seeing all of the unique institutional arrangements you have created. Congratulations on completing the first step of the simulation by participating in the Hamiltonia Constitutional Convention!

Key Terms

court of last resort (142)
chief justice (139)
general jurisdiction courts (140)
appellate courts (140)
limited jurisdiction (140)
civil cases (140)
criminal cases (141)
magistrate (141)
original jurisdiction (141)
legislative appointment (147)
gubernatorial appointment (147)
partisan elections (147)
nonpartisan elections (147)
merit plans (148)
retention elections (148)
trial court (157)
special jurisdiction court (160)

Assignments to Learn More about State Courts

1. In the Hamiltonia simulation you create the courts, but do not fulfill the roles you created. For this assignment, we want you to choose a prominent state court decision made in the last two years from the state you are from. Read over the legal questions and read the opinions of the justices. Now write your own opinion on the case as if you were a justice on Hamiltonia's court of last resort. Would you have decided the case differently?
2. Like the legislative and executive branches, *The Book of States* covers the salaries of judges at all levels in states in Table 5.4. At this point you may have decided the compensation for the other branches. What should judges get paid? Should it be more or less than legislators or executive branch officials? Why?
3. How is the court system set up in your home state? Analyze the number of courts and the judicial selection process in your state. Recommend at least two changes to your state's court system. Make sure to explain why you made those recommendations and the expected consequences of those changes.
4. One area we did not cover was the creation of **specialty jurisdiction courts**. Examples of specialty courts include domestic violence courts and drug courts. Specialty courts are like limited jurisdiction courts but are also highly specialized because they only handle offenses for those specific areas. In comparison family courts are limited jurisdiction courts but they can handle anything from custody agreements to adoption, to divorce. Consider whether or not Hamiltonia should have any specialty courts, and if so, which ones and why?

Tom Tillotson removes ballots for counting after midnight that were cast in the first-in-the-nation presidential primary, at The Balsams Grand Resort, Tuesday, January 10, 2012, in Dixville, NH.

SOURCE: AP Photo/Matt Rourke

Seeking Political Office and Setting a Policy Agenda at the State Level

Learning Objectives:

After reading this chapter students should be able to:

- Identify the differences between single and multimember districts.
- Explain how campaign finance restrictions differ across states.
- Describe the importance of local media and its decline.
- Discuss how policies get on the political agenda.
- Form a state government for Hamiltonia.

State Spotlight: New Hampshire

The state of New Hampshire is unique for many reasons. It is the only state to not require people in a vehicle to wear a seatbelt, it is one of only three states to have no motorcycle helmet laws (Illinois and Iowa are the other two), and it has the largest state legislative chamber at 400 members. The next closest legislative chamber in size is Pennsylvania with 203 members in their House of Representatives.[1] New Hampshire is also unique because it only has 203 legislative districts, meaning that nearly half of the districts are multimember, instead of single member. But what does that actually mean?

In much of the United States, including the federal level, we have something called **first-past-the-post single-member districts**. This means that our districts are geographically bound and when one person receives more votes than the other candidates (or a **plurality** as they say) then the candidate wins the whole district to represent. This is not the case in over

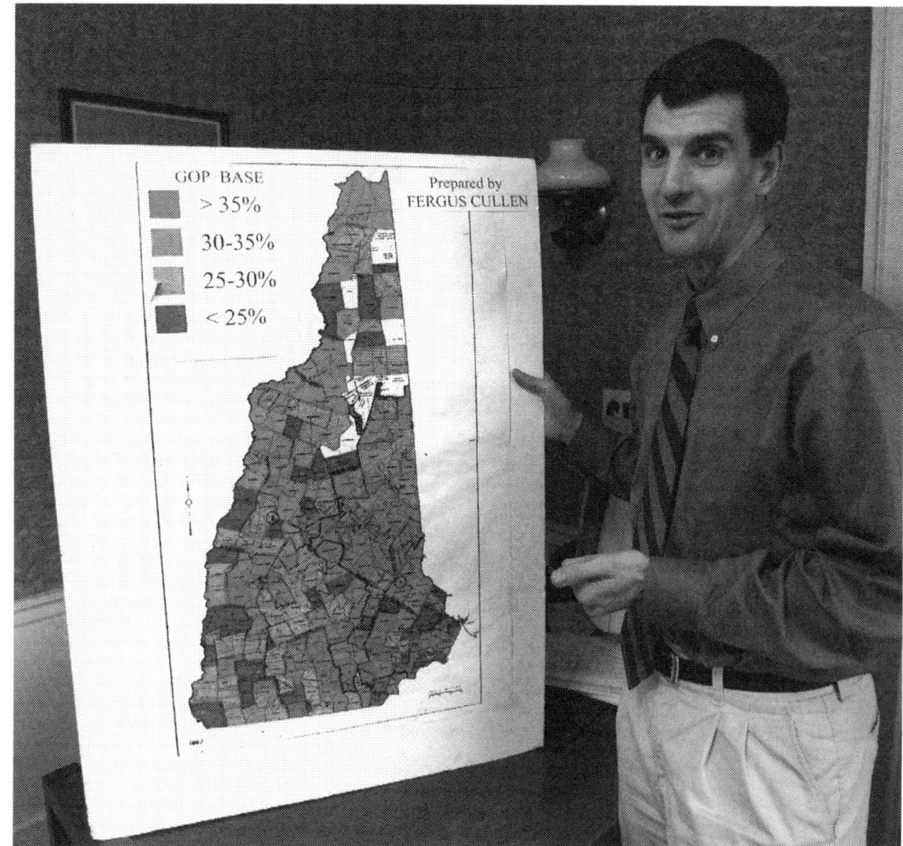

State Republican party chairman Fergus Cullen stands in Concord, NH, Tuesday, November 27, 2007, by a map of New Hampshire he hand-colored showing where Republican strongholds are. "There's all this mythology about campaigning in every hamlet in New Hampshire, but it comes down to hunting where the votes are, and 50 percent of the vote comes from something like 18 towns," said Cullen.

SOURCE: AP Photo/Jim Cole

90 of the 203 districts for the House in New Hampshire. There, depending on the size of the district, constituents can vote for more than one candidate to represent them. In fact, the thirteenth district of Rockingham has ten seats alone. In **multimember districts** voters elect as many candidates as there are seats. In the 2022 election there were 20 candidates running for the 10 seats: 10 Republicans (all **incumbents**) and 10 Democrats. All 10 Republicans won reelection to their seats.

The thirteenth district of Rockingham in the 2022 election is illustrative of two patterns in elections. First, the power of incumbency. Being an incumbent—the current officeholder—is a powerful predictor of winning an election. Over 270 of the candidates for the New Hampshire House in 2022 were incumbents. Only twenty of the incumbents running lost their seat. Second, despite being able to vote for more than one person, most people still vote in a block—which is why all the Republicans swept the Rockingham district. There are a few districts that do split their seats between the parties (Belknap 2 elected one Democrat and one Republican and Hillsborough 2 elected two Democrats and five Republicans), but in general when there is more than one seat a party will take them all.

This chapter is a transitionary chapter. In the first seven chapters of this book, you were introduced to state government and built an entire legislature, executive branch, and court system from the ground up. Now it is time to run for the offices you created and consider the policies you will want to debate in the second half of the simulation. In the first half of this chapter, we will go over the cost of running campaigns at the state level, the role of the media, and then the appointment process. We will also review the various positions you may want to seek in the Hamiltonia government.

Running for Office at the State Level

There are over half a million elected positions to run for in the United States between the local, state, and federal levels. Figure 8.1 breaks down the number of state legislative, gubernatorial, and statewide executive branch officials that are elected across the United States. As you learned in the previous chapters, states vary widely in terms of the number of legislators they elect and whether they elect or appoint certain statewide executive branch officials. Before we recap the positions available to you to seek, we want to go over two major variables associated with running for office at the state level: campaign finance and the role of the media.

Figure 8.1
Number of State Elected Positions

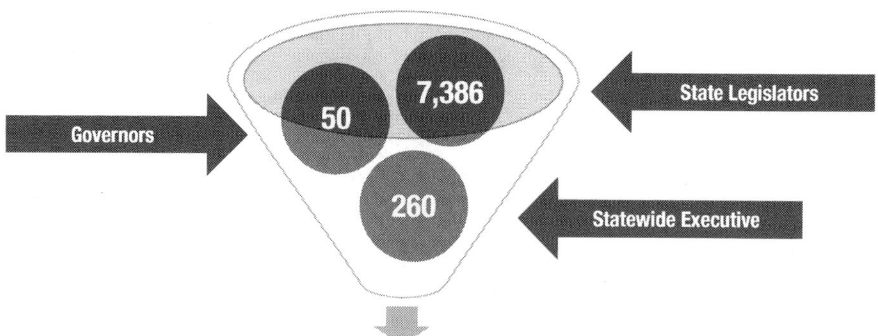

State Campaign Finance

To understand **campaign finance** at the state level we turn to the National Conference of State Legislatures (NCSL). The NCSL reported that "as of Feb. 1, 2023, more than $1.6 billion was raised and reported for state House/Assembly and Senate races in 2021 and 2022. The median amount raised in aggregate across the states for House/Assembly races was $8.7 million and for Senate races was $6.3 million."[2] Figures 8.2 and 8.3 display the individual contribution limits for the state house candidates versus statewide offices including governor.[3] There are some states that have different contribution limitations depending upon whether the person is running for the house or the senate. Connecticut, for example, sets the individual state house contribution to $250, but the state senate limit to $1,000. Eight states in total have different limits for the different legislative offices.

Note two patterns from these maps. First, the individual contribution limits for statewide races—which sometimes have same limits for governors and other officials, such as secretaries of state—are almost always higher than for state house seats. This makes sense—if you are running for a legislative district in California versus running for the governor of California to represent the whole state, then there will be a significant cost in running. Second, notice that twelve states have unlimited individual contributions. Compare this to the much more restrictive states of Colorado and Montana, for example, and the ceiling for fundraising looks quite different from state to state.

Figure 8.2
Individual Contribution Limits for State House Seats

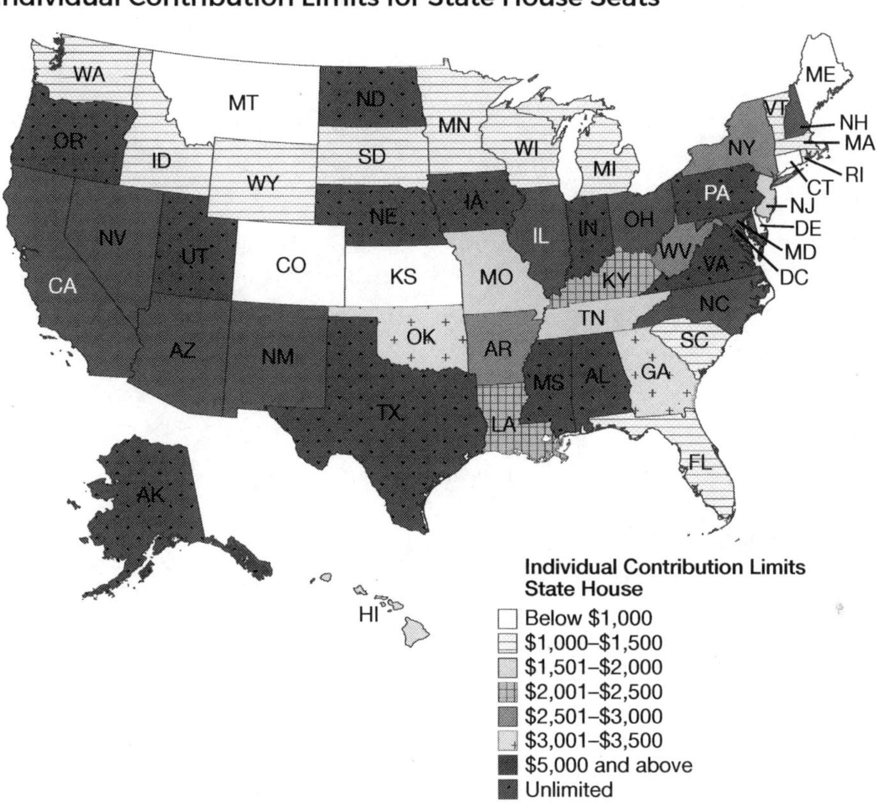

But there are also other campaign finance rules across states that set limitations from state parties, **Political Action Committees** (PACs), corporate contributions, and union contributions. While we will not go into the details of these contributions, there are a few things we want to note. First, state party contributions are set at the same rate as individual contributions (10 states), have a higher, specific amount associated with each office than individual contributions (17 states), or do not limit party contributions to candidates (23 states). Fewer states allow unlimited PAC contributions (13), and even less allow unlimited corporate or union contributions (Alabama, Nebraska, Oregon, Utah, Virginia allow unlimited for both). In fact, twenty-three states prohibit corporate contributions to candidates and twenty-one states prohibit campaign contributions from unions. Figure 8.4 displays which states prohibit corporate and union contributions to individual candidates.

Figure 8.3
Individual Contribution Limits for Statewide Seats

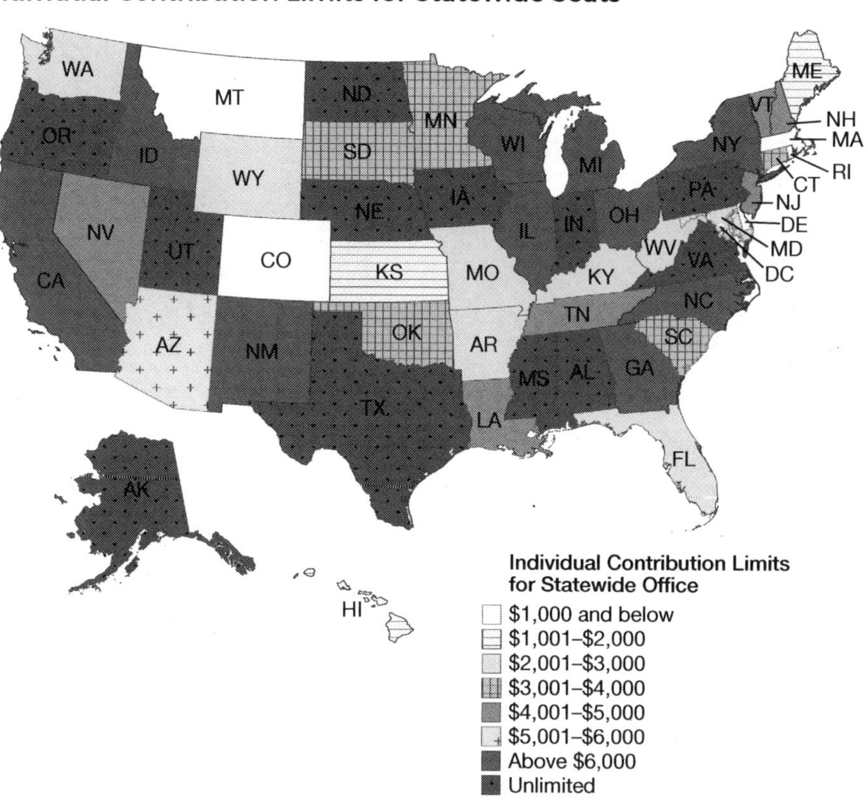

Most prohibit both, but a select few prohibit one or the other. A state's rules on campaign finance can play a role in state races.

Role of the Media

Although we often think of the media's role in national campaigns, such as for the presidency, the media also plays an important role in state elections as well, particularly for governor races. We just discussed the campaign donation limitations across states, but associated with this is the actual cost to run for office in each state. The cost of running for the governor of California, for example, is much higher than running for the governor of Rhode Island. In part this is due to the size (both population and geographic) of a state, but also has to do with **media markets**. California has major (and expensive) media markets around San Francisco, Los Angeles, and San Diego. Rhode Island has the major media market of Providence.

Figure 8.4
Union and Corporate Candidate Contributions

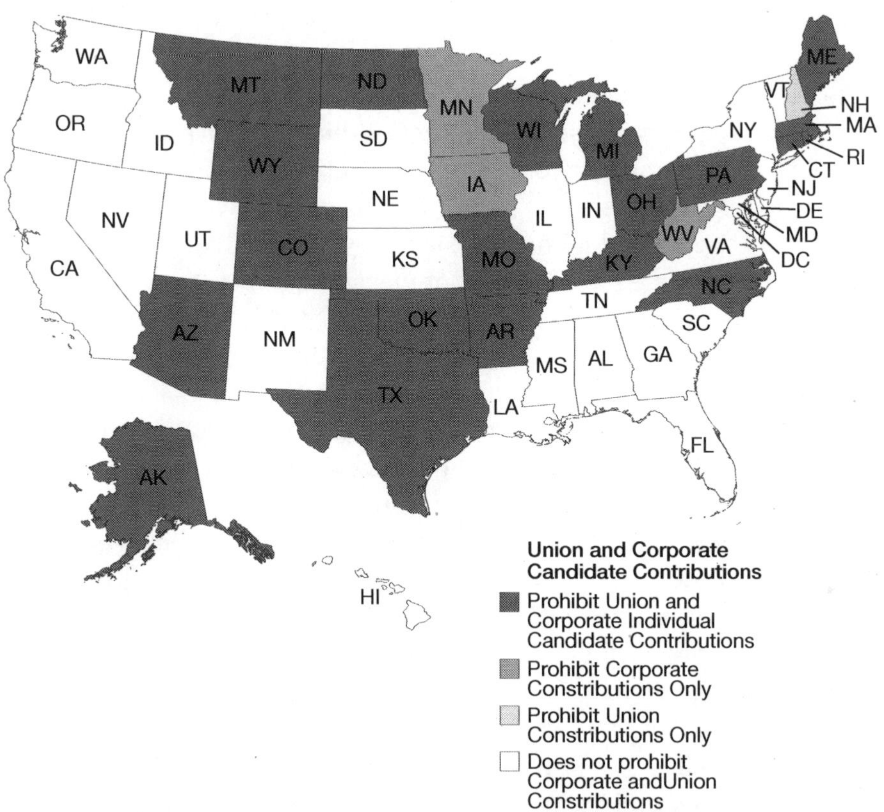

In this May 16, 2016, file photo, pedestrians walk outside the Los Angeles Times *building downtown Los Angeles Monday, May 16, 2016. Tribune Publishing, owner of the* Los Angeles Times, *is rejecting another takeover bid from* USA Today *owner Gannett on Monday, May 23, saying it's not in the best interest of shareholders.*

SOURCE: AP Photo/ Richard Vogel, File

In addition to this there is also the cost of travel, political consultants, and hosting various events to get your name out there and to fundraise. Also, remember that timing matters for the amount of attention certain governor's races may get. A 2021 NPR article titled "Here's Why the Other 48 States Care Who's Governor of Virginia and New Jersey" detailed how these gubernatorial races occur in odd numbered years, which means they not only get their local media attention, but national media attention as well.[4] And remember, if you created the opportunity for direct democracy in Hamiltonia, there is a lot of fundraising associated with that as well. Follow the Money reported that nearly $900 million was spent on fundraising associated with 162 ballot measures across 35 states in 2016. And that was not even the highest historically, in 2012 there were 185 ballot measures across 39 states that fundraised over $940 million.[5]

But it would be a mistake not to mention the major hurdles local newspapers have been facing since the dawn of the internet. Readership of local newspapers has decreased precipitously, even though many newspapers have shifted to digital news. Some newspapers, like the major newspaper of Alabama, *The Birmingham News*, made the decision in 2023 to stop circulation and only publish digitally. The University of North Carolina at Chapel Hill's Hussman School of Journalism and Media analyzed the decline in local news in 2018. In their report they find the following: The United States has lost almost 1,800 papers since 2004, including more than 60 dailies and 1,700 weeklies. Roughly half of the remaining 7,112 in the country—1,283 dailies and 5,829 weeklies—are located in small and rural communities. The vast majority—around 5,500—have circulation of less than 15,000.[6] In 2021 *Poynter* reported that over 100 newspapers closed due to the pandemic alone.[7] The Pew Research Center also tracks the circulation of locally focused news since 2015 and finds that weekday and Sunday circulation has decreased steeply from a high of twenty-eight million Sunday circulation in 2015 to just over fifteen million in 2020.[8]

If you are wondering why local news coverage matters, you have to think back to the role of the media. The media is meant to inform, but also to hold political and other institutions accountable. Who would have the resources to investigate corruption, or the details of a new state budget? When there is no local news, then the focus becomes entirely at the national level, even though so much of what affects our day to day lives happens in the halls of local and state governments. Getting the attention of the voters, therefore, may be more difficult in rural and suburban areas that no longer have their own news sources. While social media may fill the gap, it does not perform the same investigatory or interpretive functions as traditional news sources, which is something we should all keep in mind as we study state and local elections. We should also keep this in mind as we begin running the Hamiltonian government—Hamiltonians will have a difficult time finding out what their legislators are doing in session without local and state news sources.

Simulation

In the next session we will discuss running for the elected and appointed offices in the Hamiltonian government.

Running for Office in Hamiltonia

No matter what your class has decided in terms of electing or appointing certain executive branch officers, all elections in Hamiltonia start with the governor. All governors are elected in the United States, and therefore the Hamiltonia governor will be as well. Anyone running for governor (as well as any other elected office) should fill out Worksheet #1: Running for State Elected Office, and really think about what makes you the best candidate for the job. This is a leadership position and will require public speaking as well as bargaining skills with various leaders of the Hamiltonia government.

It is possible that only one person decides to run for the office, and therefore they automatically become governor. But we highly encourage multiple people to throw their hat into the ring to offer your class (aka Hamiltonia) a real choice in the election. If your class decided to have the governor share a ticket with the lieutenant governor (as happens in 26 states), then your classmates who are running for governor need to find a running mate. If the lieutenant governor is elected separately (as it is in 17 states), then after the governor's race is decided, the lieutenant governor's race begins. This allows for the candidates who did not win the governor's race to run for lieutenant governor. If you decided that Hamiltonia does not have a lieutenant governor, then the next office that would be decided if it is elected is secretary of state, followed by attorney general, and ending with the state treasurer. Once the secretary of state is elected, the elections will be run by that person.

It is possible that the only position elected in the whole of Hamiltonia's executive branch is the governor (as it is in Maine). In this case, your class would move onto the appointments process, which we will discuss in the next section. If there are other executive branch positions that your class created that are elected, then elections need to be held for those positions after the big three have been decided if they are all elected. In short, your class will hold all elections for the executive branch first, going by order of gubernatorial succession that you decided in chapter 5, Action Item 5-6. Once elections for all executive branch positions have been decided, it is now time to set the appointments for executive branch positions.

Action Item

8-1

Hold elections for governor.

- If you decided earlier in the simulation for the governor and lieutenant governor to be on the same ticket, elect the lieutenant governor as well.
- If your class has a lieutenant governor that is elected separately, hold elections for lieutenant governor after the governor is elected.

Action Item

8-2

If they are elected, hold elections for the secretary of state, attorney general, and state treasurer.

Action Item

8-3

Hold elections for remaining executive branch officials based on the order of succession set in chapter 6.

Getting Appointed in Hamiltonia

The appointment process is unique to every class's simulation. This is because you decided which positions would be appointed, and who appoints them. It is possible that some of the appointments have been given to the lieutenant governor, or one of the big three, although it is most likely that the governor gets to appoint these individuals. Students who are seeking appointed office should fill out Worksheet #2: Seeking Appointed Office. These students are in a unique position, because unlike the governor or other elected executive branch officials who must be responsive to the whole class (representing the whole state), students running for appointment are trying to convince an audience of one—the person responsible for appointing them.

Does this mean the person seeking the appointment needs to pander to the person appointing them? Of course not. In fact, a good strategy for the person seeking the appointment who does not share all the views of their appointer is to advocate for healthy debate within their administration. Either way, the students seeking appointments need to consider who is appointing them and whether they feel they could work well together. We also recommend the governor (or other appointer) seek out classmates to recruit for various executive branch positions, as this is what happens at the state level as well.

Action Item

8-4

Governor reviews applicants for executive branch appointed positions and announces their choice. If any of the other elected executive branch officials have appointments, they choose them after the governor.

State Legislature Elections

At this point in the simulation, you have a complete executive branch of Hamiltonia's government. If your class decided to have one chamber for your state legislature, then the remaining students in the class go into the legislature. If you decided to have a bicameral legislature, then the next set of elections are for senators, and once the senators have been decided the remaining students serve in the House. As a legislator, your instructor will let you know which district in Hamiltonia you will represent for the remainder of the simulation.

Once your legislature is complete, you have one more set of elections to hold, and that are the leadership positions within each chamber. These positions are decided via majority vote. Remember that the leaders of the house and senate are incredibly powerful positions. These leaders need to be able to have a coherent party position on each of the policy areas you will be debating and know how to balance the interests of not only their members but also the governor who may have veto powers on the legislation that is passed.

Once your class has decided who will be holding every position in the Hamiltonia government, it is now time to discuss which policies you will be debating in the second half of the simulation. The next section details each of the policy areas and the topics you could debate. We recommend the senate, house, and executive branch convene separately to discuss which of the policy issues each institution wants to discuss. Then the class can come back together to compare which policies they prefer, and potentially bargain for the policy they wish to put on the agenda. Policies go on the agenda via majority vote.

Action Item

8-5

If Hamiltonia has a bicameral legislature, Senate elections are held. Any students not elected to the Senate automatically serve in the House. If Hamiltonia has a unicameral legislature, all remaining students serve in the legislature.

Action Item

8-6

Senate and House leadership positions are chosen by majority vote, based on the positions created in the Hamiltonia Constitution.

Policy Agenda

Welcome to deciding the policy agenda for the state of Hamiltonia this year! The **agenda** is simply the governments to-do list. Agenda-setting is a major part of the policymaking process in the United States. Before a policy can be adopted to address an important public policy issue, it first has to make its way onto the government's agenda. Cobb and Elder (1983) examined how an issue might get on the agenda. They argue that for an issue to make it on the agenda it is important to increase the scope of an issue-mobilizing support for the issue—which will increase the overall visibility of the issue making it more likely it will get on the government's agenda.[9]

Agenda-setting is important for understanding policy change in the United States. Policymaking in the United States can be described as a process of **punctuated equilibrium** meaning that in general policymaking is very stable except for short periods of rapid change. This theory—developed by Baumgartner and Jones (1993)—can help us understand when there will be policy change in the United States.[10]

For each of the policy areas you will have a choice between two policies. Although both policies are very important to the state of Hamiltonia, not every public problem can be on the government's agenda at the same time—so you must choose. Here we will provide a brief overview of each policy to help you in making your decision. Your instructor will let you know how your class is going to decide what will be on Hamiltonia's agenda for the rest of the semester. Also see Figure 8.5 for a preview of each of the policy areas.

Education

Education is a major policy area for state governments. Not only do states spend a significant portion of their budgets on education, but they are also evaluated and judged based on their educational performance. The right to public education is enshrined in state constitutions—not the federal constitution. Therefore, this is an important policy area. You will have the choice to concentrate on either pre-k policy or higher education policy for Hamiltonia. Below we provide a brief background for each policy. Feel free to look ahead to chapter 10 for more in-depth information.

Pre-kindergarten is a year of schooling prior to kindergarten. Many of you may have participated in pre-k yourself. Pre-kindergarten has been an important area of state policymaking since the 1970s after President Nixon vetoed the Childhood Development Act—which would have created a national day care system.[11] Since then, states have developed their own pre-kindergarten programs. Most states have a targeted pre-k program where certain eligible students can go to pre-kindergarten and the state will pay for it. Other states have universal pre-k meaning

Figure 8.5
Policy Debates

Education	Universal Pre-Kindergarten
	Merit Aid Scholarships
Criminal Justice	Cash Bail Reform
	Felony Disenfranchisement
Environment	Renewable Portfolio Standards
	Lead and Water Quality
Health	Expanding Medicaid
	Addressing the Opioid Crisis

that any and all four-year-olds in the state can receive free pre-k education. Typically, states work with private childcare centers and schools to provide this education. Pre-k has received a lot of attention lately as a possible way to help reduce inequities in the k–12 education system.[12] If you choose pre-k policy, you will need to create Hamiltonia's first state-funded pre-k program. You will need to decide who is eligible, how much money Hamiltonia will spend on the program, and the quality requirements of the program.

As you all may know, higher education policy is also an important policy issue area. One of the most controversial components of higher education is its cost. If you choose higher education, you will be designing Hamiltonia's first merit aid scholarship program. In 1993, the state of Georgia used state lottery funds to start the Helping Outstanding Pupils Educationally (HOPE) program. This program provided money to Georgia students that met certain education requirements to attend in state institutions of higher education. One of the goals of merit-based scholarships is to keep the top students in the state. If you choose merit aid scholarships you will need to decide who is eligible and the requirements to keep the scholarship, how much the scholarship will be, and what schools the scholarship can be used at.

Action Item

8-7

Students choose between universal pre-kindergarten or creating merit aid scholarships for education policy.

Criminal Justice

States also play a major role in criminal justice policy. Although a lot of the news seems to focus on federal action (or inaction) in this area, states make important decisions on criminal justice from policing to jails and prisons, and to courts. We will preview the two criminal justice policy options below. If you would like more information before deciding, please skip ahead to chapter 11.

One issue on some states' agendas is cash bail reform. Cash bail is the system whereby some individuals accused—not convicted—of crimes can pay to be released from jail as they await trial. Cash bail has been criticized for creating a system whereby wealthy individuals can pay to be released while awaiting trial, but low-income individuals cannot. At the same time, reforms to eliminate cash bail have also garnered criticism for being soft on crime and releasing dangerous individuals into the community. If you choose this issue, you will need to decide how you want to reform Hamiltonia's cash bail system. You will decide if you will abolish cash bail, if so for which crimes, as well as what kind of factors a judge can consider when setting bail.

The second area you may choose is felony disenfranchisement. In the United States, states can decide whether convicted felons lose the right to vote. In some states, felons can never vote again; in others, felons can vote after their sentence is complete, and, in a couple, felons never lose their right to vote. This is an important issue because the United States has a large prison population, therefore, this issue has the potential to affect as many as nineteen million people in the United States.[13] If you choose this issue you will need to decide whether convicted felons in Hamiltonia will have the right to vote and what other requirements may be necessary for their voting rights to be restored.

Action Item

8-8

Students choose between cash bail reform or felony disenfranchisement for criminal justice policy.

Environment

Many students are interested in climate change and government responses to preserve our environment. Environmental policies include international, national, and subnational responses. For the sake of this book, we are going to focus on subnational responses at the state level. Like education and criminal justice, states have done a lot to address environmental issues. Below we provide a brief overview of two environmental issues that you can focus on. For more information, skip ahead to chapter 12.

Iowa first adopted Renewable Portfolio Standards (RPS) in 1983. Since then, thirty states have adopted renewable portfolio standards. RPS is a policy that encourages utility companies to use a certain percentage of renewable energy rather than non-renewable energy by a specific date. This is meant to require or incentivize the use of renewable energy for state energy needs. Iowa—the first state to adopt these standards—has been successful in using wind energy as a renewable energy source. If you choose this area, you will design Hamiltonia's renewable energy portfolio standards. You will decide whether the standards are a requirement or voluntary, what percent of energy needs to come from renewable sources and by what date, as well as what kinds of energy sources will count as renewable. If you choose this issue area you will create an important policy to help Hamiltonia transition from depending so heavily on non-renewable energy.

Another important area of state environmental policymaking is in water quality. The Flint Water Crisis highlighted the importance of state and local governments in ensuring water quality for residents. Additionally, the federal government has been active in this area trying to encourage states to find and replace lead pipes that cause lead in the water. If you choose this issue, you will need to decide what level of lead in the water will trigger state action, whether you are going to require an inventory of lead service lines, as well as what happens once lead service lines are found. If you choose this policy you can focus your attention on trying to eliminate lead from the drinking water in Hamiltonia.

Action Item

8-9

Students choose between renewable portfolio standards or lead and water quality for environmental policy.

Health

Health, like education, is a major component of state expenditures. Because states must balance their budgets, policies addressing one of the most—if not the most—expensive category of state spending is important. For health policy you will choose between expanding Medicaid—a state-federal program that provides insurance for low-income individuals and families—and addressing the opioid crisis. Both areas are critical for the well-being of Hamiltonians.

Medicaid was adopted in 1965. It is a state-federal program where the federal government sets certain standards and pays a large portion of the cost of Medicaid, but states administer and make major decisions for the program. State Medicaid policy changed drastically after President Obama's Affordable Care Act (ACA) was signed into law. In maybe the most significant change to Medicaid since its inception, the ACA allowed states to expand Medicaid so that more people qualified for the program. Now, individuals up to 138 percent of the poverty line could qualify for Medicaid if the state chose to expand the program. If you choose this policy, you will decide who is eligible for Medicaid in Hamiltonia, what kind of services are covered by Medicaid, and how you will pay for it. Because it is a state-federal program, state Medicaid programs look different across states. This is your opportunity to tailor Medicaid to the needs of Hamiltonia.

Hamiltonia, like the rest of the nation, has also been hit hard by the opioid epidemic. Hamiltonia was ranked in the top five states with the highest opioid overdose deaths. You may choose to focus on creating a comprehensive state strategy to address the opioid epidemic in Hamiltonia. If you choose this issue, you will decide whether you will create a drug monitoring program, whether you will restrict opioid prescriptions, how you will expand access to drug rehabilitation centers, and how the state will distribute Naloxone—an opioid overdose reversal drug.

Action Item

8-10

Students choose between expanding Medicaid or addressing the opioid crisis.

Looking Forward

We hope this chapter has given you a small glimpse into what it means to run for state-level office, and how issues end up on the agenda. Did you already start bargaining with your fellow Hamiltonians? Maybe your class decided to address the opioid crisis over expanding Medicaid because you knew your policy positions aligned more with the governor? Or maybe your class had a clear majority (unified government even) and little compromise was needed at this stage. Be prepared, however, that sharing party or ideology does not automatically mean you and your classmates will always see eye to eye. You might experience this in the next chapter on fiscal policy.

Key Terms

first-past-the-post single-member districts (162)
plurality (162)
multimember districts (163)
incumbents (163)
campaign finance (164)
Political Action Committees (165)
media markets (166)
agenda (172)
punctuated equilibrium (172)

Assignments to Learn More about State Elections and Appointments

1. Are you running for an elected office in the state of Hamiltonia? Write a stump speech where you explain the following:
   a. Your background
   b. Why you are interested in the position you are running for
   c. What qualities you bring to the table for Hamiltonia to elect you.
2. We discussed the importance of the media in state government elections. Create a storyboard for a thirty-second campaign spot. A storyboard can be completed using PowerPoint where each slide outlines what a campaign ad would look like, with visuals as examples and the dialogue you would use.
3. Interested in what it takes to run a campaign for state level office? Consider a social media fundraising strategy: What would it look like? Who would you target? Which social media websites would you use and why?
4. Go to your governor's website. What issues has he/she placed on the agenda? How long have they been on the agenda, and do you see these issues being taken up by the state legislature?

Florida Gov. Ron DeSantis addresses a joint session of the legislature, Tuesday, January 11, 2022, in Tallahassee, FL.

SOURCE: AP Photo/Phelan M. Ebenhack

The Budget

Learning Objectives:

After reading this chapter students should be able to:

- Understand how states determine and balance their budgets.
- Identify and explain the different revenue strategies states might employ.
- Explain why states might raise revenues differently.
- Identify and explain different expenditure strategies states might employ.
- Explain why states might spend money differently.

State Spotlight: Florida

In March 2023, Governor Ron DeSantis (R) delivered his State of the State address to the Florida legislature. The State of the State is an opportunity for the governor to inform the legislature of his priorities in the upcoming year. Governors also use this address to highlight their policy successes in the previous year and to outline their vision for the state's budget. In 2023, DeSantis used the State of the State to propose a two billion dollar tax cut.[1] That seems like a lot, but prior to this speech Governor DeSantis had outlined his Framework for Freedom budget which included over $114 billion in state expenditures. The prior year's budget was $110 billion so the 2023–2024 proposal did not drastically change the size of the Florida budget.[2] However, his proposal would lead to the largest budget in the state of Florida's history.

The budget outlines both the goals for **revenue** and **expenditures** for the year. Revenue is the money that the state takes in through taxes and expenditures is the money the government spends on programs, transportation, and more. Governor DeSantis' proposed budget included tax cuts such as exempting certain baby items like diapers and cribs from a sales tax, exempting gas stoves from state sales taxes, and one year sales tax exemption on certain dental products, kid's books, and more. The Framework for Freedom budget also proposed the ways in which Governor DeSantis envisioned Florida spending the money it raised in tax revenues. Some of the spending priorities of the governor included funding the state pension program for state employees, $695 million to fill positions in law enforcement and retain current law enforcement employees with pay increases, $1 billion to raise teacher pay, $451 million for the state's universal pre-k program, $10 million to provide more computer science courses, $614 million for the multifaceted Everglades Restoration project, $65 million to fight against algae blooms in the state, $145 million to protect the waterways, and much more. Governor DeSantis outlined his funding priorities in terms of education, environment, transportation, economic recovery, health, public safety, the military, and government operations in his budget.

Just because Governor DeSantis outlined his priorities in the Framework for Freedom does not mean that was the final budget for the state of Florida for **fiscal year** 2023–2024. However, Governor DeSantis was in a good political position to shape the budget. He came into office with a resounding nineteen-point victory over Democrat Charlie Crist as well as a strong Republican majority in both the Florida House and

Florida Senate.[3] Still, both the Florida Senate and the Florida House passed different budget bills, both of which were slightly more modest than the governor's proposed budget. In order to resolve the differences between these two bills—the Florida Senate's $113.7 billion and the Florida House' $113 billion budget—the legislature formed the Joint Conference Committee.[4] Both of these budgets lowered funding for universal pre-k and Medicaid because of anticipated lower enrollment, however, the amount was slightly different in both proposals. Remember from chapter 4 on the legislature, state houses and senates have to pass identical legislation. Through negotiations, the final budget passed by the legislature was slightly different from the original proposals.

The final budget was a total of $116.5 billion dollars which is the highest budget in Florida's history.[5] This was only after Governor DeSantis used his line-item veto power to eliminate over $510 million in spending from the budget passed by the legislature.[6] This means that although the House and Senate initially proposed $113 billion budgets, by the time the conference committee completed its work the budget had grown by about $4 billion.

The final budget was slightly different from the one initially proposed by Governor DeSantis. The budget provided for a $2.7 billion tax cut to Floridians instead of the original $2 billion tax cut. This included an additional $500 million for toll relief, meaning it reduced or eliminated tolls on certain roads for a certain time. The budget included slightly more for teacher pay increases but also less money for the state's universal pre-k program. The final budget also increased the per pupil spending to $8,648, whereas DeSantis had proposed $8,453. This may seem minimal, but remember Florida is a very populous state. This comes out to a total of more than $800 million dollars. The $10 million in investing in computer science remained from the governor's original proposal to the final budget for the year. DeSantis originally proposed a $6.8 billion investment in the environment, but the total ended up as $7.2 billion.[7] In Figure 9.1, you can see the chart outlining some of the differences between the initial budget and the final budget.[8]

Although the budget can be complicated, it is one of the most important components of state politics and policy. This is because the budget represents the government's—and therefore its citizens' (that's us!)—priorities for the next year. The budget details what our elected officials believe are the most pressing problems that we face and how they propose to dedicate resources to solve those problems. Without any resources, it is very difficult to address public problems. Therefore,

Figure 9.1
Florida Budget 2023

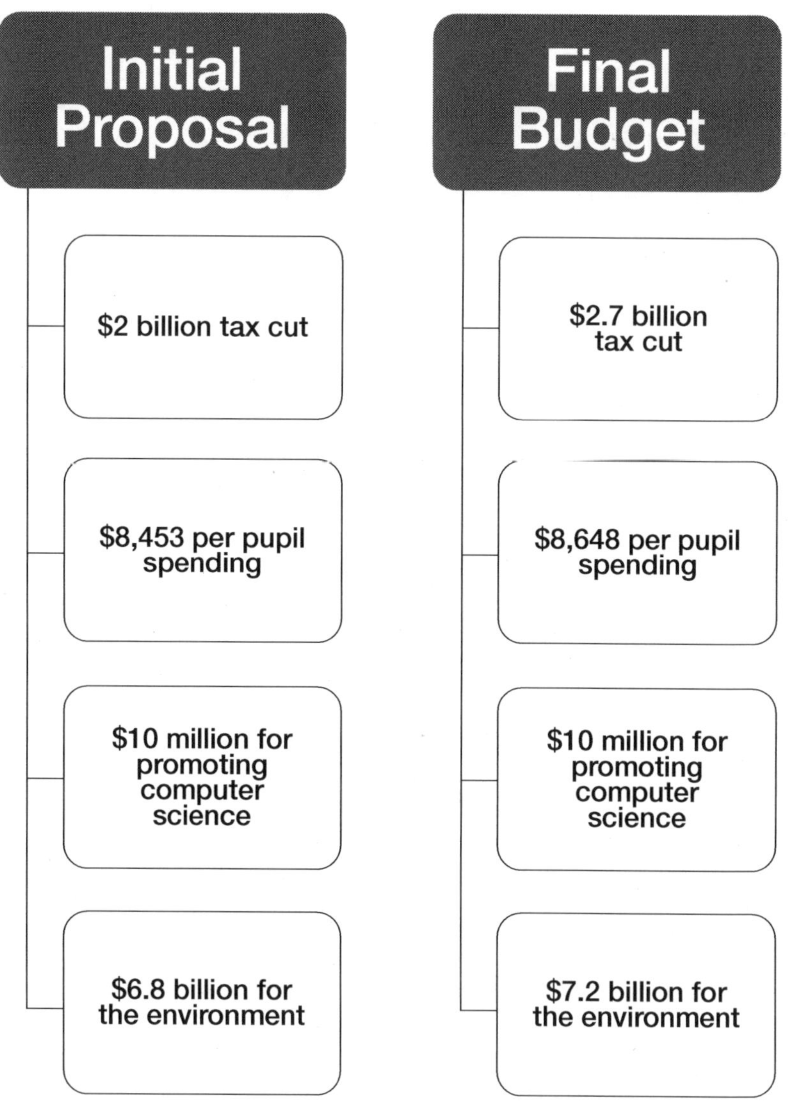

our state budget communicates the priorities of the state government for the next year. Now it is time to think about Hamiltonia's budget. What do you think the most pressing issues are in Hamiltonia? How will Hamiltonia balance raising revenue with spending on these pressing issues? Budgets are not easy, but keep in mind what you want Hamiltonia to prioritize in the next year.

Simulation

For the rest of the chapter, we will detail the various components of state budgets and you will have to decide what Hamiltonia's first official budget will look like.

Revenues

Before states can decide how much they are going to spend, they need to know how they are going to raise revenue. Unlike the federal government, most states must balance their budgets (remember all the way back to chapter 2!), meaning that they can only spend how much they take in from revenue. States have different strategies for raising money and these strategies have consequences. Some states take more aggressive approaches to raising revenues. These states are considered high tax states, but with more revenue states may be able to spend more on services to residents. Take New Jersey for example. New Jersey is a high-tax state. Combined with local revenue, in 2017 the average revenue per capita was $11,513. Florida has taken a different approach to raising revenue. Florida is a low-tax state. In 2017, the average state and local revenue per capita was $7,919. However, New Jersey ranks eighteenth in low birth weight—an important health metric—and Florida ranks thirty-fourth.[9]

Elected officials have to balance multiple interests when devising the state's taxing strategy. Elected officials must consider the economic effects, the equity effects, as well as other effects that may be realized from different strategies. For example, elected officials may not want to raise taxes too much because it could reduce family spending power in the state. Elected officials also might want to consider whether the tax is **progressive** or **regressive**. Progressive taxes are ones in which wealthier individuals pay a greater portion. Regressive taxes are the opposite in that poorer individuals pay a greater share. Sometimes taxes that seem the same across individuals might actually affect taxpayers differently. For example, if a state has a seven-cent sales tax on school supplies every family will pay an extra seven cents when buying school supplies. However, that seven cents makes up a larger portion of the income of a family making $40,000 a year compared to a family making $200,000 a year. Therefore, this might be considered a regressive tax because it has a greater impact on lower income families. Elected officials must consider the impact taxes might have on their constituents.

States have to consider the kind of strategy they want in building their revenue. Do they want to gather taxes primarily through a sales tax or an income tax? There are tradeoffs to each approach, and it may depend on the industry or natural resources of a state. In Florida, for example, one of the main industries is tourism. It makes sense that the state of Florida would want to rely more heavily on a sales tax—oftentimes paid by visitors from other states—than a direct income tax on their own residents. Similarly, if a state is trying to attract businesses to the state—let's say a business like Amazon—the state may want to reduce its revenue from a corporate income tax and rely on other sources for revenue. As representatives from Hamiltonia, you need to think through what kind of tax state you want Hamiltonia to be. We will walk through the different ways states can raise revenue. Make sure to think about what sources of revenue you think Hamiltonia should rely on.

We draw from the Urban Institute on the sources for state revenue to understand the different sources states can use to raise money. States can choose from a personal income tax, sales tax, a selective sales tax, property tax, charges and fees, and a corporate income tax. See Table 9.1 for a list and explanation for each of these taxes. For Hamiltonia, you will need to decide what percent of the revenue will be gathered from each source. Let's turn to each type of revenue.

Table 9.1
State Tax Options

TAX NAME	DESCRIPTION	AVERAGE PERCENT OF TOTAL REVENUE[1]
Personal Income Tax	Tax on resident's income	17%
Sales Tax	Tax on certain products that residents purchase	15%
Selective Income Tax	Tax on specific goods, such as cigarettes, to discourage consumption	7%
Property Tax	Tax on owned properties, such as on a home you own	5%
Charges and Fees	Fees for certain services, such as a driver's license.	11%
Corporate Income Tax	Tax on the income of a business	2%

[1] "State and Local Revenues," The Urban Institute, https://www.urban.org/policy-centers/cross-center-initiatives/state-and-local-finance-initiative/state-and-local-backgrounders/state-and-local-revenues, accessed December 15, 2023. These categories may include smaller tax categories as well.

Income Taxes

One of the most common ways states raise revenues is through a **personal income tax**. An income tax is one in which an individual's income is taxed. We pay a federal income tax, but those of us living in forty-three states also pay a state income tax. Income taxes account for about 17 percent of state revenues, but this varies by state. States may want to raise revenue this way because it is a relatively efficient and easy way to collect revenue. Taxing income, however, means that individuals will take home less pay. If you have too high of an income tax, it may hurt a family's ability to spend that money in the economy.

The Tax Foundation has provided information on how states have structured their income tax. States take two different strategies when it comes to an income tax. States can have either a flat tax (11 states) or a graduated income tax (30 states). A flat tax rate means that everyone pays the same income tax rate. For example, in Colorado the state income tax rate is 4.40 percent. This means that no matter how much income you make in Colorado your state income tax will be 4.40 percent of your income. Other states have tax brackets where you pay a different percentage of income tax based upon how much money you make. In Massachusetts if you file your taxes as an individual you would pay 5 percent if you made less than $1 million and 9 percent on income over $1 million. Different states, however, have a different number of categories and a different tax rate for each. Some states, such as Kansas, have three rates at 3.10 percent, 5.25 percent, and 5.70 percent. Other states, such as Georgia, have six categories at 1 percent, 2 percent, 3 percent, 4 percent, 5 percent, and 5.75 percent. Figure 9.2 shows the states with no tax, a flat tax, or a graduated income tax and Table 9.2 shows the top marginal income rates in each state.[10] If you use a graduated income tax you may have a progressive tax which taxes higher income individuals at higher rates.[11]

Some states may rely more or less on income taxes in their overall revenue strategy. According to the Tax Foundation, states rely on income taxes for anywhere between zero (Florida) to 42.8 percent (Oregon) of their total revenue. Many of the states' budgets consist of anywhere between 20 and 35 percent of revenue coming from an income tax. States may want to use the income tax because it is easy to collect, and states may design it to be a progressive tax. However, many states without an income tax, such as Florida, use it to attract people to the state of Florida.

Figure 9.2

Personal Income Tax across the States

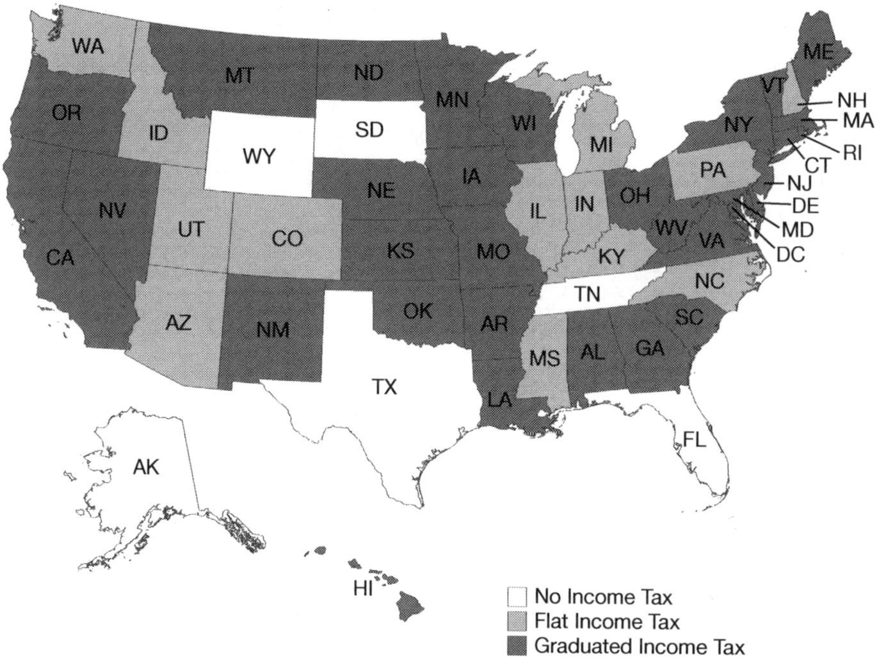

No Income Tax
Flat Income Tax
Graduated Income Tax

Action Item

9-1

What percentage of Hamiltonia's revenue will come from the personal income tax? If you have an income tax, will it be a flat rate or graduated tax?

Sales Tax

Another main way that states raise revenue is through a **sales tax**. A sales tax is a tax on items that you purchase. You may have noticed that when you go to the store to buy a new coat the tag might say $100, but when you pay at the register it comes out to $107. How did that happen? Well, the state might charge a tax on sales of items like your coat. Both state and local governments can collect sales tax revenue. What this means is that the total sales tax that you owe may depend both upon what state you are in but also what locality within the state you are in. Most states—except for five—have a sales tax. However,

Table 9.2
Percent of State and Local Revenue from Income Tax

STATE	% OF STATE REVENUE FROM INCOME TAX	STATE	% OF STATE REVENUE FROM INCOME TAX
Oregon	42.8	Alabama	23.4
Maryland	37.8	Hawaii	23.3
California	35.4	Arkansas	23
New York	34.7	Oklahoma	23
Kentucky	33.9	Nebraska	22.9
Massachusetts	33.8	New Jersey	22.8
Virginia	33.2	Kansas	22.6
Minnesota	33	Rhode Island	21.7
Connecticut	32.1	Maine	21.6
Delaware	31	Vermont	20.7
Utah	30.5	Illinois	20.2
North Carolina	29.8	Arizona	16.6
Montana	28.8	Mississippi	16.5
Missouri	28.5	Louisiana	15.9
Georgia	28.4	New Mexico	14.5
Wisconsin	28	North Dakota	6.4
Idaho	27.2	New Hampshire	1.5
Ohio	26.7	Tennessee	1.1
West Virginia	26	Alaska	0
Pennsylvania	25.9	Florida	0
Colorado	25.2	Nevada	0
Iowa	24.6	South Dakota	0
Michigan	24.5	Texas	0
Indiana	23.6	Washington	0
South Carolina	23.5	Wyoming	0

SOURCE: Janelle Fritts, "To What Extent Does Your State Rely on Individual Income Taxes," The Tax Foundation, February 10, 2021, https://taxfoundation.org/data/all/state/state-income-tax-reliance-2021/, accessed December 15, 2023.

the sales tax does differ across states. States sales tax ranges from 2.9 percent in Colorado all the way to 7.25 percent in California. Even though Colorado has a low state sales tax rate, localities in Colorado can also raise revenue through sales tax. Therefore, in Colorado residents may be paying 7.791 percent when factoring in the average local sales tax.[12]

We draw from the Tax Foundation to understand how sales tax makes up a state's overall revenue strategy. State budgets range from relying on sales tax revenue from 0 to 42.3 percent in Louisiana in their total revenues. As noted above, Florida does not have an income tax, but it does rely heavily on a sales tax. Thirty-eight percent of Florida's budget relies on sales tax revenue. This makes sense for a state that relies heavily on tourism as a main industry because visitors will be paying taxes to the state of Florida every time they buy something in the state. In this way, Florida capitalized on tourism to pay taxes. Table 9.3 shows the five states that rely most on sales tax as part of their revenue and the five states that rely on sales tax the least. This excludes the states without a sales tax.

States, however, do not necessarily tax all products. Remember from our state spotlight in this chapter that part of Governor DeSantis' budget included a tax holiday—or a suspension of the sales tax—on certain items such as baby products and kids' books.

Table 9.3
Percent of Revenue from Sales Tax

TOP 5 STATES		LOWEST 5 STATES	
State	*Percent of Revenue from Sales Tax*	*State*	*Percent of Revenue from Sales Tax*
Louisiana	42.30%	Massachusetts	13.5%
Nevada	41.30%	Virginia	13%
Tennessee	40.70%	Maryland	12%
Arizona	40.50%	Vermont	10.4%
South Dakota	39.30%	Alaska	6.9%

SOURCE: Janelle Fritts, "To What Extent Does Your State Rely on Sales Tax," The Tax Foundation, January 27, 2021, https://taxfoundation.org/data/all/state/state-sales-tax-reliance-2021/, accessed December 15, 2023.

One reason to only apply the sales tax to specific items is because a sales tax is a regressive tax. Although the sales tax applies to everyone equally, paying the sales tax requires a greater proportion of income from a low-income family compared to a high-income family. Sometimes states exempt certain necessary products to help reduce the tax burden on low-income families.[13] In Hamiltonia, you will want to think about how much the state will rely on a sales tax and whether any exemptions will be in place to ameliorate the regressiveness of the tax.

Action Item

9-2

What percentage of Hamiltonia's revenue will come from a sales tax? If Hamiltonia has a sales tax, are any items exempt? If so, which ones?

Sin Taxes

States may also raise revenue from a special type of sales tax called the selective sales tax. Selective sales taxes are also known as **sin taxes** which are taxes on certain products that are meant to discourage consumption. The most common sin taxes that states have are taxes on alcohol and cigarettes. States tax these items to raise revenue and discourage behavior as both alcohol and cigarette use can result in negative health outcomes. Tobacco taxes can be effective in reducing smoking rates especially among young people, but not necessarily among all groups including long-term smokers.[14] Just like with the personal income tax, the federal government also has its own sales tax on tobacco at $1.01 a pack.[15] States levy additional taxes on tobacco although at different rates. Four states tax a pack of tobacco at less than fifty cents a pack, nine states tax a pack under $1, eight states tax a pack under $1.50, seven states tax a pack under $2, seventeen states under $4, and three states—New York, Connecticut, and Rhode Island—tax each pack of cigarettes over $4. Mind you, this is not the total cost of a pack but the tax on top of the cost of each pack of cigarettes.

When considering a selective sales tax, states must balance reducing unwanted behavior with industry in the states. To no one's surprise, the two top producers of tobacco—North Carolina and Virginia—tax a pack of cigarettes at forty-five cents and sixty cents, respectively. This can be more complicated in other states. California, typically a high-tax state, taxes cigarettes at $2.87 a pack. However, when it comes to alcohol the state only taxes wine at $.20 but distilled alcohol at $3.30.[16] In fact, California is tied with Texas for the lowest tax on wine. This may seem out of character for California but consider California's economic landscape. California is home to Napa and Sonoma Valley which are major wine producing regions in the United States and in the world. Although California typically takes an aggressive approach to taxation, it does not do so on wine because of the industry in the state.

Action Item

9-3

Does Hamiltonia have a sin tax? If so, on what products? What percent of Hamiltonia's total revenue will come from a sin tax?

Property Taxes

States might also rely on **property taxes** for raising revenue. Property taxes are taxes on property you own. For example, if you own a house you pay property taxes on that home each year. Typically, you pay a percent of the assessed value of your home. Therefore, families living in more expensive homes typically pay more in property tax. How much you pay, however, depends both on the state and locality you live within. That's right—localities play a major role in property taxes. Therefore, the county you live in is an important component of your property taxes. For example, if you live in Bergen County in New Jersey the median property tax is over $10,000. However, if you live in Cumberland County your median property tax rate is $4,671. In some states, the median property tax rate is much lower. For example, in some counties in Louisiana the median property tax is between $200–300.[17]

How much a state relies on property taxes varies. In 2017, it ranged from 7.1 percent (Alabama) to 38.3 percent (New Hampshire).[18] Remember localities also depend upon property tax revenue to fund their expenditures. In fact, property tax is often used to fund public schools. One issue with this is that low-income areas have a hard time generating the same amount of revenue from property tax as high-income areas. Property taxes can allow you to gain income from more expensive homes, but it also has repercussions at the local level that you may want to consider. The map in Figure 9.3 shows how much states rely on property tax in their overall tax revenue strategy.

Figure 9.3
Map of Reliance on Property Taxes as a Percent of General Revenue

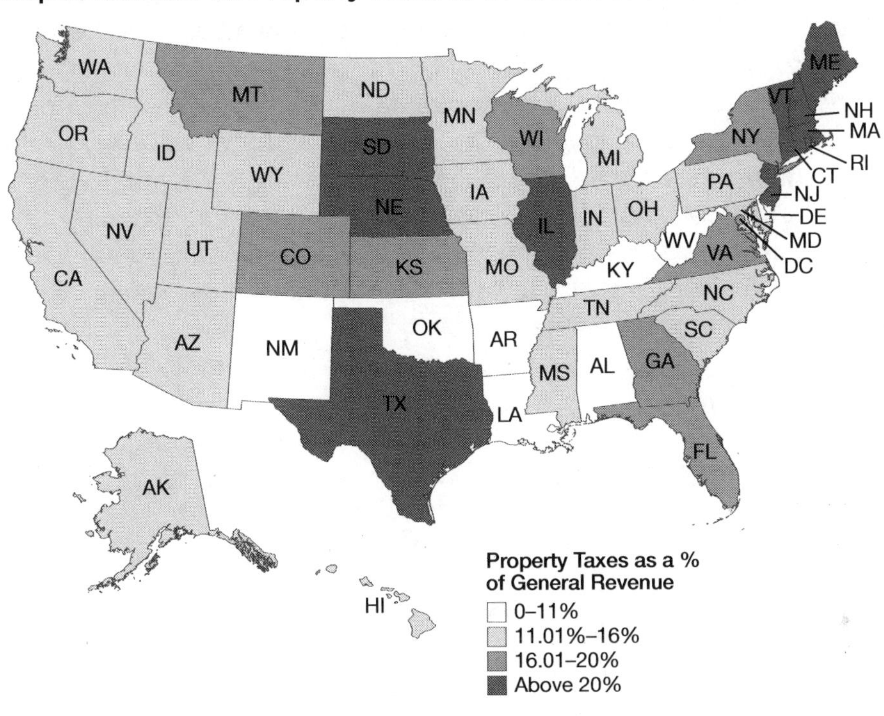

SOURCE: "Summary—State and Local Property Tax Revenue by State 2017," Lincoln Institute of Land Policy.

Action Item

9-4

Does Hamiltonia have a property tax? If so, what percentage of the total revenue will come from the property tax?

Corporate Taxes and Charges and Fees

States may tax corporate income to make up part of their revenue. The **corporate income tax** is a tax on income from businesses. Although most states—forty-six to be exact—have a corporate income tax, these taxes tend to make up a small portion of total state revenue. In fact, the Urban Institute reports that it constitutes about 2 percent of state revenue. In the majority of states, corporate income tax makes up 1–2 percent of their revenue portfolio. Some states, however, rely a bit more on corporate income tax with New Hampshire and Connecticut relying on this tax to make up 5.8 percent and 4.5 percent of their revenue, respectively.[19] In a handful of states, the state government also allows localities to gather corporate income tax. For example, New York City can levy a corporate income tax.[20] States may be hesitant to rely too heavily on corporate income taxes because states desire to attract business. Raising taxes too high on businesses may create an unfriendly business environment which states typically want to avoid. For example, Delaware has worked hard to earn the reputation of a business friendly state. CNBC reports that it "is home to more than 60% of Fortune 500 companies,"[21] Delaware has accomplished this not just through taxes, but also by having "a separate court system specifically for handling corporate cases."[22]

Finally, states may also rely on **charges and fees** to collect revenue. If you have paid a toll to drive on a road, you have paid a charges and fees tax. Remember from our state spotlight, Florida's budget included $500 million in toll relief. This was meant to alleviate the tax burden of people who travel on toll roads. Most of the charges and fees come from "hospital fees (charges collected from patients, private insurance companies, and public insurance programs such as Medicare), higher education payments (mostly tuition payments plus money spent on dormitories, athletic contests, and books)," and highways.[23] Overall charges and fees typically make up around 16 percent of the total revenue for a state. However, this varies across states. South Carolina is most dependent upon charges and fees with this tax making up 26 percent of its total revenue. Because charges and fees apply equally across individuals it may be a regressive tax. Think about tolls for example. Everyone, no matter their income, pays the same amount at a toll booth. However, this charge is a greater share of someone's income if they are low-income rather than if they are high-income.

Each state has a different approach to how it will raise revenue. This can depend on a variety of factors. Going back to our example at the beginning of this section, Florida and New Jersey are two different states with two different revenue approaches. Below in Table 9.4 you can compare the different revenue strategies of both states. This will help you think about how Hamiltonia might be characterized based on your decisions in this simulation.

You may have noticed that the percent of revenue does not add up to 100 percent. Where does the other money come from? It comes from the federal government. States increasingly rely on funds from

Table 9.4
Comparison between Florida and New Jersey Revenue Strategy

TAX	FLORIDA	NEW JERSEY
Personal Income Tax[1]	0%	10.75%
Sales Tax[2]	7.02%	6.60%
Sin Tax (Tobacco)[3]	1.339	2.7
Property Tax[4]	.91%	2.23%
Corporate Income Tax[5]	5.50%	9.00%
Intergovernmental Transfers[6]	38.0%	29.3%

[1] Vermeer, "State Individual Income Tax Rates and Brackets for 2023."

[2] "State and Local Tax Rates, Midyear 2023," The Tax Foundation, July 17, 2023, https://taxfoundation.org/data/all/state/2023-sales-tax-rates-midyear/, accessed Dec 15, 2023.

[3] "State System Excise Tax Fact Sheet," Center for Disease Control and Prevention.

[4] Yushkov, "Where Do People Pay the Most in Property Taxes?" includes "Property Taxes Paid as a Percentage of Owner-Occupied Housing Value, 2021."

[5] "State Corporate Income Tax Rates," Tax Policy Center Urban Institute and Brookings Institute, March 24, 2023, https://www.taxpolicycenter.org/statistics/state-corporate-income-tax-rates, accessed December 15, 2023.

[6] Rebecca Thiess, Justin Theal, and Kate Watkins, "Pandemic Aids Lifts Federal Share of State Budgets to New Highs," Pew, August 28, 2023, https://www.pewtrusts.org/en/research-and-analysis/articles/2023/08/28/pandemic-aid-lifts-federal-share-of-state-budgets-to-new-highs, accessed December 15, 2023.

the federal government for their state budgets. When the federal government distributes money to the states it is called **intergovernmental transfers**. Then, the state may distribute these funds to local governments. This is a key component of intergovernmental relations in the United States. State and federal programs like Medicaid—health insurance for low-income persons—are designed so that the state government runs the Medicaid program, but the federal government pays a portion of the Medicaid cost. Intergovernmental transfers are the portion of the program cost that the federal government pays to the state to continue providing the program. Sometimes the amount of the intergovernmental transfers varies across years, but it is typically around 25 percent of the state revenue. Intergovernmental transfers are a critical part of state budgets and states depend upon them to run their programs and policies.

Action Item

9-5

Does Hamiltonia have a corporate income tax? If so, what percentage of the total revenue will come from the corporate income tax?

Action Item

9-6

Does Hamiltonia use charges and fees to raise revenue? If so, what percentage of the total revenue will come from charges and fees?

As seen in Figure 9.4, the amount of intergovernmental revenue does vary a bit across states depending upon programs. Recently, intergovernmental revenue has been higher than usual because of COVID funding. For this year, Hamiltonia is receiving 25 percent of its budget from federal government transfers. Therefore, you need to determine how the other taxes will make up the other 75 percent of the state budget.

Figure 9.4

Number of States Receiving a Portion of Revenue from Intergovernmental Transfers FY 2019

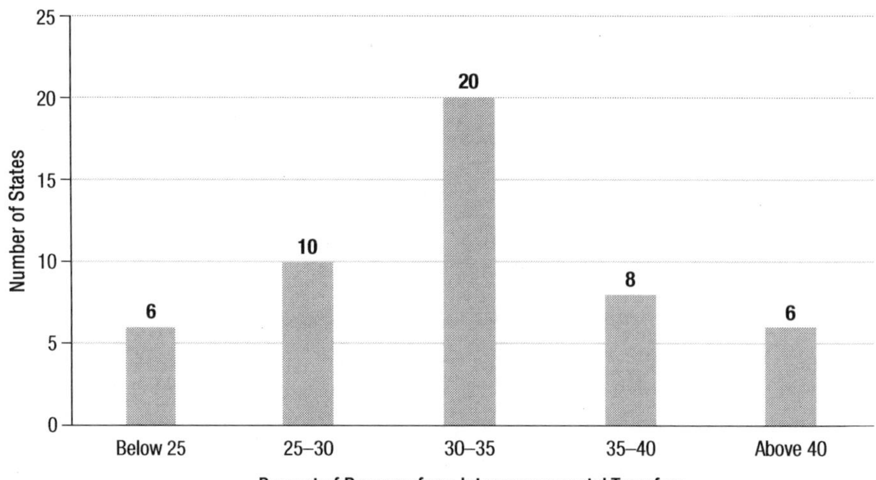

SOURCE: Rebecca Thiess, Justin Theal, and Kate Watkins, "Pandemic Aids Lifts Federal Share of State Budgets to New Highs." Pew Charitable Trusts, www.pewtrusts.org/en/research-and-analysis/articles/2023/08/28/pandemic-aid-lifts-federal-share-of-state-budgets-to-new-highs.

Expenditures

The second half of the budget includes how the state is going to spend the money that it raised in revenue. Deciding how the state is going to spend money is often contentious because we have limited resources to fund the initiatives that we care about. Remember the budget outlines our priorities so it is an important statement about what we value. To help us understand state budget priorities, we are going to discuss the large categories of state expenditures. For Hamiltonia, you will need to decide what percent of the expenditures is going to go to each of these categories.

For a long time, the largest portion of state budgets went to fund education. More recently, health has become the largest expenditure for many states. Drawing upon the Urban Institute, we are going to discuss the major categories of state spending including health and public welfare, education, highways, and police and corrections. As we discuss each of these categories, think about what you want Hamiltonia to spend the most money on. What is the most pressing issue in Hamiltonia? In your district? Make sure to consider the interests of your constituents if you are a legislator and the interests of your department if you are part of the governor's cabinet.

Health and Public Welfare

Health and public welfare have become one of the largest categories of expenditures in recent history. The program that makes up a large part of state health expenditures is the Medicaid program. Medicaid is a state-federal program that provides health insurance to low-income Americans. The federal government provides financial support for the Medicaid program—the amount depends on the per capita income of the state—and the states provide some financial support as well as are responsible for running the program. Your eligibility for Medicaid depends on certain criteria including your income. Therefore, some states have more or less Medicaid beneficiaries. The program that makes up a large portion of public welfare spending is Temporary Assistance for Needy Families (TANF)—what we traditionally think of as welfare. TANF is also a state-federal program where states can make important decisions about how the program operates. The federal government provides financial support (intergovernmental transfers) for the program.

Health and public welfare are a major expenditure category for the states. In 2020, the combined share of expenditures that went to health and hospitals and public welfare was about 32.5 percent of all state expenditures. Because this category includes Medicaid and TANF, intergovernmental transfers provide some of this expenditure money. However, states may have a more difficult time cutting spending in this category. According to the rules of the program, some individuals or families may qualify for Medicaid or TANF and are thus entitled to these benefits. States do try different innovations to lower the cost of Medicaid or reduce the number of individuals on Medicaid, but there are certain federal requirements that prevent states from disqualifying certain individuals. For example, the federal government requires states cover pregnant women at 133 percent of the federal poverty line.[24] Because of this, some portion of the cost of Medicaid is dependent upon how many residents qualify for the program in a given year. As we saw in the state spotlight, the Florida legislature lowered the amount of money for Medicaid because they anticipated lower enrollment in the coming year. You need to decide how much of Hamiltonia's expenditures will go to health and welfare, but you are not able to assign less than 25 percent to this area because of federal eligibility requirements.

Action Item

9-7

What percent of expenditures will be dedicated to health and public welfare?

Education

The next major expenditure category that states have to consider is education. States have long spent a large share of their expenditures funding their public K–12 education system and higher education system. As we saw from the state spotlight in this chapter, education spending including money for teacher salaries and computer science classes are a major part of a governor's focus. In 2020, states spent about 21.2 percent of their revenue on K–12 education and 9.2 percent of revenue on higher education. States share the cost of education with localities as well. In 2021, about 44 percent of K–12 funding was provided by local governments. The federal government also makes intergovernmental transfers in this area but it only accounts for about 11 percent of K–12 spending.[25] Although localities fund a portion of the school cost, the state is also responsible for providing a significant share of resources.

The percentage each state dedicates to education and the per pupil expenditures differ across states. The more a state spends per pupil, the more money the state will spend on education. Remember

Florida's budget fight? The final budget raised the amount of spending per pupil by about $200 from the governor's original proposal. This does not seem like much, but it led to an increase of about $800 million to the total budget. Figure 9.5 shows how much states spend per pupil. Most states spend between $10,000 and $20,000 per pupil, but this varies. For example, Idaho, Utah, Arizona, and Oklahoma all spent less than $10,000 per pupil in 2020. Other states, however, spent more than $20,000 per pupil including Vermont, New York, New Jersey, and Delaware.[26] Of course the total education spending depends upon the amount spent per pupil and the total number of pupils in the state.

Because funding comes from local, state, and federal sources, there is variation in spending across states but also within states. The way that states choose to fund their schools has the potential to alleviate or exacerbate inequities in school funding. The Education Trust reports that:

> In 20 states, the highest poverty districts received at least 5 percent more in state and local funds than the lowest poverty districts. In six states, the highest poverty districts received at least 15 percent more funding per student than the lowest poverty districts. . . . At the other end of the spectrum, there are four states where the highest poverty districts received substantially less in state and local funding than their lowest poverty counterparts.[27]

Figure 9.5

Spending per Pupil

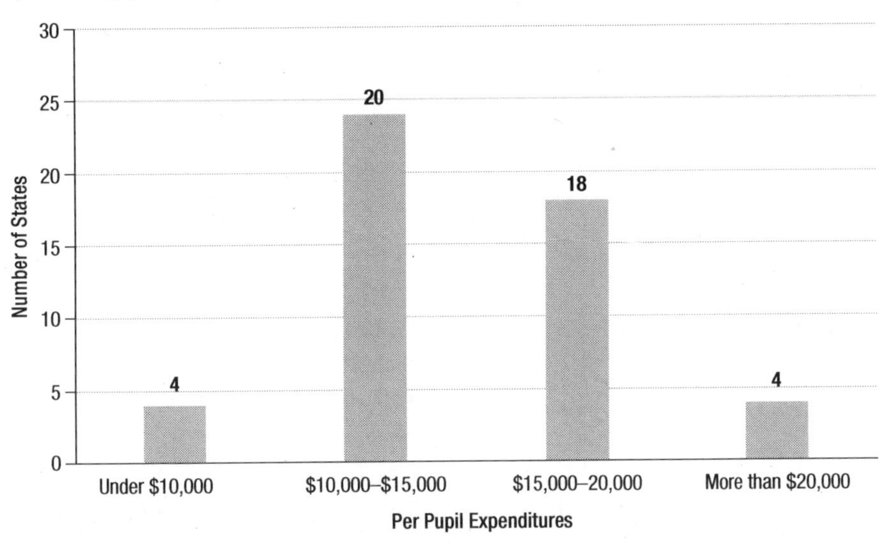

SOURCE: www.urban.org/policy-centers/cross-center-initiatives/state-and-local-finance-initiative/state-and-local backgrounders/elementary-and-secondary-education-expenditures

In Hamiltonia, you may want to consider how state education funding may address equity in education funding. Remember from chapter 1 that Hamiltonia has just under 1.1 million K–12 students and is ranked nineteenth and twenty-sixth based on fourth grade reading and math tests. Think about what percent of the budget you want to go to education knowing that will determine the amount of money the state spends per pupil.

Action Item

9-8

What percent of expenditures will be dedicated to education? Will district funding vary on high or low poverty status? If so, how much more will high-poverty districts receive in state funding than low-poverty districts?

Highways and Roads

Another major category of state expenditures are highways and roads. The Urban Institute reports that in 2020 almost 6 percent of expenditures were dedicated to highways and roads. This spending is divided into two categories. More than half of the spending (57%) went to building new roads while about 43 percent went for maintenance and safety.[28] States are not the only ones on the hook for roads. Local governments also contribute about 40 percent of the spending. Still, states differ on what percent of their expenditures is dedicated to highways and roads. Having roads that are safe and well maintained is important to Hamiltonia's residents' overall experience in the state. Poor roads can damage cars and lack of roads can hurt transportation efforts.

A recent survey conducted by the Hamiltonia Department of Transportation (HDT) found that 61 percent of residents agreed Hamiltonia needed to do more to improve road quality (i.e., fixing potholes). Because local governments are typically responsible for local roads, this varies by locality. Residents in Charlestown, Burr City, and Reynolds were most likely to agree that Hamiltonia needed to improve the roads. Charlestown has seen significant growth in the past three years which has been causing traffic issues. Interstate 70 has been crowded and there are proposals to add a lane on both sides of the highway to reduce congestion. The estimated cost is $1 billion.

Roads and road quality are important components of local and state governance. It matters not only for Hamiltonia families but also for industries to be able to transport goods efficiently. Just recently, the Rhode Island Department of Transportation closed a bridge that supports 96,000 vehicles each day. Part of the bridge was failing which could have led to "'catastrophic failure,' RIDOT Director Peter Alviti said."[29] Maintaining roads and bridges is an important function of state government and makes an important impact on residents' lives.

Action Item

9-9

What percent of expenditures will be dedicated to highways and roads?

Criminal Justice

A final spending category we want to cover is the criminal justice system. States spend significant expenditures on police, corrections, and the courts. Combined, these categories make up 7.7 percent of expenditures. As you will see in chapter 12 on the criminal justice system, the police, jails and prisons, and the courts all make up different components of criminal justice.

This is another area of expenditures that localities and states share. State expenditures largely contribute to highway patrols and localities are responsible for funding their local police forces.[30] States are responsible for more of the corrections spending which is spending dedicated to prisons. Criminal justice spending also includes spending on the courts—funding public defenders and prosecutions. This spending, however, varies by state. Florida spends the greatest portion of its budget (7.3%) on police and corrections. This comes out to about $15.1 billion. Other states that spend a lot on police and corrections include Nevada (7%), Maryland (6.3%), and California (5.7%). Other states, such as Kentucky and Iowa, spend less per capita.

As discussed in chapter 1, Hamiltonia overall has lower crime rates than other states. However, this is due to lower property crime. Hamiltonia's violent crime rate is 339 per 100,000 and they rank twenty-eighth overall in gun violence. One of the reasons that the violence crime rate is high is due to the murder of females which is primarily a result of domestic violence. The Hamiltonia chapter of the Municipal Police Association is lobbying for $300 million to train police in domestic violence response with the hopes of reducing domestic violence rates in the state.

Action Item

9-10

What percent of expenditures will be dedicated to police and corrections?

Looking Forward

Great job! You have just outlined the priorities of Hamiltonia this year and figured out how you were going to pay for all the important work that a state government does. Deciding how to raise revenue and how to spend taxpayer money is no easy task. These decisions have consequences for Hamiltonia residents both in terms of how much they pay in taxes and the kinds of services that they receive. This is an area that can be highly polarizing, leading to budget delays, like in North Carolina in 2023. Despite having veto-proof majorities in the House and Senate, the Republican majority in both chambers could not come to an agreement over tax cuts as well as certain spending measures. However, the delay in the budget meant other areas suffered as well, particularly teacher salary raises that were meant to attract more teachers to a field that is understaffed.[31] This is why it is so important to understand the state budgetary process.

Throughout the chapter you may have noticed that the federal and local governments also play a large role in state revenues and expenditures. States rely heavily on federal government money to provide some of the programs that their residents depend on such as Medicaid. At the same time, the federal government can rely on the states to pursue some of its priorities by providing money to run important programs. Local governments are important in these dynamics as well.

North Carolina Attorney General Josh Stein speaks at a news conference while state House Democratic members watch at the Legislative Building in Raleigh, NC, Wednesday, July 12, 2013. Stein and other Democrats criticized Republican legislators for failing to approve a two-year state budget before the new fiscal year began July 1.

SOURCE: AP Photo/Gary D. Robertson

Local governments also raise revenue and contribute important funding for a variety of services including roads, police, and K–12 education spending. It would be very difficult for a state to pursue its priorities without working with both the federal and local governments.

Now that you have decided the overall budget for Hamiltonia, you will be getting into the nitty-gritty of policymaking in the areas of education, health, environment, and criminal justice. In this chapter you have set up how much money each policy area has been allocated, now it is time to decide where that money should go. We start first with education policy.

Key Terms

revenues (180)
expenditures (180)
fiscal year (180)
progressive tax (183)
regressive tax (183)
personal income tax (185)
sales tax (186)
sin tax (189)
property tax (190)
corporate income tax (191)
charges and fees (192)
intergovernmental transfers (193)

Assignments to Learn More about State Budgets

1. What does your home state's budget look like this year? What are the major initiatives that the governor or legislature emphasized? Did your budget change from the governor's original proposal? How?
2. Choose a public problem that you care about. Choose two states to compare and contrast their budgeting strategies with regard to the public problem that you chose. What are the two states doing to address this important issue?
3. Choose an expenditure category and research the ways in which localities, states, and the federal government contribute funding to that category. Which level of government plays the most significant role in funding this category? What are some of the advantages and disadvantages of funding in a federal system?

Lorena Paulino, center, a senior at Charlestown High School students, walks out of her high school in Boston on March 7, 2016. Dozens of Charlestown High School students participated in a walk-out to protest public school funding cuts in Boston on March 7, 2016. The students joined other Boston public school students in a march through the Boston Common to the Massachusetts State House.

SOURCE: Photo by Dina Rudick/The Boston Globe via Getty Images

10 Education Policy

Learning Objectives:

At the end of this chapter students should be able to:

- Understand and explain the role of state government in education policy.
- Explain ways that states are active policy makers in early childhood education and higher education.
- Explain differences in pre-k policy approaches across states.
- Explain differences in merit-based scholarship approaches across states.
- Understand the different ways states expand access to early childhood education and higher education.

State Spotlight: Massachusetts

Massachusetts is seen as a leading state in education and has been since before the founding of the nation. In the 1640s, Massachusetts established an elementary school that was free and funded by taxes. As elementary and secondary schools were established, local governance played a large role. After the nation was founded, schools were seen as essential for the development of citizenship. In the 1840s, Horace Mann became the secretary of the new State Board of Education and began to institute his philosophy in the Massachusetts education system including providing an education for all students funded by taxes and the professionalization of teaching.[1] During this time Massachusetts focused on expanding access to education including to those who were handicapped. For example, in 1867 Boston established a school for the deaf named after Horace Mann. In the 1870s, Massachusetts allowed women to attend university.[2]

Investing in public education not only benefits children but is also one of the most important—and expensive—services state governments provide. This means making policy in the area of education in the state of Hamiltonia is a fundamental responsibility of state governments, and one that should not be taken lightly. In fact, your right to a public education exists in state constitutions, not the federal constitution. Chapter 5 Section II of the Massachusetts Constitution states:

> Wisdom, and knowledge, as well as virtue, diffused generally among the body of the people, being necessary for the preservation of their rights and liberties; and as these depend on spreading the opportunities and advantages of education in the various parts of the country, and among the different orders of the people, it shall be the duty of legislatures and magistrates, in all future periods of this commonwealth, to cherish the interests of literature and the sciences, and all seminaries of them; especially the university at Cambridge, public schools and grammar schools in the towns; to encourage private societies and public institutions, rewards and immunities, for the promotion of agriculture, arts, sciences, commerce, trades, manufactures, and a natural history of the country; to countenance and inculcate the principles of humanity and general benevolence, public and private charity, industry and frugality, honesty and punctuality in their dealings; sincerity, good humor, and all social affections, and generous sentiments among the people.[3]

States, therefore, play a fundamental role in education policy.

Today, Massachusetts has the Department of Elementary and Secondary Education which is tasked with the role of overseeing **K–12 public education** in the state. The department is led by the commissioner who is responsible for about 400 school districts.[4] Massachusetts also has a Board of Education made up of a student, nine members, and the secretary of education. The Board's mission is to "approv[e] learning standards, vot[e] on charter school applications, decid[e] when to intervene in the state's lowest-performing districts, and hir[e] the commissioner."[5] In addition, Massachusetts also has departments focused on early childhood education called the Department of Early Education and Care and higher education called the Department of Higher Education. In 2005, Massachusetts became "the first state in the nation to have a state-level department focused wholly on early education and care."[6] By creating additional departments, Massachusetts has designed its administrative departments to ensure an entire department is focused on each stage of a student's educational journey.

In the 2022–2023 school year Massachusetts had almost one million elementary and secondary education pupils, and thirty thousand pre-kindergarten students.[7] About 9 percent of their students are African American, 7 percent are Asian, 24 percent are Hispanic, and 54 percent are white. Their overall high school graduation rate was 90.1 percent but this varies among subgroups. Among low-income students the graduation rate was 83.2 percent and among English language learners the rate was 73.1 percent.[8] Figure 10.1 shows the racial and ethnic makeup of students in Massachusetts.

We also cannot forget that public schools are also an important source of employment in states. The Massachusetts Department of Education reported that there were 79,124 teachers employed in the state in 2023. These numbers do not include the 346 superintendents and 1,916 principals across the state. The average teacher salary in Massachusetts in 2021 was $87,071 and the total amount spent by the state on teacher salaries in that year was over $6 billion.[9]

Primary and secondary education are not the only levels of education state governments are responsible for; they also provide many postsecondary education opportunities for those who live in their state and for those who are interested in attending a public institution from outside of the state. In 2021, 26 percent of Massachusetts high school graduates attended a public four-year university, 25 percent a private four-year university, and 11 percent a two-year public university. In 2020, Massachusetts enrolled about 160,000 students in its public universities and 67,000 in their community colleges.[10] In the 2000s, Massachusetts adopted a state-funded merit-aid scholarship program called the John and Abigail Adams Scholarship.[11] Students in Massachusetts who score "Advanced" in math or English and score in the top 25 percent of the

Figure 10.1

Racial and Ethnic Diversity in Massachusetts

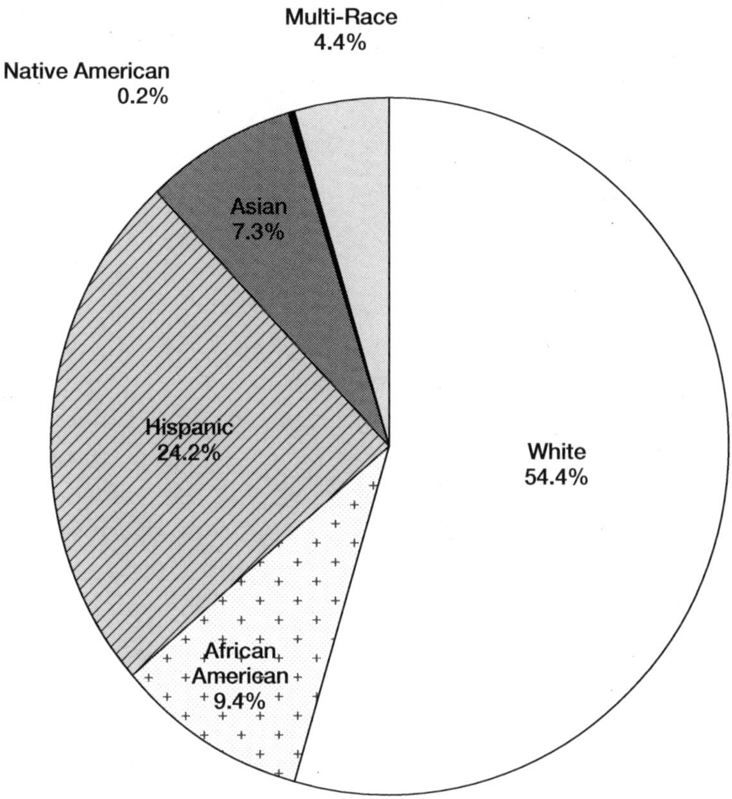

district are eligible for this scholarship to attend an in-state public university or college. Students must also be a citizen or have authorization from the federal government. The award amount is different based on the tuition at the institution that a student attends but is about $1,500 for a University of Massachusetts (UMass) school.[12]

In 2020, Massachusetts spent $18,733 per pupil while the national average was $13,494.[13] **Spending per pupil** varies by state and region, however. This can be seen in Table 10.1. Compared to the national average Massachusetts spends more per pupil. However, compared to the average in the region Massachusetts actually spends less per pupil. Massachusetts funds their schools using a combination of local, state, and federal funds. Funding alone, however, does not necessarily translate into better outcomes. Massachusetts may spend less per pupil than its neighboring states, but in 2022 students in Massachusetts performed better on national standardized tests.[14]

Table 10.1
Spending per Pupil by Region 2020

REGION	PER PUPIL SPENDING IN 2020
Midwest	$13,535
Northeast	$21,123
South	$10,954
West	$12,802

Massachusetts tends to be one of the top states in educational performance. Because states have primary authority over education, each state has different curriculum, standards, and ways of measuring academic performance. In Massachusetts students take the MCAS (Massachusetts Comprehensive Assessment System) once a year when they are in grades 3–8 and then again when they are in grade 10.[15] Students take an English and Language Arts and Mathematics exam.[16] In 2022, 6 percent of third graders exceeded expectations on the ELA exam, 38 percent met expectations, 41 percent partially met expectations, and 15 percent did not meet expectations. It is important to note that states themselves determine the testing and which scores count as exceeding or meeting expectations.[17] Students across the country also take what is called the National Assessment of Educational Progress (NAEP) in fourth, eighth, and twelfth grade. In 2022, the national average score on the grade four reading exam was 216 (out of 500). However, the average in Massachusetts was 227 which was the highest state average in the country. Massachusetts is ranked second in fourth grade math scores behind Wyoming.[18]

States are primary policy actors in education policy ranging from early education policy, K–12 policy, and higher education policy. States have taken many different policy approaches in attempting to provide high quality public education to its residents. The funding formula, curriculum, and standards are different across states. Where you live can play a big role in the types of educational programs that you have access to. Two ways states have been trying to expand educational opportunities is by providing pre-kindergarten education to residents and to provide state scholarship funding to attend in-state college and universities.

In the following sections we provide a background in each of these policy areas. Your class will have decided earlier in the simulation which education policy you will debate as the members of the Hamiltonia state government. After completing the reading below, the members of the legislature will work together to write a bill that will be reviewed and amended. The appendix contains the bill template that the legislature will use. At this same time, the governor will convene their cabinet where the members of the cabinet will discuss their stance on the issue and collectively will draft a memo to the legislature outlining the administration's priorities.

After the legislature has created a draft of the bill, the leadership will need to meet with the governor to discuss any differences between the law that has been drafted and what the governor wants in the bill. The governor and the legislative leadership should keep in mind the governor's veto powers that are outlined in the Hamiltonia Constitution. The legislature will then need to take a formal vote on the bill. If it passes it goes to the governor where they will need to decide whether to sign it, or veto it, with the extent of the veto power having been decided earlier during the Constitutional Convention. If the bill does not pass then the Hamiltonia legislature did not enact any education laws this legislative session and the simulation can move onto the next policy area.

Local Spotlight

A billboard with the current Dover Area School Board seeking reelection is seen above Main Street in Dover, PA, on election day Tuesday, November 8, 2005.

SOURCE: AP Photo/ Carolyn Kaster

As we discussed above, states have a lot of responsibility to provide a public education within the state. However, they do not work alone. Local governments also play a major role in education within the United States which began with the state of Massachusetts.[19] In addition to the federal Department of Education and state-level departments of education, school boards at the local level also make important policy decisions. Most states are divided into school districts which are run by school boards. The first school board was established in Massachusetts in 1826. The school board consists of a group of elected representatives that make decisions for the school district. The Illinois Association for School Boards notes three purposes including that the school board "legislates rules, it hears charges stemming from violations of those rules, it employs a superintendent and delegates the authority to administer the day-to-day operations of the schools to that person."[20] There are 19,254 school districts in the United States with a total of 98,609 schools. This, of course, differs across states. For example, Maryland has 25 school districts with 1,421 schools and Colorado has 272 school districts with 1,927 schools.[21]

School boards make decisions that affect the lives of K–12 students such as curricular and budgetary decisions. Because of this, school boards can be quite contentious. School boards have been in the center of controversy as we grapple with questions about how to approach critical race theory, mask mandates, what books should be allowed, and transgender rights in our schools. Much of the citizens' interaction with government will involve local government bodies such as school boards.

In many states it is possible for school board members to be **recall**ed. Remember from chapter 2 a recall election is an election to remove an elected official from their position prior to their term ending. Recall election rules are different across states, but they typically occur after a designated number of signatures in support of the recall election are gathered. Recall elections of school board members have been increasing.[22] Ballotpedia reports that in 2023 there were forty-eight school board recall elections. In 2022, voters in San Francisco recalled three board members for numerous controversial decisions including dedicating resources to renaming schools in the middle of the pandemic and changing admissions standards to the top high school in the district.[23] Because local school boards make such important decisions for the schools, they are often sites of controversy as a community with diverse views comes together to try to determine what we teach and how we teach our children.

Simulation

The rest of this chapter outlines the two different policies you could choose from for the area of education. We begin with pre-k policy. If your class chose to discuss college scholarships, head to that section.

Pre-K Policy

If you have chosen to put **pre-kindergarten** policy on Hamiltonia's agenda, you will want to read and consider this section carefully. We describe the history of pre-kindergarten policy as well as some of the components of a pre-kindergarten program that you may want to consider. If you are a legislator, make sure to check the demographics of your district and consider how important a pre-k program might be to your constituents. Keep in mind that even if your district has a lower number of school-age children, a considerable number of your constituents may work for a public school in some capacity.

Hamiltonia is considered a laggard in pre-k education. Although most states have a state-run and state-funded pre-k program, Hamiltonia does not. Advocates for pre-k have made attempts to establish a program, but budget difficulties have prevented the state from investing in early childhood education programs. The federal government has started programs like Race to the Top Early Learning Challenge and the Preschool Development Grant to help states fund and expand their pre-k programs. However, because Hamiltonia does not have a state-run program, it has not been able to take advantage of these funds.

Hamiltonia has 374,520 children (6% of the population) ages 0–5 who may benefit from a state funded pre-k program. Currently, Hamiltonia is ranked nineteenth in the nation based on fourth grade reading scores and twenty-sixth based on fourth grade mathematics scores. In 2023, 46 percent of kindergarteners were not prepared for kindergarten in Hamiltonia. Students who live in poverty and students who are English language learners are less likely to begin kindergarten prepared.[24] Fifty-four percent of African American students, 61 percent of Hispanic students, and 39 percent of white students were unprepared for kindergarten in Hamiltonia. Parents of young children tend to be in support of expanding early education opportunities. Childcare is expensive in Hamiltonia, costing families on average $9,480 per year or $7,110 for nine months. A lack of childcare or its expense is one reason some women decide to stay home with their children. As the Center for American Progress reports, "Mothers who were unable to find a childcare program were significantly less likely to be employed than those who found a childcare program, whereas there was no impact on fathers' employment."[25] This is a pressing policy issue for the government of Hamiltonia.

Background

In 1971, President Nixon vetoed the Childhood Development Act which sought to "establish a national system of comprehensive child development and daycare."[26] Congress was not able to override the veto, but activists did not stop there. Rather, proponents of early childhood education turned to the states to pursue their policy goals.[27] And, in response, states began adopting state funded pre-k programs in the 1980s, 1990s, and early 2000s. State pre-k programs are programs that are directed by the state whereby the state provides funding for education opportunities to four-year-olds at least two days per week.[28] Currently, forty-four states and Washington, DC have some form of state funded pre-k program. However, each program may have different components, requirements, and standards.

There are a number of arguments advocates make for expanding the government's role in early childhood education, particularly pre-k education. Many arguments rest on the Perry/High Scope and the Abecedarian study from the 1960s and 1970s that showed more positive outcomes for individuals that attended these early education programs such as better earnings, a greater likelihood of owning a home, and a greater likelihood of finishing high school.[29] These findings do not necessarily extend to different early childhood education programs. For example, a study conducted by Vanderbilt found that the benefits from pre-k did not last beyond third grade.[30] Others may argue that expanding pre-k opportunities may help boost kindergarten readiness—particularly among the most vulnerable four-year-olds—and reduce the achievement gap between African American and white students.[31] And still others may argue that expanding early educational opportunities can help women who want to enter the workforce, thereby helping families with the high cost of childcare.[32] Overall, state pre-k programs have garnered bipartisan support with both red and blue states adopting and expanding programs. However, there may be some disagreement in terms of how programs should be designed, who they should serve, and how much money the state should invest. We discuss these issues below.

There are two types of pre-k programs that states may have: universal and targeted programs. **Universal pre-k programs** are state programs that fund pre-k education for all four-year-olds in the state. Families and children do not have to qualify in any way to participate in the state funded program. Universal pre-k began in the state of Georgia in the 1990s. The governor, Zell Miller, wanted to establish a state lottery system. In order to overcome opposition to state sponsored gambling, Miller decided proceeds from the lottery would fund two education initiatives including a universal pre-k program. Since that time, a number of states have adopted universal pre-k programs.[33] Most states have adopted a **targeted pre-k program**. What this means is that four-year-olds must qualify in some way to participate in the state-funded program. Typically, requirements might include income level. However, states also have additional eligibility requirements such as English language learning status, disability, homelessness, a history of abuse, or other risk factors. Figure 10.2 shows the different kinds of programs states have.

Figure 10.2
State Pre-K Programs

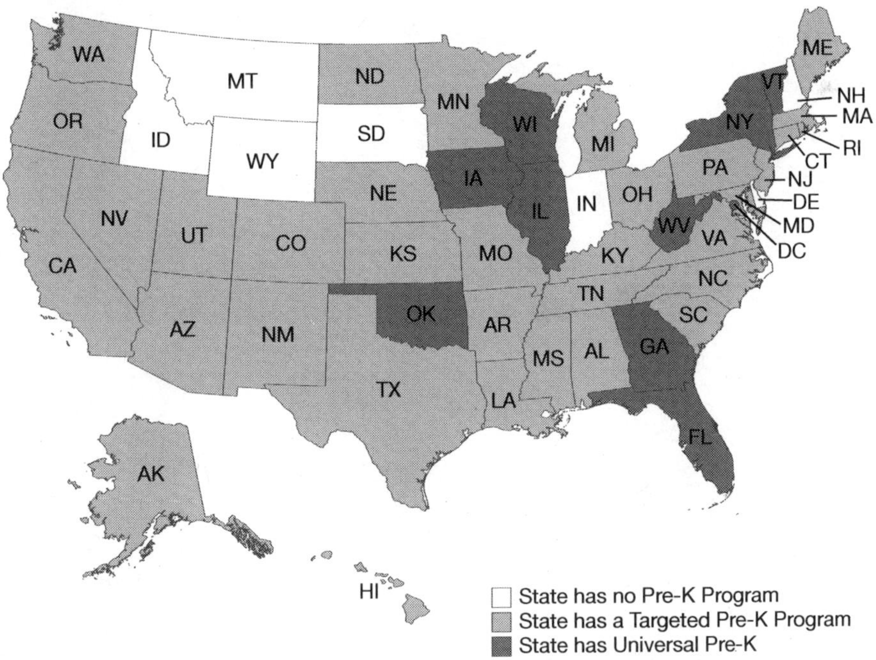

SOURCE: Steve Barnett and Rebecca Gomez, "Universal Pre-k: What Does It Mean and Who Provides It?" National Institute for Early Education Research, 2016, nieer.org/2016/01/06/universal-pre-k-what-does-it-mean-and-who-provides-it#:~:text=At%20present%2C%20only%20in%20Vermont,the%20state's%20pre%2DK%20program. There is debate over which states have universal pre-k. For example, Massachusetts used to have a universal pre-k grant. Alabama may or may not be considered to have universal pre-k. They do not have an income requirement, but do require a competitive grant process. Some states are moving toward universal pre-k. See state specific details in "The State of Preschool Yearbook 2022," https://nieer.org/the-state-of-preschool-yearbook-2022.

State programs vary in a variety of different ways including student eligibility, financial investment, and quality. The first major difference between state programs is their eligibility criteria. Surprisingly, states with universal pre-k do not always enroll more students than states with targeted programs. The map in Figure 10.3 shows the percentage of four-year-olds enrolled in each state's program. As you can see, some states with universal pre-k enroll a large percentage of four-year-olds like Florida (58%). However, states that have targeted programs have also been successful in enrolling many students. States like Kansas (39%) and Texas (41%) enroll many students without a universal program.

Eligibility

States with targeted programs may have different requirements meaning that you could live in one state and be eligible for the pre-k program and, in another state, not be eligible. For example, a student in Colorado qualifies for pre-k if their family income is 185 percent of FPL (federal poverty level) or they are on free or reduced-price lunch and in Delaware

Figure 10.3

Enrollment in State Pre-K Programs in 2021

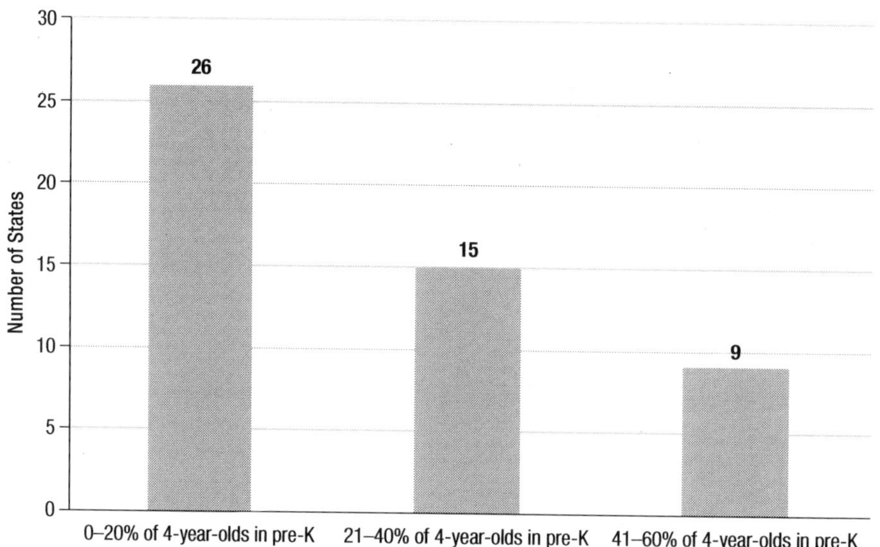

SOURCE: Data from Table 2 in Allison H. Friedman-Kraus, W. Steven Barnett, Karin A. Garver, Katherine S. Hodges, G. G. Weisenfeld, Beth Ann Gardiner, Tracy Merriman Jost, "The State of Preschool Yearbook 2021," National Institute for Early Education Research Rutgers Graduate School of Education, 2022, https://nieer.org/wp-content/uploads/2022/09/YB2021_Full_Report.pdf, pg. 15.

it is 100 percent of FPL. In Nevada, the income requirement is 200 percent of FPL but districts have flexibility in determining "eligibility based on highest need, which can include children from low-income families, those who are homeless, English Language Learners, or children receiving special education services" (111). In Utah, for example, a variety of risk factors can be considered for eligibility including homelessness, exposure to abuse, or other eligibility such as qualifying for free or reduced-price lunch or being an English Language Learner. In some states, such as Alabama, all four-year-olds are eligible if the district offers the state pre-k program.[34] States can consider all of these eligibility factors when implementing state pre-k programs. Furthermore, they can devolve authority and allow districts flexibility in determining who is eligible for the program. When states have fewer restrictions on eligibility, they may be able to enroll more students in the program. However, being able to enroll more students in the state's pre-k program also depends on state financial investment in the program. We take up finances below.

Action Item

10A-1

What type of pre-k program will you establish in Hamiltonia? Targeted or universal?

Action Item

10A-2

If targeted, who is eligible? Does the state determine eligibility or the districts?

Action Item

10A-3

What is the name of Hamiltonia's pre-k program?

Finances

States are typically different in the total amount of funds they dedicate to their pre-k program and in the amount they pay per student. This can be for a variety of reasons including fiscal constraints. Overall, in 2021 states spent almost 9 billion dollars on pre-k in 2021 and the average cost per pre-k student was $7,011. This varies widely across states, however. For example, Nevada spent about $18 million in 2020–2021 and about $9,000 per student. Other states, such as Florida, spent $302 million dollars and a little over $2,000 per student. States with universal programs or with a larger portion of the population under five will need to spend more resources on pre-k. Spending per pupil may include costs such as materials, teacher salaries, and curriculum. However, this can also depend on how much the state invests in each student. If states spend more per student, such as New Jersey at around $15,000 per student, the overall cost of pre-k each year will increase. States range in cost per student from $420 in North Dakota to $19,000 in DC.[35]

Some states have more or less control over how much money they dedicate to pre-k. Governor Miller pioneered universal pre-k by linking its funding to the state lottery. Many states have followed the governor's lead dedicating revenues from the state lottery system to education initiatives. In this funding scheme, states can only dedicate as much money as the lottery system generates to pre-k each year. Therefore, it may be difficult to increase the number of pre-k spots because it depends on how much money is raised through the lottery. However, linking the state lottery to pre-k spending may have advantages. States revisit their budget annually and, each year, programs may be cut or expanded. When the program funding is not connected to each year's budget decision, you may insulate the program by funding it through state lottery revenues. States have taken different approaches to funding pre-k. A few states, such as Connecticut, use funding from tobacco settlements to fund their pre-k programs. South Carolina has a 1 percent sales tax that funds its program.[36] Think about what funding structure would be the best for Hamiltonia.

Action Item

10A-4

How much will Hamiltonia invest per pre-k student?

Action Item

10A-5

Will Hamiltonia's pre-k program be funded by the state lottery?

Quality

Just as states have different rules for eligibility and different levels of funding, states also have varying levels of quality in terms of their state pre-k programs. Quality in pre-k programs is particularly important because it may help pre-k programs have stronger and longer lasting effects.[37] The National Institute for Early Education Research (NIEER) emphasizes ten quality benchmarks for state pre-k programs. These benchmarks are in Figure 10.4.

States have taken different approaches in balancing quality and enrollment. For example, Florida established its universal pre-k program, called VPK, after a constitutional amendment in 2002. In order to fulfill its responsibility, the state of Florida was very successful in expanding access to pre-k education in the state. However, Florida has only met two quality benchmarks including having early learning standards and a maximum class size. Rhode Island has taken a different approach. Rhode Island's pre-k program started in 2009. The state focused on quality first, reaching all ten benchmarks in 2010. However, Rhode Island only enrolls about 21 percent of students in pre-k in 2022.[38]

It takes time, money, expertise, and effort for states to establish high-quality programs. During that period of time, some students may not be able to access pre-k opportunities. This may ensure that

Figure 10.4

Pre-K Quality Benchmarks

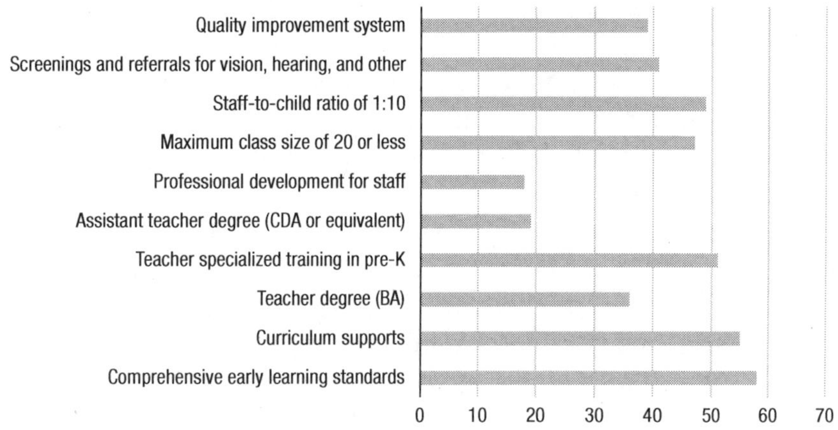

SOURCE: Data from Allison H. Friedman-Kraus, W. Steven Barnett, Karin A. Garver, Katherine S. Hodges, G. G. Weisenfeld, Beth Ann Gardiner, Tracy Merriman Jost, "The State of Preschool Yearbook 2021," National Institute for Early Education Research Rutgers Graduate School of Education, 2022, https://nieer.org/wp-content/uploads/2022/09/YB2021_Full_Report.pdf, pg. 15. Some states have more than one state funded pre-k program which is why in some cases there are more than 50 initiatives meeting the benchmark.

students experience high-quality learning opportunities, but some students may miss out. States may be able to concentrate on expanding enrollment first, however, it may be difficult to ensure all those opportunities are high quality. Which do you think Hamiltonia should focus on first—enrollment or quality?

Action Item

10A-6

Which, if any, of the above quality benchmarks will Hamiltonia's pre-k program be required to meet?

Higher Education State Scholarship Programs

If you chose to concentrate on **higher education** policy, this section is for you. We will describe the background of state scholarship programs and provide information on different policy components you might want to consider for your program in Hamiltonia. If you are a legislator, make sure to look at your district demographic information to best represent your constituents as you attempt to address higher education issues in Hamiltonia.

States have played a major role in higher education policy. Recently, it has become a more pressing problem for families and students as tuition rises. Currently, Hamiltonia is ranked twenty-fifth for highest in-state tuition and fees. Some advocates are pushing for a broad-based merit-aid program that would give students scholarships to attend in-state colleges and universities. Advocates argue that this will help expand access to higher education and help families overcome poverty. Although there is broad support for increasing access to education, other advocates disagree with a broad-based merit-aid program. They argue that Hamiltonia should focus on providing scholarships based on financial need and not based on merit.

Currently the state of Hamiltonia does not have a state scholarship program. Hamiltonia has fifteen public universities, twenty private universities, and twenty community colleges. The average cost of one year of tuition at a public university is $10,000 for in-state residents and $19,000 for out-of-state residents, $26,000 for a private institution, and $5,500 for a community college. The median income in Hamiltonia is $62,900. Hamiltonia has a graduation rate of 85.96 percent and about 59 percent go on to a four-year college or university. Currently the state population of under eighteen-year-olds is 1,373,239 which is 22 percent of the state population.

Background

Remember Governor Zell Miller who established a universal pre-kindergarten program in Georgia in the previous section? Well, universal pre-k is not the only issue area that he innovated in. Governor Miller took a bookend approach to using lottery funds for education initiatives. Part of the funds of the state lottery program went to funding universal pre-k and the other part of the funds went to establishing the brand-new state-funded and **merit-based higher education scholarship** for Georgia residents called HOPE (Helping Outstanding Pupils Educationally). Therefore, he used the funds to bookend K–12 education.

HOPE was a brand-new type of broad-based scholarship program. Using state lottery funds in 1993 students with a B average and a family income of $66k or less were eligible for a state scholarship that paid two years of tuition at a state university or college. Governor Miller pioneered this program for three reasons: to encourage high school students to improve their grades, to prevent the "brain drain" (when top talent leaves the state), and to help equalize the opportunities

Former governor of Georgia, Zell Miller

SOURCE: Photo by Alex Wong/Getty Images

for students based on socioeconomic status and race.[39] Just like with universal pre-k, because the funds for the HOPE program are linked to the state lottery the state has been able to expand the program as the state lottery has generated more revenue. The program expanded by eliminating the income cap in 1995 and over time increased the amount of scholarship that could be used at private colleges and universities.[40] By 2007, the HOPE program had awarded one million scholarships to Georgia residents.[41]

Following Georgia, Florida established its own merit-based scholarship program called Bright Futures in 1997. Bright Futures was very similar to HOPE in that it used state lottery funds to pay for the program. However, Florida established different requirements for the two scholarships it offered. Under Bright Futures, students would be awarded the Florida Academic Scholars Award which covered 100 percent of tuition and some money for books. To receive this award students needed a 3.5 GPA and 1270 on the SAT or 28 on the ACT. Students would be awarded the Florida Merit Scholars Award that covered 75 percent of tuition if they earned a 3.0 GPA and a 970 or 20 on the ACT.[42] Bright Futures had three primary goals: "1. to serve as an incentive for high school students to take rigorous courses and perform better academically; 2. to direct lottery dollars to improve postsecondary education in a way that was readily visible to the public; and 3. to improve access to postsecondary education."[43] By 2008, Florida had also awarded one million scholarships. Bright Futures, however, has been criticized for its unequal impact on students based on race and socioeconomic status. White students receive more scholarships than Black and Hispanic students and some criticize the program for wasting money on students who can afford tuition.[44]

After HOPE, states began adopting these programs in the 1990s and 2000s. Since 1993, thirteen states have merit-based scholarship programs.[45]A map of the states with these programs is shown in Figure 10.5. Although each state's program is a bit different, they typically have three goals. These include improving access to higher education, motivating students to perform well in high school, and keeping high achieving students in the state.[46] Additionally, some states recognize that these programs may have a special role to play in not only increasing access to higher education but increasing that access particularly to students who are in traditionally underrepresented groups.

Figure 10.5
State Broad-Based Merit-Aid Programs

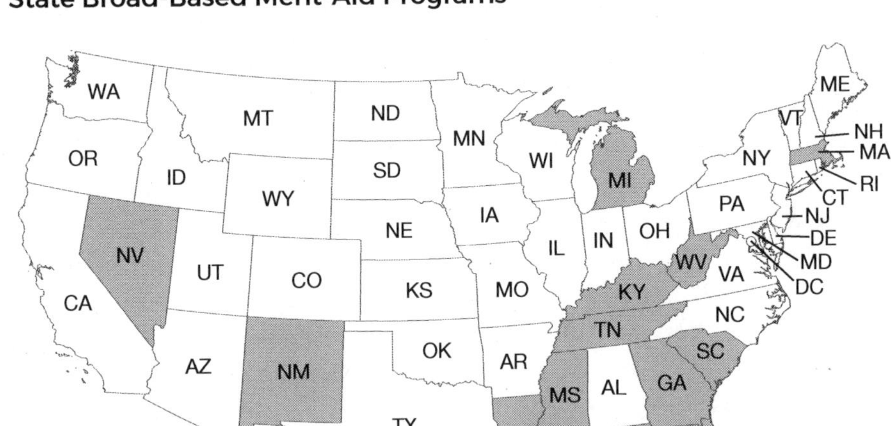

In some states merit-based scholarship programs can improve higher education enrollment.[47] Other states, however, have had cross-cutting success in achieving these goals. For example, New Mexico's program has not necessarily increased access, but there is some evidence to suggest that it has kept students in the state, therefore decreasing "brain drain."[48] However, Binder, Ganderton, and Hutchins' research suggests that the Native American community has benefited from the program. In a comparison of Florida and Michigan's program Heller and Rasmussen found that "the groups of students least likely to be awarded these scholarships are the populations who have been traditionally underrepresented in higher education" suggesting that even if the programs have increased access, they have not done so in a way that improves equity.[49]

State broad-based merit-aid programs are designed a bit differently. States typically take different approaches in determining who is eligible for the scholarship, the size of the award and how it can be used, and how the funding of the program works. All of these policy decisions may impact the program's success in achieving its three main goals: increasing access, motivating students, and preventing bright students from leaving the state. In the next section, you need to decide how to design Hamiltonia's broad-based merit-aid program.

Eligibility

As mentioned above, states have different requirements to be eligible for their merit-aid program. Some of the main eligibility requirements include GPA, standardized test scores, community service, and citizenship or residency status. For example, the Kentucky Educational Excellence Scholarship (KEES) requires a 2.5 GPA. However, the award amount increases based on academic performance.[50] Florida, on the other hand, requires you be a citizen of the United States, a Florida resident, have a 3.5 GPA, earn a 29 on the ACT or 1330 on the SAT, and complete 100 hours of community service. Meeting these requirements will allow students to earn a scholarship worth 100 percent of tuition costs and $300 for books. Students with a 3.0 GPA, 25 on the ACT or 1210 on the SAT with 75 hours of community service receive 75 percent of tuition costs. Students who decide to attend private colleges or universities in states may use a comparable award at their private institution.[51] In Tennessee's HOPE program students must be Tennessee residents, earn a 3.0 GPA, and a 21 on the ACT or 1060 on the SAT. Some states also have requirements for the scholarship to be renewed. For example, in Tennessee students must "achieve a cumulative GPA of 2.75 after attempting 24 and 48 semester hours" and after 72 hours you need a 3.0 and in Georgia they must maintain a 3.0.[52] Table 10.2 compares three states and the different requirements they use for their state funded program.

Eligibility requirements are important because they determine who may have access to the program. As you make eligibility requirements stricter, fewer students will qualify. This will likely decrease the cost of the program, but it may also make it more difficult to fulfill the goal of increasing access to higher education opportunities. Remember, some advocates complain that these merit-based scholarships pay for students who were already planning on attending college or could afford college. You may want to consider the ways in which your eligibility criteria help expand access to students who have been underrepresented in higher education. For example, using standardized test scores may disadvantage students from low-income backgrounds. In Florida and in Michigan, students who attend high-performing high schools are more likely to qualify for the

Table 10.2
Eligibility Requirements for State Merit-Aid Programs

	MASSACHUSETTS ADAMS SCHOLARSHIP[1]	WEST VIRGINIA PROMISE[2]	LOUISIANA TOPS[3]
GPA	None	B average	2.50 in core curriculum
Standardized Test Scores	Advanced score in an ELA, Math, or STE on MCAS and rank in top 25% of MCAS scores in district	ACT 21 or 1080 on the SAT	ACT or SAT score at the average state ACT or SAT score of the prior year
Residency/ Citizenship	U.S. citizen or authorized to live and work in US	Resident for 12 months	U.S. citizen or permanent resident and Louisiana resident
Community Service	None	20 hours (encouraged not required)	None

[1] "John and Adam Abigail Adams," Massachusetts.gov, https://www.mass.gov/info-details/john-and-abigail-adams-scholarship. Student also needs to score proficient or advanced in the other two tests.

[2] "West Virginia Promise Scholarship," College for West Virginia, https://www.collegeforwv.com/programs/promise-scholarship/community-service/.

[3] "The TOPS Opportunity Award," Louisiana Office of Student Financial Assistance, https://mylosfa.la.gov/students-parents/scholarships-grants/tops/the-tops-opportunity-award/.

scholarship.[53] These concerns are one reason why Massachusetts' requirements include students who score in the top 25 percent of their district.[54] You may want to consider these requirements based on the goals of the program.

Action Item

10B-1

What is the name of Hamiltonia's broad-based merit scholarship?

Action Item

10B-2

What are the goals of the program?

Action Item

10B-3

What are the eligibility requirements for earning a merit scholarship? Make sure to consider:

- GPA
- Standardized Test Scores
- Residency or Citizenship
    - If a residency requirement, how long does a student have to be a resident of Hamiltonia?
- Community Service
- Any other requirements?

Action Item

10B-4

Will recipients need to meet any requirements to maintain the scholarship? If so, what are they?

Award Size

States also vary on the generosity of the scholarship award. This is important because it may be that higher awards are more effective at keeping students in the state, one of the main goals of these programs.[55] States, however, must balance the award amount with the total cost of the program. If you provide a higher scholarship amount to each student, the program will be more expensive.

Some states provide more generous funding. For example, Florida's program covers 100 percent of tuition at a public college or university. If you attend a private institution in Florida, you may use a comparable award for tuition although it may not cover 100 percent of the cost at a private institution.[56] Other states pay a set amount. For West Virginia's PROMISE program, you can receive "$5,200 per year or the cost of tuition and mandatory fees, whichever is less, at any eligible institution."[57] Massachusetts bases the award on the institution the student attends. For example, if you attend UMass Amherst you will receive $1,701, which covers about 10 percent of student charges, but if you attend Framingham University you will receive $970 which covers about 9 percent of student charges.[58] You may want to consider the average cost of college in Hamiltonia as well as the residents' ability to pay for higher education in determining the award amount of the scholarship.

Action Item

10B-5

If a student meets the qualifications, what will be the amount of the awarded scholarship?

Action Item

10B-6

Are there any restrictions on which institutions students can apply the scholarship to? Make sure to consider:

- In-state four-year public colleges and universities
- In-state two-year public colleges and universities
- In-state private colleges and universities
- In-state trade or vocational schools

Funding

The total cost of state merit-aid scholarship programs depends upon student eligibility and on the total award amount. If Hamiltonia establishes a state merit-aid program, it needs to be prepared to pay for these scholarships. In 2010, Tennessee's program cost $297 million, Florida's program cost $423 million, and West Virginia's cost $46 million. To give some context, in that same year Tennessee served over 100,000 students, Florida served over 179,000 students, and West Virginia served just under 10,000 students.[59] In other words, West Virginia spent the least, but each student received the most money whereas Florida spent the most but gave each student the least money.

States have also paid for their programs in different ways. Following Georgia, a number of states use state lottery funds to pay for their broad-based merit-aid scholarship program including Florida, West Virginia, and Tennessee.[60] In some ways, this can help protect the program from annual budget discussions. At the same time, tying program funds to lottery revenues can potentially limit the total amount the state can award in the program. For example, in 2011, the governor of Georgia eliminated some of the HOPE scholarship award, such as additional money for books, because of budget issues.[61] Figure 10.6 shows the share of lottery appropriations each year that went to Bright Future Scholarships. Below consider how you want to fund the scholarship program in Hamiltonia.

Figure 10.6

Florida Lottery Contributions to Student Financial Aid (Bright Futures)

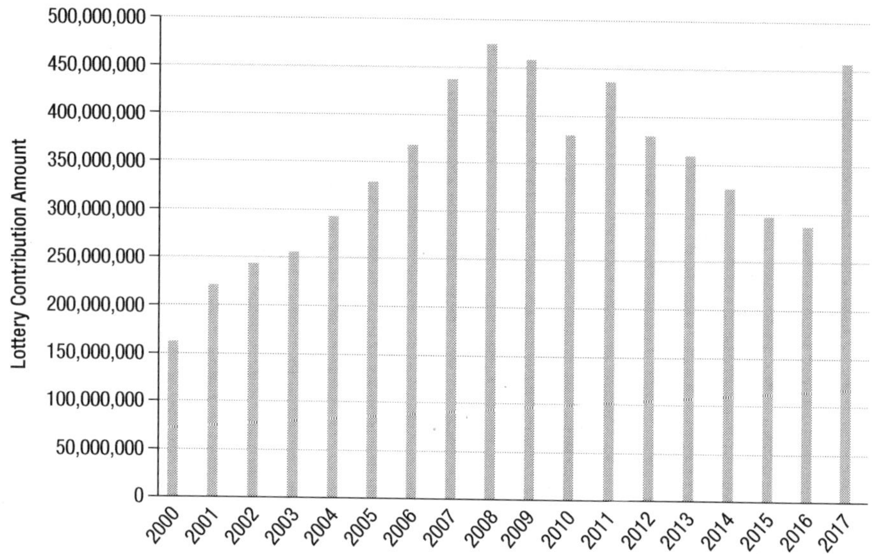

SOURCE: Data is from Budget Department, "Florida Lottery Facts: Where Does the Money Go?" The School District of Palm Beach County, https://www.palmbeachschools.org/cms/lib/FL50010848/Centricity/Domain/426/Lottery-FY2018.pdf accessed May 25, 2023. This includes the Other category which "consisted of totally Student Financial Aid, primarily the Bright Futures Scholarships Program." Each year represents a school year so that data for 2000 includes 2000–2001 data.

Action Item

10B-7

How will Hamiltonia fund the scholarship program? Will it use lottery revenues or will funding be approved in the annual budget process?

Action Item

10B-8

If you make the program part of the annual budget, how do you propose paying for the program? Will you raise taxes? If so, which ones?

Looking Forward

Congratulations on your participation in the education policy simulation for Hamiltonia! Creating, writing, and passing education legislation is challenging at the state level. You and your classmates may have been successful in establishing a new pre-k program or new state scholarship program. It is also possible that you and your classmates were not able to pass a new program in the time allotted. Do not lose hope; next week you will be able to start again with a new policy problem facing the state of Hamiltonia.

Passing legislation is a difficult task and doing so under time constraints can be even more challenging. Remember, state legislatures typically have sixty-day sessions. It can be difficult to pass major reforms or create new programs from scratch with such time limitations. Sometimes gubernatorial leadership, like in the case of Governor Zell Miller, can play an important role in policy innovation. Other times, however, that might not be enough given the time and political limitations that elected officials face. Having completed the education simulation, it may be helpful for you to reflect on all or a few of the following questions as you prepare for next week's simulation.

Key Terms

K–12 public education (203)
spending per pupil (205)
recall (208)
pre-kindergarten (209)
universal pre-k program (210)
targeted pre-k program (211)
higher education (216)
merit-based higher education scholarship (217)

Assignments to Learn More about Education Policy

1. Consider these discussion questions reflecting on this portion of the simulation deciding education policy.
   - What was the most challenging part of today's simulation? What was the least challenging? What do you think made the task more or less challenging?
   - How well did you fulfill your role in today's simulation? Did you consider the interests or needs of your constituents? What other pressures did you face in your role?
   - Did you have to convince a fellow classmate to agree to a component of the new program? What worked the best in trying to convince others of your ideas? What did not work well?
   - What were some of the institutional features that made it harder or easier for you to accomplish your goals? Why?

2. Choose two states and examine the state constitution to find the right to education. Compare and contrast the language in each of the state constitutions. Does one constitution provide a more encompassing right to an education? Why? Now write the right to education that you think should be used in Hamiltonia's constitution.
3. Consider the path not taken: What is your policy position on the policy your class did not debate? Look over those agenda action items and answer the questions.
4. Choose either the state where you are from, or if different, the state your college is in.
   a. Look up the higher educational landscape in that state and answer the following:
      i. How many institutions of higher education are there in your state?
      ii. How many are public vs. private and how many are two vs. four-year colleges?
      iii. What is the percentage of citizens in your state with an associate vs. bachelor's degree?
      iv. Does your state have a merit-aid program? If so, how is it set up?
   b. Read the National Education Association's Higher Ed State Funding Report: https://www.nea.org/he_funding_report. How do you think trends in state funding of higher education affect citizen access to postsecondary education?

An external view of the Northern State Prison in Newark, New Jersey, is seen on January 18, 2021. Federal prisons across the United States have been placed under temporary lockdown ahead of U.S. president-elect Joe Biden's inauguration which takes place on January 20, 2021.

SOURCE: Photo by Kena Betancur / AFP via Getty Image

Criminal Justice Policy

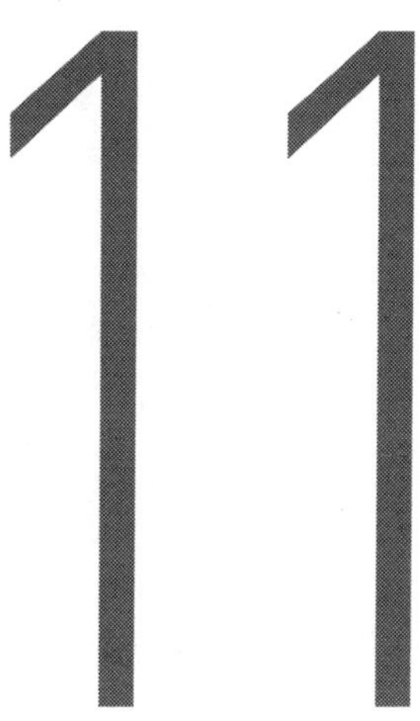

11

Learning Objectives:

- Understand how states enact criminal justice reform.
- Evaluate the role of each branch of government in criminal justice reform.
- Understand what cash bail is and how it is used in the criminal justice system.
- Evaluate the ways in which criminal justice reform can affect democracy.

State Spotlight: New Jersey

Currently about 1.2 million people in the United States are confined in prison, amounting to about 350 people per 100,000 residents.[1] To truly understand the scale of the number of people imprisoned in the United States, this number is greater than the populations of Montana, Rhode Island, and Delaware. The United States has the second highest prison population in the world.[2] The U.S. prison population grew rapidly starting in the 1970s. This growth has not been equitable across groups as "Black Americans are incarcerated in state prisons at nearly 5 times the rate of white Americans."[3] Thinking about the **criminal justice system** nationally ignores the fact that about 82 percent of prisoners are in *state* prisons, not federal prisons.[4] States vary widely in their imprisonment rates which can be seen in Figure 11.1. For example, Missouri's imprisonment rate is 374 people per 100,000 residents and Washington's imprisonment rate is 176 people per 100,000. The Black/White disparity in prison population is also different across states with Missouri's disparity at 3.6 to 1 and Washington's at 5.5 to 1.[5] One reason for these differences is that states have a lot of power to make criminal justice policies.[6]

Figure 11.1

State Imprisonment Rates per 100,000 People

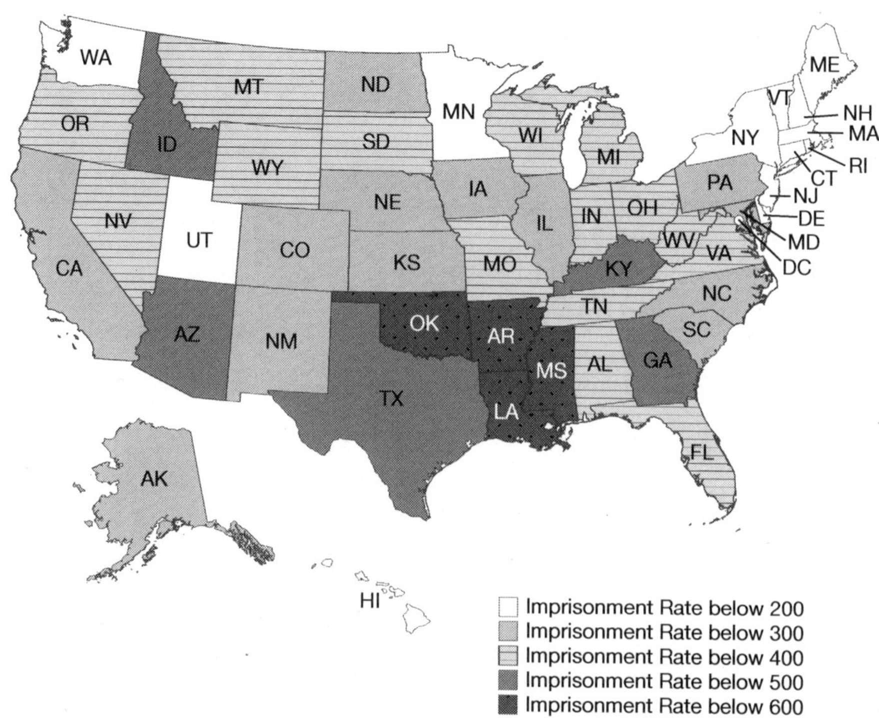

When someone commits a **crime**, they are breaking the law. This could be anything from stealing, to harassment, to assault. As we covered in chapter 7, there are two sides to our justice system, civil and criminal cases. We will be delving deeply into criminal justice in this chapter. Levels of incarceration are an important part of this area of public policy in the United States.

Let's look more deeply at New Jersey's imprisonment rate, as an example. There are 135 per 100,000 people behind bars in New Jersey. New Jersey ranks fifth in the nation with the lowest imprisonment rate. However, it has a 12.5 to 1 Black/white incarceration ratio putting New Jersey as the state with the highest disparity between Black and white imprisonment rates.[7] In 2020, there were nearly 165,000 violent and property crimes with 329 murders and 1,277 rapes or attempted rapes.[8] Figure 11.2 shows the total number of crimes from 2014 to 2020. In 2016, 14 percent of the homicides were domestic violence homicides.[9] In New Jersey, "35.8% of New Jersey women and 27.4% of New Jersey men experience intimate partner physical violence, intimate partner rape and/or intimate partner stalking in their lifetimes."[10]

Figure 11.2

Crimes in New Jersey 2014–2020

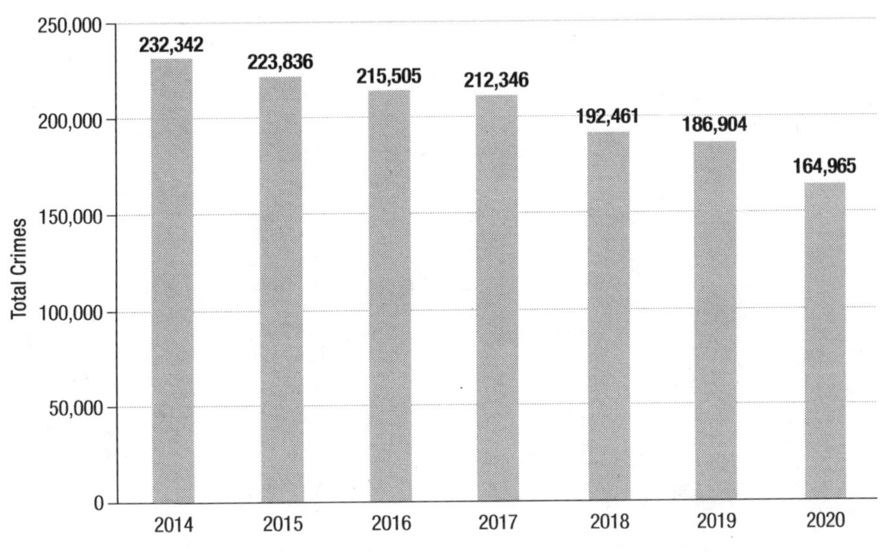

SOURCE: "Crime Data," New Jersey government, https://www.nj.gov/nj/safety/features/crimedata.html, accessed June 23, 2023.

The state Supreme Court had been working on a way to revolutionize **cash bail** because of the way it can "criminalize poverty."[11] The court created a new division that investigated ways in which judges could use a risk factor index to determine whether someone should be held on bail or not. Judges can use a rubric that gives each defendant a number to determine the risk of releasing each defendant before deciding on cash bail.[12] The idea is to reduce holding defendants in jail due to their inability to pay and rather on their risk status.

In 2014, the legislature—after Governor Christie called them into a special legislative session—proposed a constitutional amendment on criminal justice reform to the people.[13] New Jersey residents have the right to amend their constitution by voting on constitutional amendments referred to them by the state legislature. Three-fifths of the New Jersey legislature has to approve the constitutional amendment and then it can go before the general public for a majority vote.[14] The amendment gave the court the power to deny bail in criminal cases (previously the court could only deny bail in capital punishment cases, but New Jersey eliminated capital punishment in 2007), and it "authorizes the Legislature to pass laws concerning pretrial release and pretrial detention."[15] New Jersey residents approved the amendment with 61.81 percent of the vote and initiated a new era of criminal justice reform in the state.

Former New Jersey Governor Chris Christie.

SOURCE: Romer Jed Medina from Newark, NJ, United States

Governor Chris Christie (R) and the Democratic-controlled legislature got to work and passed significant bail reform in the state.[16] Because the people amended the state constitution to allow the legislature to pass laws dealing with bail, they did just that. The legislature passed and Governor Christie signed into law the Criminal Justice Reform Act which "made the state among the first in the nation to effectively eliminate cash bail."[17]

Overall, the reforms have been effective in reducing the jail population. Twenty-two percent fewer people are waiting in New Jersey jails today because of the reforms in 2017.[18] New Jersey became a leading state in bail reform. Soon, other states began to follow New Jersey with New York, California, and Illinois all adopting bail reform.[19] However, since New York "eliminated bail for most misdemeanors and non-violent felonies," the state has walked back those reforms multiple times.[20] Concerns of increasing crime by the public has placed pressure on New York lawmakers to give judges more power in detaining defendants. Although New Jersey has had a much less politically fraught and more successful reform than New York, the increase in crime following COVID-19 and spillover from New York's failed bail reform has opened the door for backsliding on these reforms. Although bail reform passed with bipartisan support, recently two Democrats have started to push back on the reforms. In 2022, Senators Paul Sarlo (D) and Joseph Lagana (D) introduced Senate Bill 3347 which "expands the list of crimes for which there is a rebuttable presumption of pretrial detention and requires pretrial detention of a defendant who violates the conditions of pretrial release"[21] Overall the bill makes it more difficult for some defendants to be released without bail and easier for the prosecution and judge to detain a defendant prior to trial. Currently the bill has been referred to the Senate Judiciary Committee.

We do not know yet whether New Jersey will continue as a leading state in bail reform or if it will begin to chip away at some of its earlier reforms. The example of New Jersey is illustrative though. A state became a clear policy leader in addressing a policy problem—the problem that income determined whether someone had to sit in jail while awaiting trial. New Jersey used a bipartisan compromise to develop a new system to determine whether it was appropriate to release a defendant on bail. After New Jersey implemented these reforms, other states attempted their own reforms. However, recent events suggest that New Jersey's reforms may be sensitive to the policies and politics of its neighbor, New York. Although states can take the lead on enacting serious reform, they are not immune to the policies and problems beyond their borders.

Simulation

In this chapter we are going to tackle criminal justice policy in the state of Hamiltonia. Your class will need to decide whether they want to pass a cash bail reform bill or restore voting rights for felons. Both policies deal with questions of race, justice, and equal treatment under the law.

Cash Bail Reform

Hamiltonia

Hamiltonia ranks twentieth in the nation on public safety—just above average. What drives this better than average ranking is low levels of property crime. However, Hamiltonia is ranked twenty-sixth in the nation for violent crime. Hamiltonia has 290 incarcerated persons per 100,000 in population or about 18,000 residents in jails or prisons. Overall, Hamiltonia has a lower **imprisonment rate** compared to other states. However, Hamiltonia has a high recidivism rate ranking fortieth out of fifty-one states.

Hamiltonia has nineteen prisons across the state and one federal prison. Two state prisons are for women and the rest are for men. Hamiltonians arrested and awaiting their day in court may be held in one of the sixty county jails. Once an individual is convicted of a crime and given a sentence, they are transferred to one of the state prisons. Figure 11.3 shows a map of Hamiltonia noting the locations of the prisons.

Background of Bail

Bail has been part of the criminal justice system since before the founding of the nation. In fact, the Eighth Amendment of the U.S. Constitution states that "excessive bail shall not be required."[22] When prosecutors charge someone with a crime, they are arrested and brought before a judge. At this point, the defendant—the person accused of committing a crime—may be granted bail. If the defendant can pay bail, they are released and told to come back for their court date. If the defendant cannot pay bail, they have two options. The defendant can pay a nonrefundable fee to a private bail bondsman who will post bail for them, or the defendant can stay in jail while awaiting trial. When the case concludes, the cash bail is returned to them. However, if they used a bail bondsman the individual may not receive their fee back even if they are found to be innocent. Cash bail

Figure 11.3
Map of Hamiltonia Prison Locations

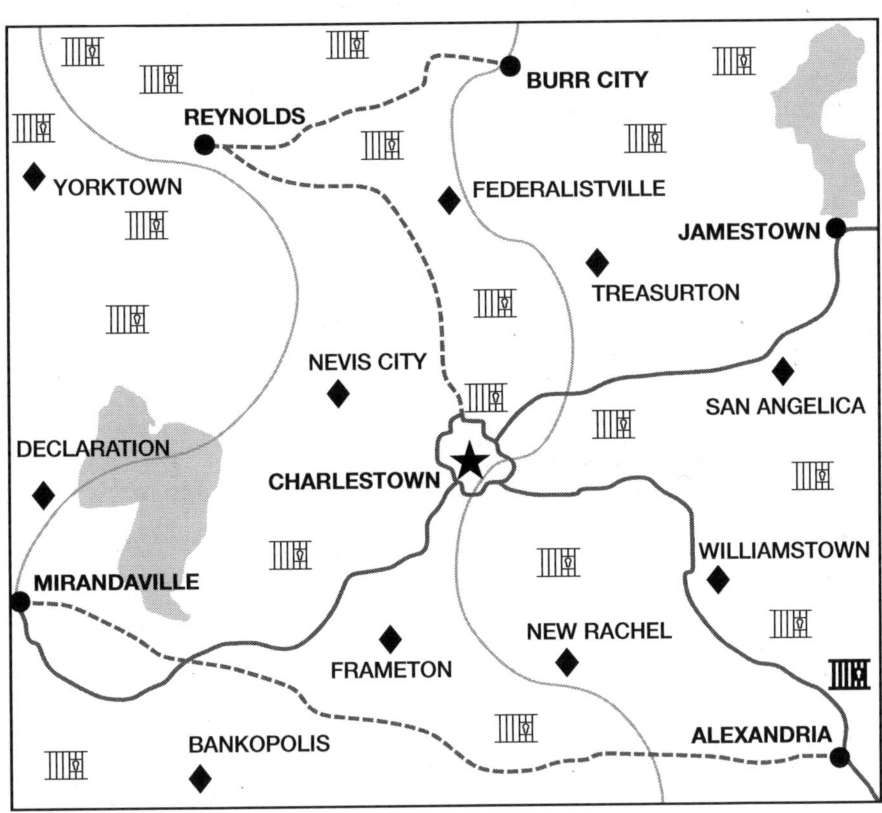

is meant to incentivize someone accused of a crime to return for their court date, but also allow the individual to continue on with their life while waiting for trial. Figure 11.4 shows these steps in the criminal justice system, although these steps may vary depending on the state.

Figure 11.4

Steps in Criminal Trials

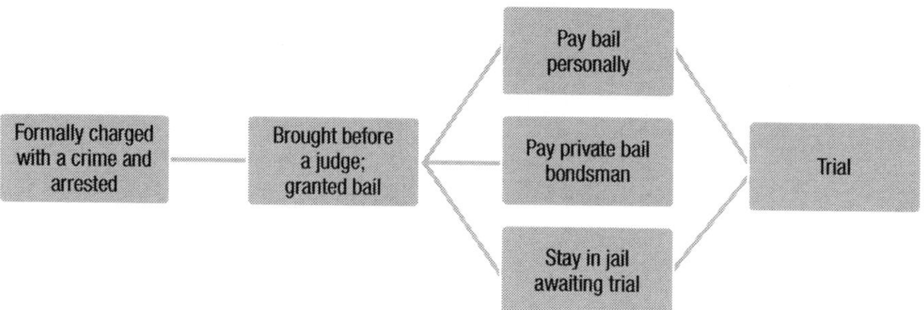

Bail, however, may be problematic in that it conditions pretrial release on the ability to pay. Therefore, people from wealthier backgrounds are able to post bail while those who do not have financial means to pay must sit in jail before they are ever convicted of a crime. If you think this is a small percentage of people facing bail, it is not. The U.S. Commission on Civil Rights issued a report in 2022 that revealed that "more than 60% of defendants are detained pre-trial because they can't afford to post bail."[23] The Commission also reported that the rates of pre-trial detention were higher for men as well as Blacks and Latinos. The number of people sitting in jails awaiting trial amounts to over 500,000 people in the United States.

Waiting in jail for trial can have serious life consequences for someone accused of a crime and their family. During that time, a defendant cannot work and may lose their job.[24] This may be devastating for some families that rely on that income. In fact, people who cannot afford bail may plead guilty so that they can return to their families and jobs.[25] Furthermore, research has shown that pre-trial detention is associated with higher likelihood of being convicted and engaging in more illegal activities in the future.[26]

Proponents of cash bail argue that some defendants pose a risk to the community if they are released from jail while awaiting trial. These proponents argue that our communities are safer if individuals accused of crimes, and particularly violent crimes, are detained until a trial has determined their guilt or innocence. However, a number of studies have not found a statistically significant relationship between bail reform and increases in felony charges.[27]

Bail is oftentimes determined by the court and can vary widely across counties and crimes. The median cost of bail for a felony is about $10,000, but this does vary widely.[28] Typically defendants standing trial for more serious crimes such as murder or rape will likely be assigned higher bail amounts than defendants accused of misdemeanors and nonviolent felonies. For example, from 1990–2004 35 percent of defendants accused of murder had bail set at above $50,000 whereas only 7 percent of defendants accused of nonviolent crimes had bail set above $50,000.[29] The higher the bail, the less likely someone will be able to pay it and be on pre-trial release. From 1990–2004, about 70 percent of defendants with bail at $5,000 or less were able to pay and be released. However, less than 10 percent of defendants were released when bail was $100,000 or more.[30] Five-thousand-dollar bail compared to $100,000 bail seems much easier to meet. But think about yourself, your family members, your friends—how many of them would be able to afford $5,000 in bail if they were arrested today?

Since 2011, seven states have adopted a risk assessment in assigning bail including the state of New Jersey.[31] New Jersey used a previously developed risk assessment that assigns a score from one to six to each defendant (see Figure 11.5). The score the defendant receives then determines whether the individual is released without bail or not. The assessment is meant to use a standardized process to determine the risks of letting a defendant out on bail in the pretrial period. The idea is that by considering whether the defendant has past criminal

Figure 11.5

New Jersey Public Safety Assessment Factors

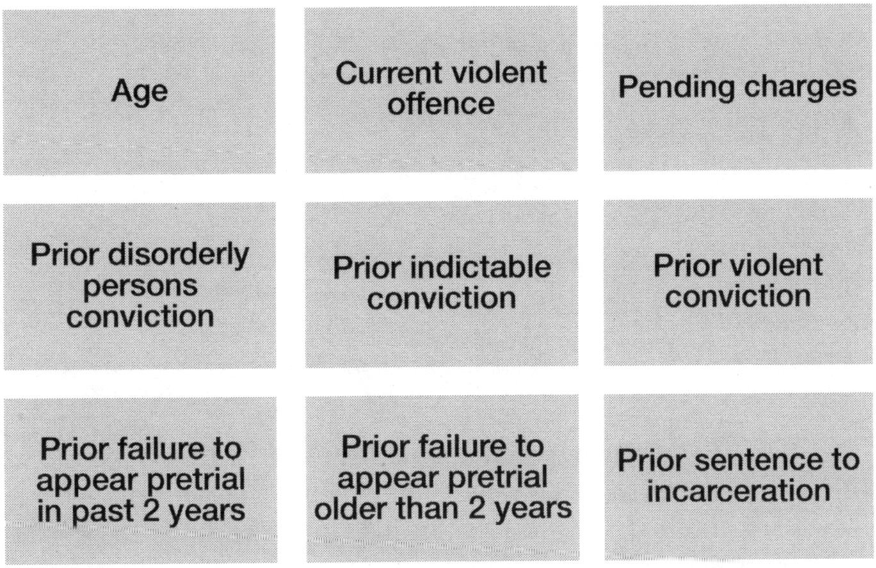

Age	Current violent offence	Pending charges
Prior disorderly persons conviction	Prior indictable conviction	Prior violent conviction
Prior failure to appear pretrial in past 2 years	Prior failure to appear pretrial older than 2 years	Prior sentence to incarceration

offenses or a history of not appearing in court, whether the defendant has any other pending charges against them or has been charged with a very serious crime, the state can release individuals who are not at high risk to commit other crimes or not show up to court.[32] However, some activists have concerns that the inputs used in risk assessments can disproportionately hurt African Americans by making it more likely they will be classified as high risk and, thus, more likely to have to pay bail than white defendants.[33]

Action Item

11A-1

Will you abolish cash bail for all crimes? If not, are there certain crimes where cash bail will not be allowed?

- Felonies (examples include murder and kidnapping)
- Misdemeanors (examples include drunk driving and trespassing)
- Nonviolent felonies (examples include drug trafficking and burglary)

Action Item

11A-2

Is there a maximum amount of bail that is allowed? If so, what is it?

Action Item

11A-3

If bail is allowed, is the judge obligated to assign bail? If not, what can the judge consider or not consider in assigning bail?

- Past offenses,
- Past failure to appear in court,
- Pending charges,
- The offense,
- Age,
- Ability to pay bail,
- Any other risks such as domestic violence charges?

One part of the **constitutional amendment** in New Jersey allowed for judges to deny bail to certain defendants depending on whether they were facing criminal charges. Prior to this, the constitution in the state gave individuals a right to bail. This amendment gave judges more power to hold defendants in jail while they awaited trial if there were concerns about the defendant appearing for court or committing violent crimes during the pretrial period.[34] Do Hamiltonians have a right to bail? Or are there scenarios where the court should have the power to detain individuals while they await trial? Take up these questions below.

Action Item

11A-4

Does the court have the power to deny bail? If yes, does it have the power to deny bail in all cases or only certain cases such as capital punishment cases?

Local Spotlight

The criminal justice system does not only span federal- or state-level courts; rather, it is a complicated system that begins at the local level. Typically, when individuals are held on cash bail they are held in county jails. For example, in the state of Florida, the sheriff of a county is responsible for the county jail. Overall county governments are responsible for and run 87 percent of the jails in the United States.[35] Typically, it is local-level police departments, locally elected district attorneys, local judges, and county jails that make up an individual's first experiences with the criminal justice system even though these criminal justice proceedings may be about violations of *state* law.

If you are arrested on a criminal charge, you may be arrested by local law enforcement. This includes police officers that work for cities or county-level law enforcement like sheriff offices. Typically, the leader of the local policy force is called the chief of police and the sheriff is an elected position that is responsible for the sheriff's office.[36] The FBI estimates that there are "more than 18,000 local police departments in the United States"[37] and there are over 3,000 sheriffs.[38] If you are charged with a crime, the charge will come from the local district attorney or prosecutor. The district attorney will represent the state and prosecute you according to the charges that have been brought. In forty-five states, you elect your local district attorney (sometimes called the state attorney).[39] Some states have partisan elections like Florida and others have nonpartisan elections for this position like Oregon.[40] The state of Florida elects twenty prosecutors across twenty circuits to prosecute individuals by representing the state.[41] States also typically have a chief prosecutor sometimes called the attorney general, which we learned about in chapter 6.

Local prosecutors have been in the spotlight after some progressive local prosecutors ran on criminal justice reforms such as limiting prosecution of low-level or certain drug offenses. After increases in crime, these prosecutors have been under pressure to establish law and order. For example, in San Francisco where a progressive prosecutor was elected in 2019, voters recalled that same district attorney in 2022.[42] Remember that even local prosecutors are prosecuting individuals for violations of *state* law. This can lead to conflict like what we have seen in the state of Florida. Florida Governor Ron DeSantis suspended two local, Democrat state attorneys (local prosecutors) who had been elected to their positions. Governor DeSantis criticized those state attorneys for not prosecuting violations of state law.[43] After the state passed a fifteen-week abortion ban, state attorney Andrew Warren planned not to prosecute on this issue.[44] Governor DeSantis claimed this was neglect of Warren's duty as state attorney. Warren argued he was duly elected in the position and the governor should not remove elected officials for political purposes.[45] Local district attorneys are elected by the people and represent the state in criminal proceedings. Again, the criminal justice system extends into local jurisdictions.

The district attorney will bring a case in the state's judicial system. State judicial systems often have county-level courts that operate with county-level judges. For example, New Jersey has municipal courts that hear cases on drunk driving and shoplifting. The local government is responsible for these courts and even appoints the judges on these courts.[46] New Jersey also has what they call Superior Courts which are housed in counties. These courts hear many criminal cases and consist of over 400 judges.[47] Even if you face a state-level criminal charge, you will likely have your bail set and case heard before a court and judge that are housed in local governments. Many criminal justice reforms, including cash bail reforms, depend upon local police, local district attorneys, and local judges in local courts.

Restoration of Voting Rights

Hamiltonia

Hamiltonia has 290 incarcerated persons per 100,000 in population or about 18,000 residents in jails or prisons. Prosecutors in Hamiltonia achieve a conviction in about 62 percent of cases. There were 127,000 felony cases in the state of Hamiltonia last year and about 94 percent of those cases ended in the defendant pleading guilty. Seventeen percent of people who have been convicted of a felony in Hamiltonia have been convicted of violent crimes. Hamiltonia's law states that people convicted of felonies permanently lose their right to vote unless pardoned by the governor. In the last election about 7 percent of the adult population could not vote due to **felony disenfranchisement**.

Background

States treat prisoners differently, especially when it comes to voting rights. Typically, residents lose their right to vote when they have been convicted of a felony. A large number of states disenfranchise felons when they are imprisoned but they are able to vote again once they are released. In two states, Maine and Vermont, felons can still vote while serving their sentence in prison. However, in a few states, people convicted of certain felonies are permanently disenfranchised meaning that even after serving the terms of their sentence, they may still be barred from voting.[48] Figure 11.6 shows different policies toward convicted felons and their voting rights.[49]

Figure 11.6

State Policies on Felony Disenfranchisement

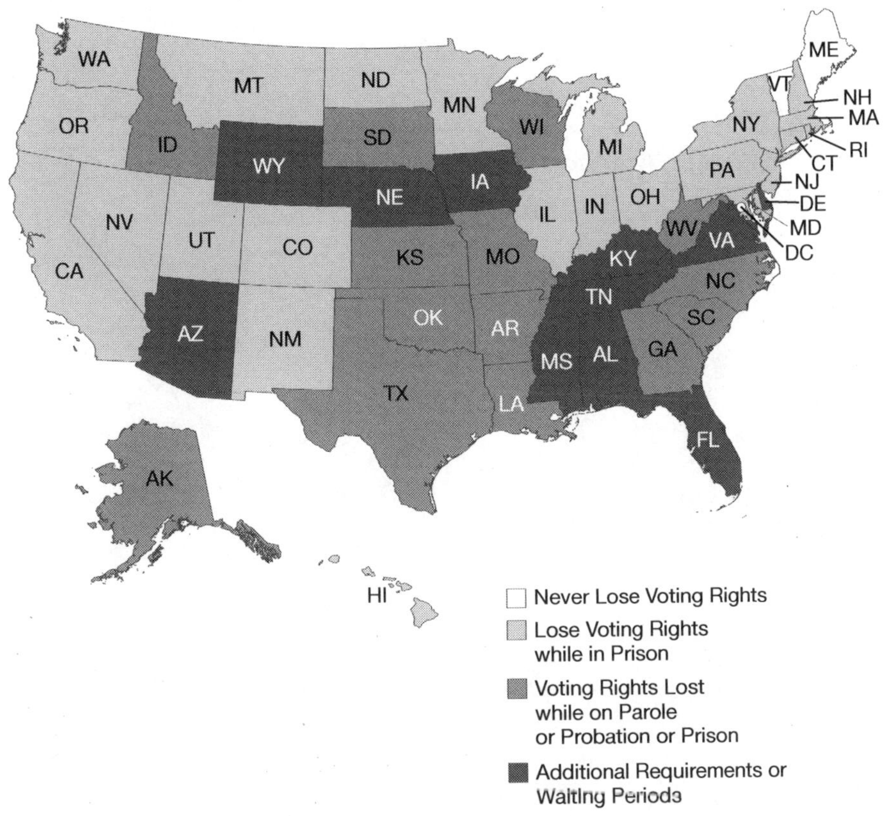

Policies on felony disenfranchisement have important racial implications. African Americans are disenfranchised at the highest rates with 6.2 percent of the population disenfranchised which is "3.7 times greater than non-African Americans."[50] Different states, however, experience different racial implications from felony disenfranchisement. As mentioned at the beginning of the chapter, not only do states have different imprisonment rates, but their Black/white imprisonment disparity also varies. These imprisonment disparities can continue to have effects on democracy long after a prisoner completes his sentence. Figure 11.7 below shows the regional average of the percent of African Americans disenfranchised.[51]

Although states have taken different approaches to felony disenfranchisement, over time states have been trending in the direction of expanding voting rights for felons. New Jersey, our state spotlight for this chapter, is a good example of this. Prior to 2019, convicted felons in New Jersey had to serve their prison sentence as well as their parole or probation before being allowed to vote. In 2019, a new law allowed voting rights to be automatically restored when a convicted felon was

Figure 11.7

Percent of African Americans Disenfranchised

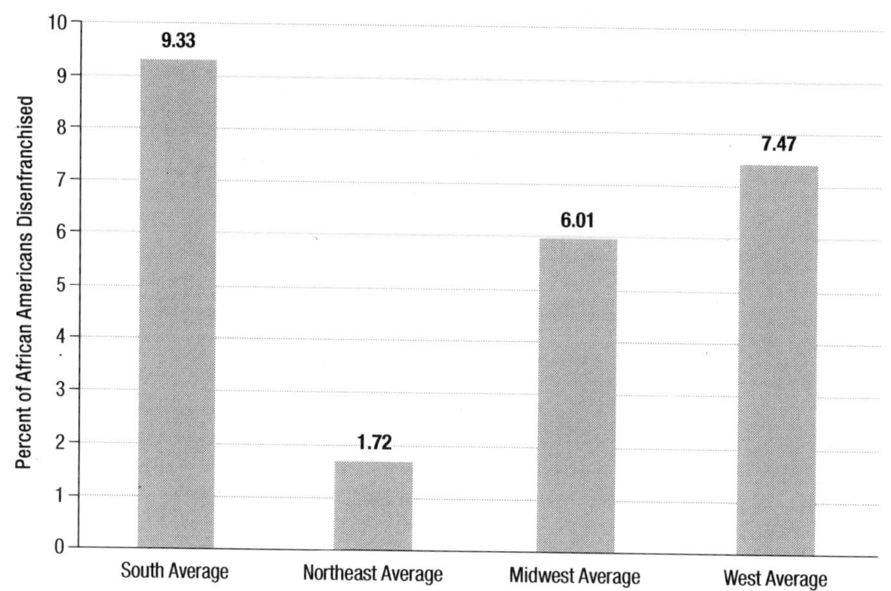

released from prison.[52] NPR estimates that about 80,000 more people in the state of New Jersey were able to vote in 2020 because of this policy change.

States have to consider a number of issues when determining when and how felony voting rights can be restored. One of the first questions to answer is when can voting rights be restored. Figure 11.8 shows that states have typically taken one of four approaches. States can decide to never disenfranchise convicted felons, allowing them to vote while in prison. States can also decide to disenfranchise convicted felons while they serve their sentence in prison, but automatically restore voting rights once they have been released from prison. This means that even while a convicted felon is serving **parole** he or she can vote in elections. States can be more restrictive and decide to disenfranchise convicted felons while they serve their sentence in prison, but also while they are on parole or on probation. Finally, states may also decide to require payment of court fines and fees, to add a waiting period even after a felon has completed prison time and parole, or to permanently disenfranchise felons for certain crimes.

Florida has had a different experience expanding felony voting rights than New Jersey. Table 11.1 compares Florida and New Jersey in terms of their imprisonment rates and disenfranchisement of felons. In 2018, Florida residents approved Amendment #4 with 64.55 percent of the vote. The ballot summary states, "This amendment restores the voting rights of Floridians with felony convictions after they complete all terms of their sentence including parole or probation. The amendment would not apply to those convicted of murder or sexual offenses, who would continue to be permanently barred from voting unless the Governor and Cabinet vote to restore their voting rights on a case-by-case basis."[53] This seems like a clear expansion of felony voting rights.

Figure 11.8

Approaches to Voting Rights for People Convicted of Felonies

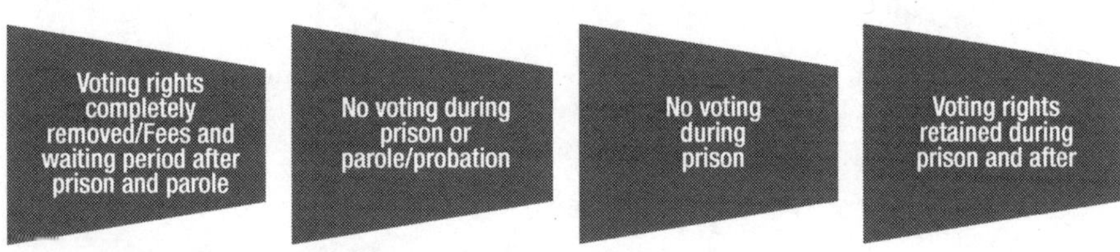

Table 11.1
Comparison of Florida and New Jersey

	FLORIDA	NEW JERSEY
Imprisonment Rate	367	135
Black/white Disparity	4.1:1	12.5:1
Latino/white Disparity	0.7:1	2:1
Felony Disenfranchisement Rate	8%	0%

Action Item

11B-1

When are voting rights restored for convicted felons in Hamiltonia?

Do convicted felons ever lose their voting rights? If yes,

- Are voting rights automatically restored when the convicted felon is released from prison?
- Are voting rights restored when the convicted felon has been released from prison and has completed parole?
- Are voting rights ever restored to a convicted felon or is disenfranchisement permanent?

Action Item

11B-2

Are there any other restrictions or requirements for the restoration of felony voting rights?

- Are felons of certain crimes excluded from voting? Such as murder or rape? If so, which crimes disqualify a felon?
- Does the felon need to pay full restitution of any fines imposed by the court before being able to vote?
- Does the felon need to wait a period of time before voting rights are restored after the completion of the sentence? If so, how many years is the waiting period?

In this, Monday, October 22, 2018, photo, people gather around the Ben & Jerry's "Yes on 4" truck as they learn about Amendment 4 and eat free ice cream at Charles Hadley Park in Miami. Amendment 4 asks voters to restore the voting rights of people with past felony convictions. More than 1.5 million adults in Florida are ineligible to vote because they have felony convictions.

SOURCE: AP Photo/ Wilfredo Lee

But the story does not end with the passing of the constitutional amendment. After the amendment was passed, the Florida legislature began working on passing legislation to implement the new law. The Florida legislature passed, and the governor signed into law, a new bill interpreting the phrase "all terms of their sentence" to include payment of restitution and any court fees before voting rights were restored. This was controversial because many read the amendment to mean that "all terms of their sentence" was just that an individual had completed their parole or probation period. Including the payment of fees and fines as completion of a sentence made it more difficult for individuals to have their voting rights restored. Governor DeSantis asked for an advisory opinion from the state Supreme Court. In January 2020, the Florida State Supreme Court upheld that requiring convicted felons to pay restitution and court fees as part of "all terms of their sentence" was appropriate.[54] Florida's expansion of voting rights to convicted felons has two qualifications. First, restoration of voting rights depends on the felony conviction with those convicted of murder or sexual crimes being permanently disenfranchised. Second, it has additional requirements to completing parole including paying court fines and fees. Florida lacks a centralized system so it may be difficult for people who have been convicted of felons to find out what they owe the state.

This is incredibly problematic because no state database means inaccurate and incomplete records creating the possibility that counties allow people to vote not knowing they are causing an individual to commit voter fraud because no one knows they are eligible to vote based upon the fees. One study of Brevard County showed that the majority of convicted felons who had been released owed $500 or more.[55] This may be a major barrier to convicted felons in restoring their voting rights.[56]

Action Item

11B-3

Does the governor have the power to restore voting rights on a case-by-case basis?

As we have seen throughout this book and this chapter, the state you live in can have a major impact on your life. If you are convicted of a felony, the state you live in can determine when and even whether you can participate via voting. There are differences in how people convicted of felonies are treated within states as well. As seen above, states may treat different felonies differently. For example, in some states, being convicted of certain felonies such as murder can permanently bar you from voting. Another distinction states make in their felony disenfranchisement policies is in the number of felonies someone has been convicted of. Typically, when a state does make this distinction it is easier for first-time offenders to vote again rather than offenders with multiple felony convictions. For example, in Wyoming first-time felony offenders can vote after probation, but a multiple felony offender needs to be pardoned.[57] What do you think? Should it be easier to have your voting rights restored if you are first-time rather than a second-time offender? Take up the questions below to decide what the laws will be in Hamiltonia.

Action Item

11B-4

Do the decisions made on the above action items apply to all people convicted of felonies? Are there different restrictions based on the number of felonies someone has committed? If so,

- What are the restrictions for first-time offenders?
- What are the restrictions for those convicted of multiple felony counts?

Looking Forward

Congratulations! At this point we hope that you were able to pass significant criminal justice reform in Hamiltonia. If you were successful, take some time to reflect on why the legislature and executive branch were able to work together to accomplish this goal. If you were not successful, reflect on what challenges lawmakers in Hamiltonia faced. Are they similar to the challenges that lawmakers across the states face? Why or why not?

Criminal justice policy is an important and often overlooked area of state policymaking. As discussed in the beginning of this chapter, states are where a lot of the criminal justice activity happens. Most people in prison are held in *state* prisons and are convicted in *state* courts. When thinking about how to improve the criminal justice system, starting at the state level may be an effective way to begin affecting change.

Key Terms

criminal justice system (228)
crime (229)
cash bail (230)
imprisonment rate (232)
constitutional amendment (236)
felony disenfranchisement (239)
parole (241)

Assignments to Learn More about Criminal Justice

1. Now that you have passed a law, consider what needs to happen to implement that law. Act as a bureaucrat for the state of Hamiltonia and write two rules that you think need to be established for a smooth implementation of either bail reform or expanding voting rights.
2. Start looking into the story of New York's experience with bail reform. Compare and contrast New York and New Jersey's bail reform experience. What was different about what happened in New York and what happened in New Jersey? Why do you think bail reform was successful in New Jersey? What is one lesson political leaders should take away from these two states?

3. Spend some time looking into the crime and incarceration statistics of your home state or the state your college or university is in. Does the state have a large prison population compared to other states? What about equity in the criminal justice system? What is the Black/white imprisonment ratio? Has your state undergone any recent criminal justice reforms? If so, what are they, how did they come about, and have they been successful? Utilize the research funded by the Sentencing Project: www.sentencingproject.org to better understand the intersection between race and incarceration in the United States.

Windmills lining the Altamont Pass generate electricity on Sunday, May 12, 2013, near Livermore, CA.
SOURCE: AP Photo/Noah Berger

Environmental Policy

12

Learning Objectives:

After reading this chapter students should be able to:

- Identify and describe the role of intergovernmental relations with regard to environmental policy.
- Understand and assess the role of local and state governments in addressing environmental issues.
- Understand how state policies on the environment can spread across states.
- Assess the government's responsibility in ensuring the environmental health of its citizens.

State Spotlight: California

California has long been viewed as the state for progressive environmental policies. So much so that scholars created the term the "California effect" to describe the ways in which California's progressive environment policies affect other state's policies and the nation as a whole. For example, the state of California was first to set vehicle emissions standards—even before the federal government's Clean Air Act. Why would California pioneer emissions standards? Why did they become a leader in the first place? Why was the federal government taking cues from state policy?

States have often been on the front lines of environmental issues because environmental problems tend to appear locally first. Take California for example. California's leadership in emission standards all started when the city of Los Angeles had severe smog in the 1940s. Initially, the local government took action. This led to state action in the 1960s with the creation of the Bureau of Air Sanitation and the passage of emissions standards.[1] The state faced an environmental issue, developed state capacity to address the issue, and adopted standards to improve environmental conditions. The Clean Air Act of 1970 (at the federal level) even allowed states to bypass the waiver process if they adopted California's emission standards.[2] Seventeen states adopted California's standards which are even stricter than the federal governments.[3]

The process by which one state's policy spreads to another is called **policy diffusion**. Policy diffusion can occur through different mechanisms such as competition with other states or by **policy learning**.[4] For example, a state can learn about the policy success in California and adapt that policy to its own state's needs. The process of policy diffusion can occur in environmental policy as well as other policy areas. Policy diffusion, however, can span our federal system whereby the federal government can encourage the spread of ideas across states and states themselves can learn from local policies.[5] In fact, local government environmental policies can also spread across other local governments, like in the case of water rights in Colorado.[6]

Local governments play an important role in environmental policy. Local government agencies are usually on the front lines of making sure county water systems meet state- and federal-level standards, help ensure air quality standards, and help ensure other aspects of environmental health. States have environmental experts in their state environmental departments, but they rely on local or regional branches to implement policies. For example, one of California's state-level agencies that addresses environmental issues is called the California Environmental Protection Agency. One of the major divisions of this state-level agency is the California Water Resources Control Board, created in the late 1960s. This board is tasked with the mission "to preserve, enhance, and restore the quality of California's water resources and drinking water for the protection of the environment, public health, and all beneficial uses, and to ensure proper water allocation and efficient use, for the benefit of present and future generations."[7] The state board consists of five members that have been appointed by the governor as well as having been approved by the Senate. Interestingly, the members must fulfill specific specialties including "representing the public, engineering expertise, water quality expertise, and water supply."[8] One of the main tasks of the Water Resources Control Board is to oversee the regional control boards. California has nine regional Water Control Boards. Each of these regional boards has seven members. To serve on the board, the governor must appoint you and the California Senate must confirm your appointment. As opposed to members on the state board, these members work for the regional board on a part time basis.[9] These local boards make important decisions on water policy including passing regulations, enforcing of water control plans, enacting requirements for water discharge, as well as other responsibilities.[10] The California Environmental Protection Agency relies on these more local Water Control Boards to help regulate and implement environmental policies throughout the state.

Simulation

Hamiltonia's officials have some important decisions to make about environmental policies in the state. Your class has decided to either focus on renewable portfolio standards or water quality. States have a responsibility to enact and implement policies to address both of these environmental issues. Below you will outline the state of Hamiltonia's approach to one of these pressing issues. Good luck!

Renewable Portfolio Standards

As discussed above using the example of California, many times state policy leads federal policy. **Renewable portfolio standards (RPS)** are a good example of this. A renewable portfolio standard is a policy that encourages utility companies to use renewable energy rather than non-renewable energy. The RPS policy typically specifies a target of what percent of energy generated should come from renewable sources. This is an environmental policy meant to help limit our use of fossil fuels. The purpose of the standards is for states to "diversify their energy resources, promote domestic energy production and encourage economic development."[11] The idea of a renewable portfolio standard started at the state level, specifically in Iowa in 1983.

Currently, thirty states have some sort of renewable portfolio standard as seen in Figure 12.1. States have differed in whether they lead in innovation in their renewable portfolio standards or follow other states. Different political pressures factor into these decisions. For example, ideology is an important predictor for whether a state is going to innovate in their RPS policy, but legislators that are vulnerable to losing their seats are more likely to borrow from other states.[12] As we will see below, although thirty states have adopted these standards, the RPS vary significantly across states.[13]

Renewable portfolio standards were first adopted by the Iowa state legislature in 1983. The Alternative Energy law established the first renewable portfolio standards in the nation. The RPS targeted investor-owned utility companies in the state to generate 105 megawatts of renewable energy. To put this in perspective, this was roughly 50 percent of energy demand for each of the companies.[14]

Figure 12.1

Map of States with Current or Expired Renewable Portfolio Standards

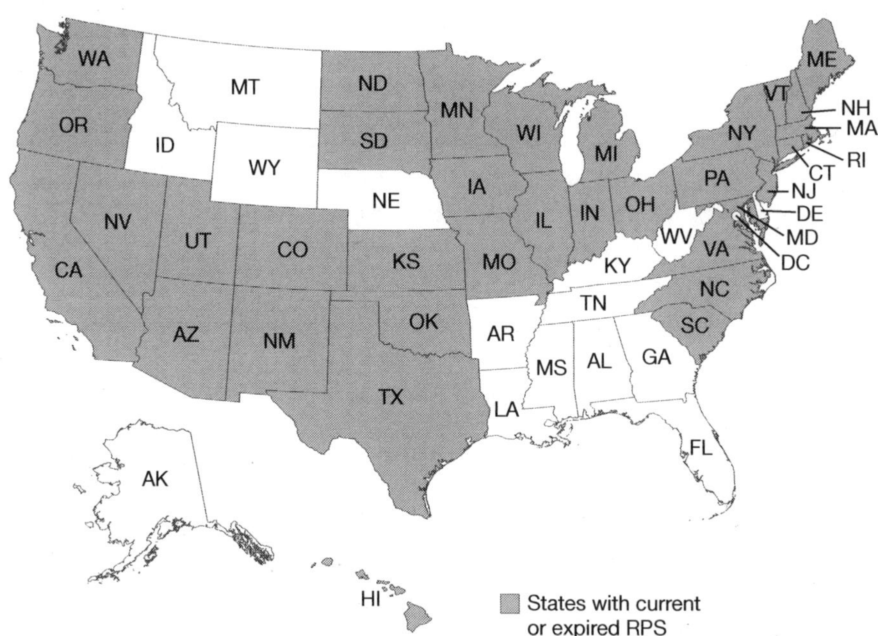

RPS have generated the use and production of more renewable energy. Across the United States, "Roughly half of the growth in U.S. renewable energy generation since the beginning of the 2000s can be attributed to state renewable energy requirements."[15] In Iowa alone, wind power produces 55 percent of its energy generation. And Iowa is first "in the nation for share of electricity sourced from wind, solar, and energy storage."[16] Prior to RPS in Iowa, Iowa was dependent upon other states for its coal-powered energy needs. Now, Iowa is less dependent on other states and instead has successfully harnessed its renewable energy resources—particularly wind power—to generate its own energy.

Although thirty states have adopted RPS, they vary in a number of important ways. We will use the National Conference of State Legislatures to consider the different ways states have established their RPS. The first factor states have to think about when adopting an RPS is how much renewable energy to generate by a specific date. This is what is called the target. In Iowa, the initial target was 105 megawatts although they have long since surpassed that goal.[17] Typically when states adopt an RPS, they use a percentage of the power generated as the target. All states with an RPS have a target rate of at least 40 percent. This means that the goal is for the state to generate 40 percent of its energy from renewable sources. However, some states set even stricter target rates with many states such as California, New Mexico, and Colorado setting their targets at 100 percent. States also set different time parameters for when the state needs to generate the target percentage of renewable energy. Some states set the standards incrementally and others have a goal by a specific date, such as 2045 in California. Keep in mind that more ambitious targets may be more difficult to reach and more costly.

Another way that states vary in their RPS policy is whether the standards are voluntary or mandatory. Voluntary standards are less severe and may have fewer consequences than mandatory targets. Setting the RPS with voluntary targets means that energy companies are not required to meet the target. Rather, the policy is a suggestion for these companies to try to meet the targets. Currently only three states—South Carolina, Indiana, and Utah—have voluntary standards. Mandatory targets are stricter in that they require companies to meet the targets by a specific date. Most states have set mandatory requirements rather than voluntary requirements. However, several states have also let their RPS expire including North and South Dakota. Table 12.1 shows which states have mandatory or voluntary standards as well as the states that have let their RPS policy expire.

Table 12.1
Renewable Portfolio Standards across States

STATES WITH RPS	STATES WITH VOLUNTARY RPS	STATES WITH EXPIRED RPS	NEVER ADOPTED RPS
Washington	Utah	North Dakota	Idaho
Oregon	Indiana	South Dakota	Montana
California	South Carolina	Kansas	Wyoming
Nevada		Oklahoma	Nebraska
Arizona		Iowa	Arkansas
New Mexico		Wisconsin	Louisiana
Colorado		Montana (repealed)	Mississippi
Texas			Alabama
Missouri			Georgia
Minnesota			Florida
Illinois			Tennessee
Michigan			Kentucky
Ohio			West Virginia
North Carolina			
Virginia			
Maryland			
Pennsylvania			
Delaware			
New Jersey			
New York			
Connecticut			
Rhode Island			
Massachusetts			
New Hampshire			
Vermont			
Hawaii			

States also need to decide what types of energy sources will be considered renewable in their portfolio standards and whether these sources have to be both renewable and clean. States may consider certain energy sources as renewable depending upon their own natural resources and production. Typically, states include solar, wind, and geothermal energy in their RPS. This means that the production of energy from these sources counts toward the percentage target set out in the standards. Some states also include hydroelectric energy in their RPS. The ability for a state to generate energy from these sources depends, in part, on their own geography and natural resources. For example, Iowa has been very successful at generating energy from wind.

Action Item

12A-1

What is the target for the renewable portfolio standards?

Action Item

12A-2

Are the RPS voluntary or required?

Action Item

12A-3

What is the year the targets should be met?

Action Item

12A-4

What type of energy should be included as renewable? Wind, solar, biomass, geothermal, or hydroelectric?

Some states have pushed their RPS even further by not only requiring the use of renewable energy but **clean energy** as well. California is a good example of this. By 2030, 60 percent of their energy production is required to be from renewable sources, but by 2045 100 percent of that energy must be clean as well.[18] This means that these sources

Action Item

12A-5

Does renewable energy also have to be clean energy?

produce zero carbon emissions. For example, biomass energy, where we burn natural materials, may also produce carbon emissions and, therefore, may not be clean energy.[19] Requiring clean energy in addition to renewable energy is one extra step that utility companies have to meet, potentially making it harder for these companies to reach the mandatory targets. You want to make sure to think about the geography and natural resources available in Hamiltonia when designing these standards. Figure 12.2 compares Indiana and Colorado's renewable portfolio standards.

Figure 12.2

Indiana and Colorado Renewable Portfolio Standards

Indiana	Colorado
• Adopted: 2011 • Voluntary 10% • Applies to "IOUs, municipalities, cooperatives, and retail suppliers"	• Adopted: 2004 • Mandatory • Requires "100% clean energy by 2050 for utilities serving 500,000 or more customers"

Energy Usage in Hamiltonia

Hamiltonians use a lot of energy! In terms of energy usage per capita, Hamiltonia ranks thirteenth in the nation. This is because Hamiltonia experiences both cold winters as well as hot and humid summers due to its position in the United States. Although the heating and cooling needs of the population are high, it is the industrial and transportation sectors in the economy that use the most energy in the state. Hamiltonia uses coal for energy production but can only produce very little of it and relies on coal imported from other states. Because of the geography, wind energy is the most abundant renewable energy in Hamiltonia. The state experiences cold and dark winters so solar energy is not as abundant as wind energy. However, the southern part of the state receives the most sunshine and may be a site for solar energy expansion. Hamiltonia does contain vast farmland, particularly in the western part of the state. The main crop of Hamiltonia farms is corn. This has the potential to help produce more biomass energy.

When adopting RPS, states also must decide which entities the standards apply to. States typically have **investor-owned utility companies** (IOUs), but they may also have municipalities—which are **publicly owned**—or **electric cooperatives** that generate energy. Investor-owned utility companies are by far the largest producers of energy for the United States. Investor-owned utility companies "are large electric distributors that issue stock owned by shareholders." They serve about 72 percent of all energy consumers in the United States. Overall, there are 168 investor-owned utilities throughout the states.[20] IOUs are profit seeking companies that are beholden to their shareholders. Municipalities may also provide utilities and are considered publicly owned utilities. Although there are over 1,900 public utility companies throughout the United States, they tend to serve fewer residents than IOUs. One of the largest municipal utility companies is the Los Angeles Department of Water and Power.[21] This reiterates the importance of localities in energy policy and consumption. The last kind of entity the RPS can apply to are energy cooperatives. Cooperatives tend to be nonprofits and are formed and led by the community that they serve. Cooperatives provide electricity to about forty-two million people throughout the United States. The National Rural Electric Cooperative Association argues that cooperatives can respond to local needs and have been building up capacity to offer more renewable energy sources over the years.[22]

Hamiltonia has a mix of investor-owned utility companies, municipalities, and energy cooperatives. The two investor-owned utility companies in the state are the Washington Electric Company and the Madison Company. The Washington Electric company serves about 36 percent of homes and businesses in Hamiltonia, including the capital Charlestown. The Madison Company is a bit smaller and serves about 24 percent of Hamiltonia including Burr City and Reynolds. There are also a few energy cooperatives in the state, although these are more common in the southwestern portion of the state. Mirandaville, Frameville, and Banktopolis have their own energy cooperatives serving about 18 percent of the total residents in Hamiltonia. The Abigail Cooperative out of Mirandaville is the largest cooperative. Traditionally, these cooperatives have been able to provide energy at slightly lower cost than the IOUs and the municipality owned utilities. A few municipalities also have their own public utility companies including Reynolds, Federalistville, and Yorktown. These municipalities serve roughly 22 percent of the residents in Hamiltonia. These companies, cooperatives, and municipalities will be most affected by the RPS that Hamiltonia decides to adopt.

One of the concerns about renewable energy is the cost—particularly the cost to the consumer. Paying an energy bill is something that you and your constituents have to do every month. When the price of energy increases, many families living paycheck to paycheck may be unable to absorb that cost. One way that states have tried to address the cost of renewable energy is by putting a cost cap on constituents' energy bills. A few states require that cost cannot increase by more than 2 percent for the consumer.[23] For example, Colorado and Illinois have a 2 percent cost cap but Connecticut has a 6 percent cost cap.[24] A cost cap might help constituents feel more comfortable with the state adopting renewable portfolio standards and to ensure costs do not increase quickly and substantially. However, the Climate Policy Initiative warns that when cost caps are not done strategically, it can make the policy more complicated and could even prevent renewable energy that has been generated from being sent to homes.[25]

Renewable portfolio standards are just one way that states seek to reduce carbon emissions and improve the capacity and use of renewable—and sometimes clean—energy sources. Although there are many different forms of renewable energy, states might be constrained in whether and how it uses renewable energy due to its geography and economy. Make sure to consider Hamiltonia and its unique resources as you design standards for the state.

Action Item

12A-6

To which entities do the renewable portfolio standards apply to? Investor owned, municipalities, and/or electric cooperatives?

Action Item

12A-7

Will you institute customer cost caps? If so, what will the cap be?

Water Quality

Water and air quality are other aspects of environmental policy that states seek to address. Below we will focus on the importance of water quality, particularly efforts to reduce lead in the drinking water.

Local Spotlight

Water quality is not only an environmental indicator, but also an important component of health. This is something that the residents of Flint, Michigan, know all too well. Flint, Michigan, is a city that is northwest of Detroit. Flint has about 80,000 residents; 56 percent of

Demonstrators outside of the Fox Theater before the Republican presidential debate in March 2016.

SOURCE: Photo by Chip Somodevilla/Getty Images

those residents are Black. Furthermore, 7 percent of the population is under five with 35 percent of Flint residents living in poverty.[26] In 2014, in efforts to save money, Flint officials began using the Flint River as the water source for residents and businesses. The water from the Flint River began to corrode pipes which allowed for lead and other contaminants to enter the drinking water because officials did not take the proper steps to treat the water from the Flint River.[27] After the city had problems addressing bacteria in the water, the Detroit Water and Sewerage Department offered Flint the opportunity to revert back to using water from Lake Huron (which had been used previously) without having to pay a reconnection fee. However, Flint officials decided against this measure because of the long-term cost of working with the Detroit Water and Sewerage Department. By the beginning of 2015, tests revealed that there were elevated levels of lead in the water. One woman's water had 397 ppb (parts per billion) of lead. To put this in perspective, the federal limit is 15 ppb.[28] By the end of March, the city council voted to stop using the water from the Flint River.

That might have been the end of the story. But Flint residents remained with water from the Flint River when the emergency manager from the state did not agree to stop using the Flint River.[29] As the EPA and a Virginia Tech team expressed concern of widespread elevated lead levels, the Michigan Department of Environmental Quality and the mayor of Flint continued to assert the safety of the drinking water.[30] Once Dr. Mona Honna-Attisha found high levels of lead in children in Flint and multiple schools tested for elevated lead levels, the governor of Michigan, Rick Snyder, finally ordered Flint to use water from the Detroit Water and Sewerage Department again. Since this time, there have been class action lawsuits against the EPA and against state officials. Furthermore, multiple officials have been charged criminally for their role in the **Flint Water Crisis**. Eventually, many of these charges were dismissed including the charges against Governor Rick Snyder.[31] Overall, the Flint Water Crisis exemplifies the failure of the local, state, and federal government to ensure the safety and health of Flint residents with long-lasting health and political consequences.

Flint, Michigan is not the only place in the United States where lead may enter into the drinking water. The National Resources Defense Council (NRDC) estimates that every state in the United States has lead pipes, although the amount of lead pipes varies widely.[32] Lead pipes are dangerous because lead from the pipe can flake off into the water as water passes from the water main into your home. Consumption of lead can lead to a number of negative health outcomes including high blood pressure and kidney problems.[33] However, lead exposure to children has the most serious consequences with irreversible developmental, growth, and behavioral issues. Lead exposure can lower children's IQ and create hearing problems.[34] Therefore, Hamiltonia is particularly concerned about the risk of elevated levels of lead among children in the state.

There are roughly 9.2 million lead pipes across the United States today, but the presence of lead pipes varies by states.[35] To give this context, it is about 9 percent of the pipes that bring water into people's homes. It is difficult to know where lead pipes throughout the United States are because they are buried deep in the ground. A service line takes water from the water main to the internal plumbing of the house. Even when you find lead pipes, it can still be a challenge to replace them because of the cost. The average cost of replacing a lead service line is over $4,000, but it can range up to $12,000.[36] Therefore, it is a very expensive endeavor to dedicate resources to both find and replace **lead service lines (LSLs)**.

Hamiltonia estimates that it has 349,850 lead pipes which is about 10.4 percent of its water pipes. Hamiltonia ranks in the top ten states for the most lead pipes per 100,000 residents. The estimated cost to replace all the lead service lines in the state is $2.1 billion. Currently, Hamiltonia does not know where most of the lead service lines are in the state. However, we do know that lead service lines are more common in houses that were built before the 1960s. We also know that Burr City, Jamestown, and Federalistville were the first cities founded in Hamiltonia and, therefore, have the oldest homes in the state. Other than that, we do not know where the nearly 350,000 lead pipes are throughout the state.

Again, we draw from the National Conference of State Legislatures to think through state action in this area.[37] First, Hamiltonia must decide what level of lead in the water will trigger state action and what kind of state action will be taken. The Lead and Copper Rule, established in 1991, structures the federal response to lead in drinking water. This rule, promulgated by the **Environmental Protection Agency (EPA)**, requires that water systems act if 10 percent of the sampled water has 15 parts per billion (ppb) of lead. In 2007, the Lead and Copper Rule was updated to include a trigger level of 10 ppb. The first item that Hamiltonia needs to decide is to what level of lead in the water triggers a state response (see Figure 12.3). Although the federal limit is 15 ppb for water systems, lead in the water is not safe at any level. States follow the limits outlined in the Lead and Copper Rule from the

Figure 12.3

Possible Elevated Lead Level Requirements

- Notify the public of response to elevated levels of lead.
- Require a lead service line inventory.
- Requires sampling of schools and childcare facilities.
- Notify homeowners of the lead test results.
- Require water system to treat for corrosion.

EPA. However, since no level of lead in the water is safe, the state of Hamiltonia may want to consider being an environmental leader in this area and develop its own acceptable limit for how much lead can be in the water. You also need to decide what kind of action the state must take if lead is found in the water. The EPA proposes that homeowners are notified if 15 ppb of lead is found in the water, that "water systems ... locate and replace sources of lead when a sample tap site exceeds 15 ppb," and requires "targeted sampling at schools and childcare facilities."[38] The EPA requires water systems to respond in this way if lead is found in the water. But what does Hamiltonia require? Hamiltonia can abide by the EPA regulations, but Hamiltonia also could trigger certain action at lower levels of lead in the water as well.

As noted above, elevated levels of lead can create negative and irreversible health consequences, particularly among children. Lead pipes can also service commercial buildings, not just homes. States have begun to take more proactive steps to protect children from lead in the water by focusing on schools and childcare centers. For example, in 2021, the state of Washington passed a new law that required schools that have plumbing from before 2016 to test for lead in their drinking water.[39] Some of these rules have applied to school districts or school boards which are local-level bodies. California as well as other states "require school districts to report elevated levels of lead to parents."[40] If the school finds a lead risk in California, the school has to use state certified companies to resolve the lead issue.[41] Hamiltonia must decide how it will regulate lead drinking water in schools and childcare facilities. The state may want to require schools to test for lead at certain intervals. If it does, the state should decide what needs to happen next. If lead is found in the water, should the state require that school districts inform parents and does the district have to inform the state?

The main issue with reducing lead in the drinking water is finding the lead pipes throughout the country. Several states have begun passing legislation to require water systems to find lead service lines in their jurisdiction called an inventory. Hamiltonia needs to decide whether they will require water systems to identify the lead service lines in the state. Finding the lead service line is just the first step, however. What needs to be done if a lead service line is found? Hamiltonia needs to consider whether the water system has to notify the homeowners of the lead service line, whether the municipality has to replace its portion of the lead service line, whether they will require homeowners to replace the lead service line, and whether homeowners will have to disclose the lead service line when selling their home (see Figure 12.4). Finding the lead service lines is only half of the battle. The state has a compelling interest in replacing these lines once they are found to reduce the risk of lead from the pipes flaking off into the water. However, it is quite expensive. Requiring both the municipality and the homeowner to replace the line could be very costly. We take up how the state might help both municipalities and homeowners pay for these repairs below.

Action Item

12B-1

What level of lead in the water will trigger state action from Hamiltonia? If action is triggered, which state action is automatically triggered?

- Community outreach,
- Required to create a replacement program,
- Require all schools and day-care centers to test for lead.

Action Item

12B-2

Are schools required to test for lead?

- How often do they have to test for lead?
- If lead is found, do the schools have to notify parents?

Figure 12.4
Possible Options after an LSL Is Identified

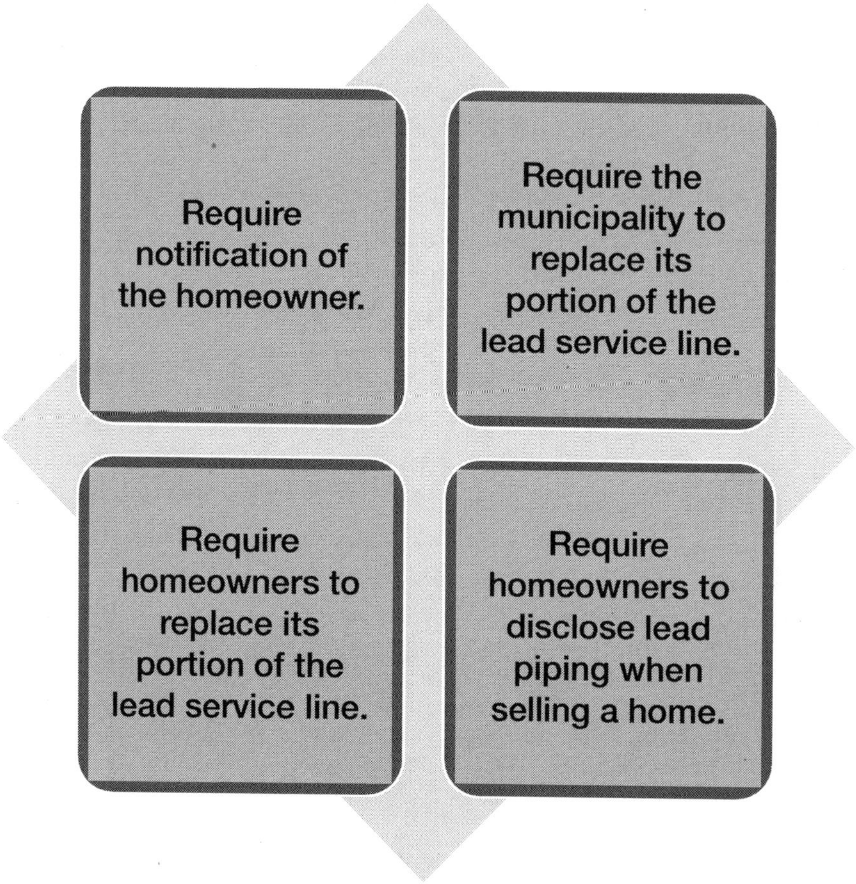

Require notification of the homeowner.

Require the municipality to replace its portion of the lead service line.

Require homeowners to replace its portion of the lead service line.

Require homeowners to disclose lead piping when selling a home.

Action Item

12B-3

Are you going to require an inventory of lead pipes? If an LSL is identified, does the homeowner have to be notified?

- Does the line have to be replaced?
- Are homeowners required to disclose the lead pipes when selling their house?
- Does the state have to be notified?

The state of Hamiltonia might want to consider the importance of transparency when deciding what utilities have to do in the face of identifying an LSL. Trust in government was eroded in Flint, Michigan, after the Flint Water Crisis.[42] It is unclear whether that trust can ever be rebuilt between residents of Flint and local, state, and federal officials. Hamiltonia may want to consider the option of creating its own online database that can inform citizens of where LSLs have been identified. For example, the Environmental Defense Fund reports that the state of Indiana conducted a voluntary survey of water utilities about LSLs. From those responses, the Environmental Defense Fund created a map from that survey so that residents of Indiana can visualize the presence and location of lead service lines throughout the state.[43] The state might want to systematically collect and report data from local governments about their inventory and replacement of LSLs to improve the transparency around the process. It is up to you to structure how the state of Hamiltonia will work with local governments to address this issue and how and when the state will communicate with its citizens.

Replacing lead service lines can be expensive. As noted above, the average cost is around $4,700.[44] If Hamiltonia requires that the LSLs be replaced, the state needs to consider whether there will be any financial assistance given to homeowners. Not all homeowners can necessarily afford a $4,700 lead service line replacement. The state of Hamiltonia needs to decide if it will dedicate any money to help homeowners replace LSLs. Hamiltonia legislators may want to consider the median income in their district to consider whether their residents would be able to afford this unexpected expense. They may also want to consider the average age of the homes in their area, since we know that homes of a certain age are more likely to have LSLs. If Hamiltonia does provide reimbursement to homeowners, Hamiltonia should decide whether local governments are responsible for distributing the funds or if the state's environmental agency should distribute the funds to homeowners. If the state gives money to localities to distribute, then localities will have more control over how to prioritize and spend that money. Essentially, it gives more local control to the issue. However, the state may choose to maintain more control over the distribution of funds and have its environmental agency directly oversee reimbursement for LSL replacement.

Homeowners are not the only parties that may be responsible for expensive lead line service replacements. Local governments may need to replace their portion of the lead service line and they typically have to dedicate limited resources to finding the lead pipes in the first place. This can be a significant barrier to replacing LSLs.[45] Some states have begun to provide grants to localities for these kinds of projects. For example, the state of Indiana has a program that offers low to no interest loans to localities to replace their lead service lines.[46] Finding and replacing LSLs is a local issue but one that can be enhanced by state and federal fiscal support. Hamiltonia may wish to create a program, similar to Indiana, that gives loans to local governments to work on this issue. If you choose to do so, the state government of Hamiltonia should decide how much money will be available in this program and how it will distribute funds. First you should decide if you want to give loans to homeowners, localities, or both. Once you have figured out who qualifies for the program you might want to decide how the funds will be distributed. For example, will Hamiltonia provide each locality with the same amount of money, or will you dedicate funds based on need? It is up to the state government to decide.

States also have several federal funding sources to draw from to help with the identification and replacement of lead service lines. Hamiltonia needs to develop a strategy for whether and how it will pursue federal funding for these local lead service line replacements projects. The newest source of funding comes from the Infrastructure Investment and Jobs Act passed under President Biden which dedicates $15 billion to assist states and localities in addressing the problem of lead service lines. Not all states, however, are using this money.[47] Hamiltonia is eligible for $82 million under the Infrastructure Investment and Jobs Act. Hamiltonia needs to decide whether it will accept these funds and how much of the $82 million will be distributed to each municipality in the state for the replacement of lead service lines. The federal government also has the Drinking Water State Revolving Loan Fund. This fund is "a powerful partnership between EPA and the states."[48] Starting in 1996, the program allows the EPA to provide funds to states—with states matching at a 20 percent rate—based on their drinking water infrastructure. In 2019 alone, this fund gave over $41 billion to states.[49] Based upon the assessment, the EPA plans to give Hamiltonia $10 million this year to improve the safety of drinking water. The state needs to decide how it is going to distribute the $82 million from the Infrastructure Investment and Jobs Act and the $10 million from the EPA to localities to address lead levels in the drinking water.

Quality drinking water is an intergovernmental issue with the federal, state, and local governments involved. As witnessed from the Flint Water Crisis, mismanagement of water quality and resources can have important political, social, and health effects. Hamiltonia has an important responsibility to its citizens to take action to protect the state from elevated levels of lead. However, the state cannot do this without relying on the help of both the federal government and local governments.

Action Item

12B-4

If a lead service line is identified, will you reimburse homeowners for lead line replacement?

- If so, how much will the reimbursement be per homeowner?
- Who will be responsible for distributing these funds? Local government or state environmental agency?

Action Item

12B-5

To help pay for the identification and replacement of lead service lines which of these federal programs will Hamiltonia pursue? If you do take federal money, who will qualify to receive the money and how will you distribute it?

- Infrastructure Investment and Jobs Act (up to $82 million) Drinking Water State Revolving Loan Fund

Looking Forward

Congratulations! I hope that you—the leaders of Hamiltonia—have taken steps to address either renewable energy or water quality in the state. As we have seen from this chapter, states make important decisions in environmental policy. Think back on how your class made decisions creating a new environmental policy for your state. Did you consider creating a voluntary survey for local governments to identify LSLs once you learned that was Indiana's approach? Or did you decide to not only require renewable energy but clean energy when you learned that was what California did? Did you use any of the other state approaches to inform what Hamiltonia was going to do to address either renewable energy or water quality? If so, you participated in policy learning and helped diffuse some of the innovations from other states into Hamiltonia. Did you develop a new idea that no other state has tried before? If so, you just made Hamiltonia a laboratory of democracy. Whether you participated in policy learning or you created a new policy innovation, you just participated in policy diffusion. This is an important dynamic for state policymaking in multiple policy areas.

As climate concerns continue to grow, states will continue to be prominent players in our federal system. Addressing environmental problems is complicated and relies on the involvement of every level of government in the United States. If you were unsuccessful in passing a new environmental policy, take time to reflect on what made it challenging to accomplish this goal. Remember, leaders in the other fifty states experience cross-political pressures when engaging in policymaking. It is not an easy task!

Key Terms

policy diffusion (248)
policy learning (248)
renewable portfolio standards (RPS) (249)
clean energy (253)
investor-owned utility companies (255)
publicly owned utility (255)
electric cooperative (255)
Flint water crisis (258)
lead service lines (LSLs) (259)
Environmental Protection Agency (EPA) (259)

Assignments to Learn More about State Environmental Policy

1. Go to your home state or the state your college is in and review its renewable portfolio standards. Are the standards different from the ones you developed for Hamiltonia? How so? Are they stricter? Think about any lessons you may take from your own state's RPS and whether they should be applied to Hamiltonia.
2. Go to your home state or the state your college is in and assess what state action is being taken to reduce lead in the drinking water. Does the state require an inventory of LSLs? Is it using money from the Infrastructure Investment and Jobs Act? If so, how is it using that money? What other policies do they have to reduce lead in the water? Are any of these the policies that you have in Hamiltonia?

3. Assess the most important environmental needs in your state. Now, act as a state environmental employee and write a proposal to the EPA for funds to solve that problem. How much money will you ask for? How will the funds be distributed? How will the funds help solve the environmental problem?
4. Spend time studying the EPA. Assess the history of the EPA, its mission, and the ways in which it regulates and partners with states. What are some ways that the EPA and state work together in environmental policy? What are some areas in which the EPA and states might have conflict in environmental policy?

Former Ohio Governor John Kasich

SOURCE: Photo by Rick Friedman/rickfriedman.com/Corbis via Getty Images

13 Health Care Policy

Learning Objectives:

After reading this chapter students should be able to:

- Understand the differences in health policies and outcomes across states.
- Describe the financial cost of various state health care policies.
- Understand what Medicaid is and explain how and why it is different across states.
- Explain and evaluate state responses to the opioid epidemic.

State Spotlight: Ohio

In 2013, Republican Governor John Kasich was frustrated with the Republican-controlled Ohio state legislature for not expanding **Medicaid**—a joint state-federal program that provides health insurance for low-income Americans. At that time, states could opt in to expand Medicaid to anyone—even adults without children—earning below 138 percent above the federal poverty line fully on the federal government's dime. Two years after expansion Ohio would need to start contributing more money to Medicaid, but the federal government would still cover 90 percent of the expansion cost. At this time, Governor Kasich needed to get the legislature on board with **Medicaid expansion**. This was difficult because expanding Medicaid was seen as supporting President Obama's Affordable Care Act (ACA)—a Democratic initiative. Indeed, the party of the governor is a strong predictor of opting into Medicaid expansion with Democratic states much more likely to expand Medicaid under the ACA.[1] Why would a Republican governor in the Midwest be pioneering a Democratic initiative in a Republican controlled state? Governor Kasich claimed it was a moral imperative and it could save money,[2] but Ohio was also facing a severe opioid epidemic and expanding Medicaid could help the state defray some of the cost of trying to address the opioid epidemic.[3]

Governor Kasich decided to go around the legislature to expand Medicaid. This was advantageous as it shielded Republicans in the legislature from having to vote on Medicaid expansion.[4] Instead, Kasich went to the Ohio Controlling Board which is a body within the Ohio Office of Budget and Management that "provides legislative oversight over certain capital and operating expenditures by state agencies."[5] The law allowed for Kasich to do this because state agencies can "spend federal funds that have been approved either by the Ohio General Assembly or the seven-member state Controlling Board."[6] The maneuver around the legislature worked and Ohio expanded Medicaid. The uninsured rate in Ohio went from 13 percent to 8 percent from 2013 (when Ohio expanded Medicaid) to 2021.[7]

In 2021, Ohio paid 25.8 percent and the federal government covered 74.2 percent of the $247 billion in total Medicaid cost for the state.[8] In 2022, Ohio covered 22 percent of its population with Medicaid and **CHIP**. CHIP is the Children's Health Insurance Program passed under President Clinton. CHIP is designed like Medicaid in that it is a state and federal program with the federal government contributing funds for states to insure children in families whose parents earn too much money to be on Medicaid, but not enough money to afford private insurance. Many states have folded CHIP into their Medicaid program. Ohio's uninsured rate is 8 percent which is 2 percent lower than the federal average.[9]

Medicaid expansion has been effective in lowering the uninsured rate in the state. There are four ways you can qualify for Medicaid/CHIP in Ohio. You can qualify if you are a child living below 211 percent above the federal poverty line (FPL), a pregnant woman living 205 percent of FPL, parents or childless adults living 138 percent of FPL, and an elderly or person with disabilities 74 percent of FPL. The federal poverty line is "$24,680 for a family of three; $14,580 for an individual."[10] This means that an individual without children qualifies for Medicaid if they make less than $20,120 a year.

Sixty-eight percent of Ohioans on Medicaid are working. As is typical, the elderly and disabled make up 22 percent of enrollees but account for 52 percent of the Medicaid expenditures in the state. Medicaid is particularly important for women and for pregnant women. In Ohio, 20 percent of women of child-bearing age (15–49) are covered by Medicaid and Medicaid covers 41 percent of the births in the state.[11]

Even though opting into Medicaid expansion has led to more people being covered by health insurance, Ohio is still facing a number of health issues. In Ohio, the infant mortality rate was 6.5 per 1,000 live births in 2021 and the maternal mortality rate was 21.3 per 100,000 live births in 2020.[12] The leading cause of death in Ohio is heart disease. Their drug overdose death rate was 48.1 per 100,000 and their firearm death rate was 16.5 per 100,000 in 2021.[13] These health issues, however, are not necessarily equitable across the United States. Take maternal mortality for example. Not only is maternal mortality in the United States high compared to other countries (by some estimates ten times higher than similar countries), but within the United States African American women die from childbirth at nearly three times the rate of white women.[14] Table 13.1 shows these health statistics compared to the national average and the national average broken down by race.

Ohio has been one of the hardest-hit states by the **opioid epidemic**. Between 2010 and 2015, almost 13,000 Ohioans died from drug overdoses.[15] In 2014, Ohio had the most heroin deaths compared to any state in the United States.[16] From 2017 to 2020, the drug epidemic was improving somewhat. However, COVID-19 has made it

Table 13.1
Ohio and National Health Statistics

	OHIO (2021)	NATIONAL (2021)	NATIONAL AVERAGE WHITE/BLACK
Infant Mortality (per 1,000 live births)	7.06	5.4[1]	4.4/10.6
Maternal Mortality Rate (per 100,000 live births)	21.3	32.9[2]	26.6/69.9
Opioid Overdose Rate (per 100,000)	29.6	24.7	28.4/33.5[3]
Firearm Death Rate (per 100,000)	16.5	14.6[4]	12.3/36.0[5]

[1] "Infant Mortality," Center for Disease Control, June 22, 2022 https://www.cdc.gov/reproductivehealth/maternalinfanthealth/infantmortality.htm, accessed July 6th, 2023. Infant mortality by race is from 2021.

[2] Donna Hoyert, "Maternal Mortality Rates in the United States, 2021," Center for Disease Control and Prevention, March 16, 2023, https://www.cdc.gov/nchs/data/hestat/maternal-mortality/2021/maternal-mortality-rates-2021.htm#:~:text=In%202021%2C%201%2C205%20women%20died,20.1%20in%202019%20(Table), accessed June 7, 2023.

[3] "Opioid Overdose Deaths by Race and Ethnicity," Kaiser Family Foundation, https://www.kff.org/other/state-indicator/opioid-overdose-deaths-by-raceethnicity/?dataView=1&activeTab=graph¤tTimeframe=0&startTimeframe=3&selectedDistributions=overall--white--black--hispanic--asian--american-indian-or-alaska-native&selectedRows=%7B%22states%22:%7B%22ohio%22:%7B%7D%7D,%22wrapups%22:%7B%22united-states%22:%7B%7D-%7D%7D&sortModel=%7B%22colId%22:%22Location%22,%22sort%22:%22asc%22%7D, accessed January 19, 2024. Data is from 2021.

[4] "Deaths Due to Injury by Firearms per 100,000 Population," Kaiser Family Foundation, https://www.kff.org/other/state-indicator/firearms-death-rate-per-100000/?currentTimeframe=1&sortModel=%7B%22colId%22:%22Location%22,%22sort%22:%22asc%22%7D, accessed June 7, 2023.

[5] "Total Deaths due to Firearms by Race/Ethnicity," Kaiser Family Foundation, https://www.kff.org/other/state-indicator/firearms-death-rate-by-raceethnicity/?dataView=1¤tTimeframe=0&sortModel=%7B%22colId%22:%22Location%22,%22sort%22:%22asc%22%7D, accessed January 19, 2024.

worse. From 2019 to 2020 there was a 22 percent increase in drug overdoses.[17] The opioid epidemic has far-reaching effects on state governance. With the rise in opioid abuse, Ohio's foster care system has faced increasing pressure. In Ohio, there has been an 11 percent increase in children needing foster care placement and a 20 percent increase in costs. The public children's health association of Ohio reported that "50% of children taken into custody in 2015 had parental drug abuse."[18] Ohio also saw an eight-fold increase in neonatal abstinence syndrome—when a baby has to withdraw from drugs when born from 2006 to 2015.[19]

Former Ohio Governor John Kasich speaking about Medicaid expansion in Ohio, one of the policy tools that would help respond to the opioid epidemic in the state.

SOURCE: AP Photo/Tony Dejak

Ohio has taken a number of policy approaches to address the opioid epidemic. In 2011, Governor Kasich established the Governor's Cabinet Opiate Action Team. To limit access to prescription opioids (opioids that are prescribed by doctors), Ohio has created prescription guidelines for physicians and limited opioid prescriptions to seven days, has created a drug monitoring system where doctors and pharmacists can track the opioids used by patients to limit abuse, and has attempted to eliminate pill mills.[20] A pill mill illegally distributes opioids without the proper medical documentation or authorization. Ohio has also expanded the use and access of free naloxone (an opioid overdose reversal drug) across the state and has given grants to emergency departments to develop systems to better address patients with an opioid disorder.[21] Expanding Medicaid is also an important response to the opioid epidemic because Medicaid recipients may receive substance use disorder benefits to help treat opioid addiction.[22]

Health policy at both the national and state level has two important implications for democracy. First, the way that our programs are designed and implemented can affect an individual's participation. Because Medicaid is unequal across states, it can lead to unequal political participation.[23] Individuals can learn political lessons when they engage in Medicaid which can affect their participation. Overall, individuals on Medicaid are less likely to participate in politics.[24] However, we have also seen increases in voter registration and, to a lesser extent voting, in states that expanded Medicaid.[25] Therefore the types of health programs that we have and how they are implemented can affect subsequent political action by beneficiaries. Second, health has an important relationship to participation in that healthy individuals are more likely to vote.[26] This includes both physical and mental health as well as both objective and subjective measures of health.[27] For example, new research has also shown that depression can make voting less likely.[28] The health of Hamiltonia's residents, then, is an important consideration for the health of our democracy.

Simulation

For this final public policy area your class will either expand Medicaid eligibility or address the opioid crisis. Both are incredibly important public policy problems that have unique challenges.

Medicaid and CHIP Expansion

At this point, Hamiltonia has not expanded Medicaid under the **Affordable Care Act (ACA)**. About 14 percent of Hamiltonians do not have any health insurance coverage, 44.7 percent get health insurance through their employer, and 14.3 percent are on Medicaid. The median income is $62,900 which is 148 percent above the federal poverty line. Last year, Hamiltonia spent $2,988,000,000 on Medicaid. Because Hamiltonia has not expanded Medicaid, about 8 percent of residents are in the coverage gap meaning that they do not qualify for Medicaid but also do not qualify for federal subsidies to purchase health insurance on healthcare.gov.

Hamiltonians are facing a number of health issues. The infant mortality rate is 6.1 per 100,000 live births, but there is disparity between white and Black children. The infant mortality rate of white children is 6.2 and the infant mortality rate of Black children is 14.88. Hamiltonia ranks thirty-seventh in maternal mortality meaning that it is not the safest place for a woman to have a child. There is also a large disparity in this health outcome as Black women in Hamiltonia are 2.6 times more likely to die from childbirth than white women.

Hamiltonia is also facing a rise in diabetes, obesity, and depression. There were 50,000 new cases of diabetes in 2023. In total, 12.5 percent of the population in Hamiltonia has diabetes. $5.1 billion dollars was spent in the state on direct medical costs associated with diabetes last year. Unfortunately, about 34 percent of Hamiltonia residents have pre-diabetes. This suggests that diabetes will continue to be a health issue in Hamiltonia for years to come. Associated with the rise in diabetes is the rise in obesity. In Hamiltonia, 32 percent of the population is obese and 31 percent of children are obese or overweight. Hamiltonia also faces mental health challenges, particularly a rise in depression. About 33 percent of the population expressed symptoms of depression with 16 percent of twelve to eighteen-year-olds reporting depression. Although Hamiltonia is facing a rise in mental health challenges, the state has also been at the forefront of expanding services for behavioral health. Taking advantage of federal support during COVID, Hamiltonia's Medicaid program now covers telehealth visits for depression and anxiety. Hamiltonia has also created a new program based on OhioRise, which coordinates and provides care for youth with behavioral health needs.

Background on Medicaid

In 1965, President Johnson signed the Medicaid program into law which created a state-federal program to provide health insurance to low-income families. Medicaid was built off an earlier law called the Kerr-Mills Act (1960). The pressing public problem was that hospital stays were very expensive, especially for poor, elderly Americans. The Kerr-Mills Act sought to address this problem by creating a federal–state program where the federal government provided funds for states to use to help elderly Americans who were on welfare with their health costs. Although this program was very limited, twenty-eight states signed on to participate in Kerr-Mills.[29] This policy design led to our modern-day Medicaid program. Medicaid has become one of the most important programs in the United States and is a major site of state and federal relations.

Medicaid provides health insurance to low-income Americans. In 2023, over 85 million Americans were enrolled in Medicaid. However, enrollment varies by state. For example, New York enrolls 28 percent and Florida enrolls 18 percent of its population in Medicaid (see Figure 13.1).[30] Why? Because Medicaid is a federal *and* state program. What this means is that the federal government has established minimum requirements for who is eligible and what Medicaid has to cover, but states are responsible for implementing the program and creating additional requirements or coverage decisions. Therefore, New York and Florida's Medicaid programs actually cover different

Figure 13.1
Florida and New York Medicaid Comparison

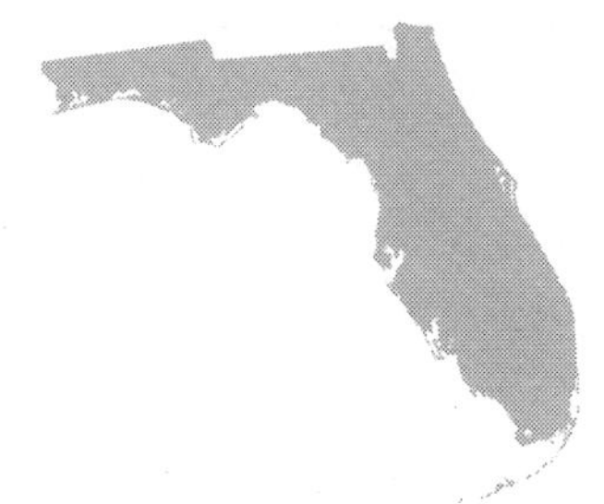

Florida

- 31% population is low income
- 4,978,001 residents on Medicaid
- 45% births paid for by Medicaid
- No expansion
- 388,000 in the coverage gap

New York

- 28% population is low income
- 7,491,311 residents on Medicaid
- 46% births paid for by Medicaid
- 2.5 million adults covered through expansion
- No coverage gap

SOURCE: "Medicaid in Florida," Kaiser Family Foundation, June 2023, https://files.kff.org/attachment/fact-sheet-medicaid-state-FL, accessed January 19, 2024, and "Medicaid in New York," Kaiser Family Foundation, June 2023, https://files.kff.org/attachment/fact-sheet-medicaid-state-NY, accessed January 19, 2024.

services and have different eligibility requirements. Some states cover hearing aids and dental services, and others do not. Your access to Medicaid and what your Medicaid insurance covers, then, depends upon which state you live in.

Enrollment in Medicaid is also a function of the amount of poverty in the state. Eligibility for Medicaid is tied to income levels. States with a greater number of families in poverty will also have higher enrollment in Medicaid because more people qualify. The federal government pays a portion of the state's Medicaid cost based on the per capita income of the state. In states with lower per capita income, like Mississippi, the federal government pays 85.2 percent of the Medicaid costs. In other states with higher per capita income, like Massachusetts, the federal government pays 64.3 percent percentage of the cost.[31] Either way, states are attracted to offering Medicaid because the federal government pays a large portion of the cost. Overall, health costs have surpassed education costs as the largest share of state budgets. Typically, states spend between 20 and 40 percent of their revenues on health costs which is mostly Medicaid. Figure 13.2 shows the percent of people covered in Medicaid and CHIP by state.

Enrollment

The Medicaid program has gained substantial public support and has expanded over time. This is surprising because Medicaid is a means-tested program. This means that people have to be eligible in some way to receive the benefits. Traditionally, we have expected programs such as Medicare—health insurance for elderly Americans—to have

Figure 13.2

Percent of Medicaid and CHIP Coverage 2021

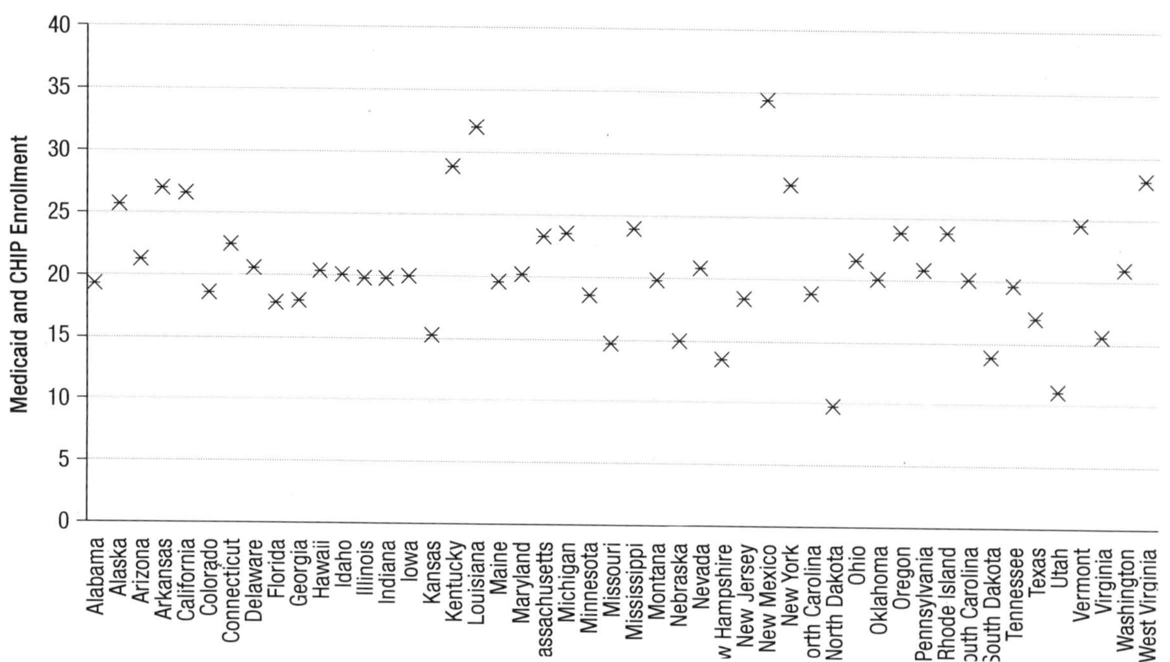

SOURCE: "Medicaid Expenditures as a Percent of Total State Expenditures by Fund," Kaiser Family Foundation, https://www.kff.org/interactive/medicaid-state-fact-sheets/, accessed January 19, 2023.

greater political stability because they are universal meaning everyone has access to the benefits. This makes it more likely that the program will have widespread support. We also expect means-tested programs to be more politically precarious because they only apply to a segment of the population which can limit widespread support.[32] This has not necessarily been the case for Medicaid. Since the 1960s, Medicaid has expanded its coverage to include pregnant women, children, and low-income adults. In fact, Medicaid covers about 41 percent of the births in the nation.[33] Medicaid also has substantial public support. Overall, 76 percent of Americans say they have a very favorable or somewhat favorable view of Medicaid.[34]

One of the most significant changes to Medicaid came under the Affordable Care Act (ACA) passed under President Obama. One component of the ACA was to require states to expand Medicaid eligibility to 138 percent of the federal poverty line including families and single individuals. Prior to the ACA, Medicaid had only been available to low-income families and pregnant women. The ACA threatened to take away all Medicaid funding if states did not comply. Numerous states brought a lawsuit against this component of the ACA and, in *National Federation of Independent Business v. Sebelius* the U.S. Supreme Court ruled that this was a coercive use of federal power. Since then, states have had the option to opt into Medicaid expansion.

States have adopted Medicaid expansion through a variety of ways including legislative enactment, but also by direct democracy like in South Dakota in 2022. As of 2023, ten states have not expanded Medicaid which can be seen in Figure 13.3. These states still have the Medicaid program, but single adults are not eligible, and the income eligibility may be higher than in states that have adopted Medicaid expansion. Overall, more people are eligible for Medicaid in expansion states than non-expansion states. Democrat-controlled states have been more likely to expand Medicaid. However, some Republican-controlled states have also signed on to expand Medicaid.[35] One of the reasons for this is the opioid epidemic. States experiencing the most severe opioid epidemic rely on Medicaid funding to help with the cost of providing substance abuse treatment. In some cases, this has been enough for Republican-controlled states to opt into Medicaid expansion.[36]

States that have opted out of Medicaid expansion have faced a new issue after the ACA. The ACA was designed to increase access to health insurance through a number of mechanisms including expanding eligibility for Medicaid, providing subsidies for individuals to purchase health insurance on online marketplaces (like healthcare.gov), expanding

Figure 13.3
State Medicaid Expansion Decisions

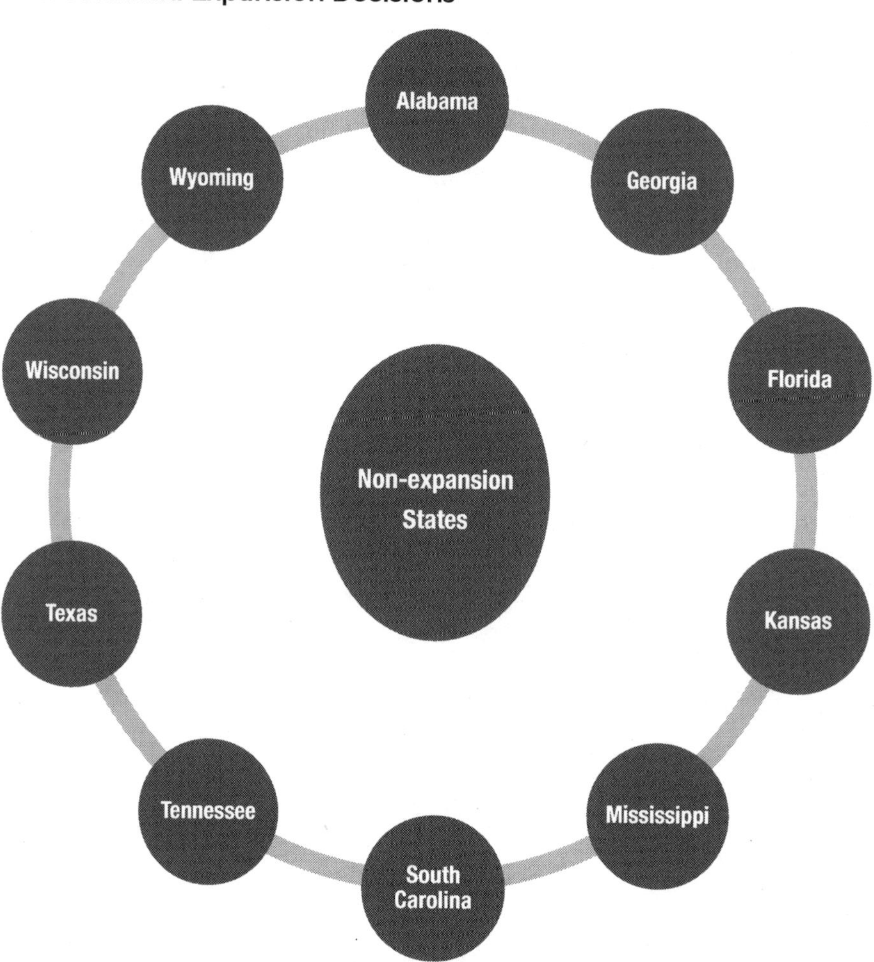

SOURCE: "Status of State Medicaid Expansion Decisions: Interactive Map," Kaiser Family Foundation, December 1, 2023, https://www.kff.org/medicaid/issue-brief/status-of-state-medicaid-expansion-decisions-interactive-map/, accessed January 19, 2024.

employer-based health insurance, and assigning a tax penalty to individuals that did not buy health insurance.[37] Because some states have not expanded Medicaid, this has created the coverage gap. In non-expansion states, there are individuals who do not qualify for Medicaid (because they are single or make too much money) but also do not qualify for the tax subsidies to purchase insurance on healthcare.gov (because they make too little money to qualify). The **coverage gap** does not affect people equitably. Only citizens living in non-expansion states can be in the coverage gap and people of color make up 61 percent of the adults in the coverage gap.[38] Based upon what you have just learned, you will have to make important decisions regarding Hamiltonia's expansion of Medicaid.

Action Item

13A-1

Who will be eligible for Medicaid in Hamiltonia?

- Do residents have to be citizens?
- Do residents have to earn a certain income? What is that income?
- Do these same requirements apply to children?

Services

State Medicaid programs can also differ in the kinds of services that they provide. The federal government requires state Medicaid programs offer certain benefits such as physician visits, hospital stays, nursing facility stays, X-ray services, lab services, pediatric care, and family planning. States are required to provide these benefits if a resident qualifies for Medicaid. However, states have a lot of flexibility in their programs and can offer more services if they desire. States may do this because they are able to offer more services with the federal government paying a large portion of the cost. Some of the optional services that state Medicaid programs can offer include prescription drug benefits, physical therapy sessions, occupational therapy, dental services, optometry services, eyeglasses, and speech and hearing services.[39] This means that the same person will have access to different services depending upon which state they live in. Dental services are a good example of this. Some states offer no dental benefits at all in their Medicaid programs. Other states, however, offer emergency dental services, limited dental services (for example a $500 limit like in Arkansas), or extensive benefits.[40] If you live in Tennessee—no matter how close you are to the border of North Carolina—you are not eligible for any dental benefits through Medicaid. However, if you live just over the border in North Carolina you are eligible for extensive benefits. Figure 13.4 shows the kinds of dental benefits offered in different states.

Figure 13.4

Dental Services Covered by State Medicaid Programs

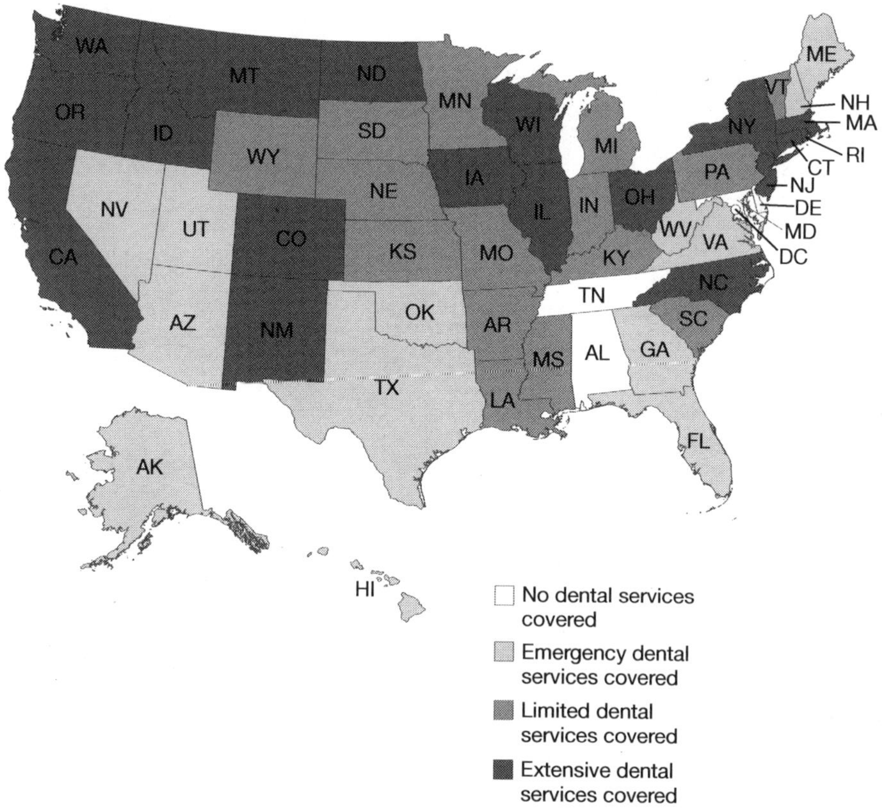

SOURCE: "Medicaid Adult Dental Benefits Coverage by State," Center for Health Care Strategies Inc, September 2019, https://www.chcs.org/media/Medicaid-Adult-Dental-Benefits-Overview-Appendix_091519.pdf, accessed July 10, 2023.

Another optional service states can provide through Medicaid is **medication-assisted treatment** (MAT). The Substance Abuse and Mental Health Services Administration defines MAT as "the use of FDA-approved medications, in combination with counseling and behavioral therapies, to provide a 'whole-patient' approach to the treatment of substance use disorders."[41] This may include medicines such as methadone or buprenorphine which can limit cravings for opioids. The ability to expand access to addiction treatment through Medicaid is one of the reasons that Ohio opted into Medicaid expansion.

Action Item

13A-2

What optional benefits, if any, will Medicaid cover in Hamiltonia?

- prescription drug benefits (66.7 billion of 4–5% of total Medicaid cost for state)
- physical therapy sessions
- dental services
- optometry services
- Medicated assisted treatment for drug addiction

Costs

Health expenditures have recently overtaken education expenditures as the largest expenditures in state budgets. Even though the federal government pays a good portion of state Medicaid costs—based on the per capita income of the state—Medicaid is still an expensive program. One reason Medicaid is expensive is because it pays a large portion of long term care costs in the United States. Individuals who are over sixty-five and are low-income can qualify for both Medicare and Medicaid. Medicaid is typically what contributes to long-term care and services. Kaiser Family Foundation reports that "In 2020, Medicaid paid 54% of the over $400 billion spent on LTSS [long-term services and supports] in the U.S."[42] The amount of Medicaid funding spent on long-term care is partly a function of the age demographics in the state. In Hamiltonia about 17 percent of the population is sixty-five and older.

In Hamiltonia, the federal government pays 71.8 percent of the total Medicaid cost and Hamiltonia pays the remaining 28.2 percent of the $10 billion spent on Medicaid. If you decide to expand Medicaid or expand the services that Medicaid offers, you will need to find a way to pay for these additional enrollees and/or additional services. In the first two years of Medicaid expansion, the government will pay 100 percent of the expansion costs. After that, Hamiltonia needs to be able to pay for 10 percent of the increase in Medicaid costs. Currently, Hamiltonia's Department of Health and Human Services expects that Medicaid expansion will cost an additional $100 million each year. States take a number of approaches to paying for Medicaid. States use money from general revenues (from tax revenues such as income or sales tax) and from taxing health services. States typically tax institutional providers, nursing facilities, and hospitals on their net patient revenues.[43] States tax anywhere between 3.5 and 5.5 percent.[44]

Action Item

13A-3

How are you going to pay for Medicaid expansion and/or additional benefits?

- General revenues? From sales tax or income tax?
- Health tax?
    - On institutional providers? What percent will the tax be on net patient revenues?
    - On nursing facilities? What percent will the tax be on net patient revenues?
    - On hospitals? What percent will the tax be on net patient revenues?

Opioid Epidemic

This section is for the Hamiltonians that have decided to focus on the opioid epidemic for their health policy. Hamiltonia has not been spared from the opioid epidemic. In 2017, it was in the top five states with the highest opioid overdose death rates. The overdose death rate had started to decrease in 2018. However, in 2021, the state began to see a rise in overdose deaths again after COVID-19. Yorktown and Frameton have the highest overdose rates in the state. They each experienced 105 overdose deaths per 100,000 people and 99 overdose deaths per 100,000 people last year. This compares to the overall state rate of overdose deaths of 45 deaths per 100,000. However, with the pervasiveness of fentanyl other areas of the state are also starting to see a rise in overdose deaths. For example, both Charlestown and Burr City have seen 45 percent increases in their overdose death rates. Last year, fentanyl was involved in 77 percent of all overdose deaths. Overdose deaths have overtaken both motor vehicle and firearm deaths as the deadliest accidental injury.

Background

The opioid epidemic has ravaged the United States. The CDC estimates that over one million Americans have died from drug overdoses since 1999.[45] There have been three waves of the opioid epidemic. The first wave began in the 1990s with an increase in use and addiction to prescription opioids. By 2010 the second wave consisted of an increase in use of and death from heroin—an illegal opioid. We are currently in wave three which is marked by an increase in use and death from fentanyl, a more potent synthetic opioid.[46] Ann Milgram of the Drug Enforcement Agency (DEA) said that "Fentanyl is the single deadliest drug threat our nation has ever encountered."[47] In 2021, over 100,000 Americans died from a drug overdose and 67 percent of the drug overdose deaths involved fentanyl. In addition to lives lost, the opioid epidemic also has economic consequences. In 2020, "the Joint Economic Committee estimates the opioid epidemic cost the United States nearly $1.5 trillion."[48]

Although the United States has suffered from the opioid epidemic, some states, such as Ohio and West Virginia, have borne the brunt of the epidemic. In 2021 alone, over 5,000 people died in Ohio (a death rate of 48.1 per 100,000 people) and 1,500 people died in West Virginia (a death rate of 90.9 per 100,000 people). Within states, white residents have made up a large portion of the opioid overdose deaths.[49] Some evidence suggests that the racial dimension to this epidemic has led to less punitive policy approaches than past drug epidemics.[50] From 1999–2015, all racial groups experienced an increase in overdose deaths from opioids with non-Hispanic whites experiencing the greatest increase.[51] This, however, may be changing with the infiltration of fentanyl into communities across the United States. From 2018–2021, all racial groups have experienced an increase in overdose death rates with Black and American Indian or Alaska Native experiencing large increases. Figure 13.5 shows the age-adjusted opioid overdose death rates (per 100,000) from 2018–2021 by racial group.

State Approaches

The federal government, state governments, and local governments have been scrambling to address the opioid epidemic. Many state and local governments were first to respond to the opioid epidemic. States have tried several policy responses to alleviate the severity of the epidemic. Below we will focus on three approaches including prescription drug monitoring, treatment approaches, and harm reduction. Hamiltonia may want to use all or some of these policy solutions. It is up to you to decide!

Prescription Drug Monitoring

The opioid epidemic began with the rise in addiction to prescribed opioids such as oxycontin. These are legal, synthetic opioids that can help with pain management. However, they can also be addictive. One issue with the introduction of prescription opioids is that prescribers and patients were not aware of the addiction risk and the labels stated that the opioids lasted longer (twelve hours) than they actually did.[52] This helped create the first wave of the opioid epidemic where many Americans became addicted to drugs that they were prescribed by doctors. States, then, have taken a number of approaches to limit

Figure 13.5
Opioid Overdose Death Rates 2018–2021 by Race

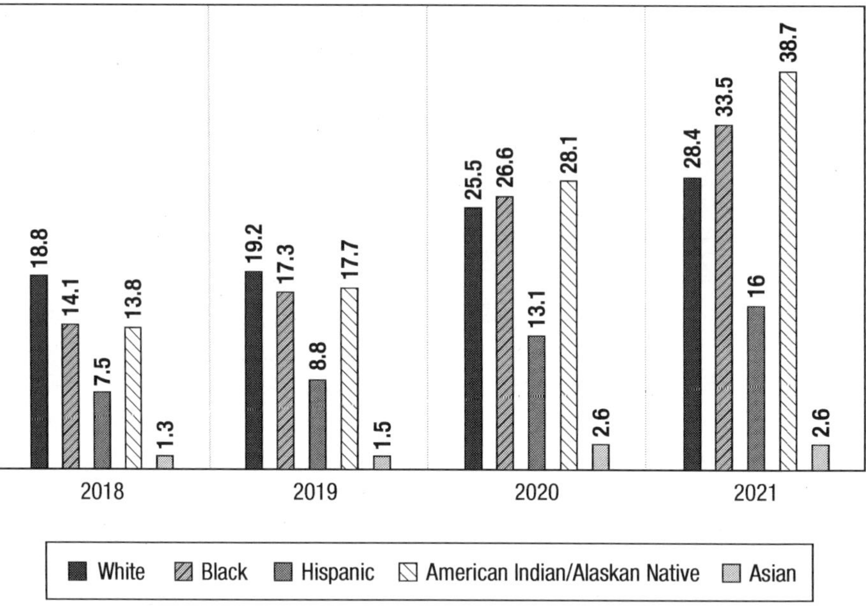

SOURCE: "Opioid Overdose Deaths by Race/Ethnicity," Kaiser Family Foundation, https://www.kff.org/other/state-indicator/opioid-overdose-deaths-by-raceethnicity/?dataView=1&activeTab=graph¤tTimeframe=0&startTimeframe=3&selectedDistributions=white--black--hispanic--american-indian-or-alaska-native&sortModel=%7B%22colId%22:%22Location%22,%22sort%22:%22asc%22%7D, accessed July 11, 2023.

the supply of prescription opioids and reduce addiction to prescription opioids.

One approach has been to institute prescription drug monitoring programs like Ohio did with its Ohio Automated Rx Reporting System (OARRS) monitoring program. A **prescription drug monitoring program (PDMP)** uses an online database to track opioid prescriptions. It is meant to help identify individuals who have a history of addiction or abuse of prescription opioids so that prescribers can take this history into account when determining care. The goal of PDMPs is to prevent individuals from shopping different doctors or pharmacies to purchase more prescription opioids. This is meant to protect individuals who may be experiencing addiction and to limit the supply of prescription opioids.

States have designed their PDMP differently in terms of how long a pharmacist has to report the dispensing of opioids and whether a prescriber is required to check the database before prescribing opioids. A state can require the pharmacist to report the dispensing of opioids in real time (immediately), in a few days, within a week, or within a month. When the pharmacist is required to report more quickly, it allows the database to have more up-to-date data. However, it does take time for the pharmacist to report each of his prescriptions. Requiring pharmacists to report in real time may slow down pharmacies. States can also decide whether to require prescribers to check the database before writing more prescriptions for a patient. Without a requirement, it is up to the prescriber whether to use the data in the drug monitoring program.

States have also tried to reduce addiction and the availability of prescription opioids by limiting doctors in the amount of opioids they can prescribe. Many states have started to limit the number of days prescribers can supply to patients. Some states restrict opioid prescriptions to three days (the most restrictive) or seven days (less restrictive). For example, Florida has a three-day prescription limit.[53] Restricting the length of prescriptions may help reduce the use of opioids. However, for some, the prescription limits create a substantial burden. Individuals with chronic pain, for example, may need opioids for longer periods of time. This may make it more difficult for them to get the care that they need.

Action Item

13B-1

Will Hamiltonia establish a drug monitoring program?

- How long will pharmacists have to report the dispensing of opioids?
- Will prescribers be required to check the program?

Action Item

13B-2

Will prescribers be limited in the time of an opioid prescription? What will the time be? Three days, five days, seven days?

Treatment Approaches

Another way that states have tried to address the opioid epidemic is by expanding access to treatment. New York has been a leading state in its approaches to the opioid epidemic. It has taken a number of policy approaches including prohibiting centers from turning away individuals who need treatment on the basis of whether they can pay, insurance companies cannot require pre-authorization for abuse services so that individuals do not have to wait to get help, and it has its own agency focused on substance abuse services.[54] Even so, New Yorkers have still struggled to access needed addiction services. Strach, Zuber, and Perez-Chicques (2020) investigated this problem. They found that although New York successfully expanded the number of treatment beds and created an online tracking tool so that residents could view which centers had available beds, there were still structural barriers to receiving treatment. Their online locator tool showed open beds, but residents had trouble accessing those beds because of issues such as treatment facilities not being open twenty-four hours a day, admission requirements such as age or sex requirements, staff shortages at treatment facilities, and logistical challenges such as finding childcare. Longer hours at treatment facilities may help individuals who seek out help outside 9 to 5 hours. However, staffing shortages are problematic for these facilities already. Longer hours would likely require even more staff. Many facilities also have requirements such as an all-female facility. This may restrict which facilities can treat certain residents.

Action Item

13B-3

Will Hamiltonia try to increase access to treatment via treatment facilities?

- Will Hamiltonia require treatment facilities to be open twenty-four hours?
- Will Hamiltonia require treatment facilities to allow young children to live in the facility with their mother?

Harm Reduction

Harm reduction is another type of approach to the opioid epidemic. **Harm reduction** is focused on "engaging directly with people who use drugs to prevent overdose and infectious disease transmission, improve the physical, mental, and social wellbeing of those served, and offer low-threshold options for accessing substance use disorder treatment and other health care services."[55] One of the more prominent harm reduction strategies is expanding access to naloxone. Naloxone is an opioid overdose reversal drug. Essentially, naloxone can be delivered to someone experiencing an opioid overdose and it can save that person's life by reversing the overdose. All states allow for the use of naloxone, but some states have different restrictions on its use and access. In most states now, naloxone can be obtained without a prescription. Some states, however, have tried to increase access to naloxone through co-prescribing requirements.

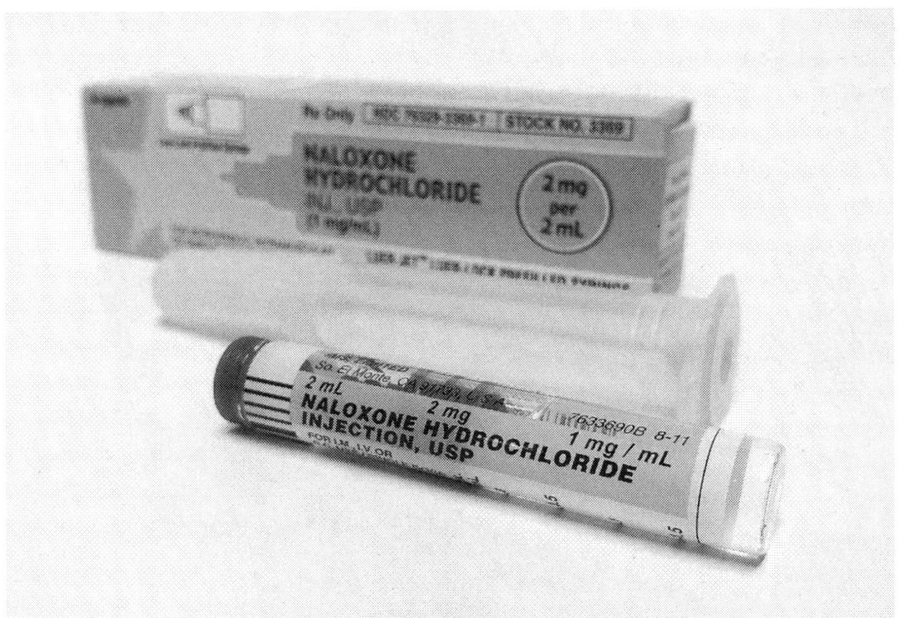

Naloxone, an opioid overdose reversal drug.

SOURCE: Intropin (Mark Oniffrey)

Co-prescribing means that when an individual gets a prescription for an opioid, they also get a prescription for naloxone. Figure 13.6 shows the different co-prescribing requirements across states.

States have also employed different strategies to make it easier to obtain naloxone. Some states require private insurance to cover naloxone which reduces the cost to residents. Other states allow schools to have naloxone on school premises and allow an adult at the school to administer naloxone in an overdose situation. Some states have taken more active measures by requiring school districts to have a naloxone policy. Requiring private insurance to cover naloxone or requiring schools to have naloxone does place a financial burden on private companies of school districts. However, it may also save lives.

Action Item

13B-4

Does Hamiltonia require a prescription for naloxone?

- If a resident is prescribed an opioid, is the pharmacist required to provide naloxone or notify the patient about naloxone?
- Does private health insurance have to cover naloxone? If so, how many doses of naloxone does it need to cover for each individual over the span of a year?

Figure 13.6

Naloxone co-prescribing requirements

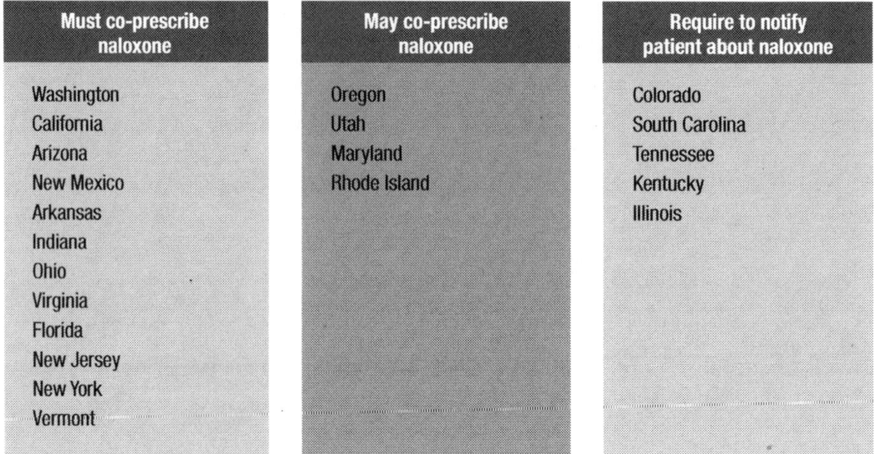

SOURCE: "Naloxone Access: Summary of State Laws," Legislative Analysis and Public Policy Association, January 2023, http://legislativeanalysis.org/wp-content/uploads/2023/02/Naloxone-Access-Summary-of-State-Laws.pdf, accessed July 11, 2023.

Local Spotlight

Addressing the opioid epidemic has involved the federal, state, and local governments. Remember, Americans live within states and, within those states, live in specific communities. These communities have had different experiences in the opioid epidemic with some facing more severe opioid addictions and overdoses. Local governments are our first responders to the opioid epidemic relying on local police departments and emergency medical personnel to save lives. Local governments also have local health departments that have played a vital role in collecting opioid epidemic data, in implementing state strategies like prescription drug monitoring programs, and providing community resources.[56]

Because the opioid epidemic is complicated, "The coordination of federal, state, and local partners, along with the engagement of community agencies and organizations, is imperative in implementing strategies to prevent and respond to opioid misuse and overdose."[57] Local health departments have been important partners to state governments to help implement state policies at the local level. In fact, states rely on localities to help support state policies on the ground. Overall, addressing the opioid epidemic has been a team effort by federal, state, and local governments.

One way localities have been supported is through state initiation of court cases to hold pharmaceutical companies responsible for their role in the opioid epidemic. For example, Mike DeWine, when he was the attorney general for the state of Ohio, brought a lawsuit that has provided $8.6 million dollars to local governments in Ohio to implement policies to slow the opioid epidemic.[58] The attorney general of Massachusetts specifically targeted Purdue Pharma, owned by the Sackler family, in her lawsuit holding pharmaceutical companies responsible for their role in the opioid epidemic.[59] Legal challenges to the Sackler family are ongoing and are currently being decided by the U.S. Supreme Court.[60] Local governments are allowed to use these funds for specific strategies to combat the crisis. In this way, local and state governments have worked together to respond to the epidemic.

In some ways, localities have tried policy solutions first to address opioid use. For example, in 2021, New York City took a new approach and started something called a safe injection site.[61] These are sites where people addicted to opioids have access to clean needles and can participate in using drugs with medical supervision. This falls under a harm reduction approach that hopes to reduce opioid overdose and other medical issues that come from using used needles. Following New York City, Providence, Rhode Island, has plans to open up a safe injection site which was approved at the state-level.[62] This is still a new, and very controversial, approach to the opioid epidemic, but one that started at the local level in the United States.

Looking Forward

Congratulations! You have finished the health policy portion of the simulation. You may have expanded Medicaid or adopted policies to address the opioid epidemic. Health policy in this country is complicated and multifaceted. There are problems including access, quality, and equity. Additionally, health policy problems include more than health insurance. Individuals face a number of different health problems and some of these problems are public health issues. Health policy is a major area of state and federal action. Remember from the beginning of the chapter, how we design and implement our health policies can have important implications for our pursuit of happiness and the health of our democracy. Take some time to consider the health policy that you considered in class. Do you think the policy will strengthen political participation? Why or why not?

Key Terms

Medicaid (269)
Medicaid expansion (269)
CHIP (Children's Health Insurance Program) (269)
opioid epidemic (270)
Affordable Care Act (ACA) (273)
coverage gap (278)
medication-assisted treatment (MAT) (280)
Prescription Drug Monitoring Program (PDMP) (284)
harm reduction (286)

Assignments to Learn More about State Health Policy

1. Choose two states in two different regions. What experience have these states had with the opioid epidemic? What kind of policy approaches have they taken to address the epidemic? Compare and contrast the two states' policy approaches.
2. Choose a Medicaid expansion state and a non-Medicaid expansion state. Compare and contrast different health measures across the two states. How do they compare on life expectancy? Diabetes and obesity rates? Infant and maternal mortality? You may want to start looking by exploring the CDC website.
3. What do you do if you need health insurance? Go on to healthcare.gov and shop for a health insurance plan. How much does each plan cost? What does it cover? Do you think you would purchase one? Why or why not?
4. Divide the class into four groups. Each group is assigned a different county in the United States, and answers the questions as if they are this person:

   - Your name is Trisha. You are forty years old living and were born and raised in your county. You love your hometown. However, you know that your hometown tends to have some health issues. You have noticed over the past few years that some of your neighbors have begun to use heroin. You have not been feeling that great lately. You have heard about Obamacare, and you think it might be a good idea to buy some insurance, but you live 120 percent above the FPL so you cannot afford a high premium plan. Before you purchase your insurance, you decide to learn more about your county and how it compares to the rest of your state. Please answer the following questions.

- The questions your group will answer are:

  What is the metropolitan classification of your county (i.e., rural/urban)?

  How large is the African American population in your county?

  How large is the Hispanic population in your county?

  What percent of residents live in poverty?

  Do you qualify for Medicaid?

  What percentage of your county is uninsured (18–64)?

  How much does Medicare spend per person?

  How many primary care physicians are in your county?

  What percentage of the county is obese?

  What percentage of the county has diabetes?

  How many of your neighbors are likely to die from overdose deaths?

  Is there anything else you find interesting about your county?

- Compare your answers with the answers from another group. Some helpful websites include: ruralhealthinfo.org, countyhealthratings.org, and kff.org
- Your teacher will divide you into four or six groups depending on the size and provide you with a county to focus on.

City of Dubois, PA

SOURCE: Doug Kerr from Albany, NY, United States

14

Reacting to Public Policy

Learning Objectives:

After reading this chapter students should be able to:

- Explain the role of the media at the state and local levels.
- Describe how traditional media sources have declined and their effect on democracy.
- Understand the different kinds of interest groups that exist in the United States.
- Create news articles and interest group strategies for legislation that was passed during the simulation.

State Spotlight: Pennsylvania

Congratulations! If you have made it to this chapter then you have successfully created and run a brand-new state-level government. We're sure there were times where you felt like you and your classmates could never come to an agreement, and maybe you didn't! But that is how the political process works; sometimes very little gets accomplished due to polarization or gridlock. Although the simulation provided insight into how to make and run a government, we felt it was important to also include how nongovernmental institutions—mainly the media and interest groups—are part of this process as well.

We touched briefly on the role of the media in state elections in chapter 8, but we will delve more deeply into the media in this chapter and challenge you to create media reports on the events that happened during the simulation, explaining the bills, who supported it and who did not, and connecting your law to a similar law in a different state. We will also explore interest groups and their role in state and local level governments. Maybe you will work for the premier Hamiltonian interest group Burr and Associates and learn how to write a persuasive memo on a piece of legislation you want passed.

But before we explore that, we wanted to discuss our final state spotlight, which focuses on the state of Pennsylvania. In November 2023 Min Xian and Angela Couloumbis of *Spotlight PA*, an independent and non-partisan news source, wrote the article "Richest Little City" about the DuBois City manager Herm Suplizio. Remember from chapter 3, city managers are powerful figures in local government, hired by city councils to run local governments.

DuBois is in Clearfield County, Pennsylvania, with a population of over 7,500 as of 2020. The article details how Suplizio was able to do the following as city manager, despite DuBois being such a small city: update and renovate ball fields, install a new city sign, and "upgrade the Tannery Dam area ... by adding lighting, restrooms, and a sidewalk." But Suplizio has been charged with corruption by the Pennsylvania Attorney General's office, which argues that he "stole hundreds of thousands of dollars in public and nonprofit funds."[1] How was the small city of DuBois able to afford such major development projects? One way was through grants, which the article details the city received far more for their size than other similarly situated cities. Why? Because Suplizio had a direct connection to a major power player in the Harrisburg capitol building—Senate Pro Tempore Joe Scarnati, who represented the state legislative district DuBois is in.

When Scarnati retired from the Senate, his new lobbying firm also contracted with the city of DuBois to represent them in Harrisburg to get more grants, another unlikely scenario for a small city.

And while the political connections in and of themselves are not illegal, they point to the unfair advantage some cities and towns have due to the relationships their leaders have with legislators. Or, alternatively, the leadership positions their representatives have in the capital. What was illegal, however, was the lack of invoices and improper bookkeeping by the city manager:

> Suplizio would allegedly sometimes pay bills submitted to the city even when they didn't have detailed invoices attached. He would also sometimes code expenses across different categories in the budget to help the fire department receive more money for equipment—but also make it hard to track what the money was being used for ... Between 2014 and 2022, Suplizio quietly gave more than $561,000 in bonuses from city coffers to key staffers ... Suplizio also rewarded himself. In fact, he was the biggest beneficiary. The records indicate he gave himself annual bonuses ranging from $8,000 to more than $64,000.[2]

There is no record of how these bonuses were decided or if the city council approved them. Furthermore, the Attorney General's office argues that Suplizio stole over half a million dollars from various city and nonprofit organizations that he ran and held positions in, which ultimately decided the outcomes of the contracts between the nonprofit and the city he managed.

Why do we care so much about the city of DuBois and its city manager beleaguered by corruption charges? Because it was local journalism that investigated the claims, and it was local journalism that helped to raise important questions of local transparency, accountability, and the relationship between state and local governments. In fact, this story is one of twenty-five different local news stories that was featured in the *New York Times* morning December 22, 2023, newsletter, which detailed the importance of local news for uncovering stories like the one in DuBois. Let's further discuss the role of the media in American democracy.

Media and State and Local Government

One of the major functions of the news media is to inform citizens of what is happening in their communities, states, and nation. The article we discussed before not only informed citizens of Pennsylvania what was happening in DuBois, but it also investigated the charges against the city manager. The reporters tracked down the grants, the financial records, and contracts of the city as well as interviewed over two dozen people related to the case over seven months of investigation. They also helped to interpret what some of their findings meant for the city and the corruption charges. Therefore, the three I's of the news media: **informing, interpreting**, and **investigating**, are lost when local journalism disappears.

Media Effects

To understand the effect the media can have on its citizens, we turn to a theory within media studies called the **not-so-minimal effects model.**[3] The not-so-minimal effects model is in direct response to an earlier media effects model called the **minimal effects model**, which argued that the media did nothing more than reinforce existing opinions.[4] However, as experiments within social science improved, researchers began to see that the media's effect on citizens could be quite significant through three separate processes: **agenda setting, priming**, and **framing**. Agenda setting should sound familiar from chapter 8, where we spoke of the policy agenda. Agenda setting for the media is similar whereby news organizations, such as the *New York Times*, only have so much space and time to cover the news of the day. On any given day there are literally hundreds of news stories to choose from, and therefore decisions must be made on which stories will be covered and which will get the coveted front-page spot.

This is like broadcast news which must decide which stories they will air first (when they have audience's attention the most), and for news websites which stories they will place at the top of their webpage with the largest font and biggest pictures. Again, it is about getting attention for specific stories. But what happens to the news stories that are not covered, or are buried in a news broadcast or within the pages of a printed newspaper? They still happened, they still matter, but they are probably not going to matter to readers or watchers of the news because they might not see it or may only glance at it. In short, the media sets the agenda and tells us what is important.

This is very closely related to priming because priming argues that whatever the media sets the agenda with will be on the forefront of our minds when we evaluate our government or vote in elections. Let's go back to the DuBois example. Let's say that *Spotlight PA* writes a series of articles about the corruption that occurred in the city of DuBois leading up to local elections. In these series of articles, like in the article we described above, the reporters discuss how loyal local elected politicians are to the city manager, and that it took a group of citizens to take the city itself to court for an injunction against continuing to pay the city manager despite being on administrative leave. Priming says that this corruption, and this loyalty to a person who at the very least was irresponsible with city funds, will be on voter's mind when they go to the polls. If these series of articles were not published, or were published far away from the election, then it would be something else that would have been on the agenda and would be on citizens' minds as they go to vote.

Finally, framing is when the media chooses a specific perspective for the articles they write. The article written about the DuBois city manager is very skeptical about the actions he took financially on behalf of the city and the various nonprofits he ran. And although they discuss the amount of support the city manager still has with the city council and other city officials, that could have been the entire perspective of the article, instead of one that raises serious questions about a government official's ethics. That is framing: how we tell a story matters for those who receive it.

Forms of Media

The other aspect of the media we need to discuss is the medium through which news is shared. In the beginning newspapers was the way information was shared throughout communities. When the radio was invented, news was also disseminated through that medium as well. However, the biggest change to media came with the advent of television. Viewers could listen and watch news stories and see events for themselves. In the beginning there were only three networks: ABC, CBS, and NBC, which meant that these news organizations could quite powerfully set the agenda. There was also a considerable amount of trust between the public and the news anchors of that time, such as Walter Cronkite and Edward R. Murrow, that has steeply declined as television has expanded.

Of course, news through the television changes over time, going from only three stations to hundreds, as well as introducing cable television which brought with it more partisan news organizations such as Fox News, MSNBC, and CNN. Many have argued that the introduction of partisan cable news stations combined with the internet has created a citizenry that only exposes themselves to the perspectives they already agree with. Why would a conservative watch MSNBC or a liberal tune into Fox News when they can listen to the broadcasts that will agree with them? This also raises the question of why citizens would watch local news broadcasts when they can tune into more global and national news that is available 24/7 at the click of a button.

But as we discussed in chapter 8, the change in media technologies has led to a decline in newspapers and local news sources. Therefore, as television and internet technology evolve we see partisan news organizations increase, local news sources decline, digital media increase, and newspaper circulation go down. Let's discuss the media landscape of Hamiltonia.

Media in Hamiltonia

The major newspaper of Hamiltonia is *The Reynolds Paper*, with a daily circulation of 99,741 and a Sunday circulation of 165,442. Every week 805,987 people visit *The Reynolds Paper* website which also has 73 million page views each month. Like many major newspapers, *The Reynolds Paper* has the sections of top news, sports, opinion, business, and entertainment. *The Reynolds Paper* has seen a decline in circulation but recognizes that investment in digital news is key to remaining relevant. The paper also strongly believes in government accountability and devotes significant attention to its investigations with success—having won multiple Pulitzer Prizes for its reporting.

WHAM is the major news and talk radio station of Hamiltonia, based out of the capital of Charlestown. While it may seem surprising to still be talking about radio as a relevant form of news, it is because it is a remarkably stable form of media. The Pew Research Center reported in August 2023 that about 82 percent of Americans listened to AM/FM radio each week. About half of those who listened received the news from the radio, although less than 10 percent of Americans prefer to receive their news from the radio itself.[5] Because of the stability of radio news, we should not ignore their listeners and how WHAM affects the stories they here and how they are framed.

Finally, KHAM is one of three of Hamiltonia's major local television stations. In addition to network affiliated programming, the station broadcasts local news forty hours each week (twenty-eight hours during the week and nine hours during the weekend plus news updates throughout the week) and has the broadcast schedule shown in Figure 14.1

The midday news broadcast has the lowest viewership, followed by the morning news, with evening news having the highest viewership. KHAM also has a digital news platform via an app that sends news updates to subscribers throughout the day. Now that we understand the news media in local and state government we can move onto exploring the role of interest groups in Hamiltonia.

Figure 14.1
KHAM Television Schedule

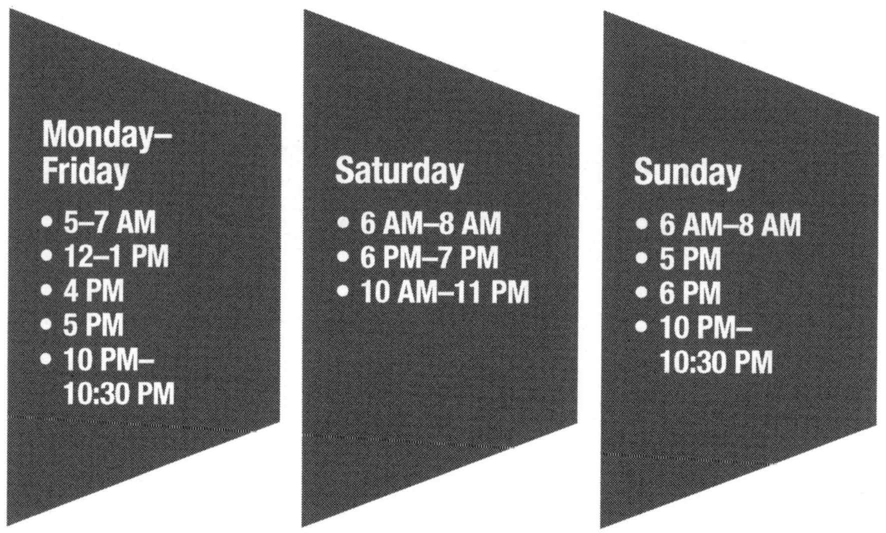

Interest Groups at the State and Local Levels

Interest groups are powerful actors at the state level. Each state's political system is composed of different interest groups pursuing different public policies. As Nownes and Freeman (1998) note, there has been an increase in interest groups and their activity since the 1950s. The interest group system in a state may look different depending upon several factors including the kinds of industry a state has and the state's public policy problems. These factors can affect the interest group dynamics in a state and their relative strength. For example, states with the initiative process tend to have more interest groups, particularly citizen interest groups.[6] The interest group system in each state is an important component of the political system.

Interest groups' main goal is to pursue the interests of their members which allows them to continue operating.[7] They do this through a host of activities including **lobbying**, testifying at legislative hearings, donating to campaigns, and supporting direct democracy initiatives. Nownes and Freeman (1998) found that lobbyists most often testify and contact officials but that "helping to draft legislation, alerting state legislators to a bill's effects, and having influential constituents contact legislators," are also common activities pursued by lobbyists.[8]

One of the important services that interest groups participate in is helping inform state legislators about bills. Remember from chapter 4, state legislators may have more or less policy expertise in a host of areas. Lobbyists may help legislators, especially those that do not serve in the legislature full time, gather information on important policy issues facing the state. Although lobbying the legislature gets the most attention, interest groups can also try to influence decisions made by the executive branch as well. Think of the importance of regulations associated with the laws legislators pass. During public comment periods of state regulation review, interest groups may submit commentary of the regulations that will affect them and their members in an effort to influence the implementation of laws.

In the sections above you learned about the importance of media in state politics. Another way that the media affects state politics is through its relationship with the interest groups in a state. Cooper et al. (2007) find that journalists and interest group representatives have relationships with one another. Journalists use interest groups as sources in their news stories and interest groups use the media to advocate for their interests.[9] Using the media to advocate for issues may help convince both government officials and the public to support the interests of their group. In Hamiltonia, you will want to think about the ways in which journalists and interest groups might work together.

There are many different types of interest groups, and they vary based on the interests that they represent. For example, some interest groups represent **trade groups or professional associations**. Even political scientists are represented through the American Political Science Association who, in 2021, had one of their strategic goals as

Chicago Teachers Union Day of Action Strike April 1, 2016.

SOURCE: Charles Edward Miller from Chicago, United States

"advocate on behalf of the discipline and political science"[10] There are also **citizen interest groups** that tend to represent broad concerns of the residents of a state such as expanding Medicaid or advocating for clean water. There are also **special interest groups** such as the National Rifle Association or Planned Parenthood. These interest groups tend to focus on one issue area. Because we have a federalist system where state governments make important policy decisions, these groups can often have strategies to advocate for their interest both at the national and subnational levels.

Governments can also lobby other governments. For example, cities can lobby state governments.[11] Essentially any group that has an interest in government decisions may pursue advocacy activities. Of course, this may be easier for some groups rather than others as E. E. Schattschneider so eloquently put: "The flaw in the pluralist heaven is that the heavenly chorus sings with a strong upper-class accent."[12] Therefore, there are concerns that although interest groups may provide another venue for representation, that representation tends to overrepresent wealthy interests.

Interest groups play an important role in our democracy by representing the interests of their members. They provide an avenue, outside of the traditional two-party structure, to express the voice of the people to government officials making consequential public policy decisions. If you do not feel well represented by the current political parties, joining an interest group may be a way for you to have your voice heard on the interests that you care most about. There are interest groups that advocate on all different kinds of topics. So, whether you are concerned about the environment, legalizing marijuana, felony rights, or more, there is likely an interest group you can join.

Interest Groups in Hamiltonia

Hamiltonia, like all states, has an active interest group system. Last year, there were 403 registered interest groups in the state. Although these groups represent a variety of interests, there are four groups in the state that we will highlight below. These groups include the teachers' union, the health care industry group, a citizen energy group, and local governments. Below we will introduce these groups and provide some background on their activities.

The largest and most active interest group in the state is the Hamiltonia State Teachers Union (HSTU). The HSTU has about 42,000 members across the state. Their membership includes K–12 teachers. Last year they spent $333,000 on lobbying. HSTU has its own lobbyists that are dedicated to advocating for the interests of teachers. These lobbyists monitored 50 bills in the prior legislative session, provided expert testimony in committee meetings, met with legislators and bureaucrats in the department of education. The main focus of the HSTU is to increase teacher pay, increase funding of the state pension system, and to increase mental health workers in the schools.

The second most active interest in Hamiltonia is the Hamiltonia Health Care Group. This group represents the two main health providers in the state including Charlestown Health and Amendment Health. These two groups have the most locations that provide health care to state residents including hospitals, doctor groups, and urgent care centers. Last year the group spent $305,000 on lobbying. The Hamiltonia Health Care Group's focus is to try to increase funding for Medicaid, reduce taxes, and increase availability of drug rehab funding.

Hamiltonia has an active energy industry represented by the Hamiltonia Energy Group. Last year this group spent $200,000 on lobbying. This group represents the interests of utility companies including the Washington Electric Company and the Madison Company. This group has been focused on advocating for more money to diversify their energy portfolios as well as more money to maintain and update the energy grid. The companies are particularly worried about weather events and cyber security. They are seeking state funding to help them invest in these areas. There is also a citizen interest group focused on expanding renewable energy in the state called Citizens for Renewable Energy (CRE). CRE does not have as many resources as the Hamiltonia Energy Group, spending about $85,000 on lobbying last year. CRE has 9,540 members in Hamiltonia. The group is focused on getting the state to invest more in renewable energy.

Although not one of the three largest interests in the state, cities and localities' interests are also represented at the state level. Charlestown and Burr City spent $110,000 on professional lobbyists this past year. These cities have focused their advocacy efforts on trying to increase state funding for a variety of projects including more money for the maintenance of roads and more money for their local police forces.

Simulation

In this part of the simulation your class will be divided between the news media and interest groups of Hamiltonia.

Becoming Part of Hamiltonia's News Media

In the first half of this chapter, we discussed the role of the media in a democracy as well as three news media outlets present in the state of Hamiltonia: *The Reynolds Paper*, WHAM the state's major talk news radio station, and KHAM one of the major news broadcast stations. Half of your class will become part of the news media group and that half will be further divided into the three media outlets. For argument's sake, if your class has eighteen students, nine will work in the media group with three students each assigned to the various media outlets.

Each group will have a designated editor. The editor makes the final decisions on which stories are covered, when they will be reported, and where they will be placed: front page, top of the hour, and so on. Be prepared to have discussions with your editor about why your story matters and why it should be emphasized out of all the other stories that are being pitched. If you are the editor of your news organization, be prepared to push your reporters to cover stories that matter, or to consider perspectives they are ignoring.

Each reporter will create a news story in whichever format is most appropriate for their news source. Working for WHAM? Be prepared to write a script for a three-minute radio news discussion. Are you the evening news anchor for KHAM? Create a story board of the news issue that will be covered at the top of the hour that includes images and audio that you plan to use. Finally, are you an investigative reporter for *The Reynolds Paper*? You will write a 500-word article on something that happened during the simulation: a deal that was brokered, a piece of legislation that failed to pass, the defeat of a particular candidate in the election. You may want to consider using an interest group representative as a source for your story.

Action Item

14A-1

Split half of the class into three groups representing each of the media outlets of Hamiltonia:

- *The Reynolds Paper*
- WHAM: News and Talk Radio
- KHAM: Local news station

Action Item

14A-2

One student from each group is to be designated the editor of their news media organization who will consult with the reporters about the story they are writing/recording.

Action Item

14A-3

The reporters for *The Reynolds Paper* are to each write a 500-word article about something that happened during the simulation. This could involve any of the following:

- Debates during the constitutional convention.
- Election/appointment results.
- Legislation that was passed or failed to pass.
- Interview with a sitting Hamiltonian official.

Action Item

14A-4

The reporters for WHAM are to each write a three-minute script to be aired on the radio station about something that happened during the simulation. The same topics are available to them as were to the reporters for *The Reynolds Paper*.

Action Item

14A-5

The anchors for KHAM are to each create a story board that will depict the news story that will air during the evening news segment. The story board should include images and audio that will be used during the broadcast.

Action Item

14A-6

The editors of the newspaper, radio show, and news station are to review the stories that have been submitted to them, decide how they will be presented (for example, which story will be on the front page of *The Reynolds Paper* or which story will lead the top of news hour), and their reasoning for the decisions they made.

Becoming Hamiltonia's Interest Groups

Now it is time to become a lobbyist yourself. While half the class is part of the media, the other half of the class will be working as lobbyists for the three major interests in the state: the Hamiltonia State Teachers Union, the Hamiltonia Health Care Group, and the Hamiltonia Energy Group. Just as above, if your class has eighteen, then nine will work in the interest group with three students each assigned to the major interests.

If you are representing the Hamiltonia State Teachers Union your job is to draft an initiative for the next election that would advance the interests of the state's K–12 teachers. You will also want to generate support for the initiative so consider reaching out to one of the journalists to get a story about your initiative in the news. If you represent the Hamiltonia Health Care Group, you will need to write a policy memo for state legislators. This should be a one-page policy memo providing information on House Bill 39 which is trying to increase the Medicaid reimbursement rates by 5 percent. If you represent the Hamiltonia Energy Group, you need to draft a two-minute elevator pitch for your upcoming meeting with the governor. Consider what the interests of the utility companies in the state may be and make your strongest argument to the top house member. Remember, you do not have a lot of time!

Action Item

14B-1

Split half the class into three groups representing each of the major interests in the state: Hamiltonia State Teachers Union, the Hamiltonia Health Care Group, and the Hamiltonia Energy Group

Action Item

14B-2

If you are part of the Hamiltonia State Teachers Union it is your job to design and draft an initiative to be voted on by the people of Hamiltonia. Make sure to use the media to generate support for your proposal.

Action Item

14B-3

If you are representing the Hamiltonia Health Care Group, you need to write a policy memo advocating for increasing the Medicaid reimbursement rates for doctors. You may also use the media to generate support for your proposal.

Action Item

14B-4

If you are representing the Hamiltonia Energy Group, you must prepare a two-minute elevator pitch for your meeting later this afternoon with the governor.

Looking Back

Over the course of the semester, you have learned about state and local governments, created your own government from the ground up, and run that government by creating new public policies. This chapter also guided you to understand the role of interest groups and the news media in forming and running a state and local government. As you were creating your government, a class somewhere else in the country was doing the exact same thing, but with different results. How might the outcomes of your Hamiltonia have been different if you had made different choices? Do you think policymaking would have been easier or harder? Do you think it mattered who was in certain positions? These are the exact same questions we could ask of the Pennsylvanian government or the Virginian government. How do the institutional rules affect governance and how do the people who fill the institutions help to make governance more or less effective? We hope this simulation helps you understand the important role of state and local government in the United States and makes you better able to understand how decisions that are chosen in your state and local governments affect you and your fellow citizens' daily lives.

Key Terms

informing (295)
interpreting (295)
investigating (295)
not-so-minimal effects model (295)
minimal effects model (295)
agenda setting (295)
priming (295)
framing (295)
interest groups (298)
lobbying (298)
trade groups or professional associations (299)
citizen interest group (300)
special interest group (300)

Assignments to Learn More about Media and Interest Groups

1. Look up the major newspaper of the state you live in. What is its name? Where is it based out of? Now look up the front page of that newspaper. What items did they place on the agenda? How do you think choosing those stories affects how readers think about their state or local governments?
2. With a partner, choose a local news station. One person should watch a half hour of a morning news segment while the other person should watch a half hour of the evening news segment. Note which stories are at the top of the hour, the order of the stories, and how long (approximately) each story is covered for. Now compare with your partner what you each noted about the morning vs. evening news. Were similar stories covered? Did something major happen during the day that became the major news story of the night? How do you think those watching only morning vs. evening news may think about the important stories of the day based on the differences between the two newscasts?
3. Look up the interest group system in your home state. What are the major interests in your state? What are they advocating for? How much do they spend on lobbying? You may want to use opensecrets.org for some information.
4. If you wanted to join an interest group in your home state, which one would it be? Think about a topic that you care about and find an interest group in your home state that represents your attitudes on the issue. What is the mission of the group? How many members do they have? What did they accomplish in the last year? Are you likely to join? Why or why not?

Glossary

529 college savings plan A state-sponsored college savings plan with specific tax benefits (131)

Affordable Care Act (ACA) This is a new health policy passed under President Obama and sometimes called Obamacare. The goal of the policy was to increase access to health insurance and lower cost. The policy made a number of changes to our health system including providing funds for states to expand eligibility to Medicaid and require the purchase of health insurance or face a tax penalty. (273)

Administrative Rules Review Committees A committee within the legislature that checks the rules that state departments and agencies pass to ensure they are in line with the intent of the legislation. (81)

advisory opinions An opinion written by the attorney general on their interpretation of a law or rule and its constitutionality. (128)

agenda Issues on the radar of public officials and/or the media. (172)

agenda setting The ability of the media to affect what citizens think about by choosing to report on certain stories while ignoring others. (295)

appellate courts Also known as intermediary courts of appeal, these are courts that review cases that have been appealed due to errors in the cases. (140)

appointment A selection mechanism whereby an executive branch official such as the governor, or the legislature, selects a person for a position in government including judgeships and executive branch positions. (117)

appointments The power of the governor to choose who serves in select executive branch positions and potentially judicial positions as well. (88)

appropriate When the legislature authorizes money to the executive branch. (81)

appropriations Bills that authorize state agencies to spend money. (89)

attorney general The chief legal officer of a state responsible for giving legal advice to state officials and protecting the public's legal interests. (109)

balanced budget requirements Standards set by states to not spend more revenue than they bring in each year. (34)

bicameral Having two legislative chambers. (71)

bill of rights A list of all rights retained by the people of a state or country. (28)

bureaucracy The organization that implements and enforces state laws composed of executive branch officials including civil servants and appointees. (109)

bureaucrats People who work for the government. (81)

campaign finance Money that is raised by candidates or for ballot measures during campaigns. (164)

cash bail This is a system whereby some defendants accused of a crime may pay an amount, set by a judge, which will allow them to be released from jail until their case has been decided. (230)

charges and fees A form of tax when residents pay a fee. When you pay a toll or a fee to renew your driver's license that is a charges and fees tax. (192)

charters An agreement between state and local governments that explains the powers the local government has been granted by the state government. (50)

chief justice The chief judge of a state supreme court. Typically handles administrative duties. (138)

CHIP (Children's Health Insurance Program) It is a state and federal program with the goal of providing health insurance to low-income children. (269)

cities A large urban area with a higher population than towns. (55)

citizen interest group This is one type of interest group that is focused on advocating for a broad interest that typically benefit most of state residents. (300)

city council The "legislative" branch of local, city governments. (45)

civil cases Cases involving disputes between private parties. (140)

civil service The merit-based system of government employment. (108)

clean energy Clean energy does not produce a carbon footprint. Energy can be renewable but not necessarily clean. (253)

commission systems A form of city or town government whereby commissioners are individually elected to run specific departments and come together as a commission to run the government. (55)

committees Organizational units of legislatures that hold hearings on bills and write legislation. (62)

concurrent powers Powers held by both state and federal government. (5)

constituent service A responsibility of state legislators where they provide assistance to their constituents in various areas including access to state services such as Medicaid and working with students. (2)

constituents The people within a legislator's district. (2)

constitutional amendment States have constitutions that can be amended in a variety of ways, depending upon the state. Constitutional amendments can sometimes make policy changes as well. (236)

constitutional convention A gathering of delegates from across a state or country to amend or create a new constitution. (33)

corporate income tax A tax on income generated from business. (191)

council–manager systems A form of city or town government whereby an elected council hires a manager to run the day-to-day operations of the government. (55)

county government Local governmental subunits located in 48 states that carry out the laws and services of the state government. (51)

court of last resort The highest state-level court that a case can be appealed to. (7, 142)

coverage gap The coverage gap is the name for the group of individuals, living in states that have not expanded Medicaid under the ACA, who make too much money to qualify for Medicaid and too little money to qualify for federal government subsidies to purchase health insurance. This group has difficulty getting health insurance. (278)

crime Breaking a law. (229)

criminal cases Cases involving breaking the law. (141)

criminal justice system The criminal justice system encompasses the government's law and order efforts. The system includes multiple components including the courts, prisons, and law enforcement. (228)

Department of Health The department in charge of addressing public health problems, licensing, and health care regulation. (110)

descriptive representation How well a representative body—like a legislature—reflects the demographics of a population, such as their race, ethnicity, sex, and age. (65)

Dillon's Rule The U.S. Constitution provides for the existence of state government powers. But local governments are products of state governments and do not have their own powers. (48)

direct democracy Mechanisms of governance whereby citizens have direct influence on the laws their government passes. (36)

direct initiatives A form of initiative whereby citizens who gain enough signature submit a law to be placed on the ballot for voter approval or denial. (37)

districts The geographical boundaries of a representative's constituency. (64)

education secretary The head of a state's department of education, sometimes known as a state superintendent. (111)

electric cooperative Provide utility services to customers who are also the owners of the cooperatives. (255)

Environmental Protection Agency (EPA) The EPA is the agency at the federal level dedicated to a number of environmental issues including clean air and water. The EPA promulgates rules for the environment but also has a number of programs to help distribute federal funds to states and localities to address environmental issues. (259)

environmental secretary The head of state's environment department. (111)

executive orders Regulations created by governors that carry the force of law. (101)

expenditures The money the government pays out. (180)

federalism The relationship between federal and state governments wherein power is shared. (4)

felony disenfranchisement This means that people who are felons are not able to participate in voting. (239)

first-past-the-post single-member districts When one candidate wins more votes than other candidates and represents the entire district. (162)

fiscal year The calendar structure for revenues and expenditures. (180)

Flint water crisis The Flint Water Crisis is a multi-level government failure to provide clean drinking water to the city of Flint, Michigan. (258)

framing The perspective from which a news article is written. (295)

general jurisdiction courts These are courts that handle various civil and criminal cases that are not assigned to limited jurisdiction courts. (140)

gubernatorial appointment A judicial selection method whereby the governor appoints a judge. (147)

harm reduction A policy approach to the opioid epidemic that focuses on trying to help individuals in the midst of their addiction and to reduce overdose deaths from addiction. (286)

higher education Higher education is the portion of the education system that is dedicated to educating students post–high school, typically colleges and universities. (216)

home rule States allocate specific powers to local governments via their State Constitution, or law. (48)

impeachment The process by which the legislature can remove a governor or executive branch official. (92)

imprisonment rate This is the total number of persons incarcerated in the United States divided by the total population. This rate gives us a sense of how large the incarcerated population is. (232

incumbents Current office holders. (163)

indirect initiatives A form of initiative whereby citizens who gain enough signatures submit a law to be reviewed by the legislature who can decide to place a competing law on the ballot at the same time for voter approval or denial. (38)

individualistic A state political culture wherein government is seen primarily as a service provider, and not an entity involved in changing society. (9)

informal powers Powers not outlined in the state constitution such as approval rating and relationship with the media. (89)

informing A responsibility of the news media where they relay what is happening in the community, state, or nation, to news consumers. (295)

initiative A direct democracy mechanism whereby citizens submit a law to be placed on the ballot as long as a certain number of signatures have been gathered. Can be direct or indirect. (32)

institutional powers Formal powers of the governor given in the state constitution. (88)

interest groups Interest groups represent the interests of its members and try to influence government decisions. (298)

interest groups Organizations that seek to influence public policy. (21

intergovernmental transfers Money that is distributed vertically across levels of government in the U.S. Typically, it is money from the federal government that is distributed to states and localities. (193)

interpreting A responsibility of the news media where they explain what is happening, what it means, and why it matters. (295)

interstate agency A governmental organization that includes two or more states. (6)

investigating A responsibility of the news media where they examine people, legislation, organizations, or governmental units for corruption or wrongdoing. (295)

investor-owned utility Utility companies that are owned by investors. These companies have a responsibility to their shareholders. They are privately owned. (255)

K–12 public education This is the education system funded by public dollars that provides education to students from kindergarten through twelfth grade. (203)

lead service lines (LSLs) Lead service lines carry water into people's homes. They can be dangerous because lead can flake off the pipe and into the drinking water. Because these lines are underground, we do not know where they are located throughout the United States. (259)

legislative appointment A judicial selection method whereby the state legislature appoints a judge. (147)

legislative professionalism A measure of state legislatures that consists of legislator salary, the number of staff, and the length of their legislative sessions. (66)

lieutenant governor The second in line to the governor's position in most states in the event of a governor's resignation or death. (88)

line-item veto A specific gubernatorial veto power that involves changes to portions of bills instead of vetoing a whole bill. (89)

litigation Pursuing legal action. (128)

lobbying One of the ways interest groups influence government decisions is by providing information to government officials. (298)

lobbyists Individuals who work to advance the needs of interest groups. (21)

magistrate judge A judge typically involved in low-level offenses or disputes or those who create protection orders and handle initial arraignments. Duties set by each state judicial branch. (141)

majority leader The second in command in state house of representatives. In state senates, a legislative leader. (83)

mayor The chief executive of a town or a city. (55)

mayor–council systems A form of city or town government whereby a mayor is elected separately from a city council. The mayor may be either weak or strong with their official powers. (55)

media markets The area or region that receives similar media offerings such as television and radio stations. (166)

Medicaid A joint state-federal program that provides health insurance for low-income Americans. (9, 63, 269)

Medicaid expansion An option under President Obama's Affordable Care Act that encourages states to expand eligibility to Medicaid to anyone—even adults without children—earning below 138% above the federal poverty line. (269)

medication-assisted treatment (MAT) This is a method to treat opioid addiction that includes, but is not limited to, using drugs such as methadone to help with addiction recovery. (280)

merit-based higher education scholarship This is a policy where the state provides scholarship money to certain seniors depending on some level of criteria. (217)

merit plans A judicial selection method whereby a bipartisan judicial committee selects a certain number of nominees for the bench based on their qualifications. The governor or legislature then chooses the judge from that pool of candidates. (148)

minimal effects model A media theory that argues that the media's effect on society is limited to reinforcing beliefs. (295)

moralistic A state political culture wherein the view of politics is positive, and government is a means to a better society. (9)

multimember districts Constituents vote for multiple legislators to represent them. (84, 163)

municipal government Local governments that include cities and towns. (51)

nonpartisan elections A judicial selection method whereby citizens cast their vote for state level judges who run without affiliating with a political party. (147)

not-so-minimal effects model A media theory that argues the media influences society via agenda setting, framing, and priming. (295)

opioid epidemic The opioid epidemic is a three-stage health epidemic that includes drastic increases in the number of people addicted to and dying from opioid use. The epidemic began in the 1990s with an increase in addiction to prescribed opioids. It expanded in the 2000s with an increase of use and death from heroin. Currently, fentanyl is the main culprit in the opioid epidemic. (270)

original jurisdiction The court that has the right to hear a case first. (141)

override The process by which a legislature passes a law despite a gubernatorial veto. (71)

oversight A power of state legislatures that is a check on the powers of the executive branch of state governments. (2)

parity Equal numbers of men and women in the legislature. (65)

parole Some inmates may be eligible for parole. This is a period of time in which an inmate may be released from prison and can resume life outside of prison as they continue to serve their sentence. Parole involves supervision by a parole officer. (241)

partisan elections A judicial selection method whereby citizens cast their vote for state level judges who run under a political party. (147)

party identification The political party an individual identifies with. (66)

personal income tax A tax on an individual's income. (185)

plurality Winning more votes than other candidates. (162)

Political Action Committees (PAC) An organization that raises and donates money for candidates running for elected office or in support or opposition to legislation. (165)

policy diffusion The spread of policies across governments. Policy diffusion helps us understand how 50 different states can share similar, or the same, policies on a host of issues. (248)

policy learning When one government learns from the policies of another government and this learning informs subsequent policy action. (248)

preamble The introduction to a state constitution. (27)

pre-kindergarten This is the year prior to kindergarten where students learn colors, numbers, letters, and more. The year is meant to prepare students for kindergarten. (209)

Prescription Drug Monitoring Program (PDMP) A policy enacted by a number of states that uses an online database to track prescribed opioids. Pharmacists input data on the prescription and the recipient to help identify areas of concern. (284)

priming The ability of the media to affect what issues citizens think about when they are evaluating government officials or candidates for public office. (295)

procedural rules The rules that govern how a legislature functions in the chamber. (2)

progressive tax A tax that has a greater effect on wealthier individuals. (183)

property tax A tax on owned property. Typically, it is calculated using the estimated value of your home. (190)

prosecution The state pursuing charges against an individual accused of breaking the law. (128)

public safety secretary The head of a state's public safety department which could include emergency response organizations, state police, and corrections. (112)

publicly owned utility Public owned utility companies are owned by the government. These utility companies have a responsibility to the citizens that they serve. (255)

punctuated equilibrium In general policymaking is very stable except for short periods of rapid change. (172)

ratification Approval and subsequent adoption of a state constitution. (32)

recall elections Elections where citizens choose to remove or retain sitting elected officials. (40)

referendums A direct democracy mechanism whereby a new law is placed on the ballot to be approved or denied by citizens. (36)

regressive tax A tax that has a greater effect on poorer individuals. (183)

renewable portfolio standards (RPS) Renewable portfolio standards are created by states that outline goals to require (or encourage) utilities to use a greater percentage of renewable energy. (249)

representative democracies Democracies whereby the citizens elect individuals to represent them in government. (36)

retention elections Elections whereby a judge is placed on the ballot with no opponents to see if the voters want to keep them on the bench. (148)

retention recall election A type of recall election whereby citizens vote to remove or retain a sitting elected official. If they vote to remove, the next in line of succession takes over the position. (40)

revenue The money states bring in, mainly through taxes and fees. (34, 180)

rulemaking The bureaucratic process that creates regulations to implement laws passed by the legislature. (130)

sales tax A tax on certain goods. (186)

school board Individuals who are elected or appointed to create the policies and budgets for school districts. (88)

school districts Locally based institutions that hire staff to run the schools and report to school boards who may be elected or appointed. (51)

secretary of state An executive branch position responsible for elections, registration of lobbyists, businesses, and filing and publishing of laws. (108)

simultaneous recall election A form of recall election whereby the vote to remove or retain an elected official happens at the same time as a replacement is chosen, if citizens choose to remove the sitting official. (40)

sin tax A tax on certain goods to discourage behavior. (189)

single-member districts Where one legislator represents one geographical area. (84)

Speaker of the House The legislative leader of a state house of representatives. (62)

special district governments A type of local government that focuses on one specific area of government. (51)

special election An election that is held outside of the typical timing of an election to replace someone who has been removed or left office. (40)

special interest group This is one type of interest group that focuses on advocating for one specific issue. (300)

Special Jurisdiction Courts These are courts that handle specific cases based on the kind of law involved, such as divorce proceedings, or the severity of the crime. (160)

spending per pupil This indicates the amount of public money spent educating each student. (205)

sponsoring The official support and submission of a bill by a legislator. (2)

standing committees Permanent committees of state houses and senates. (70)

state constitutions The governing document of a state that describes its institutions and select public policies. (27)

state treasurer The chief financial officer of a state responsible for managing state's finances including college savings plans, state pension plans, and unclaimed property. (108)

targeted pre-k program This is a state program that provides funding for four-year-olds that meet certain eligibility requirements such as an income requirement. (211)

taxing and expenditure limitations Requirements set at the state level that limit the amount of taxes a state can raise their rates by each year or limit the amount they spend each year. (35)

term limits Restrictions on the number of terms a government official can serve. (68, 95, 125)

Time, Place, and Manner Clause The clause of the Constitution giving the power to determine the time, location, and manner of elections to state governments. (5)

township governments Smaller units of local government subordinate to county governments whose functions vary widely from state to state. (51)

trade groups or professional associations This is one type of interest group focused on representing the interests of trade groups or professional associations. (299)

traditionalistic A state political culture wherein politics is for elites and the role of government is to maintain existing hierarchies in society. (9)

trial court The lowest level of state courts where most cases first enter the judicial system. These courts can be general or limited jurisdiction. (157)

unicameral Having only one legislative chamber. (71)

unitary The relationship between state and local governments whereby power is retained by the state and borrowed by local governments. (5, 26, 46)

universal pre-k program This is a state program that provides funding for four-year-olds to attend pre-k without any type of eligibility requirements such as income. (210)

veto The power of the governor to not sign a bill into law that was passed by the legislature. Can be overridden by the state legislature. (7)

zoning laws Laws that dictate how land can be used, such as for housing or for business. (4)

Notes

Chapter 1

1. Bill Chappell and Katie Riordan, "Both Black Tennessee Lawmakers Have Been Reinstated After Being Expelled by GOP," NPR, April 12, 2023, https://www.npr.org/2023/04/12/1169444850/justin-pearson-vote-memphis-tennessee-house.

2. These ground rules are partially adapted from *Camelot: A Role Playing Simulation of Political Decision Making*, Fifth Edition by James R. Woodworth, W. Robert Gump, and James R. Forrester (Cengage, 2006).

3. Port Authority of New York and New Jersey, "Governance, Ethics and Integrity," The Port Authority of New York and New Jersey, 2023, https://www.panynj.gov/corporate/en/government-ethics.html.

4. *New York State Ice Co. v. Liebmann*, 285 U.S. 262 (1932), https://supreme.justia.com/cases/federal/us/285/262/case.html, accessed May 18, 2023.

5. Craig Volden, "States as Policy Laboratories: Emulating Success in the Children's Health Insurance Program," *American Journal of Political Science* 50 (2006): 294–312.

6. Heather Trela and Laura Shultz, "In the Weeds: How States Are Legalizing Marijuana in the Shadow of a Federal Prohibition," Rockefeller Institute of Government, 2023, https://rockinst.org/InTheWeeds/.

7. "Voting Rights Restoration Efforts in Florida," The Brennan Center for Justice, May 31, 2019, https://www.brennancenter.org/our-work/research-reports/voting-rights-restoration-efforts-florida.

8. This excludes certain felony offenses including murder and sexual offenses. See Florida Division of Elections: https://dos.elections.myflorida.com/initiatives/initdetail.asp?account=64388&seqnum=1.

9. "CS/SB 7066 – Election Administration," Florida State Senate, https://www.flsenate.gov/Committees/BillSummaries/2019/html/2038.

10. "Florida Supreme Court Advisory Opinion on Amendment 4," The Brennan Center for Justice, August 9, 2019, https://www.brennancenter.org/our-work/court-cases/florida-supreme-court-advisory-opinion-amendment-4.

11. "Making the Grade: US Infrastructure Assessment," American Society of Civil Engineers, 2021, https://infrastructurereportcard.org/making-the-grade/.

12. "Making the Grade: US Infrastructure Assessment," American Society of Civil Engineers, 2021.

13. National Interagency Coordination Center. "Wildland Fire Summary and Statistics Annual Report 2022." 2022. https://www.nifc.gov/sites/default/files/NICC/2-Predictive%20Services/Intelligence/Annual%20Reports/2022/annual_report.2.pdf.

14. Cole Blease Graham Jr. and William V. Moore, *South Carolina Politics and Government* (Lincoln: University of Nebraska Press, 1994).

15. "Lobbyist Activity Report Requirements," National Conference of State Legislatures, 2018, https://www.ncsl.org/ethics/lobbyist-activity-report-requirements.

16. "Mission," Sierra Club, 2023, https://www.sierraclub.org/loma-prieta/mission#:~:text=Sierra%20Club%20Mission%20Statement&text=To%20practice%20and%20promote%20the,to%20carry%20out%20these%20objectives.

Chapter 2

1. *Official Journal of the Proceedings of the Convention of the State of Louisiana*, 1861, https://archive.org/details/officialjournal00loui/page/n6/mode/1up?view=theater.

2. "John Adams & the Massachusetts Constitution," Mass.gov, https://www.mass.gov/guides/john-adams-the-massachusetts-constitution#:~:text=The%201780%20Constitution%20of%20the,and%20became%20effective%20in%201789.

3. Sol Bloom, "Constitution Questions and Answers," National Archives, last modified July 5, 2022, https://www.archives.gov/founding-docs/constitution-q-and-a, accessed November 19, 2023. This does not include amendments.

4. "A Look at the Sizes of State Constitutions," The Texas Politics Project, The University of Texas at Austin, https://texaspolitics.utexas.edu/educational-resources/look-sizes-state-constitutions.

5. *Constitution of the Commonwealth of Pennsylvania*, https://www.legis.state.pa.us/WU01/LI/LI/CT/HTM/00/00.HTM.

6. *South Dakota Constitution*, Secretary of State, https://sdsos.gov/general-information/about-state-south-dakota/state-constitution.aspx.

7. *Massachusetts Constitution*, The 193rd General Court of the Commonwealth of Massachusetts, https://malegislature.gov/Laws/Constitution.

8. *Texas Constitution*, Texas Legislative Council, https://tlc.texas.gov/docs/legref/TxConst.pdf.

9. *Constitution of the State of Kansas*, https://www.kssos.org/other/pubs/KS_Constitution.pdf.

10. *New Jersey Constitution*, 1947, Article VIII, Section IV.

11. "The History of *Abbot v. Burke*," Education Law Center, https://edlawcenter.org/litigation/abbott-v-burke/abbott-history.html#:~:text=Taken%20together%2C%20the%201997%20Abbott,education%20for%%20low%Dincome%20schoolchildren, accessed November 20, 2023.

12. *The Constitution of the State of Hawaii*, Legislative Reference Bureau, https://lrb.hawaii.gov/constitution/#articleix.

13. *The Constitution of the State of Hawaii*, Section 7.

14. "Table 1.3: General Information on State Constitution," in *The Book of the States*, The Council of State Governments, 2022, https://bookofthestates.org/tables/general-information-on-state-constitutions-as-of-january-1-2022/.

15. "Constitutional Amendment Process," National Archives, https://www.archives.gov/federal-register/constitution.

16. "2022 Arizona Governor Election Results," Azcentral.com, January 12, 2023, https://www.azcentral.com/elections/results/race/2022-11-08-governor-AZ-3-14, accessed November 19, 2023 and "Quick Facts North Dakota," US Census, https://www.census.gov/quickfacts/fact/table/ND/PST045222, accessed November 19, 2023.

17. "Table 1.5: Constitutional Amendment Procedure: By Initiative, Constitutional Provisions," in *The Book of States*, The Council of State Governments, 2022, https://bookofthestates.org/tables/constitutional-amendment-procedure-by-initiative-constitutional-provisions/.

18. "Amending State Constitutions," Ballotpedia, https://ballotpedia.org/Amending_state_constitutions.

19. Heather Perkins, "State Constitutional Developments in 2017," The Council of State Governments Knowledge Center, accessed November 19, 2023.

20. "Convention-Land: New Yorkers' Road Map to the Constitutional Convention," New York Public Interest Research Group, 2017, https://www.nypirg.org/goodgov/concon/con_con_merged_final.pdf.

21. "Amending State Constitutions," Ballotpedia.

22. "Amending State Constitutions," Ballotpedia.

23. "Briefing Book: The State of State (and Local) Tax Policy," The Tax Policy Center, 2020, https://www.taxpolicycenter.org/briefing-book/what-are-state-balanced-budget-requirements-and-how-do-they-work.

24. "Briefing Book," Tax Policy Center.

25. "Briefing Book," Tax Policy Center.

26. "Briefing Book: What Are Tax and Expenditure Limits?" The Tax Policy Center, 2020, https://www.taxpolicycenter.org/briefing-book/what-are-tax-and-expenditure-limits#:~:text=Tax%20and%20expenditure%20limits%20(TELs,some%20combination%20of%20those%20factors.

27. *Michigan Constitution*, Article II, Section 9.

28. "Veto Referendum," Ballotpedia, https://ballotpedia.org/Veto_referendum.

29. *Massachusetts Constitution*. Article XLVII, Pt. VI, Subpt. III, § 2.

30. *Wyoming State Constitution*. Art. 3, § 52(g) and Wyo. Stat. § 22-24-401.

31. "California Governor Election Results," *Politico*, 2018, https://www.politico.com/election-results/2018/california/governor/.

32. "Petition for Recall," Secretary of State of California, 2021, https://rescuecalifornia.org/wp-content/uploads/2021/01/Recall_Gavin_Petition_8.5x11_2021_FINAL.pdf

33. "States with Gubernatorial Recall Provisions," Ballotpedia, https://ballotpedia.org/States_with_gubernatorial_recall_provisions.

34. "Newsom Recall Vote," CNN, 2021, https://www.cnn.com/election/2021/results/california.

35. National Conference of State Legislatures, "Recall of State Officials," 2021, https://www.ncsl.org/elections-and-campaigns/recall-of-state-officials.

36. "States with Gubernatorial Recall Provisions," Ballotpedia, https://ballotpedia.org/States_with_gubernatorial_recall_provisions

37. *Minnesota Constitution*, Article VIII, §6.

38. "States with Gubernatorial Recall Provisions," Ballotpedia.

Chapter 3

1. Alia E. Dastagir, "'Imagine Saying to a Room Full of Black People: It's Too Hard for Me to Watch that Trial,'" *USA Today*, April 8, 2021, https://www.usatoday.com/story/life/health-wellness/2021/04/08/derek-chauvin-trial-why-white-people-need-watch-confront-racism/7133918002/.

2. Meena Venkataramanan, "Austin City Council Cuts Police Department Budget by One-Third, Mainly through Reorganizing Some Duties Out from Law Enforcement Oversight," *The Texas Tribune,* August 13, 2020, https://www.texastribune.org/2020/08/13/austin-city-council-cut-police-budget-defund/.

3. Meena Venkataramanan, "Austin Police Release Footage Showing the Killing of Mike Ramos," *The Texas Tribune*, July 27, 2020, https://www.texastribune.org/2020/07/27/mike-ramos-austin-video/.

4. Meena Venkataramanan, "Austin City Council Cuts Police Department Budget by One-Third, Mainly through Reorganizing Some Duties Out from Law Enforcement Oversight," *The Texas Tribune*, August 13, 2020, https://www.texastribune.org/2020/08/13/austin-city-council-cut-police-budget-defund/.

5. "HB1900," State of Texas, 2021, https://capitol.texas.gov/tlodocs/87R/billtext/pdf/HB01900F.pdf.

6. "Police Department Budget Preemption Conflicts Between State and Local Governments," Ballotpedia, https://ballotpedia.org/Police_department_budget_preemption_conflicts_between_state_and_local_governments#Texas:_Governor_Abbott_signs_police_department_budget_reduction_preemption_law,_possibly_preempting_Austin's_local_budget.

7. "The Origins of Local Government and the Federal System," New York State, https://video.dos.ny.gov/lg/handbook/html/the_origins_of_local_government_and_the_federal_system.html.

8. "The Origins of Local Government and the Federal System," New York State.

9. "Dillon's Rule," Center for the Study of Federalism, https://encyclopedia.federalism.org/index.php?title=Dillon%E2%80%99s_Rule.

10. Travis Moore, "Dillon Rule and Home Rule: Principles of Local Governance," LRO Snapshot, February 2020, https://nebraskalegislature.gov/pdf/reports/research/snapshot_localgov_2020.pdf.

11. *Nebraska State Constitution*, Article 3, Section 18, https://nebraskalegislature.gov/laws/articles.php?article=III-18.

12. "County Authority Profiles," National Association of Counties, 2023, https://ce.naco.org/?dset=County%20Authority&ind=County%20Authority%20Profiles.

13. "New York County Government Overview," National Association of Counties, 2023, https://ce.naco.org/?dset=County%20Authority&ind=County%20Authority%20Profiles.

14. "Intergovernmental Relations," Suffolk County Government, 2023, https://suffolkcountyny.gov/Elected-Officials/County-Executive/Intergovernmental-Relations.

15. "Overview of the Austin City Government," March 30, 2023, https://services.austintexas.gov/edims/document.cfm?id=114612#:~:text=Austin%20is%20a%20home%2Drule,Charter%20is%20considered%20Austin's%20constitution.

16. "County Governance Project," National Association of Counties, https://www.naco.org/program/county-governance-project#national,.

17. "County Governance Project," National Association of Counties.

18. "2022 Census of Governments – Organization," U.S. Census Bureau 2022, https://www.census.gov/data/tables/2022/econ/gus/2022-governments.html.

19. Tom Geoghegan, "Is the New York Mayor the Most Powerful in the World?" BBC, 2013, https://www.bbc.com/news/magazine-23626980.

Chapter 4

1. "Michael Madigan," *Newsroom AP*, https://newsroom.ap.org/editorial-photos-videos/search?query=Michael%20Madigan&mediaType=photo&st=keyword&vs=true.

2. Austin Berg, "Illinois House Speaker Madigan Now the Longest-Serving State House Speaker in U.S. History," Illinois Policy Institute, 2017, https://www.illinoispolicy.org/illinois-house-speaker-madigan-now-the-longest-serving-state-house-speaker-in-u-s-history/.

3. Joe Tabor and Ted Dabrowski, "Madigan's Rules: How Illinois Gives Its House Speaker Power to Manipulate and Control the Legislative Process," Illinois Policy

Institute, 2017, https://www.illinoispolicy.org/reports/madigans-rules-how-illinois-gives-its-house-speaker-power-to-manipulate-and-control-the-legislative-process/.

4. Peverill Squire, "American State Legislatures in Historical Perspective," *PS: Political Science & Politics* 52 (2019): 417–21.

5. *Baker v. Carr*, 369 U.S. 186 (1962); *Reynolds v. Sims*, 377 U.S. 533 (1964).

6. "Number and Percentage of Women in State Legislatures, 1980–2023," Center for American Women and Politics, 2023, Cawp.rutgers.edu/facts/levels-office/state-legislature/women-state-legislatures-2023.

7. "Legislatures at a Glance," National Conference of State Legislatures, updated April 12, 2023, Ncsl.org/about-state-legislatures/legislatures-at-a-glance#.

8. Jeffrey M. Jones, "LGBT Identification in U.S. Ticks Up to 7.1%," *Gallup News*, February 17, 2022, News.gallup.com/poll/389792/lgbt-identification-ticks-up.aspx.

9. Michele L. Swers, "Connecting Descriptive and Substantive Representation: An Analysis of Sex Differences in Cosponsorship Activity," *Legislative Studies Quarterly* 30 (2005): 407–33; Michele L. Swers, "Pursuing Women's Interests in Partisan Times: Explaining Gender Differences in Legislative Activity on Health, Education, and Women's Health Issues," *Journal of Women, Politics & Policy* 37 (2016): 249–73.

10. Nadia E. Brown, *Sisters in the Statehouse: Black Women and Legislative Decision Making* (Oxford University Press, 2014).

11. Peverill Squire, "A Squire Index Update," *State Politics and Policy Quarterly* 17 (2017): 361–71.

12. *The Book of the States*, The Council of State Governments, 2021, 28–49.

13. Arizona legislators also receive certain mileage and per diem reimbursements.

14. Jeffrey R. Lax and Justin H. Phillips, "The Democratic Deficit in the States," *American Journal of Political Science* 56 (2012): 148–66.

15. Charles Shipan and Craig Volden, "When the Smoke Clears: Expertise, Learning, and Policy Diffusion," *Journal of Public Policy* 34 (2014): 357–87.

16. Joshua Jansa, Eric Hansen, and Virginia Gray, "Copy and Paste Lawmaking: Legislative Professionalism and Policy Reinvention in the States," *American Politics Research* 47 (2019): 739–67.

17. Gary Moncrief and Peverill Squire, *Why States Matter: An Introduction to State Politics* (Rowman & Littlefield, 2020).

18. Todd Makse, "Professional Backgrounds in State Legislatures," *State Politics & Policy Quarterly* 19 (2019): 312–33.

19. William D. Berry, Michael B. Berkman, and Stuart Schneiderman, "Legislative Professionalism and Incumbent Reelection: The Development of Institutional Boundaries," *American Political Science Review* 94 (2000): 859–74.

20. Frederick Boehmke and Charles Shipan, "Oversight Capabilities in the States: Are Professionalized Legislatures Better at Getting What They Want?" *State Politics & Policy Quarterly* 15 (2015): 366–86.

21. "Number of Legislators and Length of Terms in Years," National Conference of State Legislatures, April 19, 2021, https://www.ncsl.org/resources/details/number-of-legislators-and-length-of-terms-in-years.

22. "The Term Limited States," National Conference of State Legislatures, November 12, 2020, https://www.ncsl.org/about-state-legislatures/the-term-limited-states.

23. John Carey, Richard Neimi, Lynda Powell, and Gary Moncrief, "The Effects of Term Limits on State Legislatures: A New Survey of 50 States," *Legislative Studies Quarterly* 31 (2006).

24. *The Book of the States*, The Council of State Governments, 2021, 36–38.

25. "Number of Legislators and Length of Terms in Years," National Conference of State Legislatures, April 19, 2021, https://www.ncsl.org/resources/details/number-of-legislators-and-length-of-terms-in-years.

26. MT Code § 5-2-216 (2019).

27. "Legislative Session Length," National Conference of State Legislatures, July 1, 2021, https://www.ncsl.org/news/details/legislative-session-length.

28. Richard A. Champagne and Madeline Kasper, "The Veto Override Process in Wisconsin," The Wisconsin Legislative Reference Bureau, 2019, https://docs.legis.wisconsin.gov/misc/lrb/reading_the_constitution/reading_the_constitution_4_2.pdf, accessed April 12, 2023.

29. "How a Bill Becomes Law," Tennessee General Assembly, https://www.capitol.tn.gov/about/billtolaw.html, accessed April 12, 2023.

30. Brian J. Gerber, Cherie Maestas, and Nelson C. Dometrius, "State Legislative Influence Over Agency Rulemaking: The Utility of Ex Ante Review," *State Politics & Policy Quarterly* 5 (2005): 24–46.

31. Kevin Smith and Alan Greenblatt, *Governing States and Localities*, sixth edition (Sage Publications, 2018), 211.

32. Peverill Squire and Gary Moncrief, *State Legislatures Today*, second edition, (Rowman & Littlefield, 2015), 108.

33. "State Legislative Chambers that Use Multi-Member Districts," Ballotpedia, https://ballotpedia.org/State_legislative_chambers_that_use_multi-member_districts, accessed April 12, 2023.

34. "Single-Member Districts: Advantages and Disadvantages," The Electoral Knowledge Network, https://aceproject.org/main/english/bd/bda02a01.htm, accessed April 12, 2023.

Chapter 5

1. "Mike Dunleavy," Ballotpedia, https://ballotpedia.org/Mike_Dunleavy, accessed July 15, 2023.

2. "100 Years of Alaska's Legislature," https://w3.akleg.gov/100years/bio.php?id=1569, accessed July 15, 2023.

3. "Meet Governor Dunleavy," Office of Governor Mike Dunleavy, https://gov.alaska.gov/meet-mike-dunleavy/, accessed July 15, 2023.

4. Kavitha George and Jeremy Hsieh, "Dunleavy Poised to Win Alaska Governor's Race," *Alaska Public Media*, November 9, 2022, https://alaskapublic.org/2022/11/09/early-results-show-dunleavy-leading-in-alaska-governors-race/.

5. Becky Bohrer, "Mike Dunleavy becomes 1st Alaska Governor Reelected Since 1998," PBS *News Hour*, November 23, 2022, https://www.pbs.org/newshour/politics/mike-dunleavy-becomes-1st-alaska-governor-reelected-since-1998, accessed January 23, 2024.

6. Samuel Stebbins, "How Gov. Michael Dunleavy's Approval Compares to the Nation's Most Popular Governors." *Longview News-Journal*, https://www.news-journal.com/how-gov-michael-dunleavy-s-approval-compares-to-the-nation-s-most-popular-governors/article_e0991b15-c548-5a4f-8e7a-748ad759519f.html.

7. Kaia Hubbarb, "These States Have COVID-19 Mask Mandates," *U.S News*, March 28, 2022, https://www.usnews.com/news/best-states/articles/these-are-the-states-with-mask-mandates, accessed January 23, 2024.

8. M. C. Batinski, *Jonathan Belcher, Colonial Governor* (University Press of Kentucky, 1996), xi.

9. W. L. Morton, "The Local Executive in the British Empire 1763–1828," *The English Historical Review* 78 (1963): 436–57, http://www.jstor.org/stable/562144.

10. Alexander Hamilton, "No. 69 The Real Character of the Executive," *The Federalist Papers*, 1788, https://avalon.law.yale.edu/18th_century/fed69.asp

11. Eagleton Institute of Politics, "Governors and the White House," Center on the American Governor, Rutgers University, https://governors.rutgers.edu/governors-and-the-white-house/

12. Center for American Women and Politics, "History of Women Governors," Rutgers University. https://cawp.rutgers.edu/facts/levels-office/statewide-elective-executive/history-women-governors.

13. Center for American Women and Politics, "History of Women Governors."

14. "James Roesener Shatters Lavender Ceiling; First Trans Man Elected to a State Legislature in U.S. History," *LGBTQ+ Victory Fund*, November 8, 2022, https://victoryfund.org/news/james-roesener-shatters-lavender-ceiling-first-trans-man-elected-to-a-state-legislature-in-u-s-history/, accessed January 23, 2024.

15. There is one other area that states can set eligibility requirements, and that is whether the individual is a qualified voter, including specifying a certain number of years. Most states require an individual be a qualified voter, but they do not specify the number of years.

16. Ben Paviour, "Accused of Assaults He Denies, Justin Fairfax's Run for Va. Governor Tests #MeToo," NPR, May 31, 2021, https://www.npr.org/2021/05/31/1001713239/accused-of-assaults-he-denies-justin-fairfaxs-run-for-va-governor-tests-metoo, accessed January 23, 2024.

17. "Virginia Blackface Scandal: Ralph Northam Vows to Stay as Governor." BBC, February 10, 2019, https://www.bbc.com/news/world-us-canada-47193273.

18. Kevin Robillard, "Republican Wins Drawing to Decide Control of Virginia Statehouse," *Politico*, Jan 4, 2018, https://www.politico.com/story/2018/01/04/xxxx-wins-drawing-to-decide-control-of-virginia-statehouse-324024

19. *Book of States*, The Council of State Governments, 2021 Edition, 123.

20. Steven Walters, "Voters Drive Stake into 'Frankenstein Veto,'" *Milwaukee Journal-Sentinel*, April 2, 2008.

21. Sarah Mervosh, "With a Creative Edit, the Wisconsin Governor Raised School Funding. For 400 Years," *The New York Times*, July 6, 2023, https://www.nytimes.com/2023/07/06/us/wisconsin-school-funding-400-years.html.

22. State of Vermont Executive Department, "Executive Order No. 06–19," https://governor.vermont.gov/sites/scott/files/documents/EO%2006–19%20-%20Governor%27s%20Emergency%20Preparedness%20Advisory%20Council.pdf.

23. The adjutant general of state is typically responsible the state's national guard, veteran's affairs, and potentially emergency services depending on the state.

24. Jason Slotkin, "Michigan Supreme Court Rules Against Governor's Emergency Powers," NPR, October 3, 2020, https://www.npr.org/sections/coronavirus-live-updates/2020/10/03/919891538/michigan-supreme-court-rules-against-governors-emergency-powers.

Chapter 6

1. Marianne Levine and James Arkin, "Loeffler, Perdue Call on Georgia's Republican Secretary of State to Resign," *Politico*, November 9, 2020, https://www.politico.com/news/2020/11/09/loeffler-perdue-georgia-secretary-state-resign-435484, accessed January 23, 2024.

2. The duties of secretary of state typically go to the lieutenant governor.

3. "About State Government," Team Georgia Careers, Team.georgia.gov/careers-about-state-government.

4. "Georgia Secretary of State," Ballotpedia, https://ballotpedia.org/Georgia_Secretary_of_State.

5. *The Book of States*, The Council of State Governments, 154–56.

6. Bill Gardner, *Pillars of Public Service*, National Association of Secretaries of State, 2019, https://www.nass.org/sites/default/files/nass-history/1-Introduction-19.pdf.

7. "Past Attorneys General," National Association of Attorneys General, https://www.naag.org/attorneys-general/past-attorneys-general/, accessed January 23, 2024.

8. "What Attorneys General Do," National Association of Attorneys General, https://www.naag.org/attorneys-general/what-attorneys-general-do/.

9. "State Treasurers Count," National Association of State Treasurers, chrome-extension://efaidnbmnnnibpcajpcglclefindmkaj/https://nast.org/wp-content/uploads/FINAL_NAST_Infographic2-new-address.pdf.

10. "About the Florida Department of Corrections," Florida Department of Corrections, https://fdc.myflorida.com/about.html#:~:text=The%20Department%20has%20143%20facilities,and%20one%20basic%20training%20camp, accessed January 23, 2024.

11. Department of Public Safety, Nevada State Police, https://dps.nv.gov/.

12. For more information on women in state-level appointments see *All Roads Lead to Power: Appointed and Elected Paths to Public Office for US Women*, by Kaitlin N. Sidorsky (University Press of Kansas, 2019).

13. "Georgia's Secretaries of State," Georgia Archives, https://www.georgiaarchives.org/research/secretaries_of_state.

14. "Women Elected Officials by Position," Center for American Women and Politics, https://cawpdata.rutgers.edu/women-elected-officials/position?current=1&level[]=Statewide&race_ethnicity[]=Asian%2FPacific+Islander, accessed January 23, 2024.

15. "Women Elected Officials by Position," Center for American Women and Politics.

16. "History of the Executive Council," State of New Hampshire Executive Council, https://www.nh.gov/council/history/index.htm.

17. "Georgia Treasurer," Ballotpedia, https://ballotpedia.org/Georgia_Treasurer#:~:text=The%20treasurer%20is%20appointed%20by,filled%2C%20the%20state%20treasurer%20himself.

18. "Idaho Superintendent of Public Instruction," Ballotpedia, https://ballotpedia.org/Idaho_Superintendent_of_Public_Instruction.

19. "Georgia State Superintendent of Schools," Ballotpedia, https://ballotpedia.org/Georgia_State_Superintendent_of_Schools.

20. *The Book of States*, The Council of State Governments, volume 53, p. 157.

21. "Attorney General Opinions," National Association of Attorneys General, https://www.naag.org/issues/civil-law/attorney-general-opinions/.

22. "State Treasurers Count," National Association of State Treasurers, https://nast.org/wp-content/uploads/nastinfographic_43-states.pdf, accessed January 23, 2024.

23. "Unclaimed Property Audit Procedures," North Carolina Department of State Treasurer, updated March 2016, https://files.nc.gov/nctreasurer/documents/files/SLGFD/LGC/Resources/AuditManual/AuditPrograms/unclaimedpropertyprocedures.pdf.

24. "Governors' Relationships with Departments and Agencies," National Governors Association, https://www.nga.org/wp-content/uploads/2018/10/Governors-Relationships-with-Departments-Agencies.pdf, accessed January 23, 2024.

25. *The Book of States*, The Council of State Governments, volume 53, p. 119.

Chapter 7

1. State supreme court and state court of last resort are the same court.

2. "South Carolina State Legislature," Ballotpedia, 2023, https://ballotpedia.org/South_Carolina_State_Legislature.

3. Jennifer Berry Hawes, "How South Carolina Ended Up with an All-Male Supreme Court," *ProPublica*, April 28, 2023, https://www.propublica.org/article/how-south-carolina-ended-up-with-all-male-supreme-court.

4. Hawes, "How South Carolina Ended Up."

5. James Pollard, "Newly All-Male South Carolina Supreme Court Scrutinizes Abortion Ban Months after Tossing One Out," *AP News*, June 27, 2023, https://apnews.com/article/abortion-south-carolina-court-465924ec93cb174967656e2bafd94fbb.

6. "Circuit Court," South Carolina Judicial Branch, https://www.sccourts.org/circuitCourt/.

7. "Magistrate Court," South Carolina Judicial Branch, https://www.sccourts.org/magistrateCourt/.

8. "Probate Court," South Carolina Judicial Branch, https://www.sccourts.org/probateCourt/.

9. "Courts in New York," Ballotpedia, https://ballotpedia.org/Courts_in_New_York.

10. Amanda Powers and Alicia Bannon, "State Supreme Court Diversity – May 2022 Update," Brennan Center for Justice, https://www.brennancenter.org/our-work/research-reports/state-supreme-court-diversity-may-2022-update.

11. Powers and Bannon, "State Supreme Court Diversity – May 2022 Update."

12. Brian Frederick and Matthew J. Streb, "Women Running for Judge: The Impact of Sex on Candidate Success in State Intermediate Appellate Court Elections," *Social Science Quarterly* 89 (2008): 937–954; Margaret Williams, "Women's Representation on State Trial and Appellate Courts," *Social Science Quarterly*, 88 (2007): 1192–1204.

13. "Court of Appeals," Supreme Court of Nevada, https://nvcourts.gov/supreme/court_information/court_of_appeals.

14. "About the Trial Courts," Tennessee State Courts, https://www.tncourts.gov/courts/circuit-criminal-chancery-courts/about#:~:text=Chancery%20Courts%20handle%20a%20variety,either%20chancery%20or%20circuit%20court.

15. Connecticut Code of Laws, 2023, Sec. 51-44a, "Judicial Selection Commission. Members. Duties. Nomination of Judges by Governor," chrome-extension://efaidnbmnnnibpcajpcglclefindmkaj/https://portal.ct.gov/-/media/JSC/sec51_44a.pdf.

16. "Supreme Court Nominating Commission," Kansas Judicial Branch, https://www.kscourts.org/Judges/Become-a-Judge/Supreme-Court-Nominating-Commission.

17. Abe Kwok, "Voters Booted 3 Arizona Judges. Shouldn't We Know More Why They Deserved It?" *Arizona Republic*, November 27, 2022, https://www.azcentral.com/story/opinion/op-ed/abekwok/2022/11/27/voters-booted-3-aizona-judges-shouldnt-we-know-more-why/69672683007/.

18. "Wisconsin Supreme Court," Wisconsin Court System, 2020, chrome-extension://efaidnbmnnnibpcajpcglclefindmkaj/https://legis.wisconsin.gov/lc/media/1625/jan8supreme-court.pdf.

19. "Supreme Court of California," Judicial Branch of California, https://supreme.courts.ca.gov/efiling-and-procedures/frequently-asked-questions#:~:text=A%20decision%20to%20review%20is,a%20particular%20case%20for%20review.

20. "How Does the Indiana Supreme Court Work?," Indiana Court Records, https://indianacourtrecords.us/supreme-court/.

Chapter 8

1. "Number of Legislators and Length of Terms in Years," National Conference of State Legislatures, April 19, 2021, https://www.ncsl.org/resources/details/number-of-legislators-and-length-of-terms-in-years.

2. "Campaign Contribution Limits: Overview," National Conference of State Legislatures, updated October 4, 2019, www.Ncsl.org/elections-and-campaigns/campaign-contribution-limits-overview.

3. There are three states that set different limitations for various executive offices: Minnesota, California, and Connecticut. These state amounts are coded to the limits for the position of governor, which is $4,000 in Minnesota, $36,400 in California, and $3,500 in Connecticut (National Council of State Legislatures).

4. Ron Elving, "Here's Why the Other 48 States Care Who's Governor of Virginia and New Jersey," NPR, October 31, 2021, Npr.org/2021/10/31/1050563878/heres-why-the-other-48-states-care-whos-governor-of-virginia-and-new-jersey.

5. Linda Casey, "2016 Ballot Measures Overview," FollowTheMoney, December 12, 2017, Followthemoney.org/research/institute-reports/2016-ballot-measures-overview.

6. Penelope Muse Abernathy, "The Expanding News Desert," The Center for Innovation and Sustainability in Local Media, School of Media and Journalism, University of North Carolina at Chapel Hill, 2018, https://www.usnewsdeserts.com/.

7. Kristen Hare, "More than 100 Local Newsrooms Closed During the Coronavirus Pandemic," *Poynter*, December 2, 2021, https://www.poynter.org/locally/2021/the-coronavirus-has-closed-more-than-100-local-newsrooms-across-america-and-counting/.

8. Katerina Eva Masta and Kirsten Worden, "Local Newspapers Fact Sheet," Pew Research Center, 2022, https://www.poynter.org/locally/2021/the-coronavirus-has-closed-more-than-100-local-newsrooms-across-america-and-counting/.

9. Roger Cobb and Charles Elder, *Participation in American Politics*, second edition, (Baltimore: Johns Hopkins University Press 1983).

10. Frank Baumgartner and Bryan Jones, *Agendas and Instability in American Politics* (Chicago: University of Illinois Press 1993).

11. Andrew Karch, *Early Start: Preschool Politics in the United States* (Ann Arbor: University of Michigan Press, 2013).

12. Allison Friedman-Krauss, W. Steven Barnett, and Milagros Nores, "How Much Can High-Quality Universal Pre-K Reduce Achievement Gaps?" *American Progress*, 2016, https://www.americanprogress.org/article/how-much-can-high-quality-universal-pre-k-reduce-achievement-gaps/.

13. Ariana Freeman and Jan Crawford, "Facing a Stigma, Many Ex-Convicts in the South Struggle to Find Work," CBS News, January 31, 2023, https://www.cbsnews.com/news/ex-convicts-u-s-struggle-to-find-employment/#:~:text=Nearly%2080%20million%20Americans%2C%20or,felony%20on%20their%20permanent%20record.

Chapter 9

1. Staff, "Governor DeSantis Delivers State of the State Address," March 7, 2023, https://www.flgov.com/2023/03/07/governor-ron-desantis-delivers-state-of-the-state-address/, accessed December 15, 2023.

2. FPI Staff, "Florida House and Senate FY 2023-24 Budget Proposals: What to Know Ahead of the Joint Budget Conference," Florida Policy Institute, April 6, 2023,

https://www.floridapolicy.org/posts/florida-house-and-senate-fy-2023-24-budget-proposals-what-to-know-ahead-of-the-joint-budget-conference, accessed December 15, 2023.

3. Elise Elder, "DeSantis Wins Governor's Race by Largest Margin in 40 Years," *WUFT*, November 8, 2022, https://www.wuft.org/news/2022/11/08/desantis-wins-2022-florida-governors-race-by-largest-margin-in-40-years/, accessed December 15, 2023.

4. FPI Staff, "Florida House and Senate FY 2023-24 Budget Proposals: What to Know Ahead of the Joint Budget Conference."

5. FPI Staff, "Florida FY 2023-24 Budget: Summary by Issue Area," Florida Policy Institute, August 9, 2023, https://www.floridapolicy.org/posts/florida-fy-2023-24-budget-summary-by-issue-area, accessed December 15, 2023.

6. "2023 Veto List," Florida Government, https://www.flgov.com/wp-content/uploads/2023/06/Final-Veto-List-2023.pdf, accessed December 15, 2023.

7. "Fiscal Year 2023-24 Framework for Freedom Budget," January 31, 2023 https://www.flgov.com/wp-content/uploads/2023/02/FY-23-24-Governor-Rec-Budget-Highlights-FINAL-1.31.23.pdf, accessed December 15, 2023 and "Fiscal Year 2023-24 Framework for Freedom Budget," Draft 1, https://www.flgov.com/wp-content/uploads/2023/06/FY-23-24-Budget-Highlights-Draft-1.pdf, accessed December 15, 2023.

8. "State and Local Government Snapshot," U.S. Census, June 24, 2020, https://www.census.gov/library/visualizations/interactive/state-local-snapshot.html, accessed December 15, 2023; "Fiscal Year 2023–24 Framework for Freedom Budget," January 31, 2023, https://www.flgov.com/2023/02/01/governor-ron-desantis-announces-framework-for-freedom-budget/ and https://www.flgov.com/wp-content/uploads/2023/02/FY-23-24-Governor-Rec-Budget-Highlights-FINAL-1.31.23.pdf, accessed January 24, 2024; "Fiscal Year 2023–24 Framework for Freedom Budget," Draft 1, https://www.flgov.com/2023/06/15/governor-ron-desantis-signs-framework-for-freedom-budget/#:~:text=The%20Framework%20for%20Freedom%20Budget%20includes%20an%20additional%20%2476%20million,array%20of%20behavioral%20health%20services and https://www.flgov.com/wp-content/uploads/2023/06/FY-23-24-Budget-Highlights-Draft-1.pdf, accessed January 24, 2024.

9. "Low Birth Weight in the United States," America's Health Rankings, https://www.americashealthrankings.org/explore/measures/birthweight, accessed December 15, 2023.

10. Timothy Vermeer, "State Individual Income Tax Rates and Brackets for 2023," The Tax Foundation, Feb 21, 2023, https://taxfoundation.org/data/all/state/state-income-tax-rates-2023/#:~:text=Individual%20income%20taxes%20are%20a,Columbia%20levy%20individual%20income%20taxes, accessed December 15, 2023.

11. Timothy Vermeer, "State Individual Income Tax Rates and Brackets for 2023."

12. "State and Local Sales Tax Rates, Midyear 2023," Tax Foundation, July 17, 2023, https://taxfoundation.org/data/all/state/2023-sales-tax-rates-midyear/, accessed January 24, 2024.

13. Aiden Davis, "Options for Less Regressive Taxes in 2019," Institute on Taxation and Economic Policy, September 2019, https://leg.mt.gov/content/Committees/Interim/2019-2020/Revenue/Meetings/July-2020/HJ-35/ITEP-Options-for-a-Less-Regressive-Sales-Tax-in-2019.pdf, accessed December 15, 2023.

14. Pearl Bader, David Boisclair, and Roberta Ferrence, "Effects of Tobacco Taxation and Pricing on Smoking Behavior in High Risk Populations: A Knowledge Synthesis," *International Journal of Environmental Research and Public Health* 8 (2011): 4118–39, https://www.ncbi.nlm.nih.gov/pmc/articles/PMC3228562/.

15. "State System Excise Tax Fact Sheet," Center for Disease Control and Prevention, https://www.cdc.gov/statesystem/factsheets/excisetax/ExciseTax.html, accessed December 15, 2023.

16. "State Alcohol Excise Tax Rates," Tax Policy Center Urban Institute & Brookings Institute, February 3, 2023, https://www.taxpolicycenter.org/statistics/state-alcohol-excise-tax-rates, accessed December 15, 2023.

17. Andrey Yushkov, "Where Do People Pay the Most Property Taxes," The Tax Foundation, September 12, 2023, https://taxfoundation.org/data/all/state/property-taxes-by-state-county-2023/, accessed December 15, 2023.

18. "Summary—State and Local Property Tax Revenue by State 2017," Lincoln Institute of Land Policy, https://www.lincolninst.edu/research-data/data-toolkits/significant-features-property-tax/government-finance-data/summary-23, accessed December 15, 2023.

19. "Corporate Income Taxes," The Urban Institute, https://www.urban.org/policy-centers/cross-center-initiatives/state-and-local-finance-initiative/projects/state-and-local-backgrounders/corporate-income-taxes#:~:text=By%20using%20the%20portion%20of,the%20states%20they%20operate%20in, accessed December 15, 2023.

20. "Corporate Income Taxes," The Urban Institute.

21. Charlotte Morabito, "Here's Why More Than 60% of Fortune 500 Companies Are Incorporated in Delaware," CNBC, March 13, 2023, https://www.cnbc.com/2023/03/13/why-more-than-60percent-of-fortune-500-companies-incorporated-in-delaware.html#:~:text=Delaware%20has%20cultivated%20a%20reputation,Delaware%20their%20legal%20home%2C%20though, accessed December 28, 2023.

22. Charlotte Morabito, "Here's Why More Than 60% of Fortune 500 Companies Are Incorporated in Delaware."

23. "Charges," The Urban Institute, https://www.urban.org/policy-centers/cross-center-initiatives/state-and-local-finance-initiative/state-and-local-backgrounders/charges, December 15, 2023.

24. "Pregnant Women," Medicaid and CHIP Payment and Access Commission, https://www.macpac.gov/subtopic/pregnant-women/#:~:text=For%20more%20on%20Medicaid%20eligibility,Requirements%20and%20State%20Options%3A%20Eligibility.&text=Pregnant%20women%20must%20be%20covered%20at%20least%20up%20to%20133%20percent%20FPL.&text=States%20must%20extend%20coverage%20for,coverage%20period%20for%2012%20months, accessed December 15, 2023.

25. "How Is K-12 Education Funded?" Peter G. Peterson Foundation, August 25, 2023, https://www.pgpf.org/budget-basics/how-is-k-12-education-funded, accessed December 15, 2023.

26. "Elementary and Secondary Education Expenditures," The Urban Institute, https://www.urban.org/policy-centers/cross-center-initiatives/state-and-local-finance-initiative/state-and-local-backgrounders/elementary-and-secondary-education-expenditures, accessed December 15, 2023.

27. "Funding Gaps: An Analysis of School Funding Equity Across the U.S. and Within Each State," The Education Trust, 2018, https://edtrust.org/wp-content/uploads/2014/09/FundingGapReport_2018_FINAL.pdf, accessed December 15, 2023.

28. "Highway and Road Expenditures," The Urban Institute, https://www.urban.org/policy-centers/cross-center-initiatives/state-and-local-finance-initiative/state-and-local-backgrounders/highway-and-road-expenditures, accessed December 15, 2023.

29. Amy Russo, "Critical Failure Closes Westbound Lanes of Washington Bridge," *The Providence Journal*, December 11, 2023, https://www.providencejournal.com/story/news/local/2023/12/11/washington-bridges-westbound-i-195-providence-closed-after-critical-failure-discovered/71884771007/, accessed December 15, 2023.

30. "Criminal Justice Expenditures: Police, Corrections, and Courts," The Urban Institute, https://www.urban.org/policy-centers/cross-center-initiatives/state-and-local-

finance-initiative/state-and-local-backgrounders/criminal-justice-police-corrections-courts-expenditures, accessed December 15, 2023.

31. Gary D. Robertson, "With State Budget Talks Extending, North Carolina Democrats Criticize GOP for Delay," AP *News*, July 12, 2023. https://apnews.com/article/north-carolina-budget-delay-64958bc2b2b1c9dec84ee9ec87a6f29d.

Chapter 10

1. "Only A Teacher: School House Pioneers," PBS, May 17, https://www.pbs.org/onlyateacher/horace.html.

2. Department of Education, "The Development of Education in Massachusetts, 1630–1930," Commonwealth of Massachusetts (1930), in Selections from Archives and Special Collections, Bridgewater State University, Item 5, Available at: https://vc.bridgew.edu/selections/5.

3. *Massachusetts Constitution* Chapter 5, Section 2. https://malegislature.gov/Laws/Constitution#amendmentArticleXVIII, accessed May 23, 2022.

4. "Commissioner's Office," Massachusetts Department of Elementary and Secondary Education, https://www.doe.mass.edu/commissioner/.

5. "Education Board," Massachusetts Department of Elementary and Secondary Education, https://www.doe.mass.edu/bese/#:~:text=BESE's%20responsibilities%20include%20approving%20learning,districts%2C%20and%20hiring%20the%20commissioner.

6. "About the EEC," Department of Early Education and Care, https://www.mass.gov/orgs/department-of-early-education-and-care.

7. "School and District Profiles," Massachusetts Department of Elementary and Secondary Education, https://profiles.doe.mass.edu/profiles/student.aspx?orgcode=00000000&orgtypecode=0&, accessed May 17, 2023.

8. "School and District Profiles," Massachusetts Department of Elementary and Secondary Education, https://profiles.doe.mass.edu/profiles/student.aspx?orgcode=00000000&orgtypecode=0&, accessed May 17, 2023.

9. "School and District Profiles," Massachusetts Department of Elementary and Secondary Education, https://profiles.doe.mass.edu/profiles/teacher.aspx?orgcode=00000000&orgtypecode=0&leftNavId=815&, accessed May 22, 2023.

10. "DHE Data Center," Department of Higher Education, https://www.mass.edu/datacenter/2020enrollmentestimates.asp, accessed May 17, 2023.

11. Joshua Goodman, "Who Merits Financial Aid?: Massachusetts' Adams Scholarship," *Journal of Public Economics* 92(2008): 2121–31.

12. "John and Adam Abigail Adams," Massachusetts.gov, https://www.mass.gov/info-details/john-and-abigail-adams-scholarship, accessed May 17, 2023.

13. "U.S. School System Current Spending Per Pupil by Region: Fiscal Year 2020," United States Census Bureau, https://www.census.gov/library/visualizations/2022/comm/spending-per-pupil.html, accessed May 17, 2023.

14. New Jersey performed better in the eighth grade reading tests by one point.

15. "Participation Requirements for Students in Grades 3-8 and 10," Massachusetts Department of Elementary and Secondary Education, https://www.doe.mass.edu/mcas/participation.html?section=gr3-8and10#:~:text=Students%20in%20grades%203%E2%80%938%20and%2010%20must%20participate%20in,otherwise%2C%20results%20will%20be%20invalidated, accessed May 23, 2023.

16. In grades 5, 8, 9, and 10 students take a Science and Technology/Engineering exam. "MCAS Results," Massachusetts Department of Elementary and Secondary Education, https://www.doe.mass.edu/mcas/results.html?yr=2022, accessed May 23, 2023.

17. "Spring 2022 MCAS Tests: Summary of Results," Massachusetts Department of Elementary and Secondary Education, February 2023.

18. "State Performance Compared to the Nation," The Nation's Report Card, https://www.nationsreportcard.gov/profiles/tateprofile?chort=1&sub=MAT&sj=AL&sfj=NP&st=MN&year=2022R3, accessed May 23, 2023.

19. "The Historical Role of the School Board," Illinois Association of School Boards, 2014, https://www.iasb.com/IASB/media/Documents/HistoricPoliticalRoleBoards.pdf, accessed Jan 19, 2024.

20. "The Historical Role of the School Board," Illinois Association of School Boards.

21. "Table 2. Number of Operating Public Schools and Districts, Student Membership, Teachers, and Pupil/Teacher Ratio, by State or Jurisdiction:School Year 2020–21," NCES Common Core of Data, https://nces.ed.gov/ccd/tables/202021_summary_2.asp, accessed Jan 19, 2024.

22. Lauren Camera, "School Board Recalls at an All Time High as GOP Puts K-12 Issues in Spotlight," *U.S. News & World Report*, November 1, 2021, https://www.usnews.com/news/education-news/articles/2021-11-01/school-board-recalls-at-all-time-high-as-gop-puts-k-12-issues-in-spotlight, accessed January 19, 2024.

23. Thomas Fuller, "In Landslide, San Francisco Forces Out 3 Board of Education Members," *New York Times*, February 16, 2022, https://www.nytimes.com/2022/02/16/us/san-francisco-school-board-recall.html.

24. Emma Garcia, "Inequalities at the Starting Gate: Cognitive and Noncognitive Skills Gaps between 2010-2011 Kindergarten Classmates," Economic Policy Institute, 2015, https://www.epi.org/publication/inequalities-at-the-starting-gate-cognitive-and-noncognitive-gaps-in-the-2010–2011-kindergarten-class/.

25. Leila Schochet, "The Child Care Crisis Is Keeping Women Out of the Workforce," Center for American Progress, 2019, https://www.americanprogress.org/article/child-care-crisis-keeping-women-workforce/, accessed May 22, 2023.

26. Jack Rosenthal, "President Vetoes Child Care Plan As Irresponsible," *New York Times*, December 10, 1971, https://www.nytimes.com/1971/12/10/archives/president-vetoes-child-care-plan-as-irresponsible-he-terms-bill.html.

27. Andrew Karch, *Early Start: Preschool Politics in the United States* (Ann Arbor: University of Michigan Press, 2013).

28. Allison H. Friedman-Kraus, W. Steven Barnett, Karin A. Garver, Katherine S. Hodges, G. G. Weisenfeld, Beth Ann Gardiner, and Tracy Merriman Jost, "The State of Preschool Yearbook 2021," National Institute for Early Education Research Rutgers Graduate School of Education, 2022, https://nieer.org/wp-content/uploads/2022/09/YB2021_Full_Report.pdf, 25.

29. Lawrence J. Schweinhart, Jeanne Montie, Zongping Xiang, W. Steven Barnett, Clive R. Belfield, and Milagros Nores, "The High/Scope Perry Preschool Study Through Age 40: Summary, Conclusions, and Frequently Asked Questions," High Scope Press, 2005.

30. See Mark W. Lipsey, Dale C. Farran, and Kerry G. Hofer, "A Randomized Control Trial of a Statewide Voluntary Prekindergarten Program on Children's Skills and Behaviors Through the Third Grade," Peabody Research Institute, September 2015, https://my.vanderbilt.edu/tnprekevaluation/files/2013/10/VPKthrough3rd_final_withcover.pdf.

31. Farah Z. Ahmad and Katie Hamm, "The School-Readiness Gap and Preschool Benefits for Children of Color," Center for American Progress, 2013, https://www.americanprogress.org/article/the-school-readiness-gap-and-preschool-benefits-for-children-of-color/, accessed May 22, 2023.

32. Leila Schochet, "The Child Care Crisis Is Keeping Women Out of the Workforce," Center for American Progress, 2019, https://www.americanprogress.org/article/child-care-crisis-keeping-women-workforce/, accessed May 22, 2023.

33. As well as Washington, D.C.

34. Friedman-Kraus et al.,, "The State of Preschool Yearbook 2021."

35. Friedman-Kraus et al., "The State of Preschool Yearbook 2021."

36. Emily Parker, Louisa Diffey, and Bruce Atchinson, "How States Fund Pre-k: A Primer for Policy Makers," Education Commission of the States, 2018, https://www.ecs.org/wp-content/uploads/How-States-Fund-Pre-K_A-Primer-for-Policymakers.pdf, accessed May 22, 2023.

37. Beth Meloy, Madelyn Gardner, and Linda Darling-Hammond, "Untangling the Evidence on Preschool Effectiveness: Insights for Policymakers," Learning Policy Institute, January 2019.

38. Allison Friedman-Krauss, W. Steven Barnett, Katherine S. Hodges, Karin A. Garver, G. G. Weisenfeld, Beth Ann Gardiner, and Tracy Merriman Jost, "The State of Preschool 2022."

39. James Barlament, "HOPE Scholarship," New Georgia Encyclopedia, last modified April 10, 2021, https://www.georgiaencyclopedia.org/articles/education/hope-scholarship/.

40. Jennifer Lee and Allie Schneider, "A Brief History of Hope," Georgia Budget and Policy Institute, 2021, https://gbpi.org/a-brief-history-of-hope/.

41. Lee and Schneider, "A Brief History of Hope."

42. An additional scholarship, the Florida Gold Seal Vocational Award, covered 75 percent of tuition. "Annual Report to the Commissioner 1997–1998," Florida Department of Education Office of Student Financial Assistance, 1998, https://www.floridastudentfinancialaidsg.org/PDF/Commisioner/annualreport97-98.pdf.

43. Lyle McKinney, "An Analysis of Policy Solutions to Improve Efficiency and Equity of Florida's Bright Futures Scholarship Program," *Florida Journal of Educational Administration & Policy* 2(2009): 85–101. https://files.eric.ed.gov/fulltext/EJ930108.pdf.

44. McKinney, "Florida's Bright Futures Scholarship Program."

45. Lora Cohen-Vogel and William Kyle Ingle, "When Neighbours Matter Most: Innovation Diffusion and State Policy Adoption in Tertiary Education," *Journal of Education Policy* 22(2006): 241–62. Other scholars include Missouri as a state with a broad-based merit-aid program. See Zhang and Ness, "Does State Merit-Based Aid Stem Brain Drain," *Educational Evaluation and Policy Analysis* 32 (2010): 143–15.

46. Donald E. Heller, "State Merit Scholarship Program: An Introduction," in *Who Should We Help? The Negative Social Consequences of Merit Scholarships*, ed. Donald E. Heller and Patricia Marin (Cambridge, MA: Harvard Civil Rights Project, 2002).

47. Liang Zhang and Erik C. Ness, "Does State Merit-Based Aid Stem Brain Drain," *Educational Evaluation and Policy Analysis* 32 (2010): 143–65.

48. Melissa Binder, Philip T. Ganderton, and Kristin Hutchens, "Incentive Effects of New Mexico's Merit-Based State Scholarship Program: Who Responds and How?" In *Who Should We Help? The Negative Social Consequences of Merit Scholarships*, ed. Donald E. Heller and Patricia Marin (Cambridge, MA: Harvard Civil Rights Project, 2002), 41–56.

49. Donald E. Heller and Christopher J. Rasmussen, "Merit Scholarships and College Access: Evidence from Florida and Michigan," in *Who Should We Help? The Negative Social Consequences of Merit Scholarships*, ed. Donald E. Heller and Patricia Marin (Cambridge, MA: Harvard Civil Rights Project, 2002), 41–56, 25–40, 35.

50. "Kentucky Educational Excellence Scholarship," Kentucky Department of Education, 2022, https://education.ky.gov/districts/fin/pages/kentucky%20educational%20excellence%20scholarship.aspx.

51. Gabriel Jimenez-Ecman, "Bright Futures equirements 2022–2023," Scholarships 360, 2023, https://scholarships360.org/scholarships/bright-futures-scholarship-requirements/.

52. "Tennessee Hope Scholarship FAQS," College for TN, https://www.collegefortn.org/tennessee-hope-scholarship-faqs/; and "Hope and Zell Miller Scholarships," Georgia Student Finance Commission, https://www.gafutures.org/hope-state-aid-programs/hope-zell-miller-scholarships/hope-scholarship/academic-eligibility-in-college/.

53. Donald E. Heller, and Christopher J. Rasmussen, "Merit Scholarships and College Access: Evidence from Florida and Michigan."

54. Joshua Goodman, "Who Merits Financial Aid?: Massachusetts' Adams Scholarship," *Journal of Public Economics* 92(2008): 2121–31.

55. Liang Zhang and Erik C. Ness, "Does State Merit-Based Aid Stem Brain Drain," *Educational Evaluation and Policy Analysis* 32 (2010): 143–65.

56. Gabriel Jimenez-Ecman, "Bright Futures Requirements 2022–2023."

57. "West Virginia Promise Scholarship," College for West Virginia, https://www.collegeforwv.com/programs/promise-scholarship/award-information/.

58. "Adams Scholarship: Current and Recent Value," Office of Student Financial Assistance, https://www.mass.edu/osfa/programs/adamstable.asp.

59. "A Comparison of States' Lottery Scholarship Programs," Policy, Planning, and Research Division of the Tennessee Higher Education Commission, 2012, https://thec.ppr.tn.gov/THECSIS/Lottery/pdfs/SpecialReports/A%20Comparison%20of%20States'%20Lottery%20Scholarship%20Programs%20120717.pdf

60. "A Comparison of States' Lottery Scholarship Programs."

61. James Barlament, "HOPE Scholarship."

Chapter 11

1. Ann E. Carson, "Prisoners in 2021—Statistical Tables," Bureau of Justice Statistics, 2022, https://bjs.ojp.gov/library/publications/prisoners-2021-statistical-tables, accessed June 23, 2023.

2. Roy Walmsley, "World Prison Population List: Eleventh Edition," World Prison Brief and Institute for Criminal Policy Research, 2015, https://nicic.gov/resources/nic-library/all-library-items/world-prison-population-listeleventh-edition#:~:text=There%20are%20more%20than%2010.35,100%2C000%20of%20its%20total%20population, accessed June 23, 2023.

3. Ashley Nellis, "The Color of Justice: Racial and Ethnic Disparity in State Prisons," The Sentencing Project, October 13, 2021, https://www.sentencingproject.org/reports/the-color-of-justice-racial-and-ethnic-disparity-in-state-prisons-the-sentencing-project/, accessed June 23, 2023.

4. Laura M. Maruschak and Emily D. Buehler, "Census of State and Federal Adult Correction Facilities, 2019—Statistical Tables," Bureau of Justice Statistics, November 10, 2021, https://bjs.ojp.gov/library/publications/census-state-and-federal-adult-correctional-facilities-2019-statistical-tables#:~:text=Among%20all%20prisoners%20in%20confinement,7%25%20were%20in%20private%20facilities, accessed June 23, 2023.

5. "US Criminal Justice Data," The Sentencing Project, https://www.sentencingproject.org/research/us-criminal-justice-data/, accessed June 23, 2023.

6. "US Criminal Justice Data," The Sentencing Project.

7. "US Criminal Justice Data," The Sentencing Project, https://www.sentencingproject.org/research/us-criminal-justice-data/, accessed June 23, 2023.

8. "Crime Data," New Jersey Government, https://www.nj.gov/nj/safety/features/crimedata.html, accessed June 23, 2023. This includes uniform reporting data of murder, nonnegligent homicide, rape, robbery, and aggravated assault, burglary, larceny-theft, car theft, and arson.

9. "Domestic Violence in New Jersey," National Coalition Against Domestic Violence, 2020, https://assets.speakcdn.com/assets/2497/ncadv_new_jersey_fact_sheet_2020.pdf, accessed June 23, 2023.

10. "Domestic Violence in New Jersey," National Coalition Against Domestic Violence, 2020, https://assets.speakcdn.com/assets/2497/ncadv_new_jersey_fact_sheet_2020.pdf, accessed June 23, 2023. Data from Sharon G. Smith, Jieru Chen, Kathleen C. Basile, Leah K. Gilbert, Melissa T. Merrick, Nimesh Patel, Margie Walling, and Anurag Jain, "The National Intimate Partner and Sexual Violence Survey (NISVS): 2010–2012 State Report," 2017, https://www.cdc.gov/violenceprevention/pdf/NISVS-StateReportBook.pdf, accessed June 23, 2023.

11. Mark F. Bernstein, "How New Jersey Made a Bail Breakthrough," *Princeton Alumni Weekly*, November 2020, https://paw.princeton.edu/article/how-new-jersey-made-bail-breakthrough, accessed June 23, 2023.

12. Bernstein, "How New Jersey Made a Bail Breakthrough."

13. Bernstein, "How New Jersey Made a Bail Breakthrough."

14. *New Jersey State Constitution*, Article IX, https://www.njleg.state.nj.us/constitution, accessed June 23, 2023.

15. "New Jersey Pretrial Detention Amendment, Public Question No. 1 (2014)," Ballotpedia, https://ballotpedia.org/New_Jersey_Pretrial_Detention_Amendment,_Public_Question_No._1_(2014), accessed June 23, 2023.

16. Bernstein, "How New Jersey Made a Bail Breakthrough."

17. Matt Friedman and Joseph Specter, "New Jersey Overhauled Its Bail System Under Christie. Now Some Democrats Want to Roll It Back," *Politico*, December 11, 2022, https://www.politico.com/news/2022/12/11/new-jersey-bail-system-roll-back-00072781, accessed June 23, 2023.

18. Thomas Hanna, "The Facts on New Jersey Bail Reform," Arnold Ventures, March 1, 2023, https://www.arnoldventures.org/stories/the-facts-on-new-jersey-bail-reform, accessed June 23, 2023.

19. Bill Raferty, "Bail Reform in 2023? 2022 Efforts in 3 States May Impact the Courts," National Center for State Courts, January 4, 2023, https://www.ncsc.org/information-and-resources/trending-topics/trending-topics-landing-pg/bail-reform-in-2023-2022-efforts-in-3-states-may-impact-the-courts, accessed July 19, 2023.

20. Jesse McKinley, Grace Ashford, and Hurubie Meko, "New York Will Toughen Contentious Bail Law to Give Judges More Discretion," *The New York Times*, April 28, 2023, https://www.nytimes.com/2023/04/28/nyregion/bail-reform-ny.html, accessed July 19, 2023.

21. Senate Bill No. 3347, https://pub.njleg.state.nj.us/Bills/2022/S3500/3347_I1.PDF, accessed June 23, 2023, pg. 7.

22. U.S. Constitution, Amendment 8, https://constitution.congress.gov/constitution/amendment-8/#:~:text=Excessive%20bail%20shall%20not%20be,cruel%20and%20unusual%20punishments%20inflicted, accessed June 23, 2023.

23. "U.S. Commission on Civil Rights Releases Report: The Civil Rights Implications of Cash Bail," U.S. Commission on Civil Rights, January 20, 2022, https://www.usccr.gov/

news/2022/us-commission-civil-rights-releases-report-civil-rights-implications-cash-bail#:~:text=More%20than%2060%25%20of%20defendants,t%20afford%20to%20post%20 bail, accessed July 19, 2023.

24. Nicole Zayas Manzano, "The High Price of Cash Bail," American Bar Association, April 12, 2023, https://www.americanbar.org/groups/crsj/publications/human_rights_magazine_home/economic-issues-in-criminal-justice/the-high-price-of-cash-bail/, accessed June 23, 2023.

25. Manzano, Nicole Mayas. 2023. "The High Price of Cash Bail." American Bar Association. https://www.americanbar.org/groups/crsj/publications/human_rights_magazine_home/economic-issues-in-criminal-justice/the-high-price-of-cash-bail/#:~:text=When%20people%20with%20cash%20bail,pretrial%20detention%20has%20associated%20costs.

26. U.S. Commission on Civil Rights, 2022.

27. Isabelle Jorgensen and Sandra Susan Smith, "The Current Sate of Bail Reform in the United States: Results of a Landscape Analysis of Bail Reforms Across All 50 States," Harvard Kennedy School of Government Faculty Research Working Paper Series, 2021, https://www.hks.harvard.edu/publications/current-state-bail-reform-united-states-results-landscape-analysis-bail-reforms-across, accessed June 23, 2023.

28. Bernadette Rabuy and Daniel Kopf, "Detaining the Poor: How Money Bail Perpetuates an Endless Cycle of Poverty and Jail Time," Prison Policy Initiative, May 10, 2016, https://www.prisonpolicy.org/reports/incomejails.html, accessed June 23, 2023.

29. Thomas H. Cohen and Brian A. Reaves, "Pretrial Release of Felony Defendants in State Courts," Bureau of Justice Statistics, 2007, https://bjs.ojp.gov/content/pub/pdf/prfdsc.pdf, accessed June 23, 2023. This includes defendants from the seventy-five largest counties.

30. Cohen and Reaves, "Pretrial Release of Felony Defendants in State Courts."

31. Bernadette Rabuy and Daniel Kopf, "Detaining the Poor: How Money Bail Perpetuates an Endless Cycle of Poverty and Jail Time," Prison Policy Initiative, May 10, 2016, https://www.prisonpolicy.org/reports/incomejails.html, accessed June 23, 2023.

32. Bernstein, "How New Jersey Made a Bail Breakthrough."

33. Kelly Roberts, Freeman, Cathy Hu, and Jesse Jannetta, "Racial Equity an Criminal Justice Risk Assessment," Urban Policy Institute, March 2021, https://www.urban.org/sites/default/files/publication/103864/racial-equity-and-criminal-justice-risk-assessment.pdf, accessed June 23, 2023.

34. "Public Question Results," State of New Jersey, December 2, 2014, https://www.state.nj.us/state/elections/assets/pdf/election-results/2014/2014-official-general-public-question-1.pdf, accessed June 23, 2023.

35. Natalie R. Ortiz, "County Jails at a Crossroads: An Examination of the Jail Population and Pretrial Release," National Association of Counties, 2015, https://www.naco.org/resources/county-jails-crossroads, accessed on Oct 12, 2023.

36. "FAQ," National Sheriffs' Association, https://www.sheriffs.org/about-nsa/faq#:~:text=A%20Sheriff%20is%20generally%20(but,their%20allegiance%20to%20a%20city, accessed October 12, 2023.

37. "Policing 101," Community Relations Service, U.S. Department of Justice, https://www.justice.gov/d9/policing_101_content.pdf, accessed October 12, 2023.

38. "FAQ," https://www.sheriffs.org/about-nsa/faq#:~:text=A%20Sheriff%20is%20generally%20(but,their%20allegiance%20to%20a%20city, accessed October 12, 2023.

39. "National Study of Prosecutor Elections," The Prosecutors and Politics Project UNC Law School, https://law.unc.edu/wp-content/uploads/2020/01/National-Study-Prosecutor-Elections-2020.pdf, accessed October 12, 2023.

40. "National Study of Prosecutor Elections," The Prosecutors and Politics Project UNC Law School.

41. "FAQs," Office of the State Attorney Sixth Judicial Circuit of Florida, https://www.flsa6.gov/FAQs-10-1306222.html#:~:text=There%20are%20twenty%20elected%20State,his%20or%20her%20judicial%20circuit, accessed October 12, 2023.

42. Janie Har, "San Franscico Recalls Progressive Prosecutor Chesa Boudin," *PBS News Hour*, June 8, 2022, https://www.pbs.org/newshour/politics/san-francisco-recalls-progressive-prosecutor-chesa-boudin, accessed October 12, 2023.

43. Matt Dixon, "Ron DeSantis Suspends Second Elected Prosecutor as His 2024 Campaign Struggles," *NBC News*, Aug. 9, 2023, https://www.nbcnews.com/politics/2024-election/ron-desantis-suspends-second-elected-prosecutor-monique-worrell-rcna98968, accessed October 12, 2023.

44. Kellie Cowwan, "Warren v. DeSantis: Suspended Hillsborough State Attorney Andrew Warren Heads to Federal Appeals Court," *Fox 13 News*, May 2, 2023, https://www.fox13news.com/news/warren-v-desantis-suspended-hillsborough state-attorney-andrew-warren-fights-to-get-job-back, accessed October 12, 2023.

45. Cowwan, "Warren v. DeSantis."

46. "The New Jersey Courts: A Guide to the Judicial Process," New Jersey Courts, August 2019, https://www.njcourts.gov/sites/default/files/forms/12246_guide_judicial_process.pdf, accessed October 12, 2023.

47. "The New Jersey Courts: A Guide to the Judicial Process," New Jersey Courts.

48. "Felon Voting Rights," National Council of State Legislatures, April 6, 2023, https://www.ncsl.org/elections-and-campaigns/felon-voting-rights, accessed June 23, 2023.

49. "Felon Voting Rights," National Council of State Legislatures.

50. Chris Uggen, Ryan Larson, Sarah Shannon, and Arleth Pulido-Nava, "Locked Out 2020: Estimates of People Denied Voting Rights Due to a Felony Conviction," The Sentencing Project, October 30, 2020, https://www.sentencingproject.org/reports/locked-out-2020-estimates-of-people-denied-voting-rights-due-to-a-felony-conviction/, accessed June 23, 2023.

51. Uggen et al., "Locked Out 2020."

52. Vanessa Romo, "New Jersey Governor Signs Bills Restoring Voting Rights to More Than 80,000 People," NPR, December 18, 2019, https://www.npr.org/2019/12/18/789538148/new-jersey-governor-signs-bills-restoring-voting-rights-to-more-than-80-000-peop, accessed June 23, 2023.

53. "Voting Restoration Amendment," Florida Division of Elections, https://dos.elections.myflorida.com/initiatives/initdetail.asp?account=64388&seqnum=1, accessed June 23, 2023.

54. "Florida Supreme Court Advisory Opinion on Amendment 4," The Brennan Center, August 9, 2019, https://www.brennancenter.org/our-work/court-cases/florida-supreme-court-advisory-opinion-amendment-4, accessed June 23, 2023.

55. "Second Supplemental Expert Report of Daniel A. Smith, PhD," United States District Court for the Northern District of Florida, in the case *Kelvin Jones v. Ron DeSantis*, March 2, 2020, https://www.brennancenter.org/sites/default/files/2020-05/Smith%20Second%20Supplemental%20Report.pdf, accessed July 19, 2023.

56. "US Criminal Justice Data," The Sentencing Project, https://www.sentencingproject.org/research/us-criminal-justice-data/, accessed June 23, 2023.

57. "Felony Disenfranchisement Laws (Map)," ACLU, https://www.aclu.org/issues/voting-rights/voter-restoration/felony-disenfranchisement-laws-map, July 28, 2023.

Chapter 12

1. "History," California Air Resources Board, https://ww2.arb.ca.gov/about/history, accessed November 6, 2023.

2. "Vehicle Emissions California Waivers and Authorizations," United States Environmental Protection Agency, https://www.epa.gov/state-and-local-transportation/vehicle-emissions-california-waivers-and-authorizations#:~:text=B%2C%20%C2%A7%201074.105.-,State%20Adoption%20of%20California%20Standards,a%20waiver%20has%20been%20granted, accessed November 6, 2023.

3. "States That Have Adopted California's Vehicle Standards Under Section 177 of the Federal Clean Air Act," California Air Resources Board, May 13, 2022, https://ww2.arb.ca.gov/sites/default/files/2022-05/%C2%A7177_states_05132022_NADA_sales_r2_ac.pdf, accessed November 6, 2023.

4. Charles R. Shipan and Craig Volden, "The Mechanisms of Policy Diffusion," *American Journal of Political Science* 52 (2008): 840–57.

5. Pamela J. Clouser McCann, Charles R. Shipan, and Craig Volden, "Top-Down Federalism: Statepolicy Responses to National Government Discussion," *Publius: The Journal of Federalism* 45(2015): 495–525; Charles R. Shipan and Craig Volden, "Bottom-Up Federalism: The Diffusion of Antismoking Policies from U.S. Cities to States," *American Journal of Political Science* 50 (2006): 825–43; Kelly B. Smith, "Laboratories of Bureaucracy: How Bureaucrats Learn Across States in Setting Early Childhood Education Standards," *Publius: The Journal of Federalism* 52 (2022): 553–78.

6. Deserai Crow, "Policy Diffusion and Innovation: Media and Experts in Colorado Recreational Water Rights," *Journal of Natural Resources Policy Research* 4 (2012): 27–41.

7. "About the Water Board," State Water Resources Control Board, updated March 6, 2023, https://www.waterboards.ca.gov/about_us/, accessed November 6, 2023.

8. "About the California Water Boards," Office of Public Participation, revised February 2019, accessed November 16, 2023.

9. "About the California Water Boards," Office of Public Participation, https://www.waterboards.ca.gov/about_us/

10. "The Nine Regional Water Control Boards in California," California Water Boards, updated June 12, 2013, https://www.waterboards.ca.gov/publications_forms/publications/factsheets/docs/region_brds.pdf, accessed November 6, 2023; https://www.waterboards.ca.gov/publications_forms/publications/factsheets/docs/boardoverview.pdf

11. "State Renewable Portfolio Standards and Goals," National Council of State Legislatures, updated August 13, 2021, https://www.ncsl.org/energy/state-renewable-portfolio-standards-and-goals#:~:text=Renewable%20Portfolio%20Standards%20(RPS)%20require,production%20and%20encourage%20economic%20development, accessed November 6, 2023.

12. Srinivas C. Parinandi, "Policy Inventing and Borrowing Among State Legislatures," *American Journal of Political Science* 64 (2020): 852–68.

13. "A Brief History of U.S. Electricity Portfolio Standard Proposals," Congressional Research Service, updated February 24, 2021, https://crsreports.congress.gov/product/pdf/IF/IF11316, accessed November 7, 2023.

14. "Alternative Energy Law (AEL)," DSIRE, updated July 20, 2023, https://programs.dsireusa.org/system/program/detail/265/alternative-energy-law-ael, accessed November 7, 2023.

15. "State Renewable Portfolio Standards and Goals," National Conference of State Legislatures, updated August 13, 2021, https://www.ncsl.org/energy/state-renewable-portfolio-standards-and-goals#:~:text=Renewable%20Portfolio%20Standards%20(RPS)%20require,production%20and%20encourage%20economic%20development, accessed Nov 7, 2023.

16. "State Brief: Iowa," Center for the New Energy Economy, Colorado State University, 2022, https://cnee.colostate.edu/wp-content/uploads/2022/10/State-Brief_IA_September_2022.pdf, accessed November 7, 2023.

17. "Programs," DSIRE, https://programs.dsireusa.org/system/program/ia, accessed November 9, 2023.

18. NCSL, "State Renewable Portfolio Standards and Goals."

19. NRDC, "Renewable Energy: The Clean Facts"; NCSL, "State Renewable Portfolio Standards and Goals."

20. "Today in Energy," US Energy Information Administration, https://www.eia.gov/todayinenergy/detail.php?id=40913, accessed November 9, 2023.

21. US Energy Information Administration, "Today in Energy."

22. "Electric Co-op Facts & Figures," NRECA, https://www.electric.coop/electric-cooperative-fact-sheet, accessed November 9, 2023.

23. "Renewable Portfolio Standards- The High Cost of Insuring Against High Costs," Climate Policy Initiative, December 17, 2012, https://www.climatepolicyinitiative.org/renewable-portfolio-standards-the-high-cost-of-insuring-against-high-costs/, accessed November 9, 2023

24. NCSL, "State Renewable Portfolio Standards and Goals."

25. "Renewable Portfolio Standards: The High Cost of Insuring Against High Costs," Climate Policy Initiative.

26. "Quick Facts: Flint City, Michigan," U.S. Census Bureau, https://www.census.gov/quickfacts/fact/table/flintcitymichigan/PST045222, accessed November 9, 2023.

27. Merrit Kennedy, "Lead-Laced Water in Flint: A Step-By-Step Look at the Makings of a Crisis," NPR, April 20, 2016, https://www.npr.org/sections/thetwo-way/2016/04/20/465545378/lead-laced-water-in-flint-a-step-by-step-look-at-the-makings-of-a-crisis, accessed November 9, 2023.

28. CNN Editorial Research, "Flint Water Crisis Fast Facts," CNN, December 13, 2022, https://www.cnn.com/2016/03/04/us/flint-water-crisis-fast-facts/index.html, accessed November 9, 2023.

29. Ron Fonger, "Emergency Manager Calls City Council's Flint River Vote 'Incomprehensible'" Mlive, March 24, 2015, https://www.mlive.com/news/flint/2015/03/flint_emergency_manager_calls.html, accessed Nov 9, 2023.

30. CNN Editorial Research, "Flint Water Crisis Fast Facts."

31. CNN Editorial Research, "Flint Water Crisis Fast Facts."

32. Keith Mulvihill, "Causes and Effects of Lead in Water," NRDC, https://www.nrdc.org/stories/causes-and-effects-lead-water#problem, accessed November 17, 2023.

33. NYC Health, "Adults and Lead Poisoning," https://www.nyc.gov/site/doh/health/health-topics/lead-poisoning-adults-and-lead-poisoning.page#:~:text=Lead%20exposure%20can%20cause%20high,t%20look%20or%20feel%20sick, accessed November 17, 2023.

34. Center for Disease Control and Prevention, "Health Effects of Lead Exposure," https://www.cdc.gov/nceh/lead/prevention/health-effects.htm, accessed November 17, 2023.

35. Chris Gilligan, "States with the Most Lead Drinking Water Pipes," *U.S. News & World Report*, May 2, 2023, https://www.usnews.com/news/best-states/articles/states-with-the-most-lead-pipes#:~:text=Florida%20has%20the%20most%20lead,and%20New%20York%20(5.4%25, accessed November 17, 2023.

36. "State and Federal Efforts to Address Lead in Drinking Water," NCSL, updated December 30, 2021, https://www.ncsl.org/environment-and-natural-resources/state-and-federal-efforts-to-address-lead-in-drinking-water, accessed November 20, 2023.

37. NCSL, "State and Federal Efforts to Address Lead in Drinking Water."

38. NCSL, "State and Federal Efforts to Address Lead in Drinking Water."

39. NCSL, "State and Federal Efforts to Address Lead in Drinking Water."

40. NCSL, "State and Federal Efforts to Address Lead in Drinking Water."

41. CA Educ Code § 32243 (2019), https://law.justia.com/codes/california/2019/code-edc/title-1/division-1/part-19/chapter-2/article-4/section-32243/, accessed November 9, 2023.

42. Victor Morckel and Kathryn Terzano, "Legacy City Residents' Lack of Trust in Their Governments: An Examination of Flint, Michigan Residents' Trust at the Height of the Water Crisis," *Journal of Urban Affairs* 41 (2019): 585–601; Joanne Sobeck, Joanne Smith-Darden, Megan Hicks, Poco Kernsmith, Paul E. Kilgore, Lara Treemore-Spears, and Shawn McEllmurry, "Stress, Coping, Resilience and Trust during the Flint Water Crisis," *Behavioral Medicine* 46 (2020): 202–16.

43. "Mapping Lead Pipes by Water Utility," Environmental Defense Fund, https://www.edf.org/health/mapping-lead-pipes-water-utility, accessed November 9, 2023.

44. NCSL, "State and Federal Efforts to Address Lead in Drinking Water."

45. Michael Phillis, "Some States Reject Federal Money to Find and Replace Millions of Dangerous Lead Pipes," *PBS News Hour*, August 22, 2023, https://www.pbs.org/newshour/politics/some-states-reject-federal-money-to-find-and-replace-millions-of-dangerous-lead-pipes, accessed November 9, 2023.

46. "State Revolving Fund Loan Programs," January 2022, https://www.in.gov/ifa/srf/files/SRF-Lead-Line-Replacement-Fact-Sheet-Jan-2022.pdf, accessed November 9, 2023.

47. Michael Phillis, "Some States Reject Federal Money to Find and Replace Millions of Dangerous Lead Pipes," *Associated Press*, August 22, 2023. https://apnews.com/article/lead-epa-water-portland-toxic-bc2cb5c2df5bd73bb013674939d1ee31.

48. "How the Drinking Water State Revolving Fund Works," United States Environmental Protection Agency, updated December 7, 2022, https://www.epa.gov/dwsrf/how-drinking-water-state-revolving-fund-works, accessed November 9, 2023.

49. "How the Drinking Water State Revolving Fund Works," United States Environmental Protection Agency, updated November 17, 2023, https://www.epa.gov/dwsrf/how-drinking-water-state-revolving-fund-works.

Chapter 13

1. Charles Barrilleaux and Carlisle Rainey, "The Politics of Need: Examining Governors' Decisions to Oppose the 'Obamacare' Medicaid Expansion," *State Politics & Policy Quarterly* 14 (2014): 437–60.

2. Robin Flagg, "Medicaid Expansion: A Tale of Two Governors," *Journal of Health Politics, Policy and Law* 41 (2016): 997-1-31.

3. Colleen M. Grogan, Clifford S. Bersamira, Phillip M. Singer, Bikki Tran Smith, Harold A. Pollack, Christina M. Andrews, and Amanda J. Abraham, "Are Policy Strategies for Addressing the Opioid Epidemic Partisan?: A View from the States," *Journal of Health Politics, Policy and Law* 45 (2020): 277–308.

4. Flagg, "Medicaid Expansion."

5. "About Us," Ohio Office of Management and Budget, https://obm.ohio.gov/areas-of-interest/controlling-board/03_about-us, accessed July 6, 2023.

6. Rebecca Adams, "Ohio GOP Governor Pushes State Board to Approve Medicaid Expansion." The Commonwealth Fund, October 11, 2013, https://www.commonwealthfund.org/publications/newsletter-article/ohio-gop-governor-pushes-state-board-approve-medicaid-expansion, accessed June 7, 2023.

7. "Medicaid in Ohio," Kaiser Family Foundation, October 2022, https://files.kff.org/attachment/fact-sheet-medicaid-state-OH, accessed June 7, 2023.

8. "Federal and State Share of Medicaid Spending," Kaiser Family Foundation, https://www.kff.org/medicaid/state-indicator/federalstate-share-of-spending/?dataView=1¤tTimeframe=0&sortModel=%7B%22colId%22:%22Location%22,%22sort%22:%22asc%22%7D, accessed June 7, 2023.

9. "Medicaid in Ohio," 2022.

10. "Medicaid in Ohio," 2022.

11. "Medicaid in Ohio," 2022.

12. "Ohio," Center for Disease Control and Prevention, February 24, 2023, https://www.cdc.gov/nchs/pressroom/states/ohio/oh.htm, accessed June 7, 2023. https://www.cdc.gov/nchs/pressroom/states/ohio/oh.htm.

13. "Ohio," 2023 and "Maternal Deaths and Mortality Rates: Each State, the District of Columbia, United States, 2018–2020," Center for Disease Control and Prevention, https://www.cdc.gov/nchs/maternal-mortality/MMR-2018-2020-State-Data.pdf, accessed June 7, 2023.

14. Selena Simmons-Duffin and Carmel Wroth, "Maternal Deaths in the U.S. Spiked in 2021, CDC Reports," NPR, March 16, 2023, https://www.npr.org/sections/health-shots/2023/03/16/1163786037/maternal-deaths-in-the-u-s-spiked-in-2021-cdc-reports#:~:text=The%20U.S.%20rate%20for%202021,deaths%20per%20100%2C000%20in%202020.; Roosa Tikkanen, Munira Z. Gunja, Molly FitzGerald, and Laurie C. Zephyrin, "Maternal Mortality and Maternity Care in the United States Compared to 10 Other Developed Countries," The Commonwealth Fund, November 2020, https://www.commonwealthfund.org/publications/issue-briefs/2020/nov/maternal-mortality-maternity-care-us-compared-10-countries, accessed July 6, 2023; Latoya Hill, Samantha Artiga, and Usha Ranji, "Racial Disparities in Maternal and Infant Health: Current Status and Efforts to Address Them," Kaiser Family Foundation, November 1, 2022, https://www.kff.org/racial-equity-and-health-policy/issue-brief/racial-disparities-in-maternal-and-infant-health-current-status-and-efforts-to-address-them/, accessed July 6, 2023.

15. "2015 Ohio Drug Overdose Data: General Findings," Ohio Department of Health, https://extension.osu.edu/sites/ext/files/imce/About_docs/Opioid_Crisis/Drug%20overdose%20data-Ohio%20Dept%20of%20Health.pdf, accessed June 7, 2023.

16. Staff Writer, "Ohio Leads Nation in Overdose Deaths," *The Columbus Dispatch*, November 28, 2016, https://www.dispatch.com/story/lifestyle/health-fitness/2016/11/29/ohio-leads-nation-in-overdose/22759272007/, accessed June 7, 2023.

17. Jake Zuckerman, "New Data: Fatal Overdoses Leap 22% Last Year," *Ohio Capital Journal*, July 15, 2021, https://ohiocapitaljournal.com/2021/07/15/new-data-fatal-overdoses-leapt-22-in-ohio-last-year/, accessed June 7, 2023.

18. "The Opioid Epidemic's Impact on Children's Services in Ohio," Public Children Services Association of Ohio, Spring 2017, https://www.pcsao.org/pdf/advocacy/OpiateBriefingSlides.pdf, accessed June 7, 2023.

19. "Ohio Opioid Summary," National Institute on Drug Abuse, April 2019, https://nida.nih.gov/sites/default/files/21980-ohio-opioid-summary.pdf, accessed June 7, 2023.

20. "Key Ohio Initiatives Combating Prescription Opioid Abuse," Governor's Cabinet Opiate Action Team, https://odh.ohio.gov/wps/wcm/connect/gov/c7d588d0-33ab-4c1c-989a-68d370ba6929/Key-Ohio-Initiatives-Combating-Presciption-Opioid-Abuse.pdf?MOD=AJPERES&CONVERT_TO=url&CACHEID=ROOTWORKSPACE.Z18_M1HGGIK0N0JO00QO9DDDDM3000-c7d588d0-33ab-4c1c-989a-68d370ba6929-moLPVjT, accessed June 7, 2023.

21. "6. Treatment and Recovery Supports," Recovery Ohio, https://recoveryohio.gov/priorities/review-2021/6-2021-treament-and-recovery-supports, accessed June 7, 2023.

22. Colleen M. Grogan, Clifford S. Bersamira, Phillip M. Singer, Bikki Tran Smith, Harold A. Pollack, Christina M. Andrews, "Are Policy Strategies for Addressing the Opioid Epidemic Partisan? A View from the States," *Journal of Health Policy, Politics, and Law* 45(2020): 277–309.

23. Jamila Michener, *Fragmented Democracy: Medicaid, Federalism, and Unequal Politics* (Cambridge University Press, 2018).

24. Michener, *Fragmented Democracy*.

25. Joshua D. Clinton and Michael W. Sances, "The Politics of Policy: The Initial Mass Political Effects of Medicaid Expansion in the States," *American Political Science Review* 112 (2018): 167–85.

26. Barry C. Burden, Jason M. Fletcher, Pamela Herd, Bradley M. Jones, and Donald P. Moynihan, "How Different Forms of Health Matter to Political Participation," *The Journal of Politics* 79 (2016): 166–78.

27. Julianna Pacheco and Jason Fletcher, "Incorporating Health into Studies of Political Behavior: Evidence for Turnout and Partisanship," *Political Research Quarterly* 68 (2015): 104–16.

28. Claudia Landwehr and Christopher Ojeda, "Democracy and Depression: A Cross-National Study of Depressive Symptoms and Nonparticipation," *American Political Science Review* 115 (2021): 323–30.

29. Matthew Gritter, "The Kerr-Mills Act and the Puzzles of Health-Care Reform," *Social Science Quarterly* 110 (2019): 2209–2222.

30. "Medicaid State Fact Sheets," Kaiser Family Foundation, October 3, 2022, https://www.kff.org/interactive/medicaid-state-fact-sheets/, accessed June 7, 2023. This includes CHIP.

31. "Federal and State Share of Medicaid of Spending," Kaiser Family Foundation, https://www.kff.org/medicaid/state-indicator/federalstate-share-of-spending/?currentTimeframe=0&sortModel=%7B%22colId%22:%22Location%22,%22sort%22:%22asc%22%7D, accessed January 19, 2024. The data is from 2022.

32. Lawrence D. Brown and Michael S. Sparer, "Poor Program's Progress: The Unanticipated Politics of Medicaid Policy," *health Affairs* 22 (2003): 31–44.

33. "Births Financed by Medicaid," Kaiser Family Foundation, https://www.kff.org/medicaid/state-indicator/births-financed-by-medicaid/?currentTimeframe=0&sortModel=%7B%22colId%22:%22Location%22,%22sort%22:%22asc%22%7D, accessed June 7, 2023.

34. "5 Charts About Public Opinion on Medicaid," Kaiser Family Foundation, March 30, 2023, https://www.kff.org/medicaid/poll-finding/5-charts-about-public-opinion-on-medicaid/, accessed June 7, 2023.

35. Grogan et al., "Are Policy Strategies for Addressing the Opioid Epidemic Partisan?"

36. Grogan et al., "Are Policy Strategies for Addressing the Opioid Epidemic Partisan?"

37. Rachel Garfield, Kendal Orgera, and Anthony Damico, "The Uninsured and the ACA: A Primer," Kaiser Family Foundation, January 2019, https://files.kff.org/attachment/The-Uninsured-and-the-ACA-A-Primer-Key-Facts-about-Health-Insurance-and-the-Uninsured-amidst-Changes-to-the-Affordable-Care-Act, accessed June 7, 2023.

38. Robin Rudowitz,, Patrick Drake, Jennifer Tolbert, and Anthony Damico, "How Many Uninsured Are in the Coverage Gap and How Many Could Be Eligible if All States Adopted the Medicaid Expansion," Kaiser Family Foundation, March 31, 2023, https://www.kff.org/medicaid/issue-brief/how-many-uninsured-are-in-the-coverage-gap-and-how-many-could-be-eligible-if-all-states-adopted-the-medicaid-expansion/, accessed June 7, 2023.

39. "Mandatory & Optional Medicaid Benefits," Centers for Medicare & Medicaid Services, https://www.medicaid.gov/medicaid/benefits/mandatory-optional-medicaid-benefits/index.html, accessed June 7, 2023.

40. "Medicaid Adult Dental Benefits Coverage by State," Center for Health Care Strategies, Inc, September 2019, https://www.chcs.org/media/Medicaid-Adult-Dental-Benefits-Overview-Appendix_091519.pdf, accessed June 7, 2023.

41. "Medication-Assisted Treatment (MAT) in the Criminal Justice System: Brief Guidance to the States," Substance Abuse and Mental Health Services Administration, https://store.samhsa.gov/sites/default/files/d7/priv/pep19-matbriefcjs_0.pdf, accessed June 7, 2023, 2.

42. Priya Chidambaram and Alice Burns, "10 Things About Long-Term Services and Supports (LTSS)," Kaiser Family Foundation, September 15, 2022, https://www.kff.org/medicaid/issue-brief/10-things-about-long-term-services-and-supports-ltss/, accessed January 18, 2024.

43. "Health Care-Related Taxes in Medicaid," Medicaid and CHIP Payment and Access Commission, May 2021, https://www.macpac.gov/wp-content/uploads/2020/01/Health-Care-Related-Taxes-in-Medicaid.pdf, accessed June 7, 2023.

44. "States and Medicaid Provider Taxes and Fees," Kaiser Family Foundation, June 27, 2017, https://www.kff.org/medicaid/fact-sheet/states-and-medicaid-provider-taxes-or-fees/, accessed June 7, 2023.

45. Brian Mann, "More Than a Million Americans Have Died from Overdoses During the Opioid Epidemic," *National Public Radio*, December 30, 2021, https://www.npr.org/2021/12/30/1069062738/more-than-a-million-americans-have-died-from-overdoses-during-the-opioid-epidemi, accessed June 7, 2023.

46. "Opioid Data Analysis and Resources," Center for Disease Control and Prevention, https://www.cdc.gov/opioids/data/analysis-resources.html#:~:text=The%20findings%20show%20three%20distinct,from%20IMF%2C%20including%20fentanyl%20analogs, accessed June 7, 2023.

47. "Fentanyl Awareness," United States Drug Enforcement Agency, https://www.dea.gov/fentanylawareness, accessed June 7, 2023.

48. "The Economic Toll of the Opioid Crisis Reached Nearly $1.5 Trillion in 2020," Joint Economic Committee Democrats, September 28, 2022, https://www.jec.senate.gov/public/index.cfm/democrats/issue-briefs?ID=CE55E977-B473-414F-8B88-53EB55EB7C7C, accessed June 7, 2023.

49. Claire Klobucista, and Alejandra Martinez, "Fentanyl and the U.S. Opioid Epidemic," Council of Foreign Relations, April 19, 2023, https://www.cfr.org/backgrounder/fentanyl-and-us-opioid-epidemic, accessed June 7, 2023.

50. Jin Woo Kim, Evan Morgan, and Brendan Nyhan, "Treatment versus Punishment: Understanding Racial Inequalities in Drug Policy," *Journal of Health Policy, Politics, and Law* 45 (2020): 177–209.

51. Warner M. Hedegaard and Miniño AM, "Drug Overdose Deaths in the United States, 1999–2015," NCHS data brief, no 273. Hyattsville, MD: National Center for Health Statistics, 2017, https://www.cdc.gov/nchs/products/databriefs/db273.htm, accessed June 7, 2023.

52. Bill Whitaker, "Did the FDA Ignite the Opioid Epidemic?" *60 Minutes*, February 24, 2019, https://www.cbsnews.com/news/opioid-epidemic-did-the-fda-ignite-the-crisis-60-minutes/, accessed August 22, 2023.

53. "Tackling the Opioid Crisis: What State Strategies Are Working?" National Academy for State Health Policy, https://nashp.org/tackling-the-opioid-crisis-what-state-strategies-are-working/, accessed June 7, 2023.

54. Patricia Strach, Katie Zuber, and Elizabeth Perez-Chiques, "Why Policies Fail: The Illusion of Services and the Opioid Epidemic," *The Journal of Health Politics, Policy, and Law* 45(2) (2020): 341–64.

55. "Harm Reduction," Substance Abuse and Mental Health Services Administration, April 24, 2023, https://www.samhsa.gov/find-help/harm-reduction, accessed June 7, 2023.

56. Isabel Evans, Francis Higgins, and Stacy Stanford, "Local Health Departments on the Front Lines of the Opioid Epidemic," *Journal of Public Health Management and Practice* 25 (2019): 294–96, https://journals.lww.com/jphmp/Fulltext/2019/05000/Local_Health_Departments_on_the_Front_Lines_of_the.14.aspx.

57. Evans et al., "Local Health Departments on the Front Lines of the Opioid Epidemic."

58. "Governor DeWine Announces Local Government Payments from National Opioid Settlement Begin," July 15, 2022, https://governor.ohio.gov/media/news-and-media/governor-dewine-announces-local-government-payments-from-national-opioid-settlement-begin-07152022.

59. "Attorney General's Office Lawsuit against Purdue Pharma and Its Executives and Directors," Mass.gov, https://www.mass.gov/lists/attorney-generals-office-lawsuit-against-purdue-pharma-and-its-executives-and-directors, accessed January 18, 2024.

60. Melissa Quinn, "Supreme Court Wrestles with Legal Shield for Sackler Family in Purdue Pharma Bankruptcy Plan," *CBS News*, December 4, 2023, https://www.cbsnews.com/news/supreme-court-purdue-pharma-sackler-family-bankruptcy/, accessed January 18, 2024.

61. Carla K Johnson, "US Backs Study of Safe Injection Sites, Overdose Prevention," *Associated Press*, May 8, 2023, https://apnews.com/article/safe-injection-sites-opioids-overdose-addiction-d9bcca2500044bfc28f54330bb719ffd, accessed January 26, 2024.

62. Kate Wilkinson, "RI Prepares to Open First Injection Site Amid Onslaught of Overdose Deaths," WPRI, August 31, 2023, https://www.wpri.com/target-12/ri-prepares-to-open-first-safe-injection-site-amid-onslaught-of-overdose-deaths/.

Chapter 14

1. Min Xian and Angela Couloumbis, "Richest Little City," *Spotlight PA*, November 9, 2023, https://www.spotlightpa.org/statecollege/2023/11/dubois-pennsylvania-herm-suplizio-fraud-corruption-attorney-general/?campaign_id=9&emc=edit_nn_20231222&instance_id=110779&nl=the-morning®i_id=220090718&segment_id=153235&te=1&user_id=5a57e3f64fde4d403ead53a5f7c23228.

2. Xian and Couloumbis, "Richest Little City."

3. Shanto Iyengar and Jennifer A. McGrady, *Media Politics: A Citizen's Guide* (New York: W.W. Norton, 2007).

4. Paul Lazarsfeld, Bernard Berelson, and Hazel Gaudet, *The People's Choice* (New York: Columbia University Press, 1944).

5. Naomi Forman-Katz, "For National Radio Day, Key Facts about Radio Listeners and the Radio Industry in the U.S.," Pew Research Center, August 17, 2023, https://www.pewresearch.org/short-reads/2023/08/17/for-national-radio-day-key-facts-about-radio-listeners-and-the-radio-industry-in-the-us/, accessed January 26, 2024.

6. Frederick J. Boehmke, "The Effect of Direct Democracy on the Size and Diversity of State Interest Group Populations," *The Journal of Politics* 64 (2002): 827–44.

7. M. Olson, *The Logic of Collective Action* (Cambridge, MA: Harvard University Press, 1965).

8. Anthony J. Nownes and Patricia Freeman, "Interest Group Activity in the States," *The Journal of Politics* 60 (1998): 85–112, 91.

9. Christopher A. Cooper, Anthony J. Nownes, and Martin Johnson, "Interest Groups and Journalists in the States," *State Politics & Policy Quarterly* 7 (2007): 39–53.

10. "APSA Annual Report 2021," American Political Science Association, https://www.apsanet.org/Portals/54/annual%20report%202021/2021%20APSA%20Annual%20Report%20Draft%20MB.pdf?ver=2N59i5A520k-lqHVB_cZsg%3d%3d, accessed January 2, 2024.

11. Julia Payson, *When Cities Lobby: How Local Governments Compete for Power in State Politics* (Oxford University Press, 2021).

12. E. E. Schattschneider, *The Semi-Sovereign People* (New York: Holt, Rinehart and Winston, 1960).

Index

Page numbers in italics refer to action items, figures, photos, and tables.

N

About the Authors

Kaitlin N. Sidorsky is associate professor of political science and public policy at Ramapo College of New Jersey. She is the author of *All Roads Lead to Power: Appointed and Elected Paths to Public Office for US Women* (2019) and coauthor of *Inequality Across State Lines: How Policymakers Have Failed Domestic Violence Victims in the United States* with Wendy J. Schiller (2023). Her work has appeared in *Political Research Quarterly* and *Perspectives on Politics* and other peer reviewed journals.

Kelly B. Smith is associate professor of political science at Stetson University. Her research focuses on state politics, public policy, federalism, and policy diffusion. Her work has appeared in *Publius: The Journal of Federalism, State Politics & Policy Quarterly*, and *Perspectives on Politics*.